Microsoft®

Word 2000

Step by Step

Catapult

Microsoft® Press

PUBLISHED BY
Microsoft Press
A Division of Microsoft Corporation
One Microsoft Way
Redmond, Washington 98052-6399

Library of Congress Cataloging-in-Publication Data
Microsoft Word 2000 Step by Step / Catapult, Inc.
p. cm.
Includes index.
ISBN 1-57231-970-4
1. Microsoft Word. I. Catapult, Inc.
Z52.5.M52M494 1999
652.5'--dc21 98-48194
CIP

Printed and bound in the United States of America.

1 2 3 4 5 6 7 8 9 WCWC 4 3 2 1 0 9

Distributed in Canada by Penguin Books Canada Limited.

A CIP catalogue record for this book is available from the British Library.

Microsoft Press books are available through booksellers and distributors worldwide. For further information about international editions, contact your local Microsoft Corporation office or contact Microsoft Press International directly at fax (425) 936-7329. Visit our Web site at mspress.microsoft.com.

For Catapult, Inc.
Director of Publications: Bryn Cope
Project Editor: Cynthia Slotvig-Carey
Manuscript Editor: Peggy O'Farrell
Production Manager: Carolyn Thornley
Production/Layout: Steven Hopster, Editor; Marie Hammer, Kim McGhee, dCarter
Writers: Liz Wolk, Shellie Tucker
Technical Editors: Kelly Dengler, Marie Rosemund, Melinda Spencer, Emily MacKellen
Copy Editor: Tresy Kilbourne

For Microsoft Press
Acquisitions Editor: Susanne Forderer
Project Editor: Jenny Moss Benson

Contents

QuickLook Guide

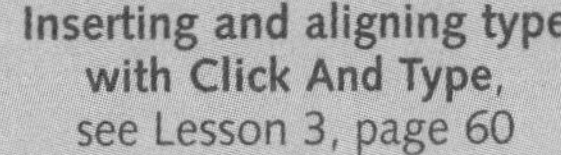

Inserting and aligning type with Click And Type,
see Lesson 3, page 60

March 1, 1999

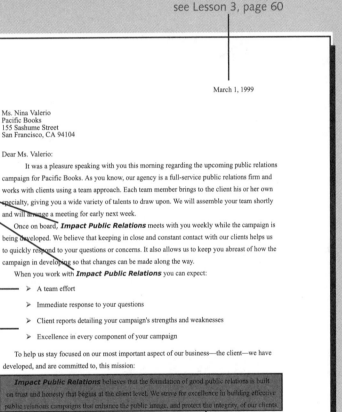

Ms. Nina Valerio
Pacific Books
155 Sashume Street
San Francisco, CA 94104

Dear Ms. Valerio:

It was a pleasure speaking with you this morning regarding the upcoming public relations campaign for Pacific Books. As you know, our agency is a full-service public relations firm and works with clients using a team approach. Each team member brings to the client his or her own specialty, giving you a wide variety of talents to draw upon. We will assemble your team shortly and will arrange a meeting for early next week.

Once on board, ***Impact Public Relations*** meets with you weekly while the campaign is being developed. We believe that keeping in close and constant contact with our clients helps us to quickly respond to your questions or concerns. It also allows us to keep you abreast of how the campaign in developing so that changes can be made along the way.

When you work with ***Impact Public Relations*** you can expect:

- A team effort
- Immediate response to your questions
- Client reports detailing your campaign's strengths and weaknesses
- Excellence in every component of your campaign

To help us stay focused on our most important aspect of our business—the client—we have developed, and are committed to, this mission:

Impact Public Relations believes that the foundation of good public relations is built on trust and honesty that begins at the client level. We strive for excellence in building effective public relations campaigns that enhance the public image, and protect the integrity, of our clients.

Sincerely,

Rebecca Smith
Impact Public Relations

Merging a form letter with a mailing list,
see Lesson 9, page 218

Applying repeated formatting with Format Painter,
see Lesson 3, page 58

Creating numbered and bulleted lists,
see Lesson 5, page 105

Changing the spacing between lines,
see Lesson 3, page 62

Inserting frequently used text,
see Lesson 6, page 134

Applying borders and shading to paragraphs,
see Lesson 3, page 68

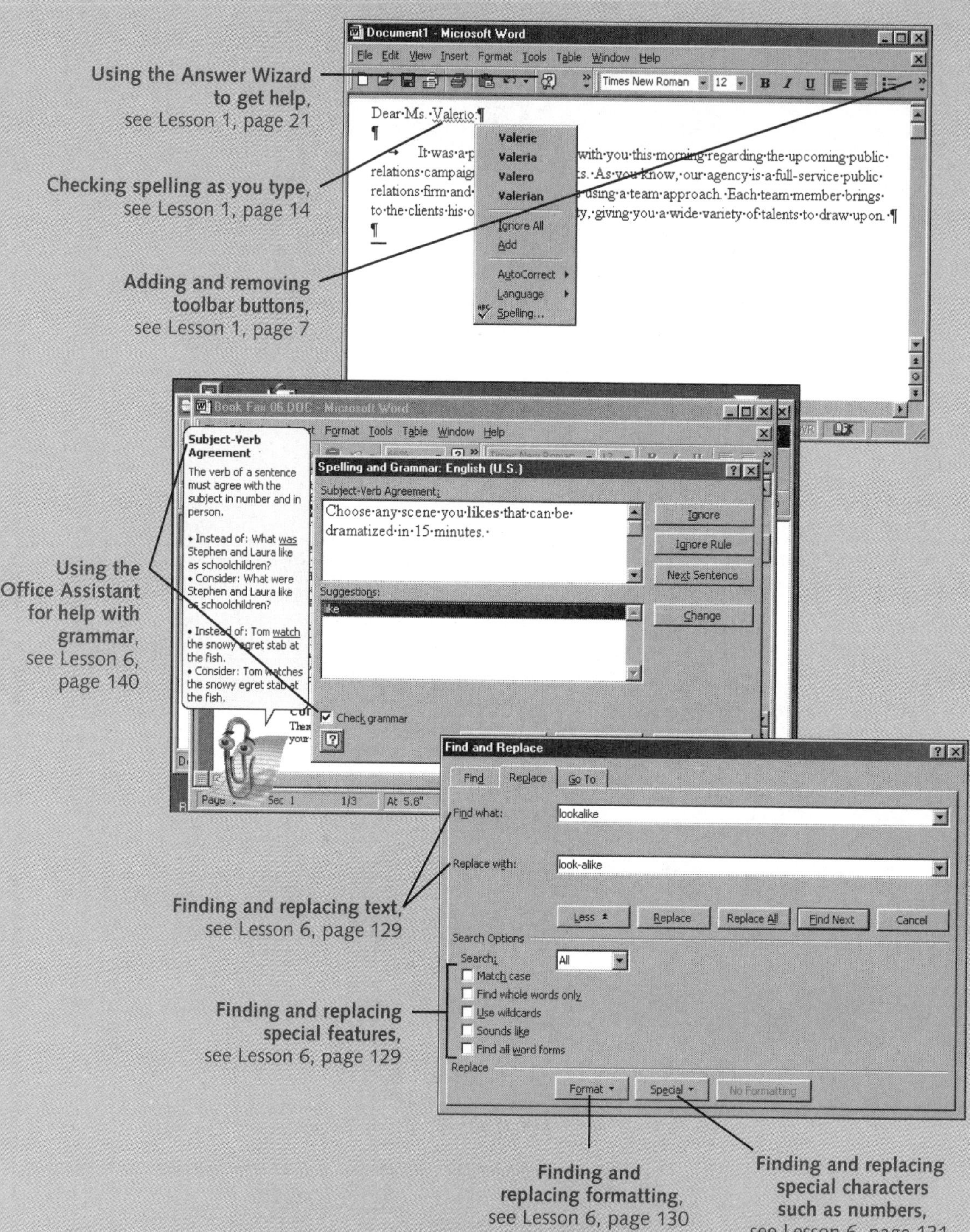
Using the Answer Wizard to get help, see Lesson 1, page 21
Checking spelling as you type, see Lesson 1, page 14
Adding and removing toolbar buttons, see Lesson 1, page 7
Using the Office Assistant for help with grammar, see Lesson 6, page 140
Finding and replacing text, see Lesson 6, page 129
Finding and replacing special features, see Lesson 6, page 129
Finding and replacing formatting, see Lesson 6, page 130
Finding and replacing special characters such as numbers, see Lesson 6, page 131
Document1 - Microsoft Word
File Edit View Insert Format Tools Table Window Help
Times New Roman
12
Dear Ms. Valerio:
Valerie
Valeria
Valero
Valerian
Ignore All
Add
AutoCorrect
Language
Spelling...
Subject-Verb Agreement
The verb of a sentence must agree with the subject in number and in person.
• Instead of: What was Stephen and Laura like as schoolchildren?
• Consider: What were Stephen and Laura like as schoolchildren?
• Instead of: Tom watch the snowy egret stab at the fish.
• Consider: Tom watches the snowy egret stab at the fish.
Spelling and Grammar: English (U.S.)
Subject-Verb Agreement:
Choose any scene you likes that can be dramatized in 15 minutes.
Ignore
Ignore Rule
Next Sentence
Suggestions:
like
Change
Check grammar
Find and Replace
Find
Replace
Go To
Find what:
lookalike
Replace with:
look-alike
Less
Replace
Replace All
Find Next
Cancel
Search Options
Search:
All
Match case
Find whole words only
Use wildcards
Sounds like
Find all word forms
Replace
Format
Special
No Formatting

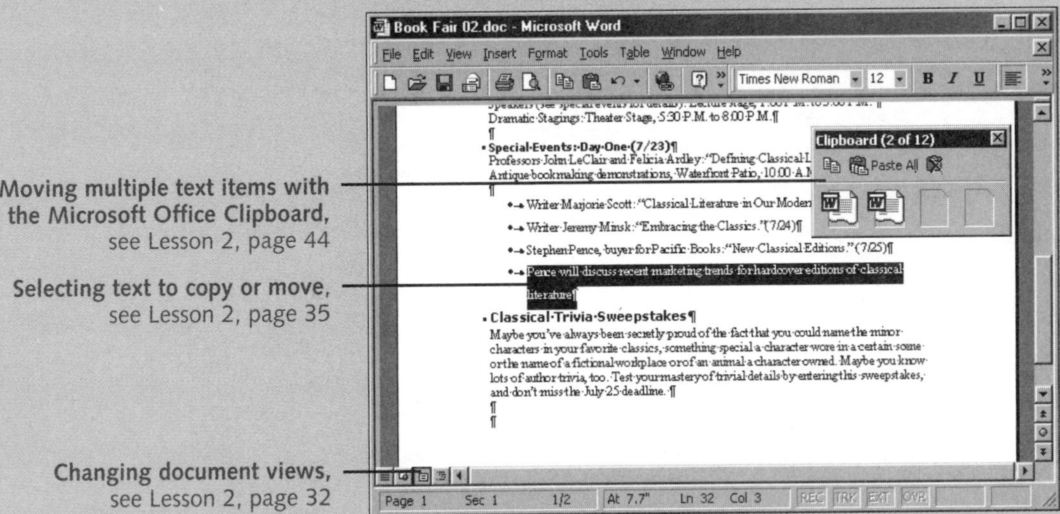
Book Fair 02.doc - Microsoft Word
File Edit View Insert Format Tools Table Window Help
Clipboard (2 of 12)
Paste All
Moving multiple text items with the Microsoft Office Clipboard, see Lesson 2, page 44
Selecting text to copy or move, see Lesson 2, page 35
Changing document views, see Lesson 2, page 32

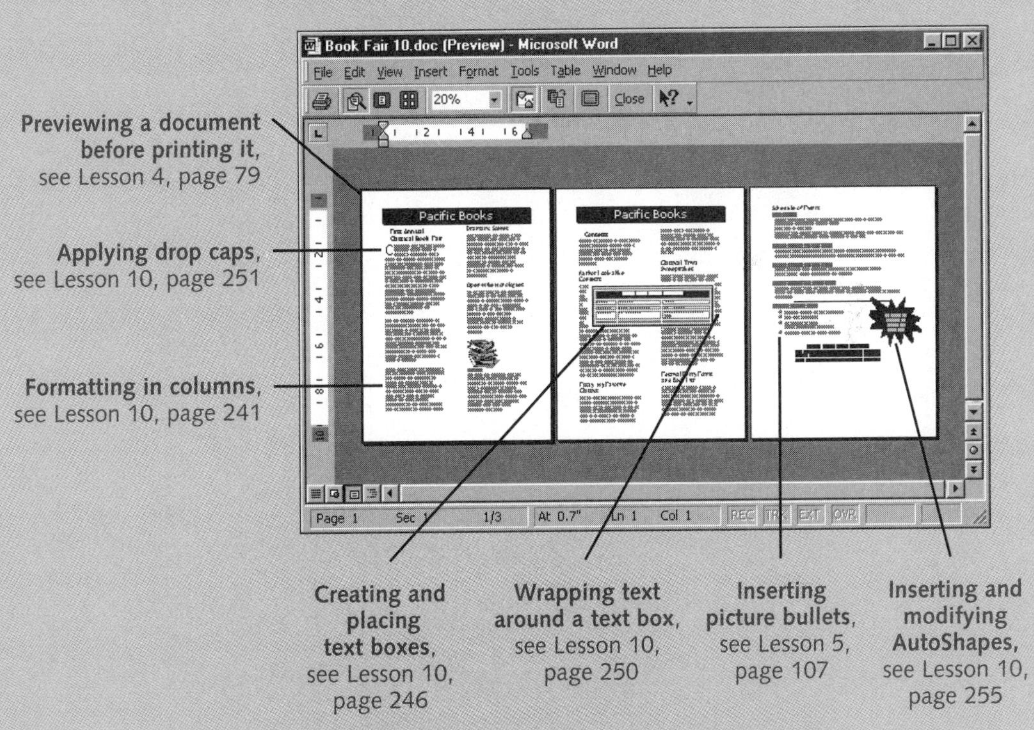
Book Fair 10.doc (Preview) - Microsoft Word
File Edit View Insert Format Tools Table Window Help
Pacific Books
Pacific Books
Previewing a document before printing it, see Lesson 4, page 79
Applying drop caps, see Lesson 10, page 251
Formatting in columns, see Lesson 10, page 241
Creating and placing text boxes, see Lesson 10, page 246
Wrapping text around a text box, see Lesson 10, page 250
Inserting picture bullets, see Lesson 5, page 107
Inserting and modifying AutoShapes, see Lesson 10, page 255

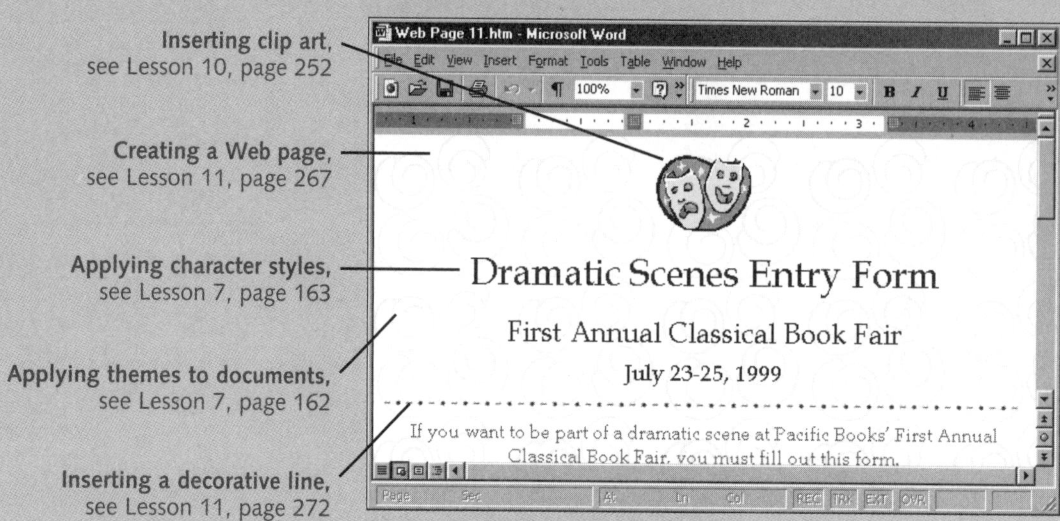
Inserting clip art, see Lesson 10, page 252
Creating a Web page, see Lesson 11, page 267
Applying character styles, see Lesson 7, page 163
Applying themes to documents, see Lesson 7, page 162
Inserting a decorative line, see Lesson 11, page 272
Web Page 11.htm - Microsoft Word
File Edit View Insert Format Tools Table Window Help
Dramatic Scenes Entry Form
First Annual Classical Book Fair
July 23-25, 1999
If you want to be part of a dramatic scene at Pacific Books' First Annual Classical Book Fair, you must fill out this form.

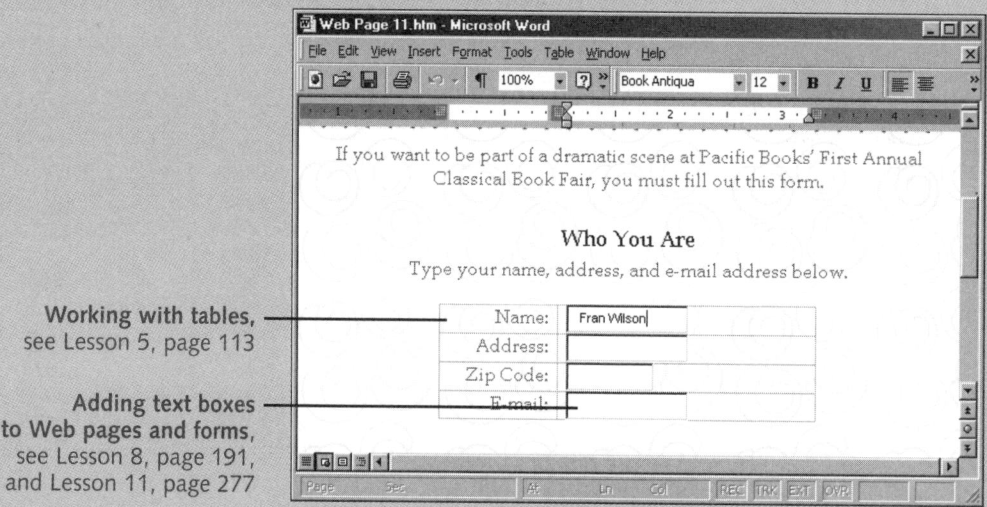
Working with tables, see Lesson 5, page 113
Adding text boxes to Web pages and forms, see Lesson 8, page 191, and Lesson 11, page 277
Web Page 11.htm - Microsoft Word
File Edit View Insert Format Tools Table Window Help
If you want to be part of a dramatic scene at Pacific Books' First Annual Classical Book Fair, you must fill out this form.
Who You Are
Type your name, address, and e-mail address below.
Name: Fran Wilson
Address:
Zip Code:
E-mail:

Finding Your Best Starting Point

Microsoft Word 2000 is a powerful word processing program that you can use to efficiently create, modify, and format documents. With *Microsoft Word 2000 Step by Step*, you'll quickly and easily learn how to use Word 2000 to get your work done.

important

This book is designed for use with Microsoft Word 2000 for the Windows operating systems. To find out which version of Word you're running, you can check the product package or you can start the program, click the Help menu, and then click About Microsoft Word. If your software is not compatible with this book, a Step by Step book matching your software is probably available. Please visit our World Wide Web site at *http://mspress.microsoft.com* or call 1-800-MSPRESS (1-800-677-7377) for more information.

Finding the Best Starting Point for You

This book is designed for beginning users of word processing, as well as readers who have had experience with these types of programs and are switching to Word or upgrading to Word 2000. Use the following table to find your best starting point in this book.

If you are	Follow these steps
New	
to computers,	1. Install the practice files as described in "Using the Microsoft Word 2000 Step by Step CD-ROM."
to graphical (as opposed to text-only) computer programs,	2. Become acquainted with the Windows operating system and how to use the online Help system by working through Appendix A, "If You're New to Windows or Word 2000" that is found on the accompanying CD-ROM.
or to Windows	3. Learn basic skills for using Microsoft Word 2000 by working through Lesson 1. Gain further basic skills by working through Lessons 2 through 4. Then you can work through lessons in the remainder of the book in any order you'd like. However, lessons in the later part of the book are generally more advanced.

If you are	Follow these steps
Switching	
from a different word processing program	1. Install the practice files as described in "Using the Microsoft Word 2000 Step by Step CD-ROM."
	2. Learn basic skills for using Microsoft Word 2000 by working through Lesson 1. Then work through Lessons 2 through 4. Lessons 5 through 16 can be completed in any order.

If you are	Follow these steps
Upgrading	
from Microsoft Word 97, Word 6, or Word 95	1. Learn about the new features of Word 2000 that are covered in this book by reading the following section, "New Features in Microsoft Word 2000."
	2. Install the practice files as described in "Using the Microsoft Word 2000 Step by Step CD-ROM."
	3. Complete the lessons that cover the topics you need. You can use the table of contents and the *Quick*Look Guide to locate information about general topics. You can use the index to find information about a specific topic or feature.

If you are	Follow these steps
Referencing this book after working through the lessons	❶ Use the index to locate information about specific topics, and use the table of contents and the *Quick*Look Guide to locate information about general topics. ❷ Read the Quick Reference at the end of each lesson for a brief review of the major tasks in the lesson. The Quick Reference topics are listed in the same order as they are presented in the lesson.

New Features in Microsoft Word 2000

The following table lists the major new features of Microsoft Word 2000 that are covered in this book and the lesson in which you can learn how to use each feature. You can also use the index to find specific information about a feature or a task that you want to perform.

The New! 2000 icon appears in the margin throughout this book to indicate these new features of Word 2000.

To learn how to	See
Use the enhanced Microsoft Office Assistant	Lesson 1
Navigate expanded menus and truncated toolbars	Lesson 1
Copy and paste several items at once	Lesson 2
Use Click And Type to quickly insert justified text anywhere in the document	Lesson 3
Print multiple pages on a single page	Lesson 4
Insert picture bullets in a list	Lesson 5
Apply a decorative theme to a document	Lesson 7
Create Web pages using the new Web Layout view and the Web Tools toolbar	Lesson 11
Save a document as a Web page	Lesson 11
Preview a Web page in a Web browser	Lesson 11
Use new Web page templates and the Web Page Wizard	Lesson 11
Insert frames into a Web page	Lesson 12
Publish a Web page to a Web server	Lesson 12
Schedule online meetings with coworkers	Lesson 13
Use e-mail to send Word documents in HTML format	Lesson 15
Apply a decorative theme to e-mail messages	Lesson 15

Corrections, Comments, and Help

Every effort has been made to ensure the accuracy of this book and the contents of the Microsoft Word 2000 Step by Step CD-ROM. Microsoft Press provides corrections and additional content for its books through the World Wide Web at

http://mspress.microsoft.com/support

If you have comments, questions, or ideas regarding this book or the CD-ROM, please send them to us.

Send e-mail to:

mspinput@microsoft.com

Or send postal mail to:

Microsoft Press
Attn: Step by Step Editor
One Microsoft Way
Redmond, WA 98052-6399

Please note that support for the Word 2000 software product itself is not offered through the above addresses. For help using Word 2000, you can call Word 2000 Technical Support at (425) 635-7070 on weekdays between 6 A.M. and 6 P.M. Pacific Time.

Visit Our World Wide Web Site

We invite you to visit the Microsoft Press World Wide Web site. You can visit us at the following location:

http://mspress.microsoft.com

You'll find descriptions of all of our books, information about ordering titles, notices of special features and events, additional content for Microsoft Press books, and much more.

You can also find out the latest in software developments and news from Microsoft Corporation by visiting the following World Wide Web site:

http://www.microsoft.com/

We look forward to your visit on the Web!

Using the Microsoft Word 2000 Step by Step CD–ROM

The CD-ROM inside the back cover of this book contains the practice files that you'll use as you perform the exercises in the book and multimedia files that demonstrate ten of the exercises. By using the practice files, you won't waste time creating the samples used in the lessons—instead, you can concentrate on learning how to use Word 2000. With the files and the step-by-step instructions in the lessons, you'll also learn by doing, which is an easy and effective way to acquire and remember new skills.

> **important**
>
> Before you break the seal on the Microsoft Word 2000 Step by Step CD-ROM package, be sure that this book matches your version of the software. This book is designed for use with Microsoft Word 2000 for the Windows operating systems. To find out which version of Word you are running, you can check the product package or you can start the software, click the Help menu, and then click About Microsoft Word. If your program is not compatible with this book, a Step by Step book matching your software is probably available. Please visit our World Wide Web site at *http://mspress.microsoft.com* or call 1-800-MSPRESS (1-800-677-7377) for more information.

Installing the Practice Files

Follow these steps to install the practice files on your computer's hard disk so that you can use them with the exercises in this book.

1. If your computer isn't on, turn it on now.
2. If you're using Windows NT, press Ctrl+Alt+Del to display a dialog box asking for your user name and password. If you are using Windows 95 or 98, you will see this dialog box if your computer is connected to a network.
3. If necessary, type your user name and password in the appropriate boxes, and then click OK. If you see the Welcome dialog box, click the Close button.

Close

4. Remove the CD-ROM from the package inside the back cover of this book and insert it in the CD-ROM drive of your computer.
5. In My Computer, double-click your CD-ROM drive.
6. Double-click Setup.exe, and then follow the instructions on the screen.

   The setup program window appears with the recommended options preselected for you. For best results in using the practice files with this book, accept these preselected settings.
7. When the files have been installed, remove the CD-ROM from your CD-ROM drive and replace it in the package inside the back cover of the book.

   A folder called Word 2000 SBS Practice has been created on your hard disk, and the practice files have been placed in that folder.

If your computer is set up to connect to the Internet, you can double-click the Microsoft Press Welcome shortcut to visit the Microsoft Press Web site. You can also connect to this Web site directly at *http://mspress.microsoft.com*

Using the Practice Files

Each lesson in this book explains when and how to use any practice files for that lesson. When a practice file is needed for a lesson, the book will list instructions on how to open the file. The lessons are built around scenarios that simulate a real work environment, so you can easily apply the skills you learn to your own work. For the scenario in this book, imagine that you're a partner in Impact Public Relations, a small public relations firm. Your company recently installed Office 2000, and you are eager to use Word 2000 for a variety of business tasks.

The screen illustrations in this book might look different from what you see on your computer, depending on how your computer is set up. To help make your screen match the illustrations in this book, please follow the instructions in Appendix B, "Matching the Exercises" that is found on the accompanying CD-ROM.

For those of you who like to know all the details, here's a list of the main practice files included on the practice CD-ROM. For the convenience of readers who won't be completing lessons from beginning to end in sequence, separate practice files are included on the CD-ROM, but they are not listed individually here.

Filename	Description
Lesson01	No practice files
Lesson02	
02A	Book fair event document for Pacific Books
02E	Pacific Books logo
Lesson03	
03A	Letter to Nina Valerio at Pacific Books from Rebecca Smith at Impact Public Relations
Lesson04	
04A	Book fair document
04E	Letter to Pacific Books from Impact Public Relations
Review & Practice 2	
RP01A	Memo to the staff of Impact Public Relations regarding time sheets for Pacific Books
Lesson05	
05A	Book fair document
Lesson06	
06A	Book fair document
Lesson07	
07A	Book fair document
Lesson08	
08A	Fax cover sheet from Impact Public Relations to Pacific Books
08B	Invoice document from Impact Public Relations to Pacific Books
Review & Practice 2	
RP02A	
Lesson09	
09A	Pacific Books logo
Lesson10	
10A	Book fair document
10H	Data for an envelope merge
Lesson11	
11A	Dramatic Scenes entry form

Filename	Description
Lesson12	
12A	Book fair document
12B	Contest Prizes Web page
Review & Practice 3	
RP03A	Data source for a mail merge
RP03B	Book fair speaker biographies
RP03C	Book fair speaker biographies
Lesson13	
13A	Book fair document
Lesson14	
14A	Pacific Books Web site outline
Lesson15	
15A	Pacific Books Web site outline
15B	Subdocument of Pacific Books Web site outline
Lesson16	
16A	Pacific Books book fair recap
16B	Activity report for Pacific Books
16C	PowerPoint slide
16D	PowerPoint slide
16E	Pacific Books book fair recap
16F	Excel spreadsheet for Pacific Books book fair recap
Review & Practice 4	
RP04A	Pacific Books home page outline
Multimedia	
ArrangeButtons	A video demonstration of how to arrange buttons on a toolbar
ClipBoard	A video demonstration of how to move two blocks of text
ClickandType	A video demonstration of how to use Click And Type to insert a date
Indent	A video demonstration of how to set indents with the ruler
InsertTable	A video demonstration of how to insert a table
StartMacro	A video demonstration of how to record a macro
ApplyTheme	A video demonstration of how to apply a theme to a document
InsertTextField	A video demonstration of how to insert a text field
CreateHyperlink	A video demonstration of how to create a hyperlink
InsertPowerPointSlide	A video demonstration of how to insert a PowerPoint slide presentation

Using the Multimedia Files

Throughout this book, you will see icons for multimedia files for particular exercises. Use the following steps to run the multimedia files.

1. Insert the Microsoft Word 2000 Step by Step CD-ROM in your CD-ROM drive.
2. On the Windows taskbar, click Start, and then click Run.

   The Run dialog box appears.
3. Click Browse.

   The Browse dialog box appears.
4. If necessary, click the Look In list drop-down arrow, and select your CD-ROM drive.

   The contents of the CD-ROM are displayed.
5. Double-click the Multimedia folder.

   The Multimedia folder opens.
6. Double-click the audiovisual file you need, and in the Run dialog box, click OK.

   Microsoft Camcorder runs the video of the exercise. After the video is finished, close Camcorder.
7. Return to the exercise in the book.

Uninstalling the Practice Files

Use the following steps when you want to delete the practice files added to your hard disk by the Step by Step setup program.

1. On the Windows taskbar, click Start, point to Settings, and then click Control Panel.
2. Double-click the Add/Remove Programs icon.

   The Add/Remove Programs Properties dialog box appears.
3. On the Install/Uninstall tab, select Microsoft Word 2000 Step by Step from the list, and then click Add/Remove.

   A confirmation message appears.
4. Click Yes or OK.

   The practice files are uninstalled.
5. Click OK to close the Add/Remove Programs Properties dialog box.
6. Close the Control Panel window.

Need Help with the Practice Files?

Every effort has been made to ensure the accuracy of this book and the contents of the Microsoft Word 2000 Step by Step files CD-ROM. If you do run into a problem, Microsoft Press provides corrections for its books through the World Wide Web at:

http://mspress.microsoft.com/support/

We invite you to visit our main Web page at:

http://mspress.microsoft.com

You'll find descriptions of all of our books, information about ordering titles, notices of special features and events, additional content for Microsoft Press books, and much more.

PART 1

Getting Started with Word 2000

Creating and Saving Simple Documents

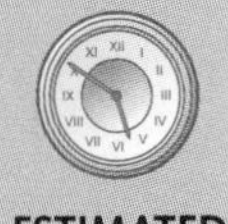

ESTIMATED TIME
25 min.

In this lesson you will learn how to:

- ✓ *Start Microsoft Word 2000.*
- ✓ *Navigate the Word menu bar and toolbars.*
- ✓ *Type and edit a new document.*
- ✓ *Correct mistakes manually and use AutoCorrect.*
- ✓ *Name and save a document.*
- ✓ *Use Microsoft Word Help.*
- ✓ *Create a new toolbar.*

Whether your task is to produce a basic memo, letter, or report, or to design a brochure, newsletter, or Web page, Microsoft Word 2000 provides powerful and easy-to-use tools. It's a snap to cut, copy, and paste text, to format and organize your documents, and to check spelling and grammar—even to correct mistakes as you type. You can work back and forth among multiple Word documents and other Microsoft Office programs. Insert graphics, tables, and charts into your documents and then publish it all to the Web if you want. You'll learn how to do all of this and more, but first let's master the fundamentals.

Using Word to Create Simple Documents

As you work through the exercises in this book, imagine that you are a partner in Impact Public Relations, a small public relations firm that specializes in designing multimedia campaigns for midsize companies. Your duties include writing and editing letters to clients, as well as many other tasks that require efficient word processing skills. In this lesson, you'll create and edit a letter to a potential client, learn how to correct mistakes manually, and work with *AutoCorrect*—a Word feature that automatically corrects some spelling and typographical errors as you type. You'll also learn how to name and save your document to a folder and how to get help with Word when necessary.

Starting Microsoft Word

There are several ways to start Word, depending on how the software is installed on your computer. If it is installed as part of the Microsoft Office 2000 suite, you can start Word from the Office shortcut bar. Or you can simply start Word using the Start button on the Windows taskbar.

Start Word from the Windows taskbar

1. On the Windows taskbar, click the Start button.

   The Start menu appears.
2. On the Start menu, point to Programs, and then click Microsoft Word.

   Word 2000 opens, and a new blank document is displayed.

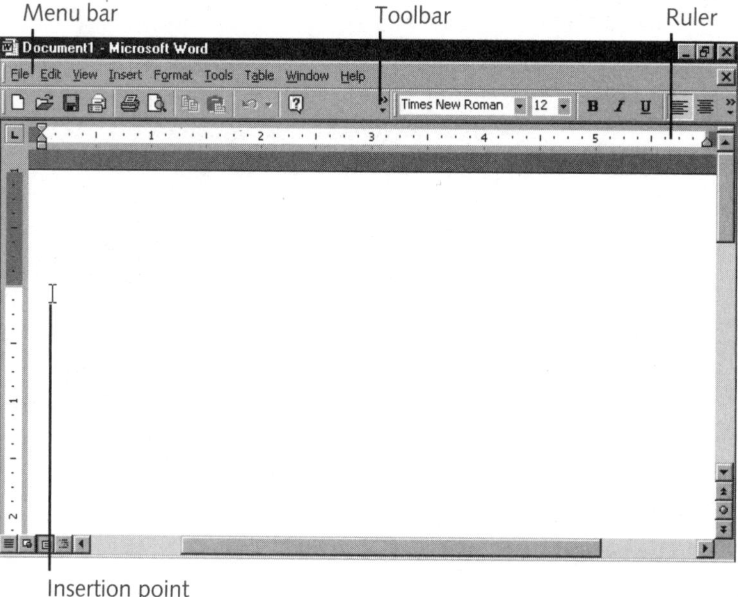

important

If the Office 2000 Registration Wizard appears, you can click Next to register the product, or you can click Register Later and then click Exit. If you choose to register later, this wizard will appear each time you start Word until you complete the registration.

Using the Office Assistant

When you start Word, an animated character named Clippit appears on your screen. Clippit is an *Office Assistant* who is there to help you produce your documents. Sometimes Clippit will recognize the task you are performing. For example, if you are typing a letter, Clippit will ask you if you would like help writing the letter. If you choose to have help, Clippit will start the Letter Wizard and continue to give you help in completing the task. Otherwise, Clippit will not give you assistance, but will remain on your screen.

You can close the Assistant by pressing the Esc key.

At other times while you're working, Clippit will give you a tip on how to complete a task. Once you have read the tip, you can click OK, and Clippit will disappear.

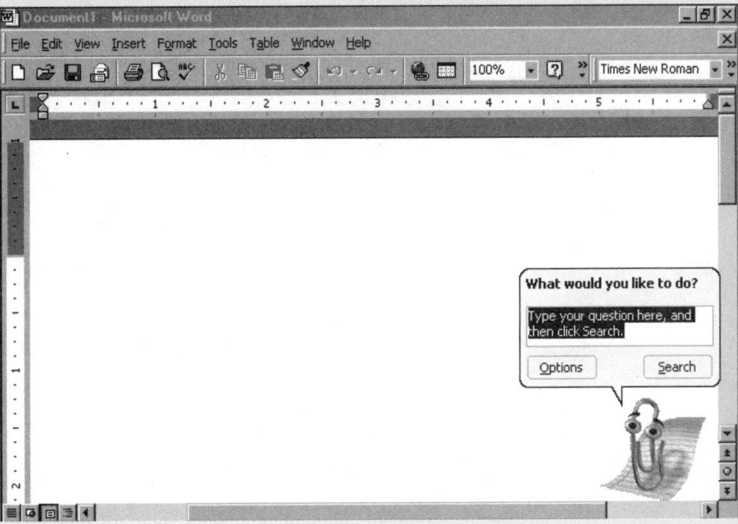

(continued)

continued

You can get help with your task at any time by simply clicking Clippit. When you do, a text box appears, allowing you to type your question. You type a question the same way you would ask someone a question, such as, *How do I save a Word document?*

Once you have asked your question, click Search and Clippit will guide you through the Help topics related to your inquiry. Clippit will remember your last question and search results so that you can easily access other Help topics related to your question. You'll find more information about using Help later in this lesson.

Customizing the Office Assistant

If the Clippit character does not suit your tastes, you can choose another character from the gallery of Office Assistants if you installed this feature during your Word program installation.

1. Right-click the Office Assistant.

   The Office Assistant shortcut menu appears.
2. Click Choose Assistant.

   The Office Assistant dialog box appears.
3. Click the Gallery tab.
4. Click Next or Back to view the gallery of Office Assistants.
5. Click OK to select an assistant.

Disabling the Office Assistant

If you choose, you can turn off the Assistant so it will not appear on your screen.

1. Right-click the Assistant.

   The shortcut menu appears.
2. Click Options.

   The Office Assistant dialog box appears.
3. Clear the Use The Office Assistant check box.
4. Click OK.

For the purposes of this book, the Office Assistant will not be shown in illustrations. If you choose to disable the Office Assistant and then want to turn it back on, on the Help menu, click Show The Office Assistant.

Navigating the Word Document Window

When you start Word, a new blank document is displayed in the program window. This window also contains a menu bar and a toolbar to help you quickly and easily turn this blank page into a useful and attractive document.

The Word menu bar organizes commands in a logical manner, making it easy for you to access features you need. For example, all table-related commands are grouped on the Table menu.

> **important**
>
> If this is your first time using Word 2000, you'll notice that when you select a menu, a short list of commands is displayed. As you continue to use Word, the list is automatically customized to your specific work habits. The commands you use most often are added to the short menu. Commands you use less often are still available but hidden until you expand the menu. You can expand the menu in two ways. Click the double arrow at the bottom of the short menu, or just keep your pointer still over the menu for a moment and the menu will expand automatically.

Viewing commands on the Word menu bar

In this exercise, you select a command from the menu.

1. On the Word menu bar, click the Format menu, and then click Theme.

   The Theme dialog box appears.
2. Click Cancel.

   The dialog box closes.

Using Toolbar Buttons

While the Word menu bar displays lists of commands, toolbars display buttons in a horizontal row across the top of the document window. Each button has a picture, or *icon*, on it corresponding to a command.

The Microsoft Word 2000 default setting for toolbars displays the most commonly used buttons from the Standard and Formatting toolbars in one row. By displaying fewer buttons for these two toolbars, more space is available to view your work. Once you use a command, its button is added to the toolbar, replacing another button that is less often used.

Clicking one of the More Buttons drop-down arrows gives you access to buttons not currently displayed on the toolbar. There are two of these buttons on the toolbar, one for the Standard toolbar and one for the Formatting toolbar.

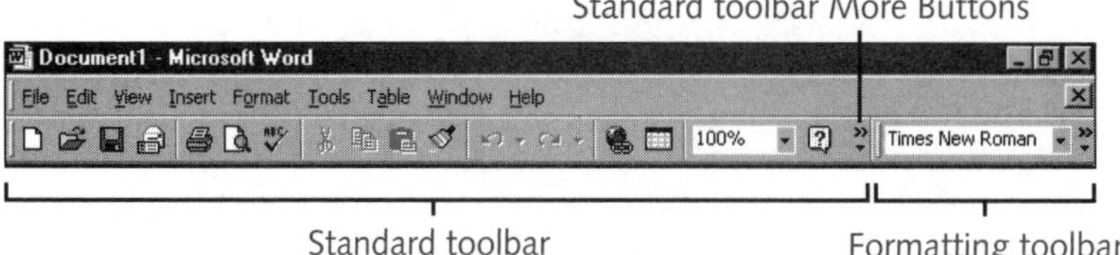

If you do not see a button name, on the Tools menu, click Customize. On the Options tab, select Show ScreenTips On Toolbars.

To see the name of any button (which also tells you its function), place your pointer on the button and wait. A ScreenTip appears showing the button name.

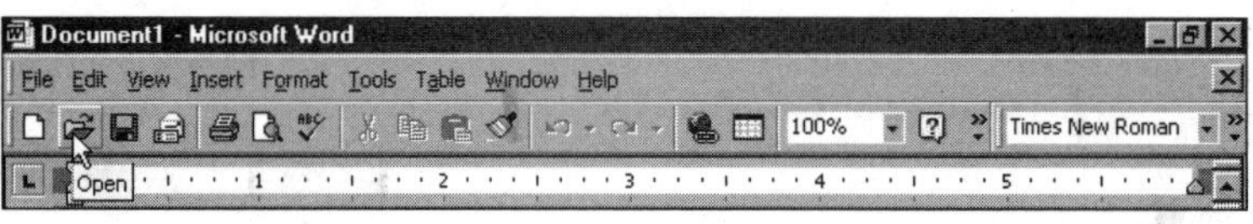

Resetting the Default Toolbar Buttons and Menu Commands

You can quickly reset the toolbar and menu bar to display the default commands. This is particularly useful when you share a computer with others. For example, you may often work with editing commands, while a coworker works with forms commands. You each could reset the toolbars for your own working convenience so that the commands you each use most frequently are displayed.

Reset the toolbars and menus

1. On the View menu, point to Toolbars, and then click Customize.

   The Customize dialog box appears.
2. Click the Options tab.
3. Click Reset My Usage Data, and click Yes when prompted.
4. Click Close.

   The Customize dialog box closes, and the toolbars and menus are reset to their default settings. If you have adjusted specific settings for any toolbars, those settings will be retained.

When you click the Open button, for example, the Open dialog box appears so you can select a file to open. Clicking some buttons, such as the Bold button on the Formatting toolbar, turns the feature either on or off. When Bold is on, all text you type or select will be formatted in bold. The instructions in this book emphasize using the toolbar buttons whenever possible and displaying the toolbars on one line.

Use a toolbar button

In this exercise, you use a toolbar button.

Open

1. On the Standard toolbar, position the pointer over the Open button.

   A ScreenTip for the button appears, showing the name of the button.
2. Click the Open button.

   The Open dialog box appears.
3. Click Cancel.

Use a toolbar button not currently displayed

In this exercise, you use a command not currently displayed on the toolbar.

More Buttons

Show/Hide ¶

1. On the Standard toolbar, click the More Buttons drop-down arrow.

   Depending on your toolbar settings, the arrow could be located anywhere from the center to the right side of the toolbar. Additional buttons are displayed.
2. Click the Show/Hide ¶ button.

   The Show/Hide ¶ button is activated and added to the toolbar.
3. On the Standard toolbar, click the Show/Hide ¶ button.

   The command is turned off.

Remove and add toolbar buttons

In this exercise, you remove a button from the Standard toolbar and then add one.

Click a check box to select (activate) or clear (deactivate) a command.

1. On the Standard toolbar, click the More Buttons drop-down arrow.

   The More Buttons menu appears.
2. Click Add Or Remove Buttons.

   The Add Or Remove Buttons menu appears.
3. Clear the Hyperlink check box.

   The button is removed from the Standard toolbar.
4. Point to the arrow at the bottom of the list.

   Additional toolbar buttons are displayed.

Close

5. Select the Close check box.

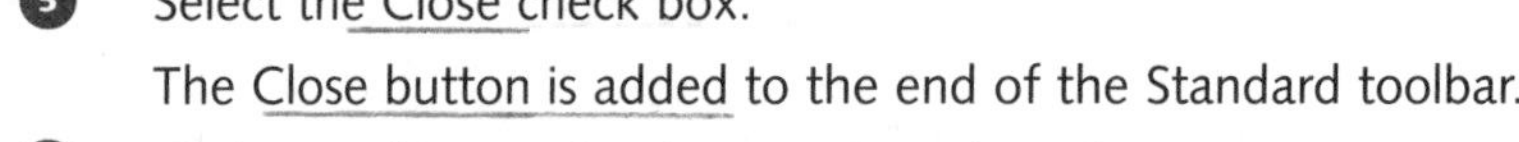

   The Close button is added to the end of the Standard toolbar.

6. Click anywhere in the document to close the menu.

For a demonstration of how to arrange buttons on the toolbar, in the Multimedia folder on the Microsoft Word 2000 Step by Step CD-ROM, double-click ArrangeButtons.

Arrange buttons on the toolbar

In this exercise, you move the Close button next to the Open button.

1. On the View menu, point to Toolbars, and then click Customize.

   The Customize dialog box appears.

2. Drag the Customize dialog box away from the toolbars by clicking the title bar at the top of the box and, without releasing the mouse button, moving the dialog box. Then release the mouse button.

3. On the toolbar, drag the Close button to the right of the Open button.

   Your screen should look similar to the following illustration.

Close

When the Customize dialog box is open, Standard and Formatting toolbars are displayed separately, and ScreenTips do not appear.

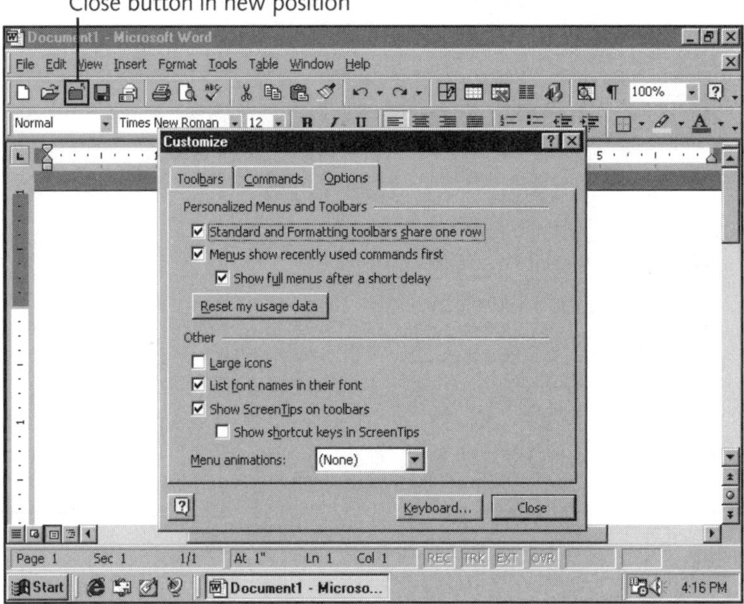

4. In the Customize dialog box, click Close.

Creating and Editing Basic Word Documents

Your responsibilities as a partner in Impact Public Relations require you to keep up regular communications with your clients. Word is an important and efficient tool for this task. To begin a letter, you start typing just as you would with a clean sheet of paper in a typewriter. There are a few things you need to know first, however.

The short, vertical, blinking line at the top of the document is the *insertion point*. The insertion point indicates where text will be entered as you type. As you create a document, you can move the insertion point to edit text anywhere in your document.

When typing long lines of text, you do not have to press Enter each time you want to start a new line. Word will automatically start a new line for you when you reach the right margin. This feature is called *wordwrapping*.

Type text in a letter

In this exercise, you begin a letter to a client, starting with the address block.

New Blank Document

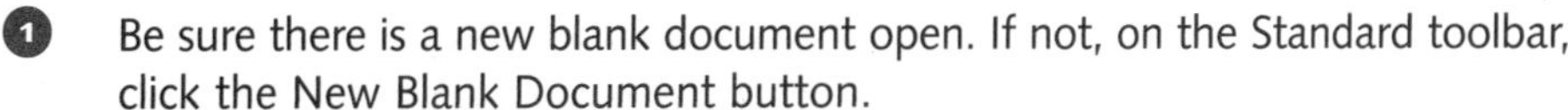

1. Be sure there is a new blank document open. If not, on the Standard toolbar, click the New Blank Document button.
2. Type **Ms. Nina Valerio** and press Enter.

   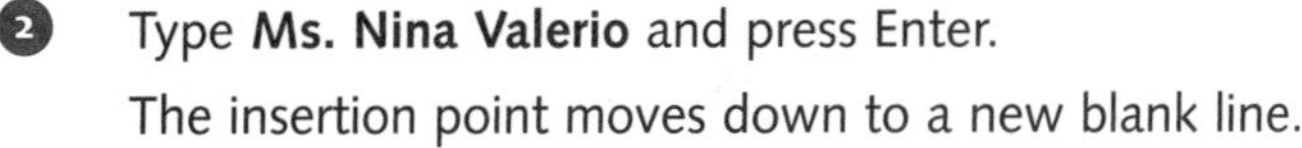

   The insertion point moves down to a new blank line.

tip

A red wavy line under a word means that the automatic Spelling And Grammar Checker is activated, and it recognizes that the underlined word might be misspelled. A green wavy line under a word or sentence indicates a possible grammatical error. You will learn more about the Spelling And Grammar Checker later in this lesson. For now, just ignore any wavy lines.

3. Type **Pacific Books** and press Enter.
4. Finish the address block by typing the following text.

   155 Sashume Street

   San Francisco, CA 94104
5. Press Enter twice to leave two blank lines after the address block.
6. Type **Dear Ms. Valerio:** and press Enter twice.

> **important**
>
> If the Office Assistant is on and it asks you if you want help writing a letter, click Just Type The Letter Without Help. Next, from the menu bar, choose Help, and then click Hide The Office Assistant. Working without the Assistant at this time will let you concentrate on mastering the typing and editing features of Word. For further information on the Assistant, see "Using the Office Assistant," earlier in this lesson.

Type a paragraph in a letter

In this exercise, you continue your letter by typing the following text without pressing Enter.

- Type the following text:

  It was a pleasure speaking with you this morning regarding the upcoming public relations campaign for Pacific Books. As you know, our firm is a full-service public relations agency and works with clients using a team approach. Each team member brings to the client his or her own specialty, giving you a wide range of talents to draw upon. We will assemble your team soon, and we will arrange a meeting for early next week.

Using Delete and Backspace to Edit Text

One of the easiest ways to edit text is to delete and retype. In Word, you can delete text in two ways: with the Delete key and the Backspace key. The Delete key deletes text to the right of the insertion point. You use the Backspace key to delete text to the left of the insertion point. The goal in either case is to place the insertion point at the correct spot to edit the document. Your mouse pointer, which is displayed as an I-beam when placed in the document, is used to move the insertion point.

Move the insertion point

In this exercise, you move the insertion point.

The insertion point is the vertical, blinking line that shows where text will be added when you type.

- Position the pointer before the word *range* and click. The insertion point is now blinking in this new location.

Use Delete and Backspace to edit text

In this exercise, you use both the Backspace and Delete keys to edit your letter.

1. Be sure that the pointer is positioned before the word *range*.
2. Press Delete five times.

   The word *range* is deleted.
3. Type **variety**
4. Click after the word *soon* (before the comma).
5. Press Backspace four times.

   The word *soon* is deleted.
6. Type **shortly**

Correcting Mistakes

You might notice red and green wavy lines under some of your text. These lines flag possible spelling and grammatical errors because the automatic Spelling And Grammar Checker is activated. Once you are finished typing your document, you can go back and edit flagged text. To do this, right-click the flagged word. A shortcut menu is displayed, giving you some correctly spelled words to choose from. You can ignore the suggestions if you like. You can also choose to add the flagged word to a customized dictionary that you build, which can include specialized terms, acronyms, and names that are not included in the standard Word dictionary. If you add the word, it will no longer be underlined as a possible spelling error in later documents.

Use the automatic Spelling And Grammar Checker

In this exercise, you use the automatic Spelling And Grammar Checker to correct spelling errors.

1. Press Ctrl+Home to move to the top of the document.

> **tip**
>
> When you hold the Ctrl key down while pressing Home, you are using a *short-cut key combination*. Doing so moves the insertion point to the top of the document. See more on shortcut keys in Lesson 6, "Automating Tasks."

2. Right-click the word *Sashume*.

   The automatic Spelling And Grammar Checker shortcut menu is displayed.

3. Click Ignore All.

   The red wavy line disappears. Now the automatic Spelling And Grammar Checker will always ignore the spelling of this word.

4. Right-click the word *Valerio*.

   The automatic Spelling And Grammar Checker shortcut menu is displayed.

5. Click Spelling.

   The Spelling dialog box appears.

6. Click Ignore.

   The Spelling And Grammar Checker will ignore this occurrence of the word. The second occurrence of *Valerio* is still flagged.

Disable the automatic Spelling And Grammar Checker

In this exercise, you disable the automatic Spelling And Grammar Checker.

1. On the Tools menu, click Options.

   The Options dialog box appears.

2. Click the Spelling & Grammar tab.
3. In the Spelling area, clear the Check Spelling As You Type check box.
4. In the Grammar area, clear the Check Grammar As You Type check box.
5. Click OK.

   The Options dialog box closes, and the automatic Spelling And Grammar Checker is turned off.

Using AutoCorrect

As you type long sections of text in a document, you may be aware of making typographical errors, but when you look at your document after you're finished, these mistakes may have been corrected. This happens because the AutoCorrect feature is activated. This Word feature corrects the most common typographical errors. For example, the most common misspelling of *and* is *adn*. As soon as you type a space or begin a new paragraph after the misspelled word, Word recognizes the misspelling and automatically corrects it.

You can customize AutoCorrect to recognize misspellings you routinely make. You can also delete any entries that you do not want AutoCorrect to change. And you can take AutoCorrect one step further, using it to recognize abbreviations or codes that you create to automate typing certain words—your full name or your company name, for example.

tip

Other corrections Word automatically makes when AutoCorrect is activated include correcting two-initial capitalization (Like THis), capitalizing the first word of a sentence and the days of the week, and correcting the accidental use of the Caps Lock key.

View AutoCorrect entries

In the following exercises, you continue working with the document you created in the previous section.

If the AutoCorrect command does not appear on the short Tools menu, wait a moment for the menu to expand.

In this exercise, you view the default list of AutoCorrect entries.

1. On the Tools menu, click AutoCorrect.
   The AutoCorrect dialog box appears.
2. Click the scroll bar arrows to scroll through the list and view the entries.
3. Click Cancel.

Add and delete AutoCorrect entries

In this exercise, you add an AutoCorrect entry to automate insertion of often-used text.

1. On the Tools menu, click AutoCorrect.
   The AutoCorrect dialog box appears.
2. In the Replace box, type **pb** and press the Tab key.
3. In the With box, type **Pacific Books**
   Note the capitalization.
4. Click Add, and click OK.

Test the new AutoCorrect entry

In this exercise, you continue your letter and test the new AutoCorrect entry.

1. Press Ctrl+End to move to the end of the document.
2. Press Enter three times.
   You should have two blank lines after the first paragraph.
3. Type **The first step to creating a public relations campaign for pb**
4. Press the Spacebar.
   The text *pb* changes to *Pacific Books*.
5. Type **is to research your company image. We believe that this research is the cornerstone of an effective public relations campaign**.

6. Press Enter twice.
   Blank lines are inserted into the document.

Delete an AutoCorrect entry

In this exercise, you delete an AutoCorrect entry.

1. On the Tools menu, click AutoCorrect.
   The AutoCorrect dialog box appears.
2. In the Replace box, type **pb**
   The entry appears at the top of the list.
3. In the Replace box, select the entry.
4. Click Delete.
   The entry is removed.
5. Click OK.

Turn off AutoCorrect

In this exercise, you turn off AutoCorrect.

1. On the Tools menu, click AutoCorrect.
   The AutoCorrect dialog box appears.
2. Clear the Replace Text As You Type check box.
   AutoCorrect is turned off.
3. Click OK.

Working with Formatting Marks

Whenever you type, special characters called *formatting marks* are inserted into the document. The two formatting marks you work with most often are paragraph marks (¶), which are placed in the document each time you press Enter, and space marks (·), which are inserted each time you press the Spacebar. These characters can be displayed on the screen, or hidden, but in either case, they do not show up in the document when it is printed. These formatting marks help you troubleshoot your document during the editing process. You can use these characters to identify extra lines between paragraphs and spaces between words, for example.

Display formatting marks

In this exercise, you turn on the formatting marks.

Show/Hide ¶

- On the Standard toolbar, click the Show/Hide ¶ button.

  Formatting marks are displayed in your open document.

  Your screen should look similar to the following illustration.

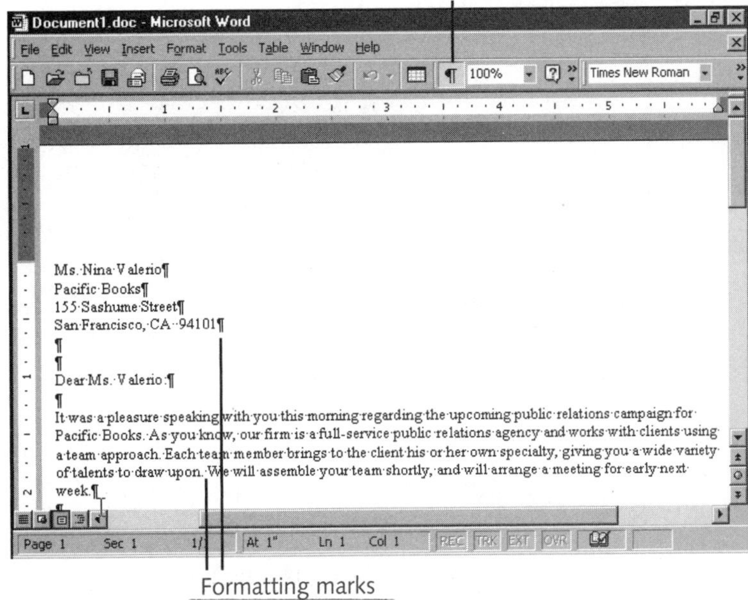

Delete an extra line between paragraphs

In this exercise, you delete an extra line between two paragraphs in your letter.

1. Be sure that the formatting marks are displayed.

2. Click before the first paragraph mark that appears between the two paragraphs.

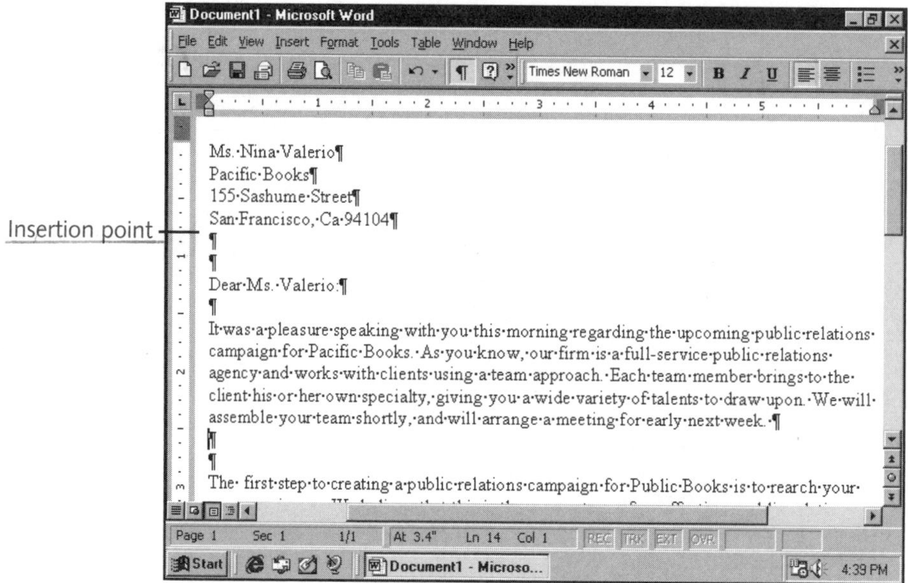

3. Press Delete.
   The paragraph mark is removed, and the lower paragraph moves up one line.

Inserting, Replacing, and Deleting Text

By positioning the insertion point anywhere in your document, you can easily add a word, sentence, or paragraph. You can also quickly select text and delete or replace it.

Insert a sentence in a paragraph

In this exercise, you add an additional sentence to the letter you created in the previous exercises.

1. Click before the sentence beginning *We believe that this research*, and type **This study includes a market analysis and a customer survey.**
2. Press the Spacebar twice to separate the sentences.

Select and replace text in a sentence

In this exercise, you change the sentence you typed in the last exercise.

To drag means to click the insertion point before text you want to select and then, while keeping the mouse button down, moving across the desired text selection.

1. Click before the sentence beginning *This study includes*.
2. Drag the pointer across *This study includes*.
3. Type **Our initial study focuses mainly on**

   The selected phrase is replaced by the new phrase you just typed.

Delete a word

In this exercise, you select and delete a word in a sentence.

1. In the new sentence, double-click the word *mainly* to select it.

   This selection technique automatically selects the spacing following the selection. This ensures the proper spacing after the text has been deleted.
2. Press Delete to remove the word.

   The remaining text in the document moves to close up the space left by the deleted word.

Saving Documents

If you want to store your document for future use, you must give it a name and save it to a hard disk, a floppy disk, or a network drive. In Word 2000, you also have the option to save documents to Web folders that collect documents that will be published as pages on a Web site.

The first time you save a new document, you will give it a name and specify where you want to store it. After that, Word automatically updates the file in that location each time you save it.

Save a document

In this exercise, you name and save the letter you created in the previous exercises. You will store it in a subfolder of the Word 2000 SBS Practice folder on your hard disk. If you have not already done so, refer to "Using the Microsoft Word 2000 Step by Step CD-ROM," earlier in this book, for instructions on installing the Word SBS Practice folder on your hard disk.

Save

1. On the Standard toolbar, click the Save button.

   Because this is the first time you have saved this document, the Save As dialog box appears.

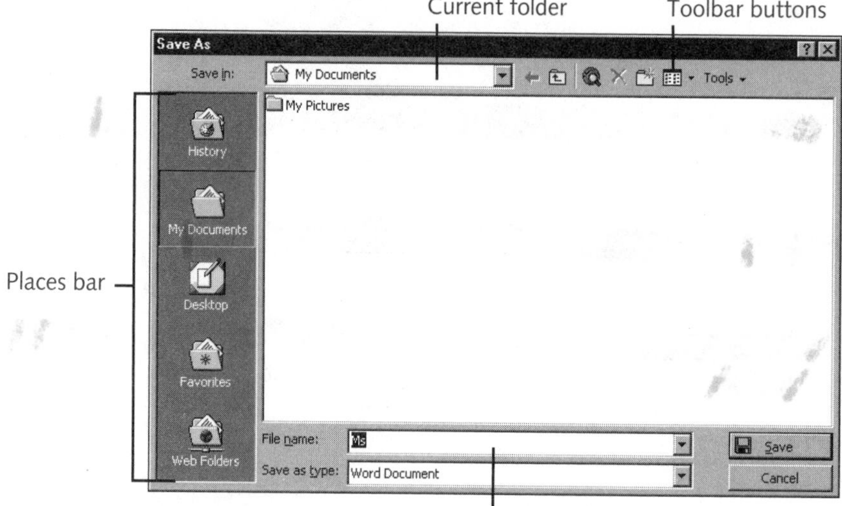

2. In the Save In box, click the drop-down arrow and select your hard drive.
3. In the list of folders, double-click the Word 2000 SBS Practice folder, and then double-click the Lesson01 folder.
4. In the File Name box, select the text and type **Client Letter 01**

> **tip**
>
> File names can be up to 255 characters and can include numbers, spaces, and other characters except the forward slash (/).

5. Click Save to complete the action, and close the Save As dialog box.

Getting Help

The new Microsoft Word 2000 Help interface makes it easier than ever for you to work with the Microsoft Word Help features. When you start Help, your screen is split into separate windows. Your document appears on the left side of the screen, and the Help window is anchored on the right. This way, both your document and Help screen are clearly visible. There are three ways to search for help in Word. You can:

- Use the Answer Wizard to type a question and let Help find topics related to your inquiry.
- Use the Contents tab to look for information in broad categories.
- Use the Index tab to type a key word about a specific topic.

Ask the Answer Wizard a question

In this exercise, you use the Answer Wizard to find out how to save your document.

1. On the Help menu, click Microsoft Word Help.
   The Microsoft Word Help dialog box appears.
2. Click the Answer Wizard tab.
3. In the What Would You Like To Do? box, type **How do I save my document?**
4. Click Search.
   The Search Results are displayed.
5. In the Select Topic To Display area, click Save A Document.
6. On the Help toolbar, click the Hide button.
7. Click the Saving Documents In Microsoft Word Format topic, and then click Save A New, Unnamed Document.
8. Close the Microsoft Word Help window.

Hide

Explore the contents of Microsoft Word Help

In this exercise, you use Help to find information on creating documents.

1. On the Help menu, click Microsoft Word Help.
   The Microsoft Word Help dialog box appears.
2. In the Microsoft Word Help dialog box, click the Contents tab.
3. Double-click Creating, Opening, And Saving Documents.
   The topic is expanded.
4. Double-click Creating Documents.

5. Click Create A Memo.

   The instructions for this topic are displayed on the right side of the Help window.

Hide

6. On the Microsoft Word Help toolbar, click the Hide button.

   The Help tabs are hidden, allowing you to work in your document while reading the Help instructions.

7. Close the Microsoft Word Help window.

Use the Microsoft Word Help Index

In this exercise, you use the Help Index to get help creating an envelope for a letter.

1. On the Help menu, click Microsoft Word Help.

   The Microsoft Word Help dialog box appears.

2. In the Microsoft Word Help dialog box, click the Index tab.
3. In the Type Keywords box, type **envelope**
4. Click Search.
5. In the Choose A Topic list, click Create And Print Envelopes.
6. On the Help toolbar, click the Hide button.

   You are ready to follow the directions to create an envelope.

7. Close the Microsoft Word Help window.

One Step Further Creating Your Own Toolbar

As you settle into your routine as a partner in Impact Public Relations, you decide to create your own toolbar displaying commands that you use most often. This toolbar will not change unless you add or remove buttons.

Create a new toolbar

If you are not working through this lesson sequentially, before proceeding to the next step, open the 01A file in the Lesson01 folder, and save it as Client Letter 01.

In this exercise, you create a new toolbar and add buttons to it.

1. On the View menu, point to Toolbars, and then click Customize.

   The Customize dialog box appears.

2. Click the Toolbars tab.

3. Click New.

   The New Toolbar dialog box appears.

4. In the Toolbar Name box, type **My Toolbar** and click OK.

   A small toolbar appears in the document. You can reposition either the new toolbar or the Customize dialog box by clicking the title bar and dragging to a new location.

   Your screen should look similar to the following illustration.

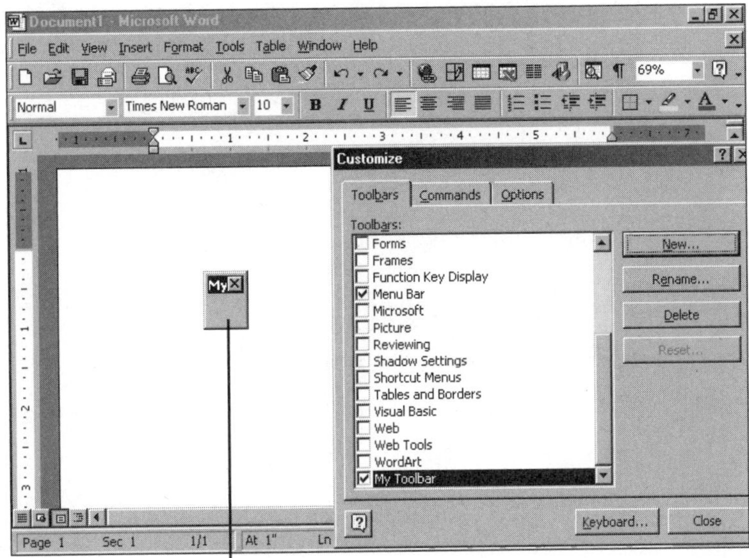

New toolbar

5. In the Customize dialog box, click the Commands tab.

New E-mail Message

6. In the Commands area, drag the New E-mail Message button to the new toolbar.

Date

7. In the Categories area, click Insert, and then in the Commands area, drag the Date button to the new toolbar.

   The toolbar is resized to accommodate the new button.

8. Finish the toolbar by adding any other buttons you want.

9. In the Customize dialog box, click Close.

   The Customize dialog box closes.

Display and use the new toolbar

In this exercise, you move your toolbar and add a date to your letter.

1. Drag the toolbar below the first button on the Standard toolbar.

   Your screen should look similar to the following illustration.

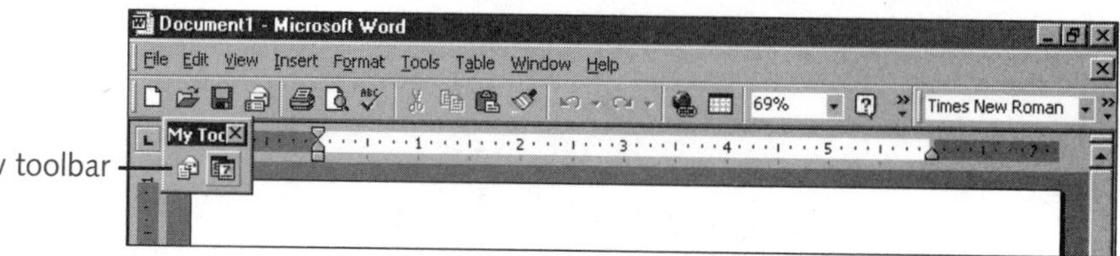

2. Press Ctrl+Home to move the insertion point to the top of the document.

Insert Date

3. Click the Insert Date button and press Enter twice.

   The date is inserted into the document.

Delete the new toolbar

In this exercise, you delete the toolbar you just created.

1. On the View menu, point to Toolbars, and then click Customize.

   The Customize dialog box appears.
2. In the Customize dialog box, click the Toolbars tab.
3. In the Toolbars list, scroll to view the My Toolbar check box.
4. Select My Toolbar.
5. Click Delete, and then click OK to confirm your action.
6. Click Close.

Finish the lesson

Save

1. On the Standard toolbar, click the Save button

   The changes to your document are saved.
2. On the File menu, click Close.
3. On the File menu, click Exit.

Lesson 1 Quick Reference

To	Do this	Button
Start Word	On the Windows taskbar, click Start. Point to Programs, and then click Microsoft Word 2000.	
Customize the Office Assistant	Right-click the Office Assistant. On the shortcut menu that appears, click Choose Office Assistant. In the Office Assistant dialog box, click the Gallery tab. Select an Office Assistant, and click OK.	
Disable the Office Assistant	Right-click the Office Assistant. On the shortcut menu, click Options. In the Office Assistant dialog box, clear the Use The Office Assistant check box. Click OK.	
Find a toolbar button not currently displayed	On the Standard toolbar, click the More Buttons drop-down arrow. Select the desired button. On the toolbar, click the button to turn it off or on.	»
Add or remove a toolbar button	On the Standard toolbar, click the More Buttons drop-down arrow. Point to Add Or Remove Buttons and select or clear check boxes to add or remove buttons.	
Reset toolbars and menus	On the View menu, point to Toolbars, and then click Customize. On the Options tab, click Reset My Usage Data. Click Yes when prompted, and click Close.	
Arrange buttons on a toolbar	On the View menu, point to Toolbars, and then click Customize. On the toolbar, drag the desired button to a new location. Click Close.	
Remove characters	Position the insertion point, and press Backspace to remove characters to the left. Press delete to remove characters to the right.	

Lesson 1 Quick Reference

To	Do this	Button
Correct a spelling error	Right-click a misspelled word. On the shortcut menu, click Spelling. Choose the appropriate option.	
Disable the automatic Spelling And Grammar Checker	On the Tools menu, click AutoCorrect. In the Options dialog box, click the Spelling And Grammer tab. Clear the Check Spelling As You Type and Check Grammar As You Type check boxes. Click OK.	
Add an AutoCorrect Entry	On the Tools menu, click AutoCorrect. In the AutoCorrect dialog box, in the Replace box, type a short letter code or abbreviation. In the With box, type the full word or phrase that will replace the code letters. Click Add, and click OK.	
Turn off AutoCorrect	On the Tools menu, click Auto-Correct. In the AutoCorrect dialog box, clear the Replace Text As You Type check box. Click OK.	
Display formatting marks	On the Standard toolbar, click the Show/Hide ¶ button.	¶
Insert a sentence in a paragraph	Click where you want to insert text, and begin typing.	
Save a document	On the Standard toolbar, click the Save button. Navigate to the folder in which you want to save your document. In the File Name box, type the document name. Click Save.	

Lesson 1 Quick Reference

To	Do this
Use Microsoft Word Help	On the Help menu, click Microsoft Word Help.
Ask the Answer Wizard a question	On the Word menu bar, click Help, and then click Microsoft Word Help. In the Microsoft Word Help dialog box, click the Answer Wizard tab. In the What Would You Like To Do? box, type your question.
Create a toolbar	On the View menu, point to Toolbars, and then click Customize. In the Customize dialog box, click the Toolbars tab, and then click New. In the New Toolbar dialog box, type the name of the new toolbar. Click OK.

LESSON

2

Working with Text

In this lesson you will learn how to:

- ✔ *Open an existing document and save it with a new name.*
- ✔ *Select a view for working in a document.*
- ✔ *Cut, copy, and paste text.*
- ✔ *Undo and redo changes.*
- ✔ *Move multiple text selections at once.*
- ✔ *Link two documents.*

ESTIMATED TIME
30 min.

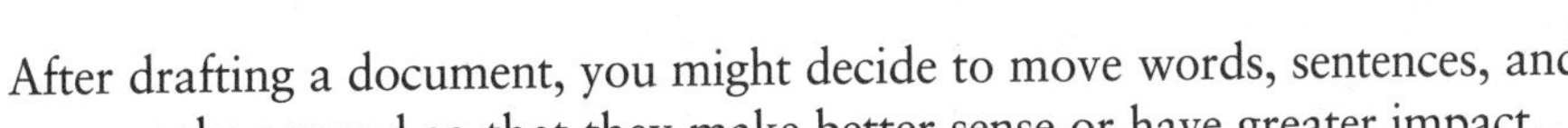

After drafting a document, you might decide to move words, sentences, and paragraphs around so that they make better sense or have greater impact.

In this lesson, you'll learn how to open an existing document and make changes to it while preserving the original file. You'll learn how to select text and move it using the mouse and the Cut, Copy, and Paste toolbar buttons. You'll also move multiple items at once with the help of the Microsoft Office Clipboard. You'll work in the Print Layout view and explore other screen display options. As you make changes, you'll also learn how to undo and redo them.

More Buttons

important

The default toolbar setting in Microsoft Word 2000 displays both the Standard and Formatting toolbars in one row at the top of your document window just below the menu bar. This gives you maximum workspace. While working through the exercises in this book, toolbar buttons you need may not initially be visible. If a toolbar button is not visible, click one of the two More Buttons drop-down arrows on the toolbar to locate the button you need. When you select a new toolbar button, it is automatically added to the visible portion of the toolbar, replacing one that is not used as often.

Opening Documents

If you have not yet installed this book's practice files, refer to "Using the Microsoft Word 2000 Step by Step CD-ROM," earlier in this book.

Normally when you open Word, a new blank document window appears. For this lesson, however, you'll open and edit a document that your partner in Impact Public Relations has already begun.

Start Word and Open a Practice File

In this exercise, you open practice file 02A and then save it with the new name Book Fair 02. By saving the file with a new name, you create a duplicate of the original file that you can edit. The original practice file remains unchanged and available for you to use again if you want to repeat this lesson. This procedure for using practice files is followed throughout the book.

1. On the Windows taskbar, click the Start button.

   The Start menu appears.
2. On the Start menu, point to Programs, and then click Microsoft Word.

   Microsoft Word opens.

Open

3. On the Standard toolbar, click the Open button.

   The Open dialog box appears.
4. Click the Look In drop-down arrow, and then select your hard disk.
5. In the list of folders, double-click the Word 2000 SBS Practice folder, and then double-click the Lesson02 folder.

   Your screen should look similar to the following illustration.

In the Open dialog box, you select the folder and document you want to open. The Look In box shows the folder that is currently selected.

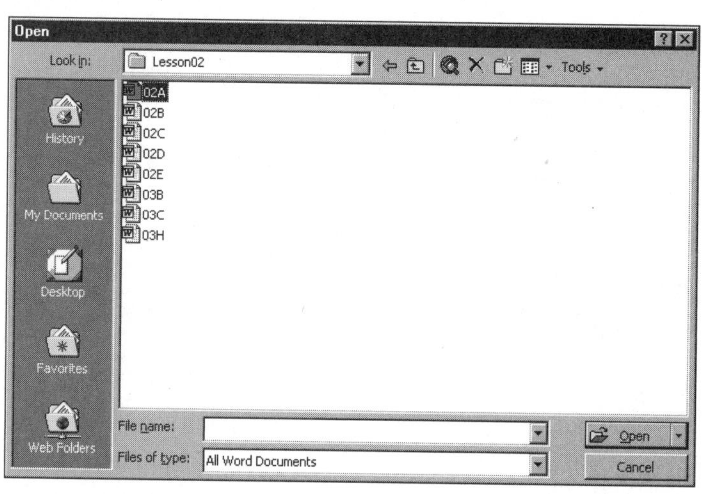

6. In the file list, double-click the 02A file to open it.

   The document opens in the document window.

Saving a File with a New Name

When you save a file, you give it a name and specify where you want to store it. Each time you open a practice file while working through the lessons in this book, you save it with a new name. By doing so, you leave the original practice file unchanged, and you can repeat the exercises as many times as you want.

Save the practice file with a new name

In this exercise, you save the 02A practice file with the name Book Fair 02.

1. On the File menu, click Save As.

   The Save As dialog box appears.

2. Be sure the Lesson02 folder appears in the Save In box.
3. In the File Name box, if the text is not already selected, select it.
4. Type **Book Fair 02**
5. Click Save to save the file and close the dialog box.

   Your file is saved with the name Book Fair 02. When the dialog box closes, your new document is open, and the new document name appears in the title bar. Word automatically closes the original document.

Display formatting marks

To make it easier to edit your document, you can display formatting marks such as paragraph marks and space marks on your screen.

Show/Hide ¶

If the Show/Hide ¶ button is not visible, on the Standard toolbar, click the More Buttons drop-down arrow to locate the button.

- If formatting marks are not currently displayed, on the Standard toolbar, click the Show/Hide ¶ button.

Opening a File from the Documents and File Menus

You can open a document directly using the Documents menu, which you display from the Windows Start menu. You might find this quicker and easier than first opening Word and then opening a file.

Open a file from the Documents menu

1. On the Windows taskbar, click Start.
2. Point to the Documents menu.

   The last 15 documents that you used are displayed in alphabetical order on the menu.
3. Click the document you want to open.

   The associated program opens and displays the document.

Opening a File from the File Menu List

When you are already working in Word, a quick way to open a recently used file is to click the File menu. Listed at the bottom of the File menu are up to nine of the most recently used files. Click a file to open it.

The default number of files listed is four. To change the default number, follow the steps below.

Expand or shorten the File menu list

1. On the Tools menu, click Options, and then click the General tab.
2. In the Recently Used File list, click the arrows to increase or decrease the number.

   The names of the selected number of files will be displayed on the File menu.
3. Click OK.

Selecting a View for Working in a Document

Word provides a range of *views*, or screen displays, that you can use to do your work. Which one you choose depends on the type of document you've created and how you want to work with it. The *Normal* view helps you focus on composition, text revisions, and basic formatting such as bold and italic text, without worrying too much about the layout of the page.

When you're applying more elaborate formatting or moving and copying text, it's helpful to work in *Print Layout* view—the default view. This view shows you the page layout and formatting so you can easily see the effects of formatting or how your document looks after you've cut or moved text.

Web Layout view shows you how your Web page will be displayed in a Web browser. *Outline* view lets you focus on document organization by highlighting headings and subheadings. *Document Map* view, discussed later in this lesson, lets you see all document headings on one side of the window. You can move around in your document by clicking the headings. *Full Screen* view fills the window with your document, and no toolbars or controls are displayed.

All of these views can be selected from the View menu. You can also open Normal, Web Layout, Print Layout, and Outline views by using the buttons on the horizontal scroll bar at the bottom left side of the document window. In this lesson, you'll work in Print Layout view.

Work in Print Layout view

Print Layout View

- If you are not already in Print Layout view, click the Print Layout View button—the third button from the left on the horizontal scroll bar.

  Your document should look similar to the following illustration.

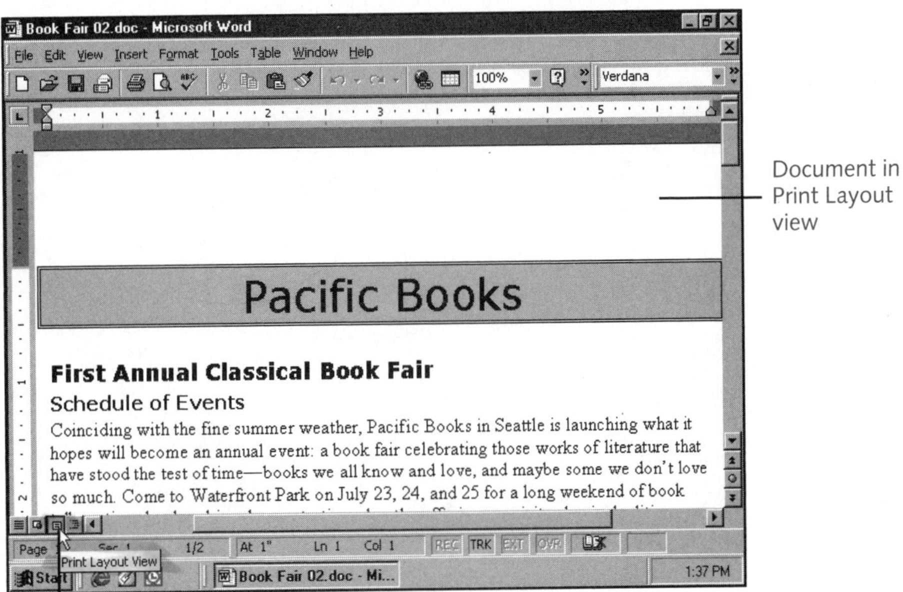

Selecting Text with the Mouse

Most editing actions require you to first select text. Microsoft Word makes text selection quick and easy. Using the mouse, you can select any amount of text, from one character to the whole document. Following is a summary of mouse text selection techniques.

To	Do this
Select a word	Click before the word, hold down the mouse button, and drag the pointer over the word, releasing the mouse button at the end of the word. Or position the pointer over the word and double-click.
Select more than one word	Select a word, and while keeping the mouse button down, drag the pointer over additional text.
Select a line	Position the pointer to the left side of the line you want to select, and when the right-pointing arrow appears, click the mouse.
Select a paragraph	Double-click to select a word, and then quickly click a third time. Or position the pointer to the left side of the paragraph, and when the right-pointing arrow appears, double-click.
Select a whole document	Position the pointer to the left side of the document, and when the right-pointing arrow appears, click the mouse three times.
Select any amount of text	Click where you want the selection to begin. Then, while holding down the Shift key, click where you want the selection to end.

On the left side of your document, there's an invisible selection bar. Click there when the right-pointing arrow appears to select a line, a paragraph, or the whole document.

Moving and Copying Text Using the Mouse

The document your partner has asked you to edit already contains several paragraphs and headings, but it still needs a lot of work. You begin to edit the document by moving a heading and copying some text to a new location.

The drag-and-drop feature in Word allows you to use the mouse to pull selected text from one place and put it in another. Dragging text is the most efficient way to move or copy it, as long as you can see the destination for the text on your screen.

Change the magnification

Before moving or copying text, you can change the magnification of your screen to see more of your text within the window.

100%

Zoom

- On the Standard toolbar, click the Zoom drop-down arrow, and then click Page Width.

Select and move a heading

If you are not working through this lesson sequentially, before proceeding to the next step, open the 02B file in the Lesson02 folder, and save it as Book Fair 02.

In this exercise, you move a heading in your document.

1. Scroll down so that the headings *Schedule of Events* and *Daily Events* show in the same window.
2. Position the mouse pointer in the selection bar, before the *Schedule of Events* heading.

   The mouse pointer changes to a right-pointing arrow.
3. Click to select the heading.

   The selected text changes to white text on a darker background.

   Your screen should look similar to the following illustration.

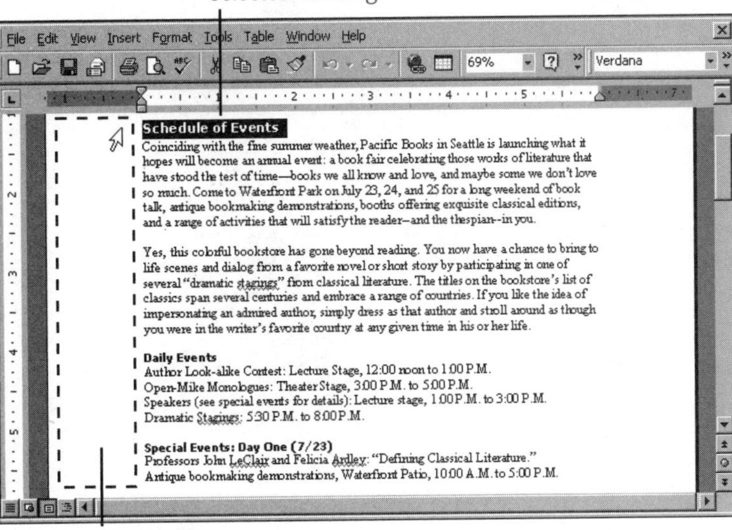

4. Position the mouse pointer over the selected heading.

   The pointer turns into a left-pointing arrow.

5. Click and hold down the mouse button.

   A small, dotted box and a dotted insertion point appear.

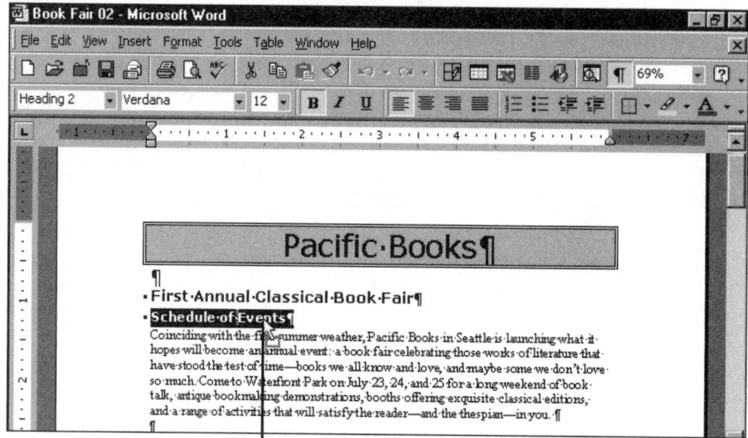

Mouse pointer ready to drag selected text

6. Drag down until the dotted insertion point is before the heading *Daily Events*, and then release the mouse button.

7. Click anywhere outside of the selected text to cancel the selection.

   Your screen should look similar to the following illustration.

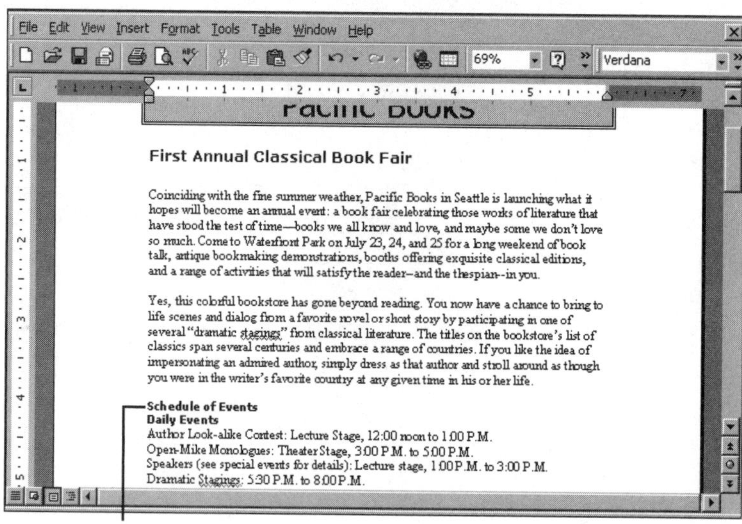

Moved text

Copy text using the mouse

In this exercise, you use the mouse and keyboard to copy text to be repeated in the document.

1. Scroll down until you can see all of the *Daily Events* section.
2. In the line that begins *Open-Mike Monologues*, select the text *Theater Stage* (including the end comma).
3. Hold down the Ctrl key.
4. Point to the selected text, and then hold down the mouse button.
5. Drag to position the dotted insertion point after the text *Dramatic Stagings* in the *Daily Events* section.
6. Release the mouse button, and then release the Ctrl key.

   A copy of the selected text is inserted. The original text is unchanged.

   Your screen should look similar to the following illustration.

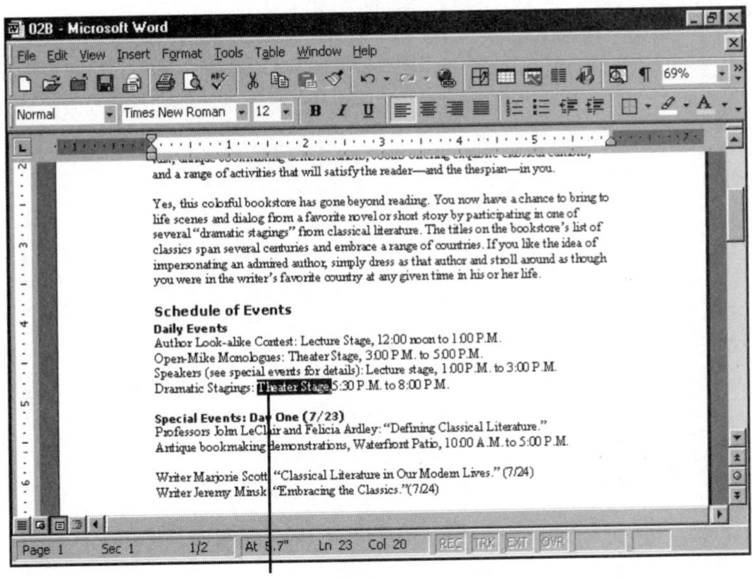

Copied text

7. Click anywhere outside of the selected text to cancel the selection.

Undoing and Redoing Changes

You can undo and redo changes after you make them by using the Undo and Redo buttons on your toolbar. The Undo button reverses your last action. You use the Redo button to reverse an Undo action. For example, if you delete a word and then click Undo, the word will be restored to your document. If you then click Redo, it will be deleted again.

You can also reverse more than one action. When you click the Undo drop-down arrow, you'll see a list of the actions you can reverse. The actions in the Undo list appear with the most recent change at the top of the list and all previous changes below it. Because several changes in sequence often depend on preceding changes, you cannot select an individual action on the list without undoing all the actions that appear above it.

You can undo most Word commands. Commands that cannot be undone include saving, printing, opening, and creating documents.

Undo the last change

Undo

You can also press Ctrl+Z to undo changes.

- On the Standard toolbar, click the Undo button to undo your last change.

  If this action did not remove the text you copied, you might have pressed another key before you clicked the Undo button. Click the Undo button until the new text is removed and the text reads as it did originally.

Redo the change

Redo

If the Redo button is not visible, on the Standard toolbar, click the More Buttons drop-down arrow to locate the button.

- On the Standard toolbar, click the Redo button to redo the action you just undid.

  The phrase you copied, *Theater Stage*, should now be replaced to where you first copied it, after *Dramatic Stagings*.

Undo all changes

- On the Standard toolbar, click the Undo drop-down arrow, and then select all the actions.

  All of the changes you made are reversed.

Redo all changes

- On the Standard toolbar, click the Redo drop-down arrow, and then select the top two changes in the list to redo your most recent paste actions.

  Your document should look similar to the following illustration.

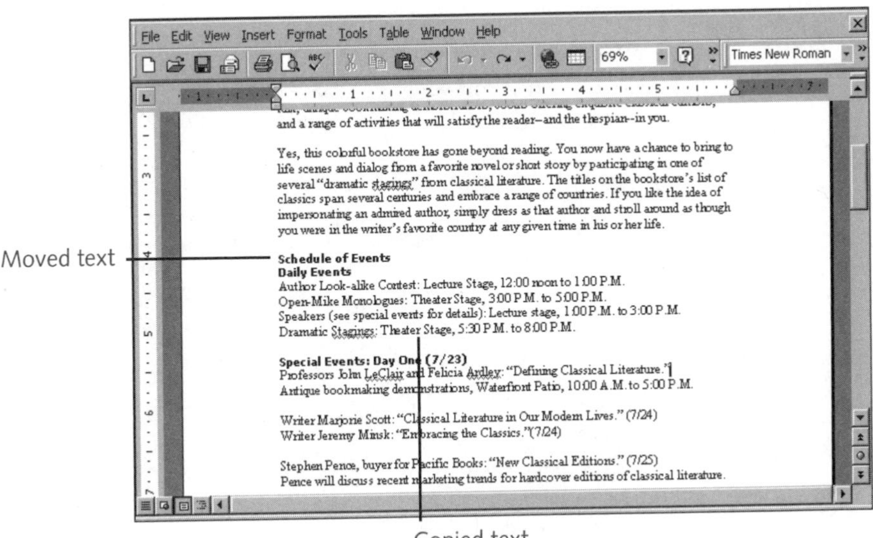

Moving and Copying Text Using Buttons

If you are not working through this lesson sequentially, before proceeding to the next step, open the 02C file in the Lesson02 folder, and save it as Book Fair 02.

If you want to move text to a location that is not visible in the document window, you can use the Cut, Copy, and Paste buttons on the Standard toolbar. The Cut button deletes selected text from your document and copies it to the *Windows Clipboard*. The Clipboard is an invisible storage area for text. If you want to copy text from a location in your document, leaving the original text as it is, you use the Copy button. Selected text is again copied to the Windows Clipboard. When you have located the point in the document where you want to move your text, you position the insertion point and then click the Paste button. This moves the text from the Clipboard.

Move text

In this exercise, you move text using the Cut and Paste buttons.

1. Press Ctrl+Home to move the insertion point to the beginning of the document.
2. In the second paragraph, select the last sentence, which begins *If you like the idea of impersonating*. Don't include the ending paragraph mark in the selection.

Cut

You can also move selected text to the Clipboard by pressing Ctrl+X.

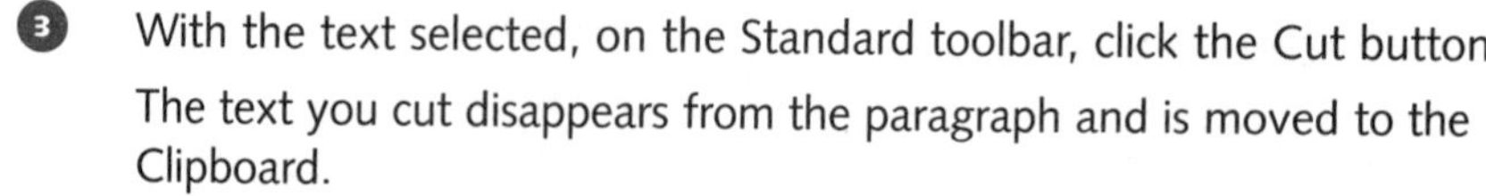

3. With the text selected, on the Standard toolbar, click the Cut button.

   The text you cut disappears from the paragraph and is moved to the Clipboard.

4. Scroll until you see the heading *Author Look-alike Contests* on page 2.
5. Click at the beginning of the paragraph before the text *The contests will take place*.
6. On the Standard toolbar, click the Paste button to insert the cut text from the Clipboard. Press the Spacebar to separate the sentences. Your screen should look similar to the following illustration.

Paste

You can also paste text by pressing Ctrl+V.

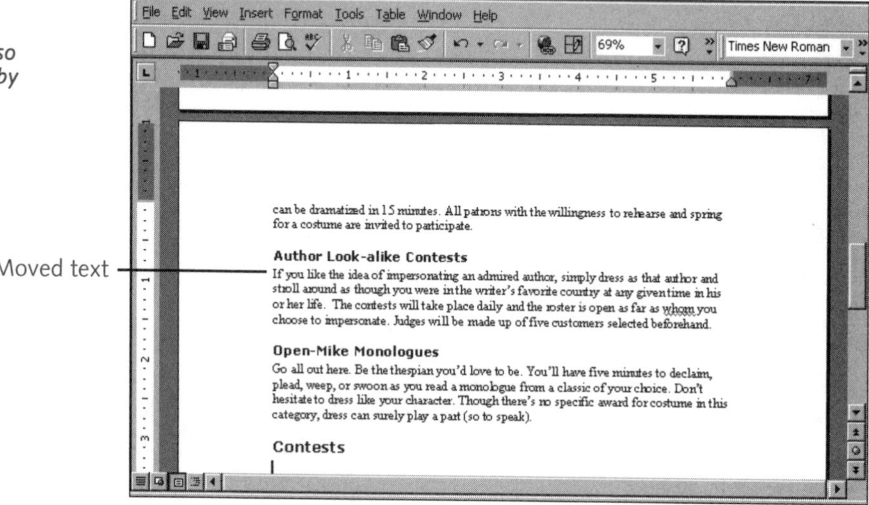

Copy and paste text

In this exercise, you copy and paste text in two places and then edit the headings.

1. Scroll up to the heading *Special Events: Day One (7/23)* on page 1.
2. Select the heading, including the ending paragraph mark.
3. On the Standard toolbar, click the Copy button.

   You see no change in the document, but a copy of the selected text is placed on the Clipboard.

Copy

You can also copy text to the Clipboard by pressing Ctrl+C.

> **tip**
>
> Microsoft Word 2000 introduces an additional type of Clipboard, the *Microsoft Office Clipboard*, that enables you to move or copy up to 12 text items at one time. See "Moving Multiple Items at One Time," later in this lesson, for more information.

4. Click before the line that begins *Writer Marjorie Scott.*
5. On the Standard toolbar, click the Paste button.

   A copy of the heading is inserted.

Paste

You can also press the F4 key to repeat your last action.

6. Click before the line that begins *Stephen Pence.*
7. Click the Paste button again.

   A copy of the heading is pasted a second time.

Edit the new headings

In this exercise, you modify the headings.

1. In the first new heading, above the name *Marjorie Scott*, select *One* and then type **Two**
2. Select the *3* in the date and type **4**

   The text *Two (7/24)* replaces the text *One (7/23)*.
3. In the second new heading, above the name *Stephen Pence*, select *One* and then type **Three**
4. In the *Special Events: Day Three* heading, select the *3* in the date and type **5**

   The text *Three (7/25)* replaces the text *One (7/23)*.
5. In the lines under each of the three *Special Events* headings, delete the dates.

   Your screen should look similar to the following illustration.

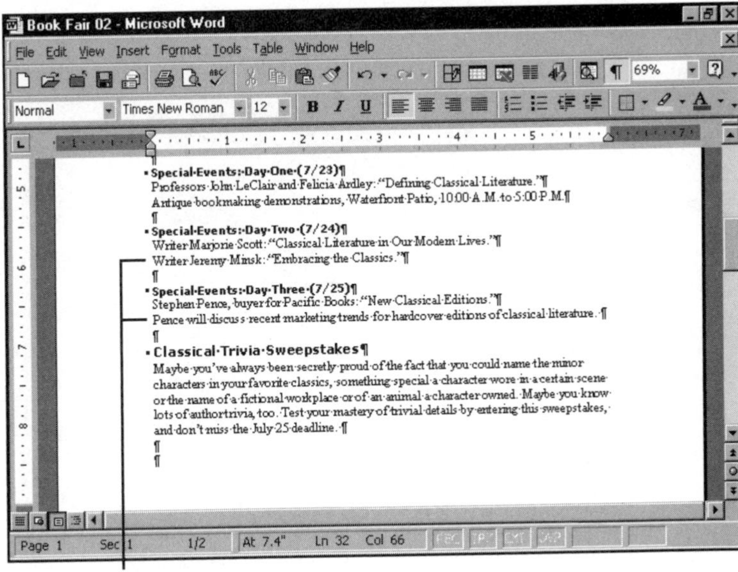

important

When you edit the headings, if the new text you type does not replace the old text, but instead appears next to it, do this: Go to the Tools menu, click Options, and then click the Edit tab. In the Editing Options area, be sure that the Typing Replaces Selection check box is selected. For more information, see the Edit Options section in Appendix B, "Matching the Exercises."

Moving Text Over a Longer Distance

When moving text over many pages in your document, you might find it convenient to work in the Document Map view. This will help you avoid the need to scroll or page up and down excessively. The Document Map view splits the window to show your document headings and subheadings on the left and your document on the right. When you click a heading on the left, the document on the right moves instantly to that heading. You can then place your insertion point in the document and paste the text you have moved or copied. By clicking the plus or minus sign next to a heading, you can expand or collapse the heading to display or hide its subheadings.

In the following exercises, you cut and paste text while in the Document Map view.

tip

In the Document Map view, you may want to turn off the ruler. To do so, on the View menu, click Ruler. If you want to see more of the left side of the window, move the pointer over the border between the two sides. The pointer turns into the two-headed *Resize* arrow. Use it to drag the border. Some headings in the left window may still not be shown completely, but when you place the pointer over one of them, a ScreenTip displays the full heading.

Switch to Document Map view

Document Map

- On the View menu, click Document Map, then press Ctrl+Home to move the insertion point to the top of the document.

  Your screen should look similar to the following illustration.

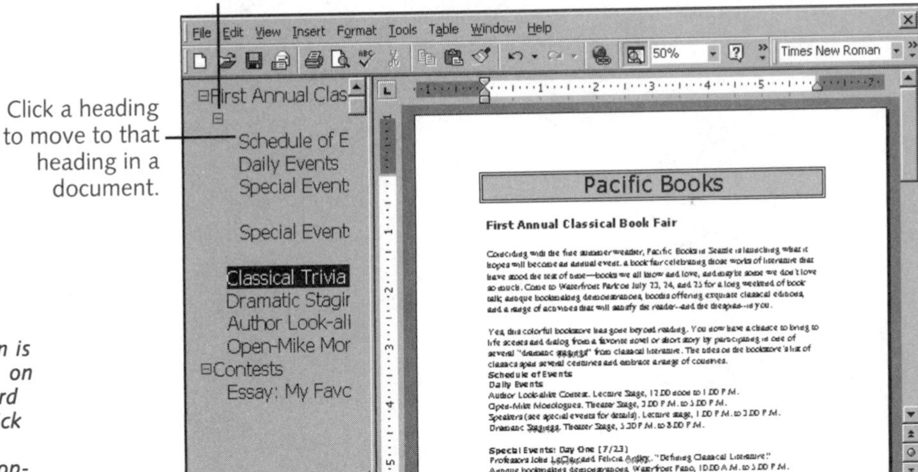

If the Document Map button is not visible, on the Standard toolbar, click the More Buttons drop-down arrow to locate the button.

Move a block of text

In this exercise, you select text and move it to the bottom of the document.

1. In the left side of the window, click the heading *Schedule of Events*.

   The view jumps to this heading in your document, and you see the heading at the top of the window on the right side, with the insertion point placed before it.

2. In the document, select the entire schedule starting with the heading *Schedule of Events* and including all text through the last special event—the line that ends *editions of classical literature*. Include the ending paragraph mark in the selection.

3. On the Standard toolbar, click the Cut button.

   Cut

   The text is removed from the document and stored on the Clipboard.

4. On the left side of the window, click the heading *Essay: My Favorite Classics*.

5. In the document, click before the first paragraph mark under the *Essay* paragraph.

6. On the Standard toolbar, click the Paste button.

   Paste

   The Schedule of Events is now the last section in the document.

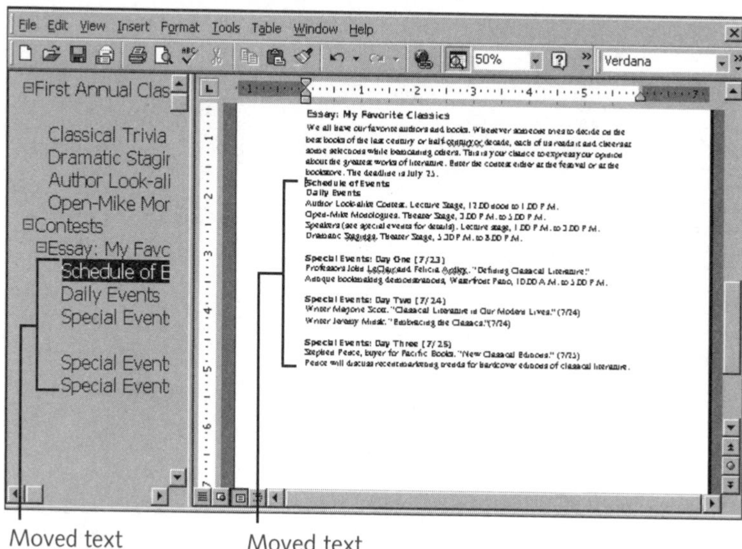

7. To add a line of space between the *Essay* and *Schedule* sections, click before *Schedule* and press Enter. The schedule moves down one line.

Moving Multiple Items at One Time

With the *Collect And Paste* feature in Microsoft Word 2000, you can move or copy up to 12 items to the Microsoft Office Clipboard. You can paste the items in any order into various documents or paste them all in one place, all at one time.

You use the Microsoft Office Clipboard toolbar when you want to collect and paste text. The toolbar displays an icon for each bit of text you have copied onto it. A ScreenTip identifies the copied text, and the text you've moved most recently is stored as the last item on the toolbar. The Microsoft Office Clipboard differs from the Windows Clipboard in that you can copy to it several items at a time rather than only one.

The Clipboard toolbar includes Copy and Paste buttons. If you want to cut the text from your document rather than copy it, use the Cut button on the Standard toolbar. The cut text will be moved to the Clipboard toolbar and cut from your document.

As you continue your edits to the book fair document while working in Document Map view, you'll see how easy it is to organize the document further by cutting and pasting.

For a demonstration of how to move two blocks of text, in the Multimedia folder on the Microsoft Word 2000 Step by Step CD-ROM, double-click ClipBoard.

Move two blocks of text

In this exercise, you move text to group similar items together.

1. On the View menu, point to Toolbars, and then click Clipboard.

   The Clipboard toolbar appears in the right side of the document window. (Drag the title bar if you need to move the toolbar over.)

2. In the left side of the window, click the heading *Author Look-alike Contests*.

   The *Author Look-alike Contests* heading now is shown at the top of the document.

3. Select the heading and the text under it, including the ending paragraph mark.

4. On the Standard toolbar, click the Cut button.

   The text is removed from the document and stored on the Clipboard.

Cut

5. On the left side of the window, click the heading *Classical Trivia Sweepstakes*.

   The heading is displayed at the top of your document.

6. In the document, select the heading *Classical Trivia Sweepstakes* and the text under it (including the ending paragraph mark), and then, on the Standard toolbar, click the Cut button.

   The Clipboard displays the items you cut from your document.

   Your screen should look similar to the following illustration.

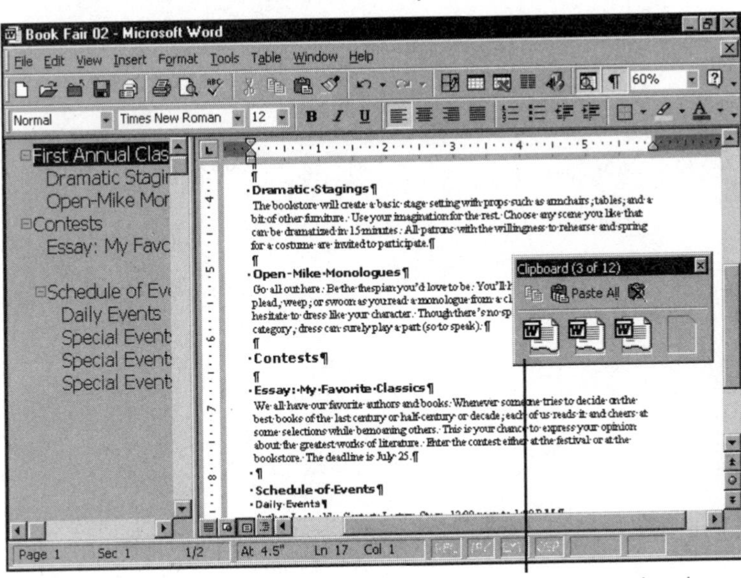

Items moved to the Clipboard and ready to be pasted

7. In the document, click before the paragraph mark above the heading *Essay: My Favorite Classics* and below the heading *Contests*.
8. On the Clipboard, click the text item *Author Look-alike Contests*.

   The text is pasted above the *Essay* heading.
9. In the document, click in front of the heading *Schedule of Events* on page 2.
10. On the Clipboard, click the text item *Classical Trivia Sweepstakes*.

    The text is pasted below the *Essay* section.

Clear the Clipboard

Clear Clipboard

1. On the Clipboard toolbar, click the Clear Clipboard button.

   Your text items are cleared from the Clipboard.
2. Close the Clipboard.

> **tip**
>
> To paste Clipboard items in a document all at once, in the same order in which they appear on the Clipboard, on the Clipboard toolbar, click the Paste All button.

Close Document Map view

Document Map

If the Document Map button is not visible, on the Standard toolbar, click the More Buttons drop-down arrow to locate the button.

- On the Standard toolbar, click the Document Map button.

Save the document

Save

- On the Standard toolbar, click Save.

  Changes made to the document are saved.

One Step Further Linking Two Documents

Your partner has created a new logo for your client Pacific Books. You want to use the logo in the book fair document. This is a perfect opportunity to use the Word feature called Paste Special. Using Paste Special, you can paste the logo and simultaneously link your book fair document to the source document you copied the logo from. After that, when anyone makes formatting changes to the logo in the source document, those changes will be reflected in your linked document.

In this exercise, you paste the logo into Book Fair 02 using Paste Special to link your document to the source document.

Open a document and save it with a new name

Open

If you are not working through this lesson sequentially, before proceeding to the next step, open the 02D file in the Lesson 02 folder, and save it as Book Fair 02.

1. On the Standard toolbar, click the Open button.

   The Open dialog box appears.
2. Be sure the Word 2000 SBS Practice folder appears in the Look In box.
3. Double-click the Word 2000 SBS Practice folder, and double-click the Lesson02 folder.
4. In the file list, double-click the 02E file to open it.

   The document contains a logo for Pacific Books.
5. On the File menu, click Save As.

   The Save As dialog box appears.
6. Be sure the Lesson02 folder appears in the Save In box.
7. In the Save As Type box, be sure Word Document appears. Select and delete any text in the File Name box, and then type **Logo Practice 02**
8. Click Save.

   You now have two documents open: Book Fair 02 and Logo Practice 02, with Logo Practice 02 currently displayed. The Windows taskbar shows a button for each open document.

Link two documents using Paste Special

In this exercise, you copy and paste the logo using the Paste Special command to link two documents.

1. In the Logo Practice 02 document, drag to select the logo and its ending paragraph mark.

Copy

2. On the Standard toolbar, click the Copy button.

   The logo is copied to the Clipboard.
3. On the taskbar, click the button for Book Fair 02 to display it.
4. In Book Fair 02, place the pointer in the selection bar next to the heading Pacific Books, and click to select it. Press the Delete key.
5. On the Edit menu, click Paste Special.

   The Paste Special dialog box appears.
6. In the Paste Special dialog box, in the As list, select Formatted Text (RTF) to reflect the type of text you are pasting from the source document.
7. Click Paste Link to create a link in your document to the source document.

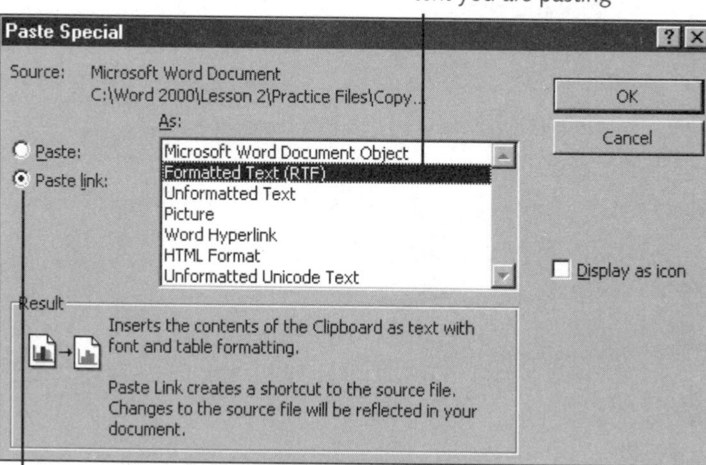

8. Click OK.

   The new logo replaces the heading in the Book Fair 02 document.

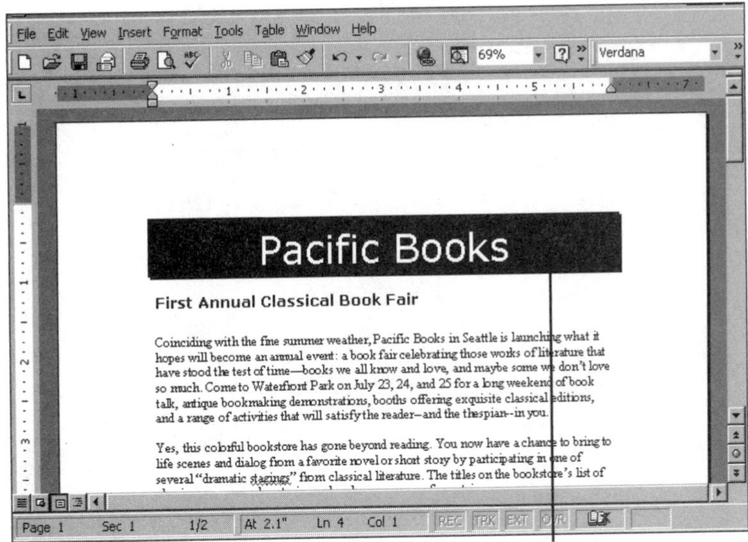

Test the link

In this exercise, you test the link between the two documents.

1. On the Windows taskbar, click Logo Practice 02, and then select the logo.
2. On the Format menu, click Borders And Shading.

   The Borders And Shading dialog box appears.
3. On the Shading tab, in the Fill area, choose a color.

   The Preview area gives a sample of the new color.
4. Click OK.

   Logo Practice 02 is displayed with the new color.
5. Click anywhere outside the selected logo to turn off the selection and view the color.
6. On the Windows taskbar, click Book Fair 02.

   The logo should reflect your change to the background color.

Finish the lesson

Save

1. On the Standard toolbar, click the Save button.

   To save your changes to Book Fair 02 and Logo Practice 02, click Yes when the message boxes ask if you want to save changes.
2. On the File menu, click Close.
3. On the File menu, click Exit.

Lesson 2 Quick Reference

To	Do this	Button
Open an existing document	On the Standard toolbar, click the Open button. In the Open dialog box, double-click folders to open and display their contents. When the file you want to open appears in the file list, double-click it.	
Save a document with a new name	On the File menu, click Save As. In the Save As dialog box, type the new file name. Click OK.	
Display a document in a different view	Click the desired view button located to the left of the horizontal scroll bar. Or, on the View menu, select the desired view.	
Adjust the screen magnification	On the Standard toolbar, click the Zoom drop-down arrow, and then select a magnification.	
Move or copy text using the mouse	Select the text. When the mouse pointer becomes a left-pointing arrow, click and hold the mouse button as you drag the text. At the new location, release the button to insert the text.	
Undo a change	On the Standard toolbar, click the Undo button.	
Redo an undone change	On the Standard toolbar, click the Redo button.	
Move or copy text using toolbar buttons	Select the text. On the Standard toolbar, click the Cut or Copy button. Click where you want to insert the text, and click the Paste button.	

Lesson 2 Quick Reference

To	Do this	Button
Work in Document Map view	On the Standard toolbar, click the Document Map button.	
Move multiple text items at once	On the View menu, point to Toolbars, and then click Clipboard. Cut or copy items to the Clipboard. Position the insertion point and then click an item to paste it.	
Link two documents	Select the item to be linked. On the Standard toolbar, click the Copy button. In the document, click where the item is to be inserted/linked. On the Standard toolbar, click the Edit Paste Special button. In the As box, select an option, and click Paste Link. Click OK.	

LESSON

3

Formatting Characters and Paragraphs

In this lesson you will learn how to:

- ✔ *Apply formatting to text.*
- ✔ *Copy formatting using the Format Painter.*
- ✔ *Change fonts, font sizes, and font effects.*
- ✔ *Modify the position of paragraphs on a page.*
- ✔ *Add borders and shading to paragraphs.*
- ✔ *Control hyphenation in a document.*
- ✔ *Create a quick logo.*

ESTIMATED TIME
35 min.

Learning how to format text will help you improve the impact of your documents. With quick and easy Microsoft Word formatting features, you can emphasize key points and reposition text for greater clarity.

In this lesson, you'll master the use of Word formatting features to enhance a letter to a new client. You'll work with the Format Painter to apply repeated formatting to text, and you'll learn how to align text and apply borders and shading to paragraphs. You'll also learn to use paragraph and line spacing, line breaks, and hyphenation rules to make your work easier.

important

The default toolbar setting in Microsoft Word 2000 displays both the Standard and Formatting toolbars in one row at the top of the document window, just below the menu bar. This gives you maximum workspace. While working through the exercises in this book, toolbar buttons you need may not initially be visible. If a toolbar button is not visible, click one of the two More Buttons drop-down arrows on the toolbar to locate the button you need. When you select a new toolbar button, it is automatically added to the visible portion of the toolbar, replacing one that is not used as often.

More Buttons

If you have not yet installed this book's practice files, refer to "Using the Microsoft Word 2000 Step by Step CD-ROM," earlier in this book.

Start Word and open a practice file

In this exercise, you start Word, open a practice file, then save it under a new name.

1. On the Windows taskbar, click the Start button.
   The Start menu appears.
2. On the Start menu, point to Programs, and then click Microsoft Word.
   Microsoft Word 2000 opens.
3. On the Standard toolbar, click the Open button.
   The Open dialog box appears.
4. Click the Look In drop-down arrow, and then select your hard disk.
5. In the list of folders, double-click the Word 2000 SBS Practice folder, and then double-click the Lesson03 folder.
6. In the file list, double-click the 03A file to open it.
   The document, a letter about Impact Public Relations to a potential client, opens in the document window.
7. On the File menu, click Save As.
   The Save As dialog box appears.
8. Be sure that the Lesson03 folder appears in the Save In box.
9. In the File Name box, select the text, and then type **Client Letter 03**
10. Click Save.

Open

Display formatting marks

To make it easier to edit your document, you can display formatting marks such as paragraph marks and space marks on your screen.

Show/Hide ¶

- If formatting marks are not currently displayed, on the Standard toolbar, click the Show/Hide ¶ button.

Changing the Appearance of Text

You can change the appearance of text by applying formatting attributes, which are available on the Formatting toolbar. Commonly used attributes include bold, italic, and underline.

You can also change the font style and font size with a click of a button. A font is the typeface applied to text, numbers, and punctuation. There are many fonts from which to choose. In Word 2000, the Font list has been enhanced to display the name of the font in its own typeface so that you can preview it before you select it. Word provides other, more complex formats that can be applied from the Format menu.

If you are not working through this lesson sequentially, before proceeding to the next step, open the 03A file in the Lesson03 folder, and save it as Client Letter 03.

Apply basic formatting

In this exercise, you enhance a letter to a client with text formatting.

1. In the first sentence of the third paragraph, select the text *Impact Public Relations*.
2. On the Formatting toolbar, click the Bold button, and then click the Italic button.
3. Click anywhere outside of the selected text to cancel the selection. *Impact Public Relations* is now displayed with bold and italic formatting.

   Your screen should look similar to the following illustration.

Bold

Italic

If the toolbar button you need is not visible, on the Formatting toolbar, click the More Buttons drop-down arrow to locate the button.

More Buttons

Bold and italic formatting applied to text

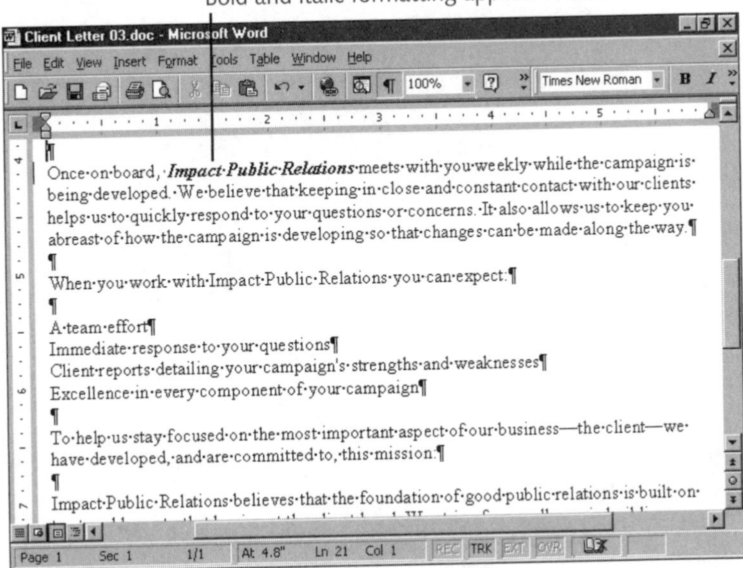

Modify the font and font size

Font size is measured in units called points; there are 72 points in an inch.

In this exercise, you change the font style and font size of your company name.

1. In the first sentence of the third paragraph, select the text *Impact Public Relations*.

If the Font button is not visible, on the Formatting toolbar, click the More Buttons drop-down arrow to locate the button.

More Buttons

2. On the Formatting toolbar, click the Font drop-down arrow to see more options.

   Your screen should look similar to the following illustration.

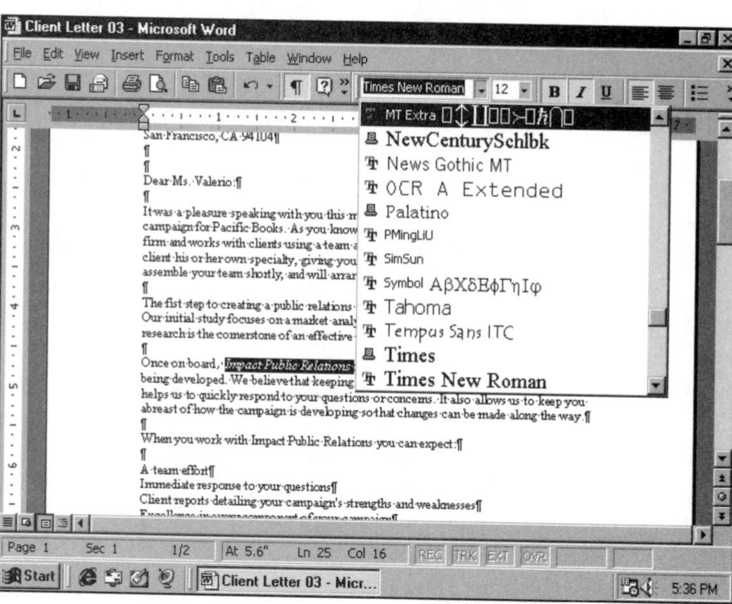

3. In the Font list, scroll down, and click Verdana.

   The selected text is changed to the Verdana font.

Font Size

4. On the Formatting toolbar, click the Font Size drop-down arrow, and then click 10.

   The size of the selected text changes to 10 points.

5. Click anywhere outside of the selected text to cancel the selection.

Using Additional Text Effects

Not all Word formatting options are available on the Formatting toolbar. You can access some additional effects only from the Format menu. Effects used to animate text are also available in Word. You might find these effects particularly useful when designing Web pages, for example. To apply these text effects, on the Format menu, click Font, and then click the Text Effects tab. Select from the following text effects.

Text effects	Description
Blinking Background	Background around text flashes on and off.
Las Vegas Lights	Blinking marquee of different colors flashes around text.
Marching Black Ants	Black dashed line moves around text.
Marching Red Ants	Red dashed line moves around text.
Shimmer	Text vibrates on the screen.
Sparkle Text	Text is randomly sprinkled with colored confetti-like shapes.

In the Font dialog box, click the Character Spacing tab to find more ways to enhance your text with these character-spacing rules:

Feature	Description
Scale	Increase and decrease the width of the characters by the percentage selected.
Spacing	Adjust the space between characters. Choose from Normal, Condensed, or Expanded. In the By box, select an exact amount of space, measured in points.
Position	Raises and lowers the selected text position in the line by increments.
Kerning For Fonts	Allows you to specify whether you want the space between characters to be adjusted automatically based on the size of the font.

Apply additional text effects from the Format menu

If you are not working through this lesson sequentially, open the 03B file in the Lesson03 folder, and save it as Client Letter 03.

In this exercise, you apply formatting from the Format menu.

1. In the first sentence of the third paragraph, select the text *Impact Public Relations*.
2. On the Format menu, click Font.

   The Font dialog box appears.
3. Click the Font tab, and in the Effects area, select the Small Caps check box.

   The formatting is applied and the result can be seen in the Preview window.
4. Click OK.
5. Click anywhere outside of the selected text to cancel the selection.

Applying Repeated Formatting

If you are not working through this lesson sequentially, before proceeding to the next step, open the 03C file in the Lesson03 folder, and save it as Client Letter 03.

The text *Impact Public Relations* appears several times in the letter. Instead of selecting the text and repeatedly applying the formatting, you can use a Word shortcut that copies formatting from text, and then pastes, or *paints*, it onto other text selections. This feature is called the *Format Painter*.

To use the Format Painter, first select the text that has the formatting you want to apply to other text selections. Once you activate the Format Painter, all the formatting attributes of the selected text will be attached to your pointer. Double-click the Format Painter button if you're going to copy the formatting to several locations, or just click the button if you're going to copy the formatting only once.

Use the Format Painter

In this exercise, you apply formatting using the Format Painter.

1. In the first sentence of the third paragraph, select the text *Impact Public Relations*.

Format Painter

If the Format Painter button is not visible, on the Standard toolbar, click the More Buttons drop-down arrow to locate the button.

More Buttons

2. On the Standard toolbar, double-click the Format Painter button, and then move the pointer around in the document.

   The pointer now has a paintbrush attached to it, which indicates that the Format Painter is active. Now any selected text will acquire formatting that matches the formatting of *Impact Public Relations*.

   Your screen should look similar to the following illustration.

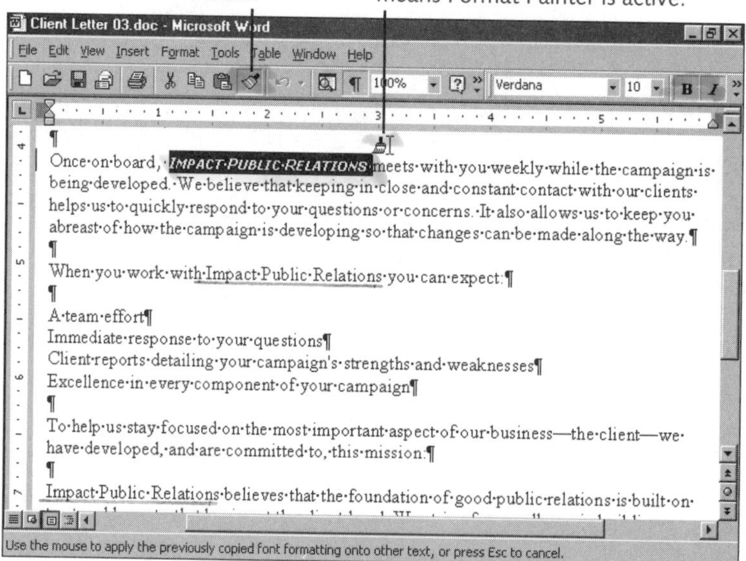

3. In the first sentence of the next paragraph, drag the pointer across the text *Impact Public Relations*.
4. Continue to scroll through the document, dragging the pointer across each occurrence of the text *Impact Public Relations*.

   The Format Painter stays active as you scroll through the document.
5. On the Standard toolbar, click the Format Painter button.

   The Format Painter is turned off.

Changing Paragraph Alignment

If you are not working through this lesson sequentially, before proceeding to the next step, open the 03D file in the Lesson03 folder, and save it as Client Letter 03.

Another way to enhance your document is to change the look of paragraphs on the page. One way you can do this is by changing the alignment of the paragraph. Paragraph alignment refers to the position of the paragraph between the left and right margins. There are four ways to align a paragraph. *Align left* means that all lines on the left side of the paragraph are aligned with the left margin, while lines on the right side end at different places. In Word, all paragraphs are aligned on the left unless you specify otherwise. *Align right* is the opposite of align left. Lines on the right side of the paragraph will be aligned with the right margin, while lines on the left side will end in different places. *Center alignment* means text is centered in the middle of the page. Text that is *justified* is aligned with both the left and right margins by spreading the words evenly between the margins. Newspapers typically align text in this way.

tip

If you change the alignment of a single paragraph, you do not need to select the entire paragraph first. Word automatically recognizes that you want to apply an alignment style to that paragraph only. Just position your insertion point anywhere in the paragraph you want to align.

Justify

If the Justify button is not visible, on the Formatting toolbar, click the More Buttons drop-down arrow to locate the button.

Experiment with different alignment techniques

In this exercise, you view the different alignment options.

1. Click anywhere in the first paragraph.
2. On the Formatting toolbar, click the Justify button.

   The paragraph is now justified with both the left and right margins.
3. On the Formatting toolbar, click the Align Left button.

   The paragraph is now back to the default setting.

Align Left

Use center alignment

In this exercise, you continue designing your letterhead by positioning the company logo.

1. Press Ctrl+Home to move to the top of the document.
2. Click the Impact Public Relations logo to select it.
   The sizing handles appear.
3. On the Format menu, click Picture.
   The Picture dialog box appears.
4. Click the Layout tab, and in the Horizontal area, click Center.
5. Click OK.
   The *Impact Public Relations* logo is centered in the middle of the line.

Center

Justifying Text by Clicking the Insertion Point

New! 2000

With the new *Click And Type* feature in Word 2000, you can set the text justification for new text in your document just by double-clicking anywhere in a blank space. Click And Type can apply left, center, or right alignment, or tabs to text entered in blank areas of your document. This feature allows you to point to any blank area of the document, double-click, and begin typing. This saves you from having to press Enter repeatedly, turn on alignment formatting, or set a tab before typing.

An icon attached to the mouse pointer shows that Click And Type is active and what type of alignment—left, center, or right—will be applied, or where a tab will be set when you double-click.

To use Click And Type to align text, be sure you are in the Print Layout view. Then position the pointer in a blank area of the document in one of three alignment zones: far left (for left alignment), center (for center alignment), or far right (for right alignment). The pointer displays an icon indicating what alignment will be applied to the new text. Once the correct icon is attached to the pointer, just double-click and begin entering text.

The following illustration shows the mouse pointer icon for left alignment.

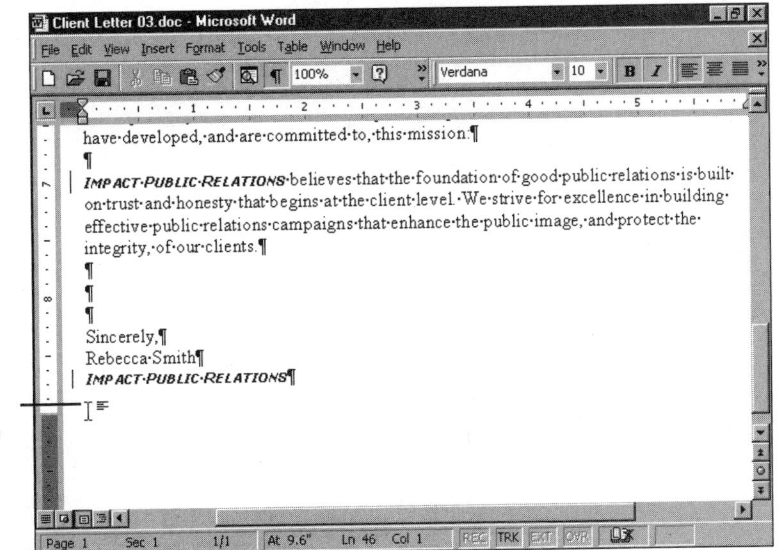

New text will be aligned on the left.

Use Click And Type to insert a date

In this exercise, you insert a date using Click And Type.

For a demonstration of how to justify text using Click And Type, in the Multimedia folder on the Microsoft Word 2000 Step by Step CD-ROM, double-click ClickandType.

1. At the half-inch vertical ruler marker, double-click in the far right side of the document.

   Your screen should look similar to the following illustration.

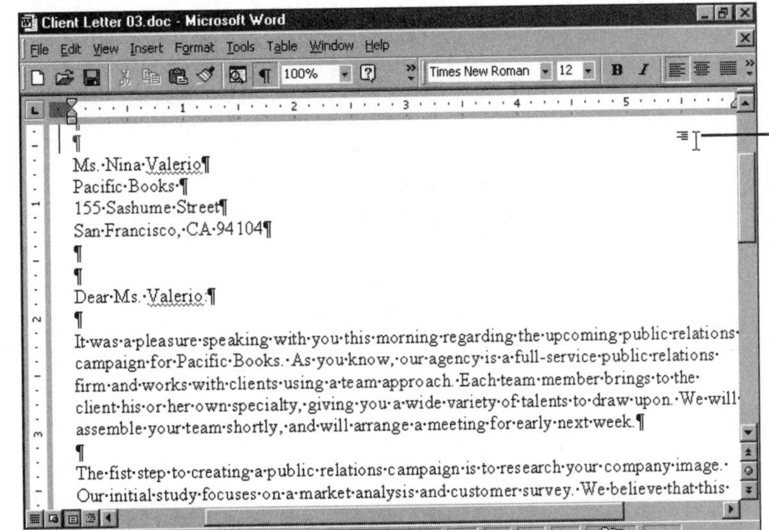
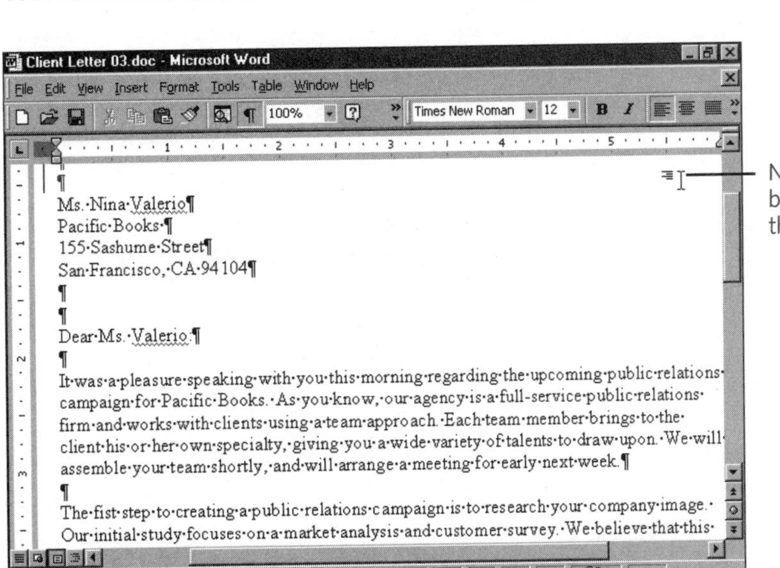

New text will be aligned on the right.

You must be in Print Layout view in order to use Click And Type, and you must click in a blank area of the document.

2. Type today's date.

   The text is right-aligned.

Changing the Spacing of Paragraphs

If you are not working through this lesson sequentially, before proceeding to the next step, open the 03E file in the Lesson03 folder, and save it as Client Letter 03.

After you've created a document, you often see ways to improve it by changing paragraph formatting. For example, you might decide that instead of double-spacing a list, one-and-a-half lines between items would look better. You also might decide that even though your final document will be single-spaced, it would be useful to print a double-spaced copy to edit. With Word, it's easy to change the line spacing of your document—temporarily or permanently—by using the Paragraph command. You can also make other changes, such as changing the spacing between paragraphs. For example, although you've selected a font size of 12 points, you might select spacing between paragraphs of 16 points.

Change line spacing

In this exercise, you change the line spacing in a list to make it stand out in your letter.

1. Select the text beginning with *A team effort* through *Excellence in every component of your campaign*.

   Your screen should look similar to the following illustration.

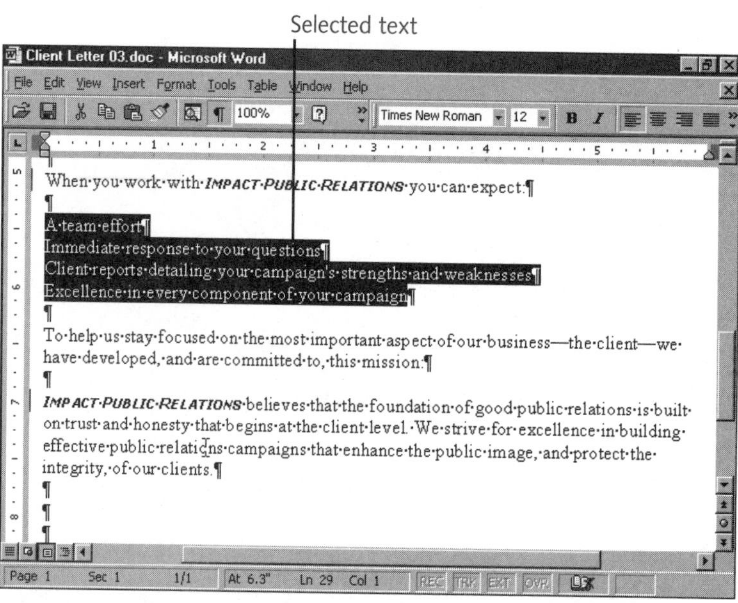

2. On the Format menu, click Paragraph.

3. In the Paragraph dialog box, be sure that the Indents And Spacing tab is selected.
4. In the Line Spacing area, click the drop-down arrow, and then click 1.5 lines.

   Your screen should look similar to the following illustration.

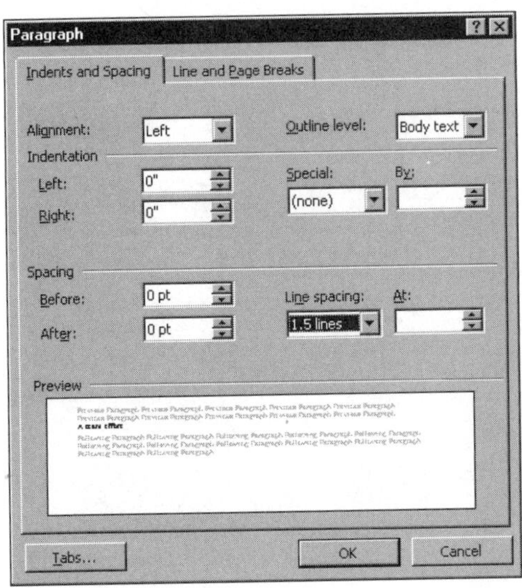

5. Click OK.

   The Paragraph dialog box closes, and the list spacing changes to 1.5 lines.

   Your screen should look similar to the following illustration.

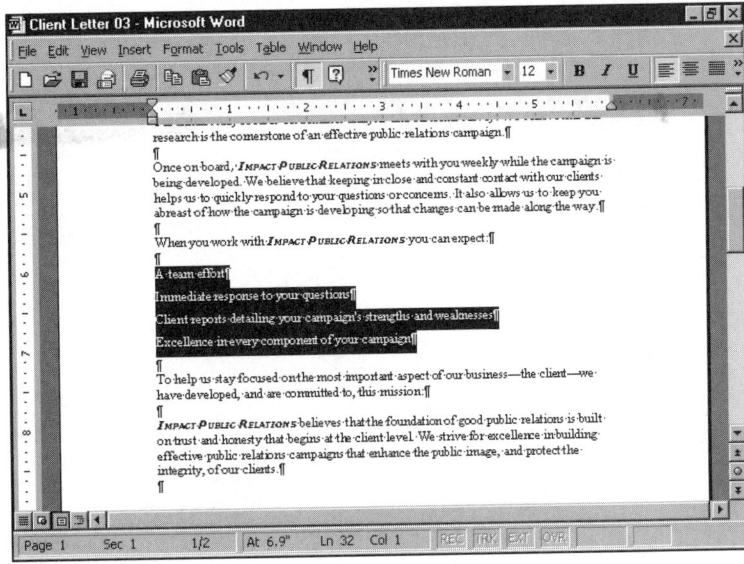

Change paragraph spacing

In this exercise, you set your own paragraph spacing and remove the paragraph marks.

1. Select the first three paragraphs of the letter.

   Your screen should look similar to the following illustration.

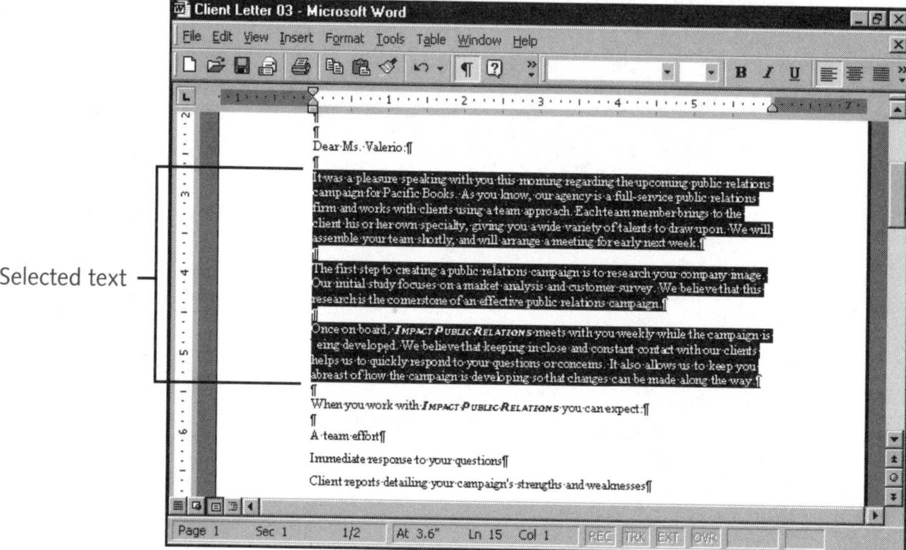

2. On the Format menu, click Paragraph.
3. In the Spacing Before box, click the up arrow until 18 pt shows in the box.
4. In the Spacing After box, click the up arrow until 18 pt shows in the box.

   Your screen should look similar to the following illustration.

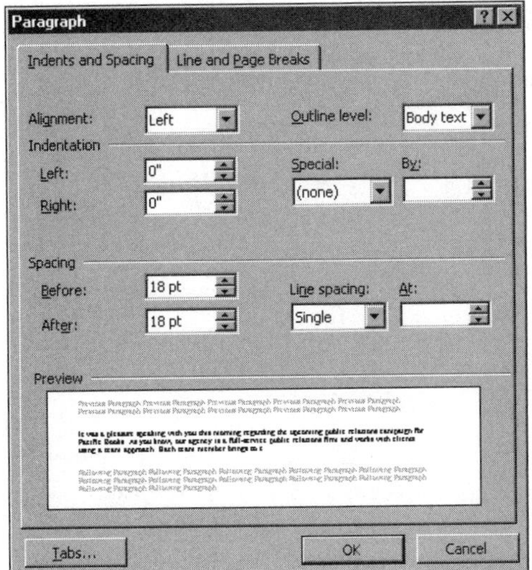

5 Click OK.

The Paragraph dialog box closes, and the spacing before and after paragraphs changes to 18 points.

6 Click anywhere outside of the selected text to cancel the selection.

Delete paragraph marks

In this exercise, you delete unnecessary paragraph marks between each paragraph.

1 Press Ctrl+Home to move the insertion point to the beginning of the document.

2 Click before the paragraph mark below the text *Dear Ms. Valerio* and press the Delete key.

The paragraph mark is removed. There is still space between the salutation and first paragraph.

3 Scroll down and delete the paragraph mark between the first and second paragraphs.

4 Scroll down and delete the paragraph mark between the second and third paragraphs.

5 Scroll down and delete the paragraph mark between the third and fourth paragraphs.

Setting Additional Paragraph Rules

When you come to the end of a page in a document, Word starts a new page by automatically placing a page break in your document. This is called a *soft page break.* Word ensures that a single line of a paragraph is not printed on a page by itself. This default feature is called *Widow And Orphan Control*. However, beyond this control of single lines, Word automatically splits paragraphs when the end of a page is reached. You can further modify the way a paragraph is printed by setting text flow options found in the Paragraph dialog box.

By selecting the Keep Lines Together option, for example, you ensure that text you want to keep on one page is not separated by a soft page break. This option is particularly useful when working with tables because it ensures that they do not get split across two pages. Besides the Keep Lines Together option, there are other paragraph rules you can apply by clicking the Line And Page Breaks tab in the Paragraph dialog box. These options are summarized as follows.

Option	Description
Widow/Orphan Control	Prevents the last line of a paragraph from being printed at the top of a new page (widow) or the first line of a paragraph from being printed at the bottom of a page (orphan).
Keep Lines Together	Keeps all lines of a paragraph on the same page.
Keep With Next	Keeps two paragraphs on the same page.
Page Break Before	Forces a page break before a specified paragraph.
Suppress Line Numbers	Suppresses line numbering to the selected paragraphs when the Line Numbering feature is active.
Don't Hyphenate	Ensures that words are not hyphenated at the end of a line.

Keep lines together

If you are not working through this lesson sequentially, before proceeding to the next step, open the 03F file in the Lesson03 folder, and save it as Client Letter 03.

In this exercise, you set line and page break options to keep a paragraph together.

1. On the View menu, click Normal.

   Your view is changed from Print Layout to Normal.

tip

When you are working with text longer than two pages, it is easier to work in the Normal view. This is because the Normal view simplifies the display of the document by not showing the top and bottom margins. As a result, all text is displayed continuously, with dotted lines indicating where pages will break when the document is printed.

2. Select the paragraph beginning with the text *Impact Public Relations believes that the foundation of*.

   Your screen should look similar to the following illustration.

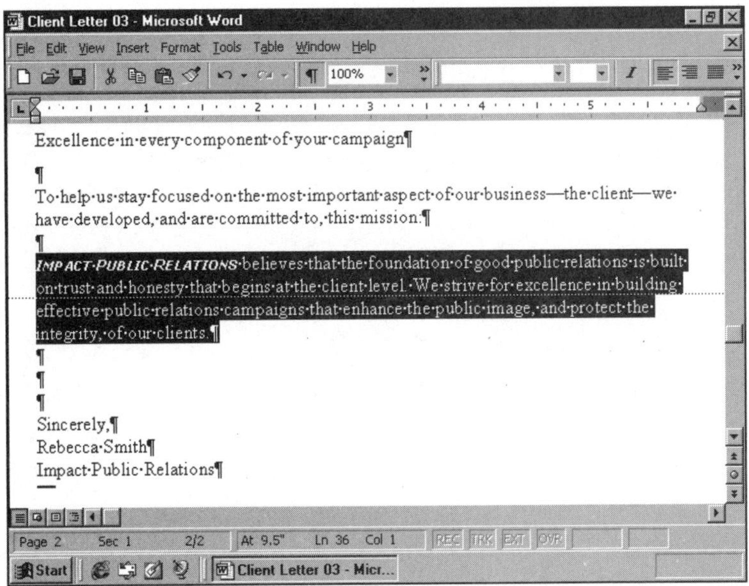

For more about setting page breaks, see Lesson 4, "Previewing and Printing a Document."

3. On the Format menu, click Paragraph.

   The Paragraph dialog box appears.
4. In the Paragraph dialog box, click the Line And Page Breaks tab.
5. Select the Keep Lines Together check box, and click OK.

   The entire paragraph is moved to the next page.
6. On the View menu, click Print Layout.

Adding Borders and Shading to Paragraphs

Once you have positioned paragraphs where you want them on the pages, you can apply borders and shading. This formatting helps draw attention to text in your document. Word has more than 20 different border styles you can choose from, and each can be displayed in line weights (thicknesses) ranging from ¼ point to 6 points. You can also choose from a variety of border colors. As you create borders, they are added to the Line Style list, making them available for future use in your document.

Do not add a border to a paragraph that must split across two pages, however, because the page break will split the border between two pages. Using the Keep Lines Together option can help prevent this.

Controlling Hyphenation

By default, Word will not hyphenate text at the end of a line. Instead, it will move the whole word down to the next line. However, if a hyphenated word occurs at a normal line break, Word will maintain that hyphenation and put the first part of the word on one line and the last part on the next line.

There are certain circumstances when you would not want Word to follow the default hyphenation rules. These include occurrences of phone numbers and hyphenated names falling at the end of a line. When you want to ensure that hyphenated text does not break across two lines, you can specify a *nonbreaking hyphen.*

To do this, click where you want to insert the nonbreaking hyphen, and press Ctrl+Shift+Hyphen. Your hyphenated text will be moved to the next line.

To ensure that proper names are not separated over two lines, you can specify a *nonbreaking space.*

Insert a nonbreaking space

1. Position your pointer between the two words you want to keep together.
2. Select the space mark between the two words.
3. Press Ctrl+Shift+Spacebar.

If you decide that you do not want Word to hyphenate under any circumstances, you can specify that rule in the Paragraph dialog box. On the Format menu, click Paragraph. In the Paragraph dialog box, click the Line And Page Breaks tab. Select the Don't Hyphenate check box, and click OK. Word will no longer hyphenate text in your document.

Display the Tables And Borders toolbar

If you are not working through this lesson sequentially, before proceeding to the next step, open the 03G file in the Lesson03 folder, and save it as Client Letter 03.

In this exercise, you prepare to add a border and shading around your company mission statement.

- On the View menu, point to Toolbars, and then click Tables And Borders. The Tables And Borders toolbar appears. If necessary, drag it to a position directly under the Formatting toolbar.

Apply a border

In this exercise, you add a border around your company mission statement.

1. Click the paragraph starting with the text *Impact Public Relations believes that the foundation of.*

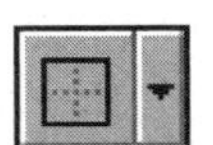

Outside Border

2. On the Tables And Borders toolbar, click the Outside Border button.

   The paragraph is surrounded by an outside border.

   Your screen should look similar to the following illustration.

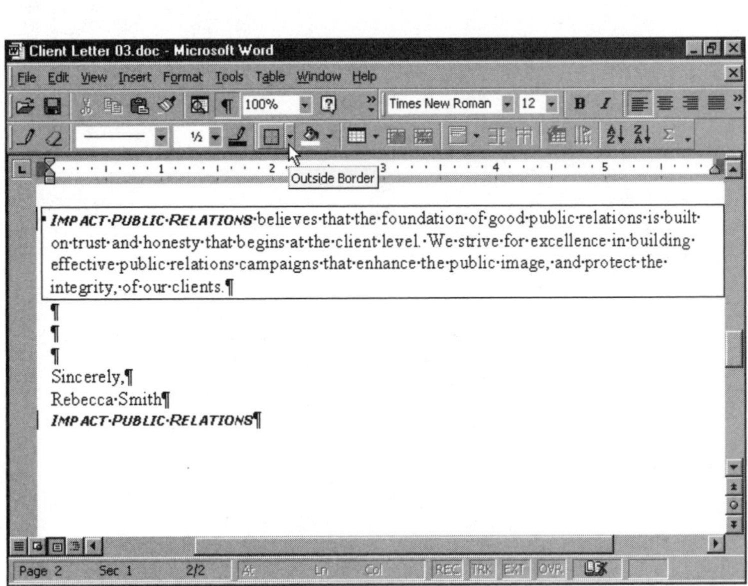

Change the border

In this exercise, you change the border style and then the line weight.

Line Style

1. Click at the beginning of the paragraph beginning with *Impact Public Relations believes*.
2. On the Tables And Borders toolbar, click the Line Style drop-down arrow to see more options.
3. Scroll to the bottom of the Line Style list and click the line style that is third from the bottom.

   Your screen should look similar to the following illustration.

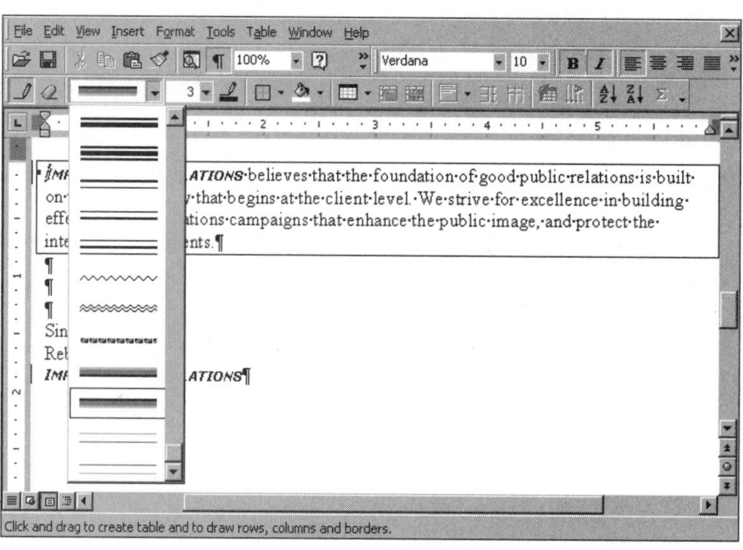

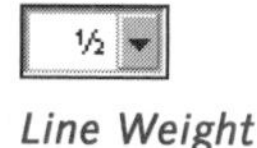

Line Weight

Border Color

4. On the Tables And Borders toolbar, click the Line Weight drop-down arrow to see more options, and then select 1½ pt.
5. On the Tables And Borders toolbar, click the Border Color button, and then click Dark Blue.

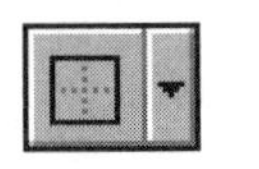

Outside Border

6. Click the Outside Border button.

   The border is updated. If you display the Line Style list, you will see that this new border style has been added.

Apply shading to a paragraph

In this exercise, you add shading around the company mission statement.

1. Click at the beginning of the paragraph starting with the text *Impact Public Relations believes that the foundation of*.

Shading Color

2. On the Tables And Borders toolbar, click the Shading Color drop-down arrow to see more options.
3. Click Gray-5%.

   The paragraph is filled with gray 5% shading.

   Your screen should look similar to the following illustration.

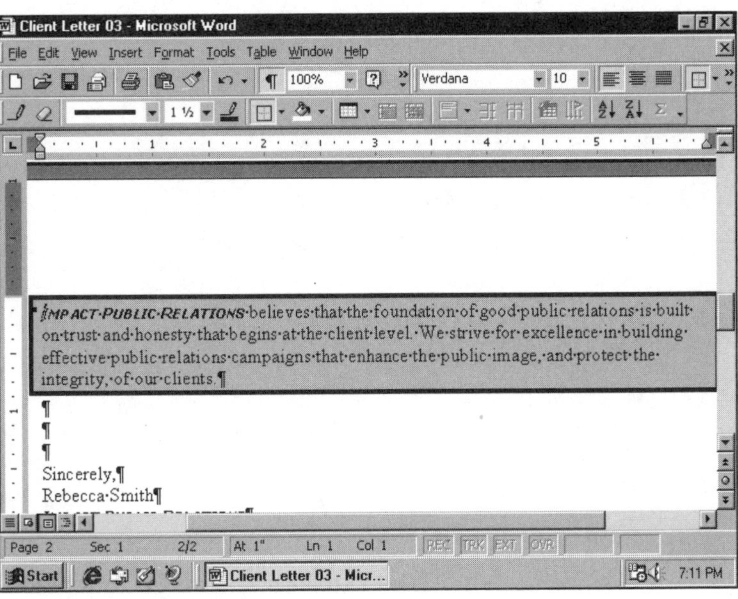

4. Close the Tables And Borders toolbar.

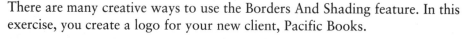

One Step Further: Creating a Quick and Colorful Logo

If you are not working through this lesson sequentially, before proceeding to the next step, open the 03H file Lesson03 folder, and save it as Client Letter 03.

There are many creative ways to use the Borders And Shading feature. In this exercise, you create a logo for your new client, Pacific Books.

Create a logo

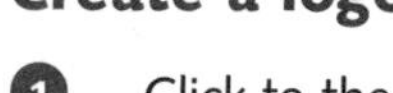

1. Click to the left of the second paragraph marker below the mission statement, and type **As per your request, I have created a logo for Pacific Books. This logo will be used everywhere, including your new Web site.** Press Enter twice.
2. Type **Pacific Books**, and press Enter.
3. Select the text *Pacific Books*.
4. On the Formatting toolbar, click the Center button.

   The text *Pacific Books* is centered.

Center

You can also press Ctrl+E to center the text.

5. On the Format menu, click Font.

   The Font dialog box is displayed.
6. In the Font list, click Verdana. In the Size list, click 36, and click OK.
7. On the Format menu, click Borders And Shading, and then click the Borders tab.
8. In the Setting area, click Shadow. In the Color list, click Dark Blue, and then click the Shading tab.
9. In the Fill palette, click Dark Blue, and click OK. Click anywhere outside of the selected text to cancel the selection.

Finish the lesson

Save

1. On the Standard toolbar, click the Save button.

   Changes made to Client Letter 03 are saved.
2. On the File menu, click Close.
3. On the File menu, click Exit.

Lesson 3 Quick Reference

To	Do this	Button
Format text in bold and italic	Select the text to be formatted. On the Formatting toolbar, click the Bold button, and then click the Italic button.	B I
Modify fonts and font size	Select the text to be modified. On the Formatting toolbar, click the Font drop-down arrow. Select a font. Click the Font Size drop-down arrow, and select a point size.	
Use the Format Painter	Select the text containing the formatting you want to copy. On the Standard toolbar, double-click the Format Painter button. Drag across the new text you want to format. On the Standard toolbar, click the Format Painter button to turn it off.	
Center text	Select the text, or click in the paragraph to be centered. On the Formatting toolbar, click the Center button.	
Use Click And Type	Be sure you are in Print Layout view. Double-click in a blank space in the document. Note the mouse pointer icon to determine how text will be aligned. Begin typing.	
Change line spacing	Select the paragraphs to be formatted. On the Format menu, click Paragraph. In the Paragraph dialog box, be sure that the Indents And Spacing tab is selected. Click the Line Spacing drop-down arrow, click the desired line spacing, and click OK.	

Lesson 3 Quick Reference

To	Do this	Button
Change paragraph spacing	Select the paragraphs to be formatted. On the Format menu, click Paragraph. In the Paragraph dialog box, click the Spacing Before arrow until the desired point size is displayed in the box. Click the Spacing After arrow until the desired point size is displayed. Click OK.	
Keep lines together	Select a paragraph. On the Format menu, click Paragraph. In the Paragraph dialog box, click the Line And Page Breaks tab. Select the Keep Lines Together check box. Click OK.	
Create a nonbreaking hyphen	Click before the hyphenated word and press Ctrl+Shift+Hyphen.	
Insert a nonbreaking space	Click between the two words to be kept together. Select the space mark between the two words. Press Ctrl+Shift+Spacebar.	
Apply a border	Click at the beginning of the paragraph to be formatted. On the Tables And Borders toolbar, click the Border drop-down arrow, and choose an outside border style. Click the Outside Border button.	
Apply shading to a paragraph	Position the insertion point at the beginning of the paragraph to be formatted. On the Tables And Borders toolbar, click the Shading Color button drop-down arrow. Click the desired shading.	

Lesson 3 Quick Reference

To	Do this	Button
Create a logo	Select the text to be used as a logo. On the Formatting toolbar, click Center. On the Format menu, click Font. In the Font dialog box, select a font and font size. On the Format menu, click Borders And Shading, and then click the Borders tab. In the setting area, select a setting. In the Color list, select a color. On the Shading tab, from the Fill palette, select a color. Click OK.	

LESSON

4

Previewing and Printing a Document

In this lesson you will learn how to:

- ✔ *Preview how your document will look when printed.*
- ✔ *Insert page breaks.*
- ✔ *Adjust margins using the ruler.*
- ✔ *Print a whole document or just a part.*
- ✔ *Print an envelope.*
- ✔ *Shrink a document to fit on one page.*

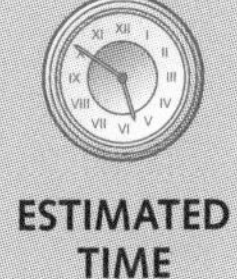

ESTIMATED TIME
20 min.

After organizing, editing, and formatting a document, you will probably want to print it. Before you do, you can make adjustments to it in *Print Preview*. This document view helps you avoid wasted print jobs, as you can see your work before printing it. In this lesson, you view the layout of a Word document before you print it; then you edit it and adjust the margins and the text flow across pages. Finally, you print the whole document, as well as just one page.

More Buttons

important

The default toolbar setting in Microsoft Word 2000 displays both the Standard and Formatting toolbars in one row, at the top of the document window, just below the menu bar. This gives you maximum workspace. While working through these exercises, toolbar buttons you need may not initially be visible. If a toolbar button is not visible, click one of the two More Buttons drop-down arrows on the toolbar to locate the button you need. The new button you select will be added to the visible portion of the toolbar, replacing one that is not used as often.

Open a practice file

If you have not yet installed this book's files, refer to "Using the Microsoft Word 2000 Step by Step CD-ROM," earlier in this book.

To begin this lesson, be sure Word is started. Follow the instructions to open a practice document named 04A, and then save it with the new name Book Fair 04.

Open

1. On the Standard toolbar, click the Open button.

   The Open dialog box appears.
2. Click the Look In drop-down arrow, and then select your hard disk.
3. In the list of folders, double-click the Word 2000 SBS Practice folder, and then double-click the Lesson04 folder.
4. In the file list, double-click the 04A file to open it.

   The document opens in the document window.
5. On the File menu, click Save As.

   The Save As dialog box appears.
6. Be sure that the Lesson04 folder appears in the Save In box.
7. In the File Name box, select the text, and then type **Book Fair 04**
8. Click Save.

Display formatting marks

To make it easier to edit your document, you can display formatting marks such as paragraph marks and space marks on your screen.

Show/Hide ¶

- If formatting marks are not currently displayed, on the Standard toolbar, click the Show/Hide ¶ button.

Previewing Documents

If you are not working through this lesson sequentially, before proceeding to the next step, open the 04A file in the Lesson04 folder, and save it as Book Fair 04.

To see exactly how your document will look when printed, use the Print Preview command. The Print Preview window shows you where lines of text break on the page and where page breaks occur. If you don't like the layout, you can make adjustments before you print, which might prevent a wasted print job.

As a partner at Impact Public Relations, you've created a document for your client, Pacific Books, that will become the basis for a newsletter and will later be part of the client's Web site. You've added headings and a logo, and included a schedule. Now you'd like to see how it will look when printed, and you want to show your partner a draft.

Preview a document

In this exercise, you preview a document before printing it.

Print Preview

If the Print Preview button is not visible, on the Standard toolbar, click the More Buttons drop-down arrow to locate and select the button.

- On the Standard toolbar, click the Print Preview button.

  The Print Preview window opens and the first page of your document is displayed. The Print Preview toolbar appears, and the Word menu bar remains unchanged.

  Your screen should look similar to the following illustration.

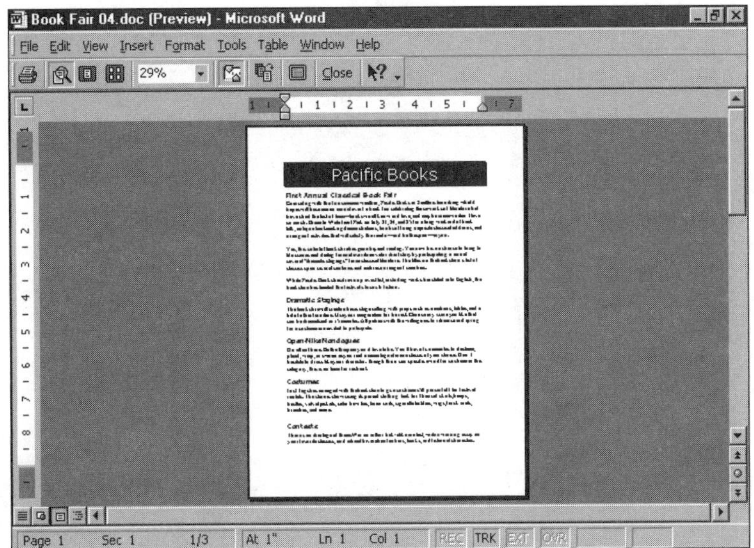

View Ruler

One Page

tip

If your screen does not match this illustration, on the Print Preview toolbar, click the View Ruler button to display the ruler. Click the One Page button if you see more than one page of the document.

View all pages

In this exercise, you view all pages of your document in Print Preview.

Multiple Pages

- On the Print Preview toolbar, click the Multiple Pages button, move the pointer across the three boxes in the top row to select them, and then click.

  Your three-page document is displayed in full.

  Your screen should look similar to the following illustration.

Multiple pages in Print Preview

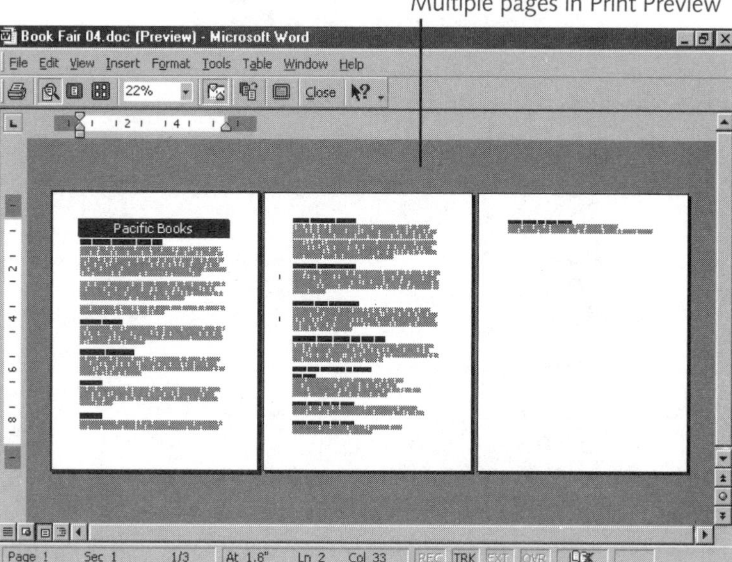

Editing While in Print Preview

If you are not working through this lesson sequentially, before proceeding to the next step, open the 04A file in the Lesson04 folder, and save it as Book Fair 04.

While viewing your document in Print Preview, you might think of text changes you'd like to make. You don't have to switch to Print Layout view or another document view to do this; you can make the changes in the Print Preview window. However, if your text or formatting changes are extensive, you might find it easier to edit using Normal, Print Layout, or Web Layout view.

As you look over Book Fair 04, you remember that there's a quotation you intended to add in the first section. To make this addition, you use the magnifier to enlarge text so you can see it more clearly, and then you add the new text. The Magnifier button is activated by default when you open the Print Preview window.

Add text in Print Preview

In this exercise, you use the magnifier to enlarge text, and then you add a quotation.

1. In the Print Preview window, move your pointer to the first page of the document.

   The pointer now looks like a magnifying glass.

Magnifier

2. On Page 1, place the pointer before the third paragraph, and click.

   The text is magnified.

   Your screen should look similar to the following illustration.

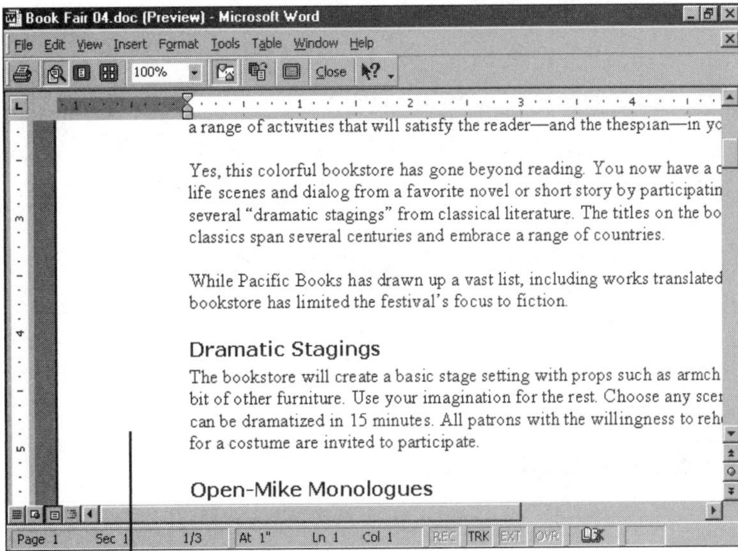

Magnified view of text in Print Preview

3. Scroll until you can see the full width of the text.
4. On the Print Preview toolbar, click the Magnifier button.

   The magnifier is turned off, and the pointer becomes the insertion point.

5. Position the insertion point after the word *fiction* in the third paragraph (after the period).
6. Press the Spacebar, and Type **Erica Thomas, manager of the Seattle store, says, "It might seem like a crime to exclude poetry, but we've already established our fall poetry festival, and we decided it was fiction's turn."**

Inserting Page Breaks

If you are not working through this lesson sequentially, before proceeding to the next step, open the 04B file in the Lesson04 folder, and save it as BookFair04.

As you type text in Word, page breaks are inserted automatically when you reach the end of a page. These are called soft page breaks. If you add or delete text on the page, the soft page break moves automatically to accommodate the increased or decreased amount of text.

A soft page break is shown in Normal view as a single dotted line across the page. In Print Layout view, you see the actual end of the page on your screen. You cannot move or delete soft page breaks except by editing the text. You can, however, create a page break exactly where you want one by inserting a hard page break. After you insert a hard page break, Word repaginates the document and changes soft page breaks appropriately.

In Normal and Print Layout views, a hard page break is shown as a dotted line with the label *Page Break*. Neither the line nor the label appears in a printed document.

When you insert a hard page break, information below the break will always start at the top of a new page. You might use the hard page break to keep certain paragraphs of your document together or to divide text more evenly across pages. It's best to insert hard page breaks only when your document is nearly final, to avoid a wasted print job.

You can also control how the text breaks across pages by setting line and page break options found in the Paragraph command on the Format menu. Lesson 3, "Formatting Characters and Paragraphs," discusses this subject further.

Insert a page break

In this exercise, you insert a hard page break.

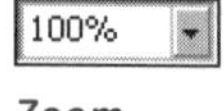

Zoom

1. On the Print Preview toolbar, click the Zoom drop-down arrow, and then click Page Width.
2. Scroll to the heading *Contests*, at the bottom of the first page, and then click before the heading.

You can also insert a hard page break by pressing Ctrl+Enter.

3. On the Insert menu, click Break.

   The Break dialog box appears.
4. Be sure Page Break is selected in the Break dialog box, and click OK.

   A hard page break is inserted, and the text following the break moves to the next page.

Multiple Pages

5. On the Print Preview toolbar, click the Multiple Pages button, move the pointer across the first three boxes in the top row to select them, and then click.

   Your document appears with its new page breaks.
6. On the Print Preview toolbar, click Close.

7. Scroll up to see the new page break at the bottom of page 1.

   Your screen should look similar to the following illustration.

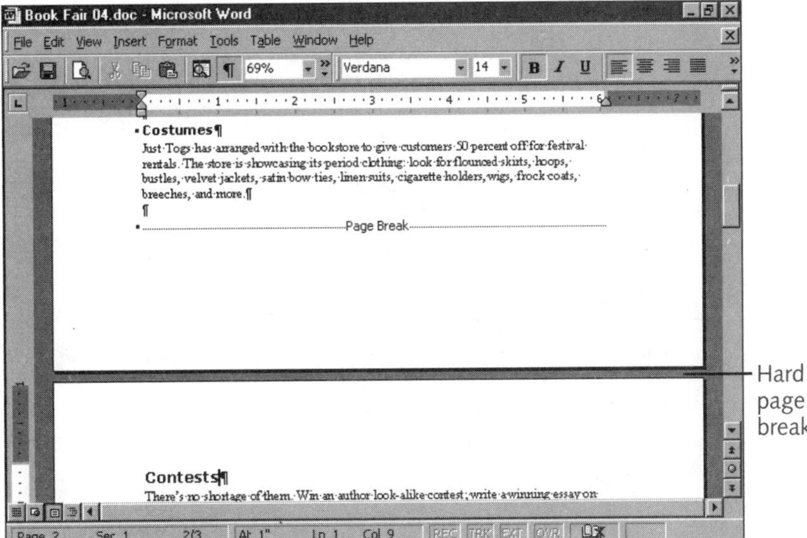

8. Save the document.

Adjusting Margins with the Ruler

If you are not working through this lesson sequentially, before proceeding to the next step, open the 04C file in the Lesson04 folder, and save it as BookFair 04.

Although you can use the Page Setup command and dialog box to specify a variety of settings for your margins, you can also adjust margins quickly by using the ruler. The Page Setup dialog box is discussed in depth in Lesson 7, "Formatting Pages and Working with Styles."

In the next exercise, you adjust the left margin to match the right margin in the Book Fair 04 document.

> **tip**
>
> On the Print Preview toolbar, you can click the Ruler button to display or hide the ruler. Also, on the View menu, you can click Ruler to accomplish the same task.

Change the left margin with the ruler

In this exercise, you use the ruler to adjust the left margin.

1. Press Ctrl+Home to move the insertion point to the top of the document.

2. Position the pointer on the left margin marker (on the left edge of the ruler). When the pointer changes to a double-headed arrow, click and hold while you press the Alt key.

   Left and right margin measurements are displayed.

3. Keeping the mouse button and the Alt key depressed, drag to the right until the width of the left margin measures 1.25 inches.

   Your screen should look similar to the following illustration.

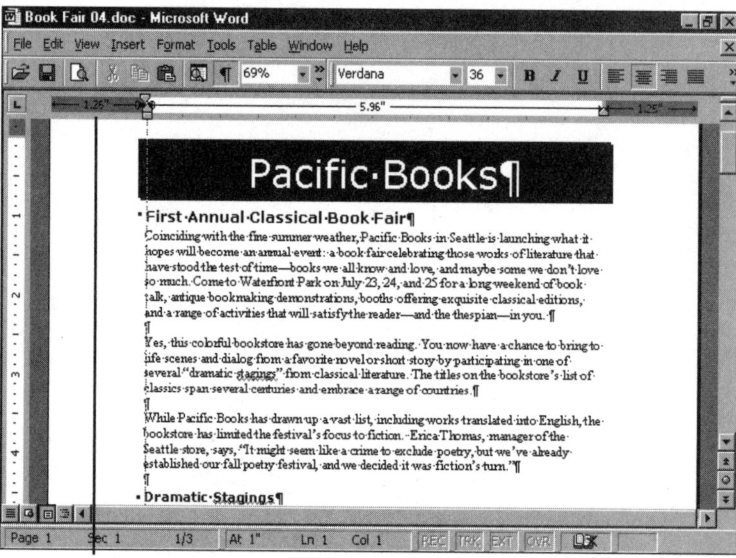

Left margin measurement

4. Release the mouse button and the Alt key.

   The left margin is now the width of the right margin on each page in the document.

5. On the Standard toolbar, click the Save button.

   Changes made to your document are saved.

Save

tip

To check to see that a margin adjustment hasn't altered any soft page breaks, view the entire document in Print Preview again before saving it. If you find that narrowing your margin has bumped text to a new page, you can either return to Print Layout view and readjust the margin or alter the margin while in Print Preview by using the mouse button and Alt key. The new margins you set will apply to all pages. You might find it more difficult to match exact measurements in Print Preview.

Setting Mirrored Margins in a Document

The Page Setup dialog box in Word enables you to set margin widths and other related options, including mirror margins. This option adjusts margins for facing pages when a document is printed or photocopied on both sides of the paper, or back-to-back.

When you print a document, you might need to leave a bit of space along one edge of the pages to accommodate binding. The space along the edge is called the gutter margin. To set a gutter margin, in the Page Setup dialog box, click the Margins tab. Set the gutter margin as wide as necessary to accommodate binding. For documents that read left to right, the binding is usually along the left edge of the pages.

When you're printing or copying back-to-back, you must also turn on Mirror Margins to place the gutter margin on facing pages rather than on the left side of every page. Set the gutter position to Left. On even-numbered pages, Word will flip the widths of the left and right margins set for odd-numbered pages so that even-page margins mirror odd-page margins.

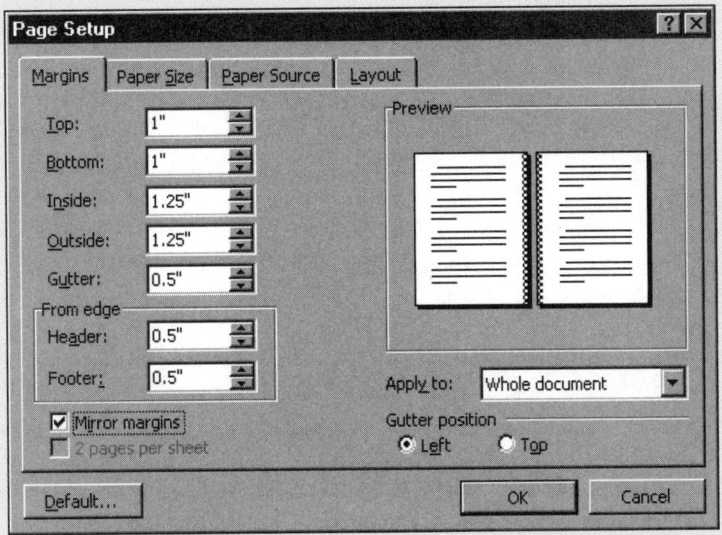

The preview area shows the gutter margin as a checkerboard on the pages. The preview shows you approximately how much of the page Word gives to the gutter margin.

Printing Documents

Another way to print the currently selected document is to click the Print button on the Print Preview toolbar. Default print settings will apply.

The quickest and easiest way to print a document is to click the Print button on the Standard toolbar. This prints the whole document using default settings. If you are connected to multiple printers, the Print button activates the default printer.

To print only certain pages or multiple copies, or to otherwise alter the default settings, use the File menu. On the File menu, click Print to display the Print dialog box, and then select specific options.

If your computer is not connected to a printer, you can skip to the end of this lesson.

> **tip**
>
> The Microsoft Windows 95, Windows 98, and Windows 2000 operating systems enable you to continue working in Word or another program as your document prints in the background—you don't have to wait for the printer to finish first. To ensure that you have background printing enabled in Word, on the Tools menu, click Options, click the Print tab, and then verify that Background Printing is selected.

If you are not working through this lesson sequentially, before proceeding to the next step, open the 04D file in the Lesson04 folder, and save it as Book Fair 04.

Print the entire document

In this exercise, you print the Book Fair 04 document.

Print

1. Be sure that the printer is on.
2. On the Standard toolbar, click the Print button.
   The document is printed.

Print one page of the document

In this exercise, you fix a typo in the document and then reprint just one page.

1. On the left side of the status bar, double-click the page number display.
   The Find And Replace dialog box appears, and the Go To tab is selected.

2. On the Go To tab, type **2** in the Enter Page Number box, click Go To, and then click Close.

   Page 2 of Book Fair 04 is displayed on the screen.
3. Click after the word *decad*, in the second line of the paragraph.
4. Type the letter **e** to fix the typo, and then, on the Standard toolbar, click the Save button.
5. On the File menu, click Print.

   The Print dialog box appears.

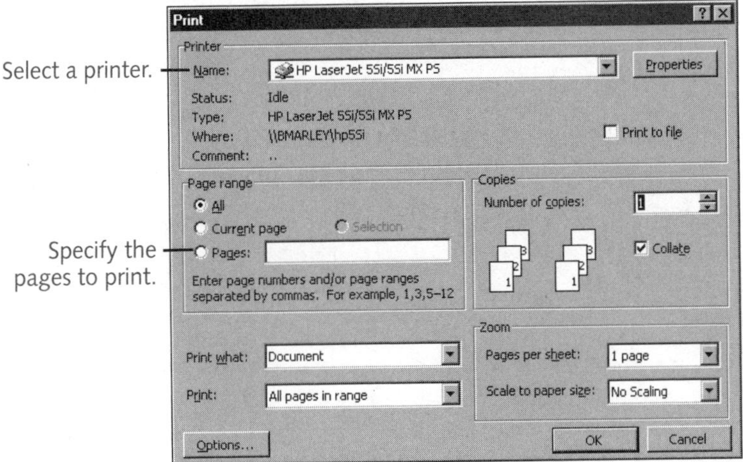

6. In the Page Range area, click Current Page.
7. Click OK to begin printing.
8. After the page has printed, on the Standard toolbar, click the Save button.
9. On the File menu, click Close.

Save

Additional Printing Options

In the Print dialog box, you can select a variety of options affecting the way your document is printed. Among your choices is a new zoom feature that prints multiple pages on one page, and allows you to scale a document to fit various paper sizes. For example, if your document page is set up for legal-sized paper, but you're printing on letter-sized paper, select Letter 8½ x 11 in the scaling list. To set your printer to adjust to a letter-sized page, on the Tools menu, click Options, and then on the Print tab, select Allow A4/Letter Paper Resizing. Following are some of the options available from the Print dialog box. To open the Print dialog box, on the File menu, click Print.

Print a few pages of a long document

1. In the Print dialog box, in the Page Range area, click Pages.
2. In the Pages area, type page numbers or a page range, separated by commas, such as *10-14, 17, 20,* and click OK.

Print selected text

1. In the document, select the text you want to print.
2. On the File menu, click Print to display the Print dialog box.
3. In the Page Range area, click Selection, and click OK.

Print and collate several copies

1. In the Print dialog box, in the Number of Copies area, type a number.
2. Select the Collate check box, and click OK.

Print multiple pages on one page

1. In the Print dialog box, in the Zoom area, select a number of pages per printed sheet. (For example, if you want two pages to print on a single page, select 2 Pages.)
2. Click OK.

Scale a document for larger or smaller paper

1. In the Print dialog box, in the Zoom area, select a paper size in the Scale To Paper Size list.
2. Click OK.

Printing Envelopes

Open

With Word, it's easy to address and print an envelope as long as your printer will accept envelopes. On the Tools menu, click Envelopes And Labels. In the Envelopes And Labels dialog box, specify the size of envelope or brand of label you want to print.

In the following exercises, you open the 04E practice file and save it as Client Letter 04. Then you print an envelope.

Open a letter and save it with a new name

In this exercise, you open a letter and save it with a new name.

1. On the Standard toolbar, click the Open button.

   The Open dialog box appears.
2. Click the Look In drop-down arrow, and then select your hard disk.
3. In the list of folders, double-click the Word 2000 SBS Practice folder, and then double-click the Lesson04 folder.
4. In the file list, double-click the 04E file to open it.

   This is a letter from your firm to a client, Pacific Books.
5. On the File menu, click Save As.

   The Save As dialog box appears.
6. Be sure that the Lesson04 folder appears in the Save In box.
7. In the File Name box, select the text, and then type **Client Letter 04**
8. Click Save.

tip

The default envelope size is a standard #10 business envelope. To print an envelope of a different size, on the Tools menu, click Envelopes And Labels. In the Envelopes And Labels dialog box, click Options. In the Envelope Options dialog box, click the Envelope Options tab. In the Envelope size area, select the appropriate size. To position your envelope for printing, consult the documentation that came with your printer. If your envelope isn't printed correctly, click the Feed area of the Envelopes And Labels dialog box and review the default settings and other position options that Word offers.

Print an envelope

In this exercise, you print an envelope.

1. Select the recipient's address at the top of the letter.
2. Place an envelope in your printer.
3. On the Tools menu, click Envelopes And Labels.

   The Envelopes And Labels dialog box appears.
4. In the Envelopes And Labels dialog box, be sure that the recipient's address and the return address, are correct. The return address is based on information you entered when you installed the software. If either address is wrong, type the corrections.
5. Click Print.

   Your printer prints the addressed envelope.

> **tip**
>
> To avoid having to add the return address each time you print an envelope, on the Tools menu, click Options. On the User Information tab, type the name and address information that you always want to use as your return address. Click OK.

One Step Further: Shrinking a Document to Fit

If you are not working through this lesson sequentially, before proceeding to the next step, open the 04E file in the Lesson04 folder, and save it as Client Letter 04.

When you view a document in the Print Preview window, you see that the last page contains only a small amount of text. You might decide that the document would look better if all the text were on one page. Rather than editing your text, you can use the Shrink To Fit feature in Print Preview to reduce the number of pages by one. Word does this by reducing the document font sizes.

> **important**
>
> To undo a Shrink To Fit command, on the Edit menu, click Undo Tools Shrink To Fit. If you have saved and closed the document after using Shrink To Fit, you will have to manually restore the document to the original font sizes.

Shorten the letter by one page

In this exercise, you use Shrink To Fit to reduce the length of a letter by one page.

Print Preview

Multiple Pages

Shrink To Fit

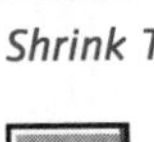

Save

1. On the Standard toolbar, click the Print Preview button.
2. On the Print Preview toolbar, click the Multiple Pages button, move your pointer over the first and second boxes to display both pages of the letter, and then click.
3. On the Print Preview toolbar, click the Shrink To Fit button.

   The letter shrinks to fit on one page.
4. Close the Print Preview window to return to Print Layout view.
5. Scroll through the letter to view the changes.
6. On the Standard toolbar, click the Save button. Changes made to Client Letter 04 are saved.

Finish the lesson

1. On the Standard toolbar, click Save.

   Changes made to Book Fair 04 are saved.
2. On the File menu, click Close.
3. If you want to quit Word for now, on the File menu, click Exit.

Lesson 4 Quick Reference

To	Do this	Button
Display a document in Print Preview	On the Standard toolbar, click the Print Preview button.	
Change from single-page view to multiple-page view	On the Standard toolbar, click the Print Preview button. On the Print Preview toolbar, click the Multiple Pages button and select the number of pages you want to display.	
Magnify text for editing in Print Preview	On the Standard toolbar, click the Print Preview button. In the Print Preview window, position the mouse pointer on the document. When the pointer changes to a magnifying glass, click the area of the document you want to magnify.	

Lesson 4 Quick Reference

To	Do this	Button
Edit text in Print Preview	On the Standard toolbar, click Print Preview. On the Print Preview toolbar, click the Magnifier button to turn the magnifying glass into the insertion point.	
Insert a page break	Click where you want the page break, and on the Insert menu, click Break. In the Break dialog box, select Page Break, and then click OK.	
Adjust margins using the ruler	Place the pointer on the edge of the ruler, where the margin marker is, and wait for the pointer to change into a double-headed arrow. Press Alt and then drag to change the margins.	
Print a whole document	On the Standard toolbar, click the Print button. Or, on the Print Preview toolbar, click the Print button.	
Print part of a document using dialog box options	On the File menu, click Print. Select the options you want in the Print dialog box. Click Print.	
Print an envelope	Open a letter file and select the recipient's address. On the Tools menu, click Envelopes And Labels. Position the envelope in your printer. In the Envelopes And Labels dialog box, click Print.	
Shrink a document to fit on one page	On the Standard toolbar, click the Print Preview button. On the Print Preview toolbar, click the Multiple Pages button, display both pages, and then click the Shrink To Fit button.	

Review & Practice

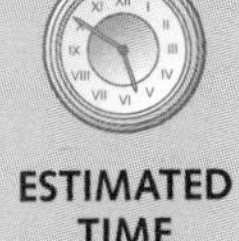

ESTIMATED TIME
20 min.

You will review and practice how to:

- *Create and save a document.*
- *Select, cut, and paste text.*
- *Apply formatting to text.*
- *Print a document.*

Before you move on to Part 2, which covers indents, tabs and tables, automated tasks, styles, templates, and electronic forms, you can practice the skills you learned in Part 1 by working through this Review & Practice section. In this section, you practice creating and saving a document, rearranging text within a document, applying formatting to text, and printing the new document.

Scenario

You have been asked by a colleague at Impact Public Relations to create an interoffice memo outlining the time sheet procedures for your firm's new client, Pacific Books. Your colleague will create the time sheet to be included in the interoffice memo distribution. The memo needs to be attractive in order to get the attention of the staff.

Step 1: Start Word and Create and Save a New Document

In this exercise, you draft the memo explaining the new time sheet procedures.

1. Start Microsoft Word.
2. Type the following memo. Use the Tab key to align text.

   Interoffice Memo

   TO: **The staff of Impact Public Relations**

   FROM: [type your name]

   DATE: **March 1, 1999**

   RE: **TIME SHEETS FOR PACIFIC BOOKS**

   Our new client, Pacific Books, has asked us to submit weekly accounts of work activity. A sample of the time sheet is attached. You will all receive this document electronically. The time sheet must be completed by Friday at 5:00 P.M. Activity after 5:00 P.M. on Friday is to be recorded on next week's time sheet.

   If you have any questions, please contact me.

   Sincerely,

   [type your name]
3. Save the document as Review Memo 01.
4. Close the document.

For more information about	See
Starting Microsoft Word	Lesson 1
Using toolbar buttons	Lesson 1
Entering text into a new document	Lesson 1
Using Delete and Backspace	Lesson 1
Saving documents	Lesson 1

Step 2: Open a Document and Rearrange Text

Your colleague has reviewed your memo and made some additions. You also want to make some adjustments in the text layout.

1. Open the RP01A document, and save it as Staff Memo 01.
2. In the Staff Memo 01 document, cut the date and paragraph mark and paste them to the left of the text *To: The Staff of Impact Public Relations.*
3. Select the sentence *You will all receive this document electronically.* Then type **This document will be sent electronically to every staff member by 10:00 A.M. on Friday.**

4. Select the second paragraph, *Our clients at Pacific Books would like each team member...*, and move it above the sentence *If you have any questions, please contact me*.
5. Delete the extra paragraph mark above the text *There are several items...*

For more information about	See
Opening a document	Lesson 2
Moving and copying text using buttons	Lesson 2
Moving and copying text by dragging	Lesson 2

Step 3: Modify the Appearance of Text

It is now your responsibility to enhance the appearance of the memo by applying some formatting, text alignment, paragraph spacing, and borders and shading.

1. Change the font type and size of all the text in the document to 14-point Garamond.
2. Select the heading *Interoffice Memo*, make it bold and underlined, and then center the heading.
3. Select the text from *DATE: March 1, 1999* to *RE: TIME SHEETS FOR PACIFIC BOOKS*, and set the paragraph spacing, before and after, to 6 points.
4. Select the three lines of text, *Weekly time sheets cover the period…, Round time to the nearest…, and Please send time sheets electronically….*
5. Apply a 2¼-point outside border with 10-percent gray shading.

For more information about	See
Changing the appearance of text	Lesson 3
Changing paragraph alignment	Lesson 3
Changing the spacing of paragraphs	Lesson 3
Adding borders and shading to paragraphs	Lesson 3

Step 4: Preview and Print the Memo

Now that the memo is complete, you want to print a copy for one final review before sending it to the staff.

1. View the document in the Print Preview window.
2. Save and print the document.

For more information about	See
Previewing a document before printing	Lesson 4
Inserting page breaks	Lesson 4
Adjusting page margins	Lesson 4
Printing a document	Lesson 4

Finish the Review & Practice

Follow these steps if you want to continue to the next lesson.

1. On the File menu, click Close.
2. When a message appears, asking whether you want to save changes, click Yes.

Follow these steps if you want to quit Microsoft Word for now.

1. On the File menu, click Exit.
2. If a message appears, asking whether you want to save changes, click Yes.

PART 2

Increasing Your Editing Skills

LESSON

5

Mastering Indents, Tabs, and Tables

ESTIMATED TIME **40 min.**

In this lesson you will learn how to:

- ✔ *Enhance a document with indents and tabs.*
- ✔ *Create bulleted and numbered lists.*
- ✔ *Control line breaks.*
- ✔ *Set customized tabs.*
- ✔ *Insert and format tables.*
- ✔ *Use a table as a graphic.*

With Microsoft Word, there are many quick and easy ways to make your documents more readable and visually appealing. Indents, tabs, bulleted and numbered lists, and tables are a few of the simplest and most effective tools you can use.

In this lesson, you continue to work on a project for your client, Pacific Books. You work with a document that promotes a book fair, enhancing its appearance using customized indents, tabs, and bulleted lists. You also organize information by formatting it in a table, and finally, you insert a table as a graphic in your document.

important

The default toolbar setting in Microsoft Word 2000 displays both the Standard and Formatting toolbars in one row at the top of the document window, just below the menu bar. This gives you maximum workspace. While working through the exercises in this book, toolbar buttons you need may not initially be visible. If a toolbar button is not visible, click one of the two More Buttons drop-down arrows on the toolbar to locate the button you need. When you select a new toolbar button, it is automatically added to the visible portion of the toolbar, replacing one that is not used as often.

More Buttons

If you have not yet installed this book's practice files, refer to "Using the Microsoft Word 2000 Step by Step CD-ROM," earlier in this book.

Start Word and open a practice file

In this exercise, you start Word and open and save a practice file with a new name.

1. On the Windows taskbar, click the Start button.
   The Start menu appears.
2. On the Start menu, point to Programs, and then click Microsoft Word.
   Microsoft Word 2000 opens.
3. On the Standard toolbar, click the Open button.
   The Open dialog box appears.
4. Click the Look In drop-down arrow, and then select your hard disk.
5. In the list of folders, double-click the Word 2000 SBS Practice folder, and then double-click the Lesson05 folder.
6. In the file list, double-click the 05A file to open it.
   The document opens in the document window.
7. On the File menu, click Save As.
   The Save As dialog box appears.
8. Be sure that the Lesson05 folder appears in the Save In box.
9. In the File Name box, select the text, and then type **Book Fair 05**
10. Click Save.

Open

Display formatting marks

To make it easier to edit your document, you can display formatting marks such as paragraph marks and space marks on your screen.

Show/Hide ¶

- If the formatting marks are not currently displayed, on the Standard toolbar, click the Show/Hide ¶ button.

Displaying the Ruler

The ruler, which stretches across the top of your document when it is displayed, makes working with indents and tabs easier. When the ruler is displayed, you can see the indent markers and tab stops that apply to your document. From the ruler, you can quickly move indent markers and set, move, and delete tab stops.

Display the ruler

In this exercise, you use the View menu to display the ruler.

- To display the ruler, on the View menu, click Ruler.

Understanding Indents and Tabs

Both indents and tabs reposition text in your document, making your document easier to read. Generally, you use indents to position paragraphs on a page, and tabs to move a single line of text or to line up columns of information. For example, you want to display a customer testimonial in a prominent position on the page. By indenting the text two inches from both the left and right margins, your text would appear as follows:

> "Impact Public Relations created an
> effective pubic relations campaign for
> Pacific Books."
> Brett Novak, Pacific Books

Tabs, on the other hand, are useful to line up columns of information. For example, you might use a tab stop placed at the 4-inch mark on the ruler to create the following list:

Name	Phone
Tom Herron	(212) 555-3944
Helen Peterson	(405) 555-7979
Paulette Miller	(419) 555-7539

Working with Indents

If you are not working through this lesson sequentially, before proceeding to the next step, open the 05A file in the Lesson05 folder, and save it as Book Fair 05.

There are three types of indents: left, right, and hanging. A *left indent* moves all lines of the paragraph to the right; a *right indent* moves all lines of the paragraph to the left. A *hanging indent* moves all lines except the first line. Hanging indents are used with numbered or bulleted lists. You can also use both the left and right indent to reformat both margins, as shown in the previous example.

There are several toolbar buttons you can use to indent paragraphs. The *Increase Indent* button indents text in half-inch increments to the right, and the *Decrease Indent* button moves text to the left in half-inch increments. The Numbering and Bullets buttons both create hanging indents. You can also use indent markers on the ruler to indent text from the left and the right.

Use the Formatting toolbar to set indents

In this exercise, you increase and decrease the indent of a paragraph.

1. Scroll down to the middle of page 2, and click before the text *BOOK FAIR SCHEDULE OF EVENTS.*

Increase Indent

2. On the Formatting toolbar, click the Increase Indent button three times.

   The text is indented to the right by 1.5 inches.

   Your screen should look similar to the following illustration.

If the Increase Indent button is not visible, on the Formatting toolbar, click the More Buttons drop-down arrow to locate the button.

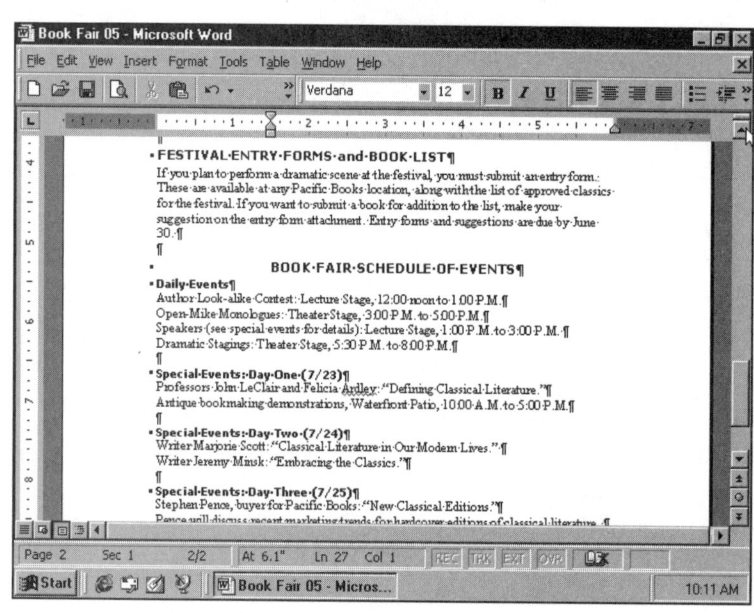

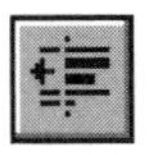

Decrease Indent

3. On the Formatting toolbar, click the Decrease Indent button.

   The text is moved one half inch to the left.

Setting Custom Indents with the Ruler

The indent buttons on the Formatting toolbar are useful to set left indents. To set both left and right indents, you move the indent markers on the ruler.

The left-indent marker on the ruler looks like an hourglass sitting on a box. In fact, it is really three separate icons. The three icons can be moved separately to set one of the following indents: a first-line indent, a hanging indent, or a left indent.

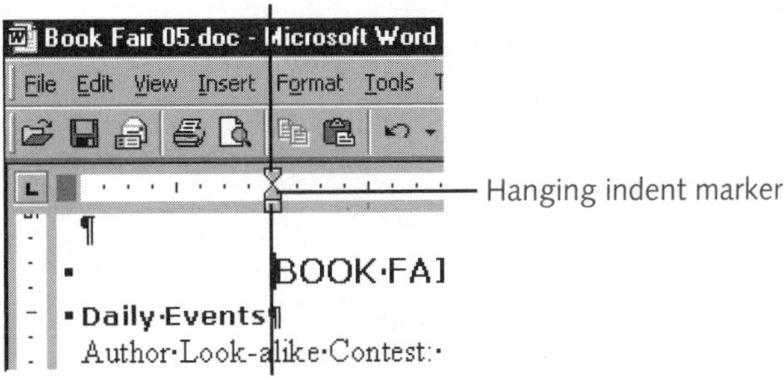

Be sure the ruler is displayed. If it is not, on the View menu, click Ruler.

There is also a right-indent marker on the ruler. This icon is at the right margin on the ruler.

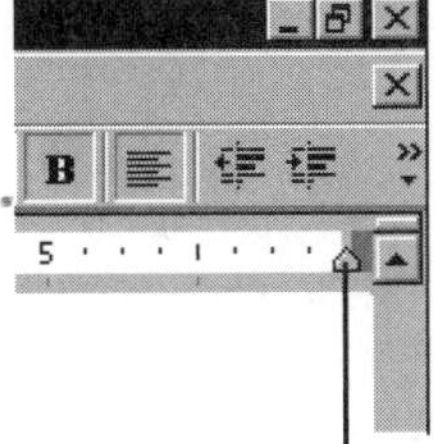

For a demonstation of how to set indents with the ruler, in the Multimedia folder on the Microsoft Word 2000 Step by Step CD-ROM, double-click Indent.

Set indents with the ruler

In this exercise, you use the indent markers on the ruler to set a left indent, a right indent, and a hanging indent.

1. Select the text *Daily Events*.
2. Drag the first-line indent marker to the 0.5-inch mark on the ruler.

Indents, Tabs, and Tables 5

3. Select the text from *Author Look-alike Contest* to *Theater Stage 5:30 P.M. to 8:00 P.M.*
4. Drag the left-indent marker to the 1-inch mark on the ruler.
5. Drag the right-indent marker to the 4.5-inch mark on the ruler.
6. Click anywhere outside of the selected text to cancel the selection.

   The paragraph has been repositioned on the page using three different types of indents.

   Your screen should look similar to the following illustration.

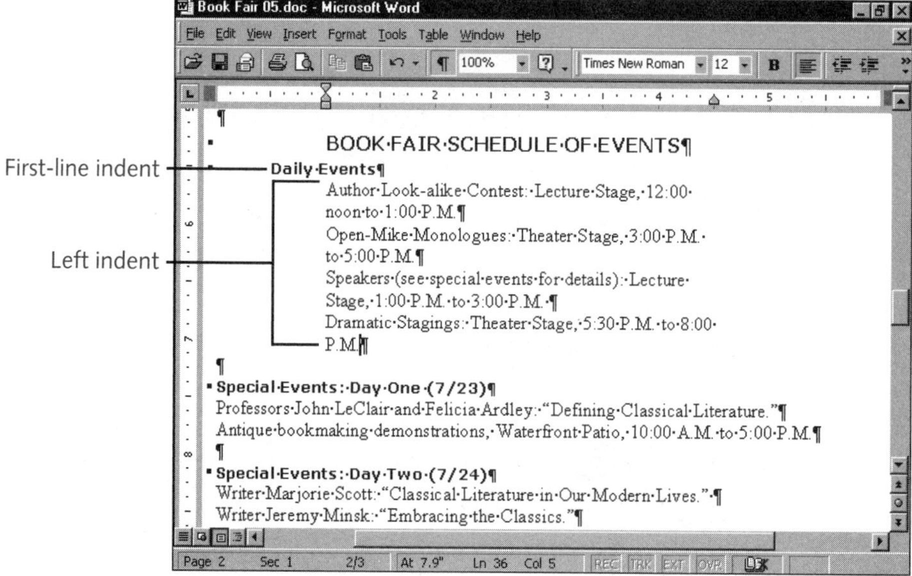

Indent several paragraphs

You can indent several adjacent paragraphs all at one time by selecting the paragraphs and then applying the formatting. In this exercise, you indent the remaining text in the document.

1. Select the text from *Special Events: Day One* to *Pence will discuss recent marketing trends for hardcover editions of classical literature*. This is the remaining text in the document.
2. Drag the left-indent marker to the 1-inch mark on the ruler.

   A left indent is set at the 1-inch mark.
3. Drag the right-indent marker to the 4.5-inch mark on the ruler, and click anywhere outside of the selected text to cancel the selection.

   A right-indent is now set at the 4.5-inch mark.

Creating Bulleted and Numbered Lists

If you are not working through this lesson sequentially, before proceeding to the next step, open the 05B file in the Lesson05 folder, and save it as Book Fair 05.

Hanging indents are used to format items such as numbered or bulleted lists, bibliographic entries, and outlines. In this formatting, the first line of a list item is not indented, while the remaining lines are indented. Hanging indents are automated in Word with two Formatting toolbar buttons. The *Numbering* button places a number at the beginning of each item in the list. You can adjust settings in the Bullets And Numbering dialog box to specify numbers, letters, or Roman numerals. The *Bullets* button places a bullet next to each item. You can choose from a variety of bullet styles, or even import your own.

Create a numbered list using toolbar buttons

In this exercise, you create a numbered list of the Pacific Books summer lectures for the Book Fair 05 document.

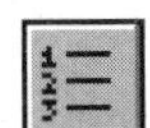

Numbering

If the Numbering button is not visible, on the Formatting toolbar, click the More Buttons drop-down arrow to locate the button.

1. Position the insertion point at the end of the document. You can press Ctrl+End as a shortcut.
2. On the Formatting toolbar, click the Numbering button.
   The number 1 is inserted in the document.
3. Type **Creative Writing for the Noncreative** and press Enter.
   The number 2 is inserted in the document.
4. Type **Best New Nonfiction** and press Enter.
   The number 3 is inserted in the document.
5. Type **Choosing Books for Young Readers**
6. Press Enter twice to end the numbered list.
   The numbering feature is turned off.

Add an item to a numbered list

You can easily add an item to a numbered list, and the list will be automatically renumbered. In this exercise, you add an item to the current list.

1. Click after the word *Noncreative* in the first list item.

2. Press Enter.

   This list item becomes the new number 2, and the other list items are renumbered.

   Your screen should look similar to the following illustration.

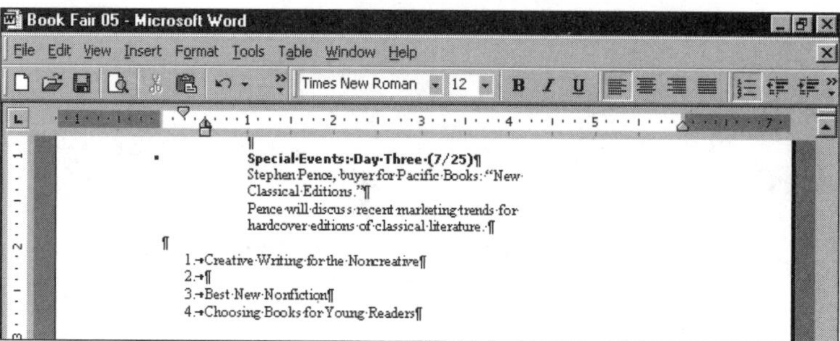

3. Type **An Evening of Poetry** and press Enter.

   An extra number is placed in the document.

4. Press Backspace three times to remove the extra number in the list.

Change numbers to bullets

In this exercise, you change the list of summer lectures to a bulleted list.

1. Position the insertion point before the word *Creative*, and drag to select the text through *Choosing Books for Young Readers*.

   Your screen should look similar to the following illustration.

Bullets

2. On the Formatting toolbar, click the Bullets button.

   This list is displayed with bullets.

Using the New Line Character

Occasionally you need to add text to an item in your numbered list, but as you saw in the last exercise, if you move the insertion point to the end of that item and press Enter, you start a new numbered item. In this case, you need to use the *new line character*. The new line character starts a new line and properly aligns it with the text above, without causing the list to be renumbered.

Insert a new line character

If you are not working through this lesson sequentially, before proceeding to the next step, open the 05C file in the Lesson05 folder, and save it as Book Fair 05.

In this exercise, you add a speaker's name to one of the items in the list created in the previous exercises by using the new line character.

1. Click after the word *Poetry* in the second line of the list.
2. Press Shift+Enter.

   The new line character is inserted.
3. Type **Jasper Greenwald, Moderator**

   The text is aligned with the line above.
4. Press Ctrl+End to move the insertion point to the end of the document.

Using Picture Bullets

Word provides a number of bullet styles to choose from, and in Word 2000, a new feature lets you select from a variety of *picture bullets,* too. Picture bullets are like small graphics and can be especially useful for documents used as Web pages. In general, when you change a bullet style, the Bullets button will apply the new bullet style thereafter.

Insert a picture bullet

In this exercise, you change the bulleted list to display a picture bullet.

1. Select the text from *Creative Writing for the Noncreative* to *Choosing Books for Young Readers*.
2. On the Format menu, click Bullets And Numbering.

   The Bullets And Numbering dialog box appears.

New! 2000

3. In the Bullets And Numbering dialog box, click the Bulleted tab.

   The bullet options are displayed.
4. Click Picture.

   The Picture Bullet dialog box appears.
5. Click the first picture bullet in the second row.

   A shortcut menu of buttons appears next to the bullet box.

   Your screen should look similar to the following illustration.

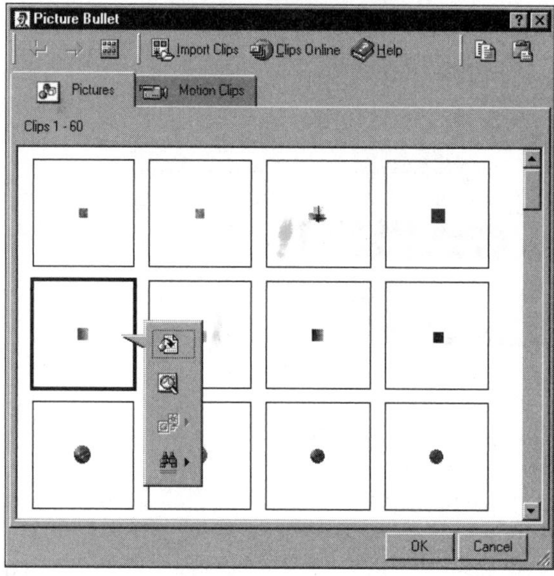

Insert Clip

6. Click the Insert Clip button.

   The bullets are changed to the picture bullet.

7. Click anywhere outside of the selected text to cancel the selection.

tip

To remove bullets or numbers from a list, select the text, and on the Formatting toolbar, click the Bullets button or the Numbers button.

Using Tabs

Tab stops are used primarily to line up columns of text. The type of tab stop you choose determines how the text is lined up in the document. There are five tab stops you can select from the ruler: left (the default), center, right, decimal, and bar. Each type of tab stop aligns the text differently. For example, a decimal tab stop is used to align a column of currency figures on their decimal points.

There are additional ways to format your document using tabs. For example, if you want items in a multicolumn list, such as a table of contents, to be separated by a horizontal dotted line, you can select various *dot leader* options. Dot leaders are also useful when creating phone directories in which a person's name is followed by a dotted line to that person's phone number. To view dot leader options, on the Format menu, click Tabs. The available dot leader options are listed in the Leader area.

Each time you press the Tab key when the insertion point is positioned on a blank line, you insert a tab stop in your document. By default, the insertion point is moved to the right in half-inch increments. Nonprinting arrows denoting tabs are placed in the document.

Use the default tab stop

If you are not working through this lesson sequentially, before proceeding to the next step, open the 05D file in the Lesson05 folder, and save it as Book Fair 05.

In this exercise, you add tab stops and text to your document using the default tab stops.

1. Position the insertion point at the end of the document. You can press Ctrl+End as a shortcut.
2. Press Tab four times.

   The insertion point is moved 2 inches to the right.
3. Type **Pacific Books Store Managers** and press Enter.

   The insertion point is moved to the next line.

Using the Ruler to Set Tabs

If you are not working through this lesson sequentially, before proceeding to the next step, open the 05E file in the Lesson05 folder, and save it as Book Fair 05.

Aligning text with the Tab key can be cumbersome, especially when you have long lists that you want to align to the far right on the page. A quicker method is to set customized tabs directly on the ruler. Tabs set on the ruler can be moved and deleted. Clicking the Tab Alignment button, at the far left of the ruler, changes the tab alignment. The tab stop options include left, center, right, decimal, and bar.

Set tab stops on the ruler

In this exercise, you align columns of information by placing tab stops on the ruler.

1. Position the insertion point at the end of the document.
2. Click the 1-inch mark on the ruler.

   A left tab is set at the 1-inch mark on the ruler.

   Your screen should look similar to the following illustration.

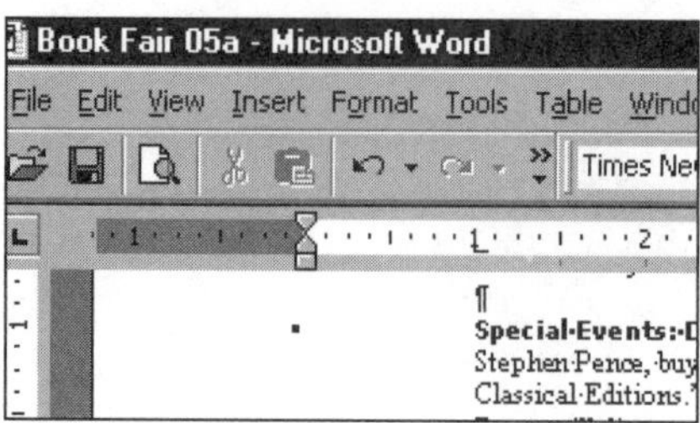

3. Position the pointer on the Tab icon to the left of the ruler.

Left Tab

It currently displays the Left Tab icon.

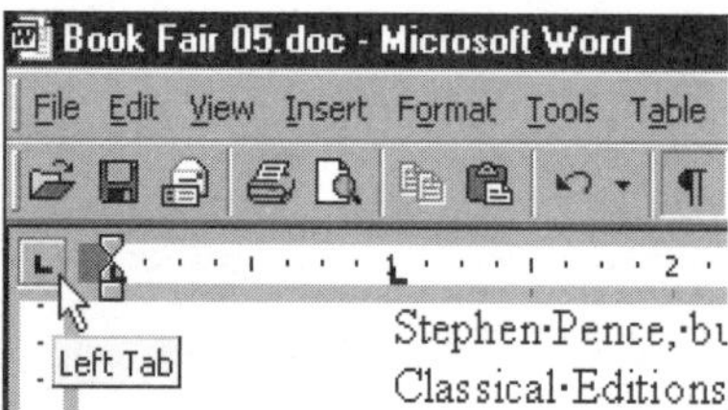

4. Click the Tab icon twice.

Right Tab

The tab alignment icon changes to Right Tab.

5. Position the pointer at the 4-inch mark on the ruler, and then click.

A right-aligned tab stop is now set at the 4-inch mark on the ruler.

Use tab stops on the ruler

In this exercise, you create a list using the preset tab stops on the ruler.

1. Be sure the insertion point is before the paragraph mark at the end of the document.
2. Press Tab.

   The insertion point moves to the first tab stop at the 1-inch mark on the ruler.
3. Type **R.H. Hiatt** and then press the Tab key.
4. Type **(415) 555-2983** and then press Enter.
5. Press Tab, and then type **Francis Lockwood**
6. Press Tab, type **(503) 555-9573** and then press Enter.
7. Press Tab, and then type **Erica Thomas**
8. Press Tab, type **(206) 555-3453** and then press Enter.

   The list is complete. All items should be aligned evenly in columns.

Move tab stops on the ruler

After you've created the list in your document, you can adjust the columns by moving the tabs on the ruler. In this exercise, you move the column with phone numbers by adjusting the tab stop on the ruler.

1. Select the text from *R.H. Hiatt* to *(503) 555-3453*.
2. Drag the tab stop on the 4-inch mark of the ruler to the 5-inch mark on the ruler.

   The column of phone numbers is moved 1 inch to the right. Keep the text selected.

   Your screen should look similar to the following illustration.

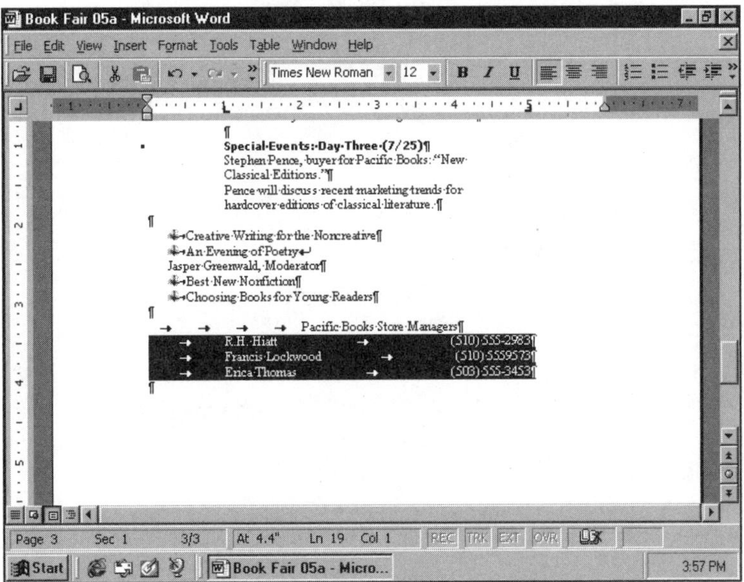

Set tabs from the menu

In this exercise, you clear a tab and replace it with a dot leader tab.

1. Be sure the text selected in the previous exercise is still selected.
2. On the Format menu, click Tabs.

   The Tabs dialog box appears.
3. In the Tab Stop Position list, select 5".

Your screen should look similar to the following illustration.

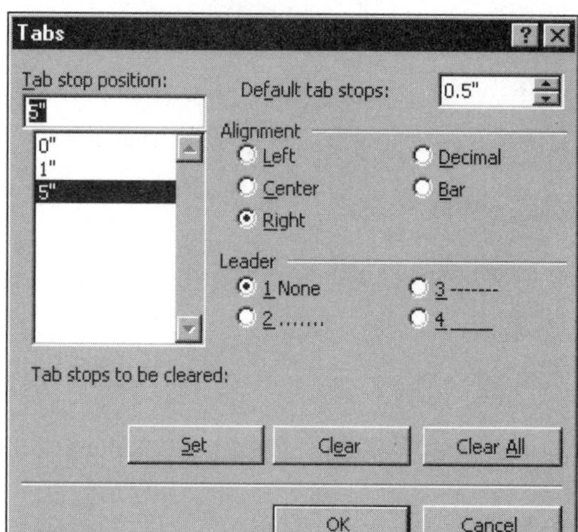

4. Click Clear.

   The tab stop at the 5-inch mark on the ruler is deleted.
5. In the Tab Stop Position box, type **5**
6. In the Alignment area, click Right.
7. In the Leader area, click 2.

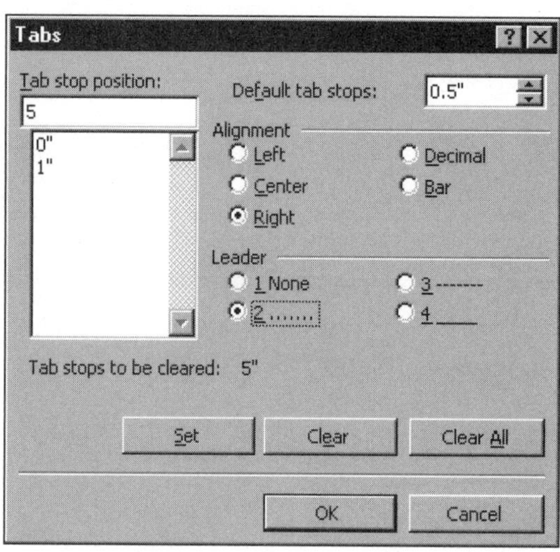

8. Click Set.

   A right-aligned dot leader tab is set at the 5-inch mark on the ruler.

9. Click OK, and then click anywhere outside of the selected text.

   Dots lead from the end of the managers' names to their phone numbers.

Remove customized tabs

When you've finished working with the customized tabs, it's a good idea to remove the tab stops at the first line below the list in order to reset the default tab stops. By doing this, you return to the default tab settings, making it easier to set up other customized tabs later on. In this exercise, you remove the tabs at the 1-inch and 5-inch marks on the ruler.

1. Press Ctrl+End to move the insertion point to the end of the document.
2. Drag the tab at the 1-inch mark on the ruler into the document.

   The tab is removed from the ruler.
3. Drag the tab at the 4-inch mark on the ruler into the document.

   The tab is removed from the ruler.

Working with Tables

If you are not working through this lesson sequentially, before proceeding to the next step, open the 05F file in the Lesson05 folder, and save it as Book Fair 05.

Using tabs to arrange a simple list is easy, but when you have many columns and rows of information, tables are easier to work with than tabs. Tables are arranged by columns and rows. You can insert tables into a document using either the Table menu or the Tables And Borders toolbar. The borders and cells of a table can be formatted, and text can be aligned—and even wordwrapped—within a cell. You can create a heading for your table and drag the table as you would a graphic to another place in your document. You can also insert and delete columns and rows, making it easy to enlarge or reduce your table if necessary.

When you insert a table, the columns are evenly divided between the left and right margins. Usually, text fills some columns but not others. You can resize each column to fit the text in that column. When you resize columns, you resize from left to right, because changes made to one column affect the column to its right.

For a demonstation of how to insert a table, in the Multimedia folder on the Microsoft Word 2000 Step by Step CD-ROM, double-click InsertTable.

To work with the table commands, you first display the Tables And Borders toolbar.

Insert a table

To insert information about Pacific Books branch stores into your document, you decide that a table would work best. In this exercise, you insert a table with four columns and three rows.

1. Press Ctrl+End to move the insertion point to the end of the document, and then press Enter twice.
2. On the View menu, point to Toolbars, and then click Tables And Borders.

   The Tables And Borders toolbar is displayed.

Insert Table

3. On the Tables And Borders toolbar, click the Insert Table button.

   The Insert Table dialog box appears.
4. In the Table Size area, in the Number Of Columns box, type **4**
5. Press Tab, and in the Number Of Rows box, type **3**
6. Click OK.

   A table with four columns and three rows is inserted into your document and the insertion point is placed in the upper-left cell of the table.

Cell Gridline End-of-cell marker End-of-row marker

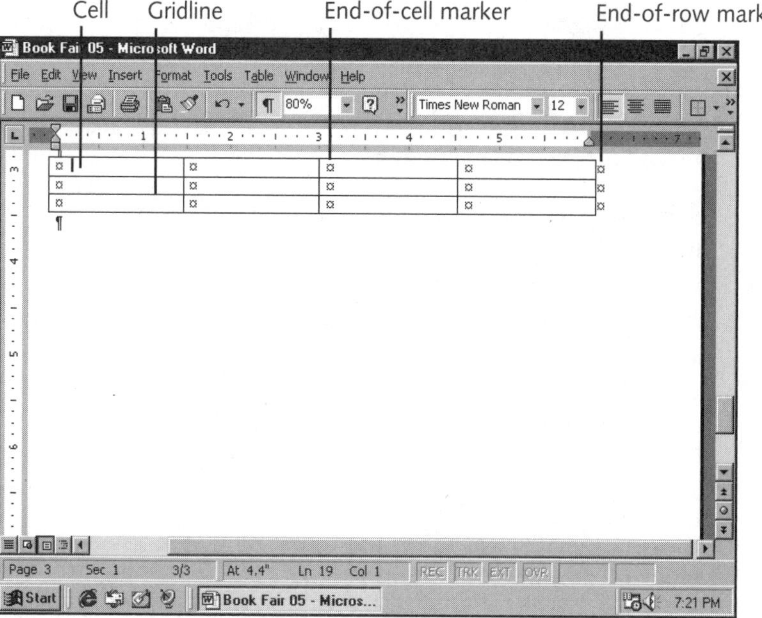

Enter text into a table

In this exercise, you fill out the table with Pacific Books branch information.

1. Type **Branch** and then press Tab.

   Type **Location** and then press Tab.

   Type **Hours** and then press Tab.

   Type **Phone** and then press Tab.

   The first row of information in the table is complete.

❷ Type **Berkeley** and then press Tab.

Type **2226 Shattuck Ave**. and then press Tab.

Type **10-10 Daily** and then press Tab.

Type **(510) 555-2953** and then press Tab.

The second row of information in the table is complete.

❸ Type **Portland** and then press Tab.

Don't worry about text not fitting into a cell; you can resize column widths later.

Type **89 Rain Way** and then press Tab.

Type **10-10 Tue – Sun, closed Mon** and then press Tab.

Type **(503) 555-9573**

The third row of information in the table is complete.

Add a row at the end of a table

In this exercise, you add an additional row to your table for one more store.

❶ Press Tab.

A new row is inserted into the table, and the insertion point is placed in the left cell of the new row.

❷ Type **Seattle**

Press Tab, and then type **41 S. Marion St.**

Press Tab, and then type **10-10 Daily**

Press tab, and then type **(206) 555-3453**

The last row of information in the table is complete.

Your screen should look similar to the following illustration.

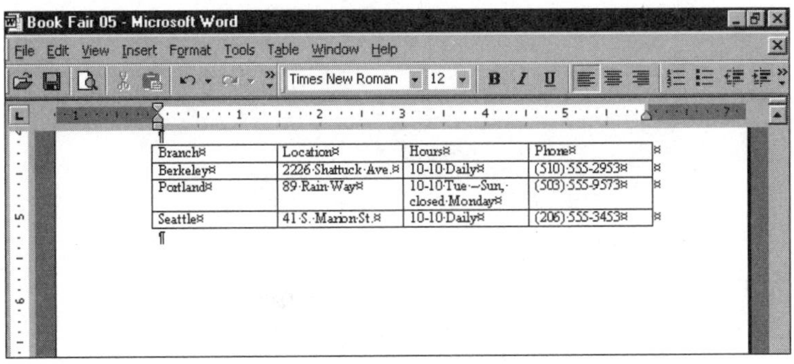

Branch	Location	Hours	Phone
Berkeley	2226 Shattuck Ave.	10-10 Daily	(510) 555-2953
Portland	89 Rain Way	10-10 Tue – Sun, closed Monday	(503) 555-9573
Seattle	41 S. Marion St.	10-10 Daily	(206) 555-3453

❸ Click anywhere outside of the table.

Delete a column

In this exercise, you delete the Phone column.

1. Click in the Phone column.
2. On the Table menu, point to Delete, and then click Columns.

   The column is deleted.

Change column widths

In this exercise, you resize the columns of your table.

1. Position the pointer on the column gridline between Branch and Location.

   The pointer changes into a double-headed arrow.

   Your screen should look similar to the following illustration.

Double-headed arrow ready to resize column

Branch	Location
Berkeley	2226 Shattuck Ave.
Portland	89 Rain Way
Seattle	41 S. Marion St.

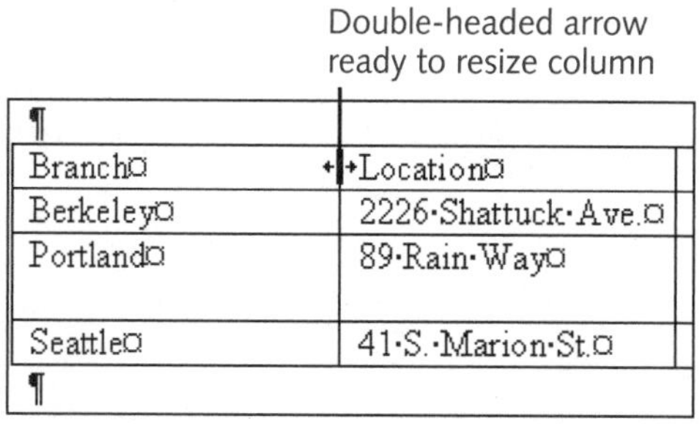

2. Drag the column gridline to the left to narrow the Branch column.

   The Branch column width is decreased, and the Location column width is increased.
3. Position the pointer on the last column gridline of the table, and double-click.

   The Hours column is automatically resized to fit all text on one line.

   Your screen should look similar to the following illustration.

Resized table

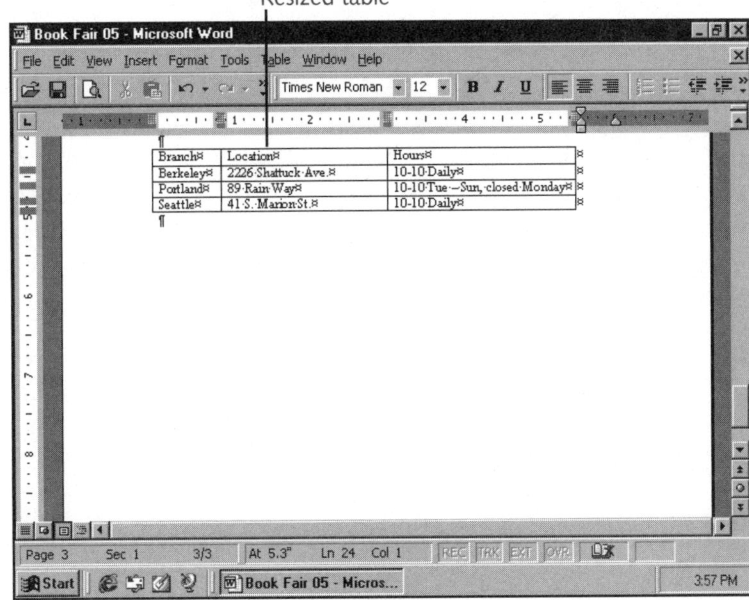

Add a row and merge cells for a table head

In this exercise, you insert a new row and merge the cells to create a heading for your table.

1. Click anywhere in the first row of the table.
2. On the Table menu, point to Insert, and then click Rows Above.

   A new row is inserted above the table, and it is selected.
3. On the Tables And Borders toolbar, click the Merge Cells button.
4. Click in the first row to cancel the selection, and then type **Pacific Books Branch Locations**

Merge Cells

> **tip**
>
> If a Table menu command or the Tables And Borders toolbar button is not available, click in the table and then check again.

Formatting Tables

If you are not working through this lesson sequentially, before proceeding to the next step, open the 05G file in the Lesson05 folder, and save it as Book Fair 05.

Two components in a table can be formatted: the gridlines making up the cells of the table, and the text within the cells. The quickest way to format a table is using the Table AutoFormat feature available on the Tables And Borders toolbar. There are a variety of table styles to choose from, including several designed specifically for Web pages. You can also format text in individual cells. You should format text within a cell after you apply formatting with Table AutoFormat, or else AutoFormat will override the individual cell formatting.

Generally, you format text in the cells the same way you format all other text. You can even use the Format Painter button to copy formatting from text in one cell to the next. One difference from regular text formatting is that when you align text in a table, it is justified within the cell—not within the page margins.

Use Table AutoFormat

In this exercise, you format a table using the Table AutoFormat feature.

1. Click anywhere in the table of the Book Fair 05 document.

Table AutoFormat

2. On the Tables And Borders toolbar, click the Table AutoFormat button.

   The Table AutoFormat dialog box appears.
3. In the Formats list, scroll down and select Web 1.
4. Click OK to close the Table AutoFormat dialog box.

   Your screen should look similar to the following illustration.

Table in Web1 formatting

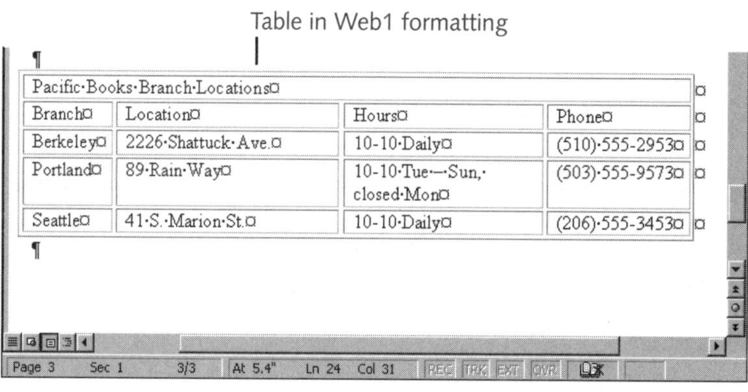

Format text in a table

In this exercise, you format the header of your table.

1. Position the pointer outside and to the left of the top row.
2. When the pointer is a right-pointing arrow, click.

   The text in the top row is selected.

Center

3. On the Formatting toolbar, click the Center button.

   The text is centered across the table.

4. On the Formatting toolbar, click the Font drop-down arrow, and then select Verdana.
5. On the Formatting toolbar, click the Font Size drop-down arrow, and then select 16.

Shading Color

6. On the Tables And Borders toolbar, click the Shading Color drop-down arrow, and then select Dark Blue.
7. Click anywhere in the table to cancel the selection of the top row.

   The text in the heading is formatted.

   Your screen should look similar to the following illustration.

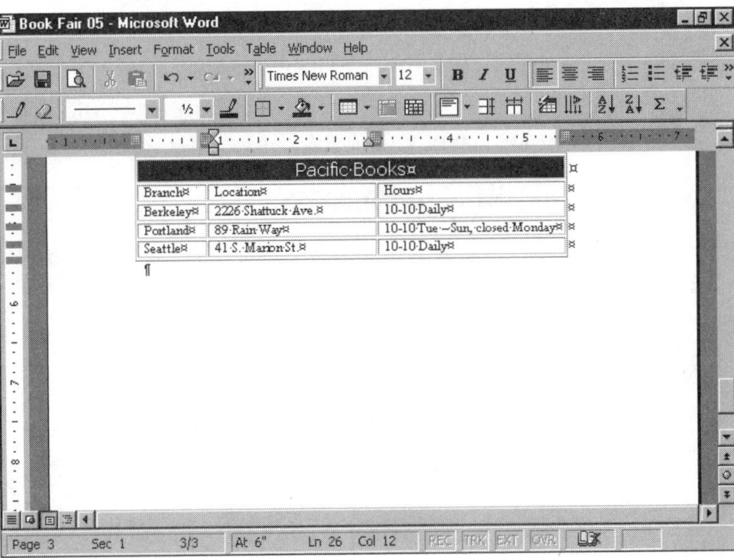

Centering a Table Across a Page

You can center a table in a document across the page, instead of leaving it aligned flush left. Centering helps to balance a document and draw attention to the table.

Center a table across a page

In this exercise, you use the Table menu to center the table across the page.

1. Position the insertion point anywhere in the table.
2. On the Table menu, click Table Properties.

   The Table Properties dialog box appears.
3. In the Table Properties dialog box, click the Table tab.
4. In the Alignment area, click Center, and click OK.

   The table is centered between the margins of the page.

One Step Further Using Tables as Graphics

If you are not working through this lesson sequentially, before proceeding to the next step, open the 05H file in the Lesson05 folder, and save it as Book Fair 05.

You can draw your own table in a document and thereby control the size of the cells. Drawing a table differs from inserting a table because you control the height of a cell and the number of columns in a row. For example, you can draw a table with two columns in the first row and three columns in the remaining rows. The Draw Table feature in Word even allows you to insert a table within a table. This is useful for specialized tables such as those used in Web pages.

Tables can also be used as graphics. You can drag and reposition a table in a document the same way you would position another type of graphic.

Draw a table in a document

In this exercise, you draw a single-cell table that can be used as a graphic in your document.

1. Press Ctrl+End to move the insertion point to the end of the document.
2. Press Enter twice. This moves the insertion point to a blank area of the document where you can insert a new table.
3. On the Tables And Borders toolbar, click the Draw Table button.

   There is now a pencil attached to the pointer.

Draw Table

4. Position the pointer on the insertion point.
5. Drag the insertion point down in the document until you have a cell about 2 inches high by 0.5 inches wide. Use the ruler as a guide.

   Your screen should look similar to the following illustration.

If your cell does not turn out right, click the Undo button and try again.

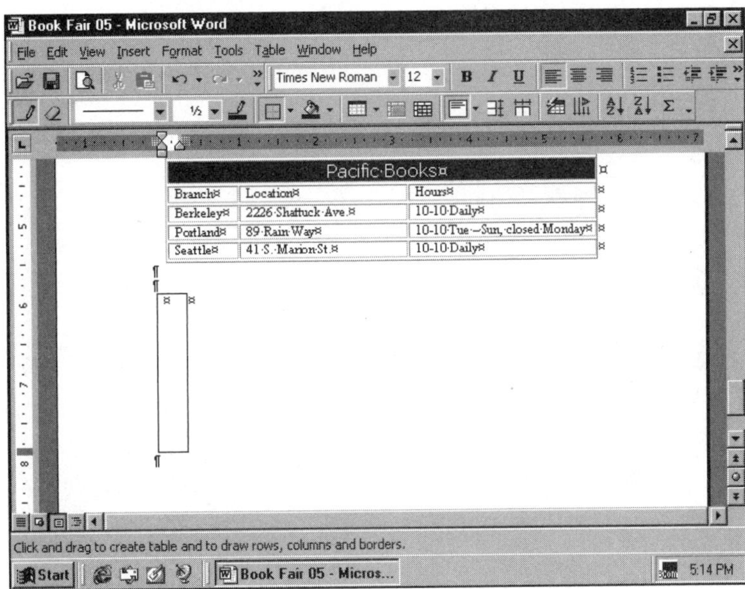

6 Click the Draw Table button to turn off the command.

7 In the cell, type **Pacific Books**

Your screen should look similar to the following illustration.

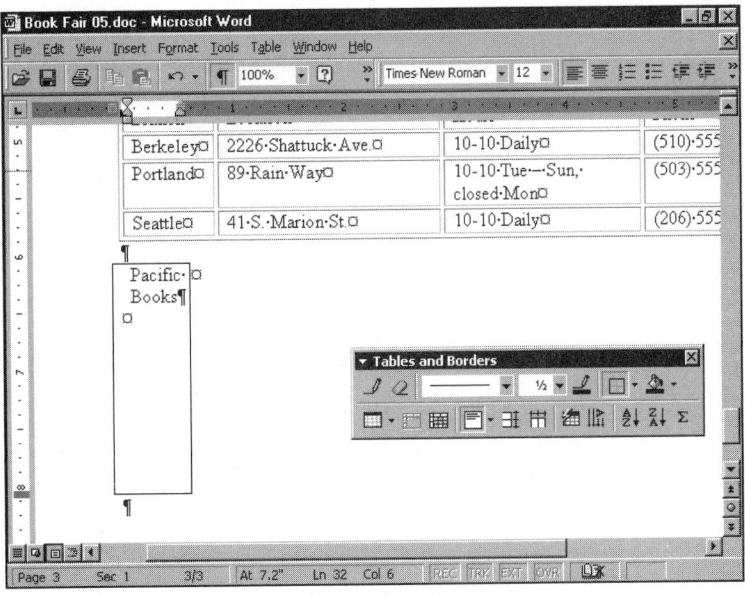

Format a table to be used as a graphic

In this exercise, you reposition the text in the cell and format it to be used as a graphic in your document.

Change Text Direction

Format Painter

Shading Color

The default is Dark Blue because it was selected previously.

Center

1. Be sure the insertion point is in the single-cell table.
2. On the Tables And Borders toolbar, click the Change Text Direction button.

   The text is changed to fit vertically within the cell.
3. Scroll back to the heading row of the Pacific Books Branch Locations table above, and then select the word *Pacific*.
4. On the Standard toolbar, click the Format Painter button.
5. Drag the insertion point over the text *Pacific Books* in the new table, and then click inside the cell to cancel the selection.

   The text is formatted.
6. On the Tables And Borders toolbar, click the Shading Color button.

   The cell is formatted in Dark Blue.
7. On the Formatting toolbar, click the Center button.

   The text is centered.
8. Click anywhere in the cell to cancel the selection.

Positioning a Table by Dragging

You can drag tables, like other graphics, anywhere in your document. When you position a table, the surrounding text wraps around it.

Move a table

In this exercise, you drag the table to the left of the Schedule of Events.

1. Click in the newly created Pacific Books table.

   The table is outlined and a move handle appears in the upper-left corner of the table.
2. Move the pointer over the move handle until a four-headed arrow appears.
3. Drag the table to the left of the heading *BOOK FAIR SCHEDULE OF EVENTS*.

   Your screen should look similar to the following illustration.

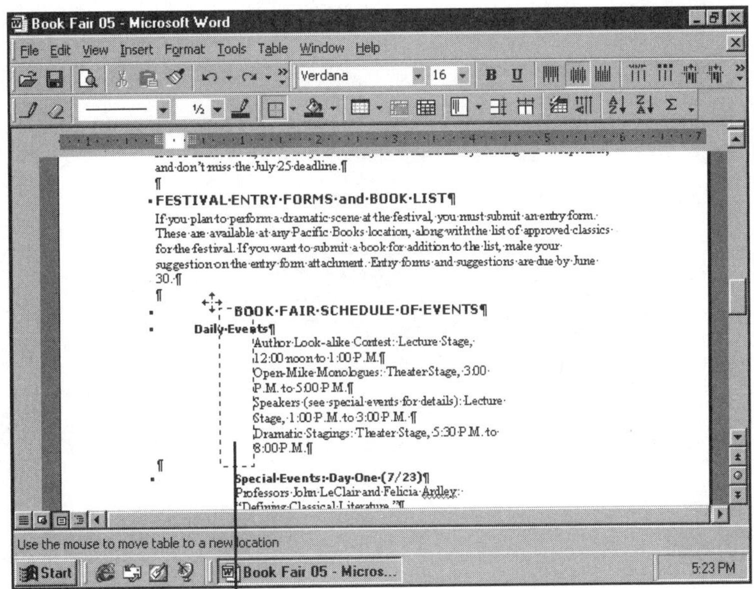

Repositioned table

4 Release the mouse button.

The text wraps around the table.

Your screen should look similar to the following illustration.

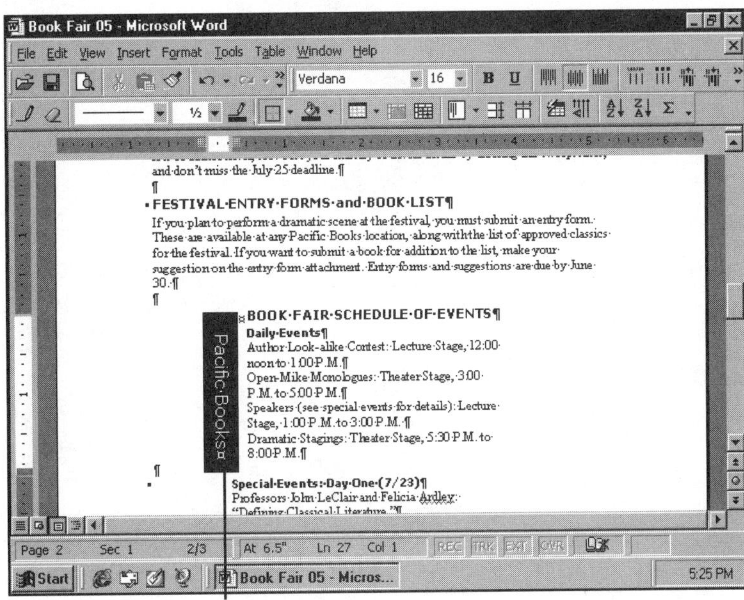

Table in new position with text wrapped

Finish the lesson

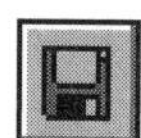

Save

1. On the Standard toolbar, click the Save button.

   Changes to Book Fair 05 are saved.
2. On the File menu, click Close.
3. On the File menu, click Exit.

Lesson 5 Quick Reference

To	Do this	Button
Display the ruler	On the View menu, click Ruler.	
Set custom indents with the ruler	Select the text to be indented. Drag the indent marker to the desired position on the ruler.	
Create a numbered list	On the Formatting toolbar, click the Numbering button. Type the first item, and press Enter. Continue until the list is complete. Press Enter twice to end the numbered list.	
Use the new line character	Position the insertion point at the end of the text in the list. Press Shift+Enter. Type the text.	
Insert picture bullets	On the Format menu, click Bullets And Numbering. In the Bullets And Numbering dialog box, click the Bulleted tab. Click Picture. In the Picture Bullet dialog box, select the picture bullet to be inserted. Click the Insert Clip button. Click anywhere outside the selected text to cancel the selection.	
Remove bullets	Select the bulleted text in the list. On the Formatting toolbar, click the Bullets button.	
Use the default tab stop	Press the Tab key.	
Set tabs from the ruler	Click the ruler where you want the tab.	
Remove customized tabs	Drag the tab marker on the ruler into the document.	

Lesson 5 Quick Reference

To	Do this	Button
Insert a table	On the Tables And Borders toolbar, click the Insert Table button. In the Table Size area, in the Number Of Columns box, type the number of columns, and then press Tab. In the Number Of Rows box, type the number of rows. Click OK.	
Enter text into a table	Position the insertion point in a table cell. Type the text and press Tab to move to the next cell.	
Add a row at the end of the table	In the last cell of the last row of the table, press Tab.	
Delete a column	Position the insertion in the column to be deleted. On the Table menu, point to Delete, and then click Columns.	
Change column widths	Position the pointer on the column grid between the columns to be resized. The pointer changes to a double-headed arrow. Drag the column grid to the left to narrow the left column, or to the right to widen it.	
Add a row and merge cells for a table head	Position the insertion point anywhere in the first row of the table. On the Table menu, point to Insert and click Rows Above. With the top row selected, on the Tables And Borders toolbar, click the Merge Cells button. Click to cancel the selection of the row.	
Use Table AutoFormat	Position the insertion point anywhere in the table. On the Tables And Borders toolbar, click the Table AutoFormat button. In the Formats list, select a table format. Click OK.	

Lesson 5 Quick Reference

To	Do this	Button
Center a table across the page	Click anywhere in the table. On the Table menu, click Table Properties. In the Table Properties dialog box, click the Table tab. In the Alignment area, click Center, and click OK.	
Draw a table in a document	On the Tables And Borders toolbar, click the Draw Table button. Click and drag the insertion point until the cell is the desired size. Continue to draw cells until the table is complete. Click the Draw Table button to turn it off.	
Drag a table into a document	Click in the table. When the move handle icon appears at the upper-left corner of the table, move the pointer over the move icon until the pointer becomes a four-headed arrow. Drag the table to a new place in the document.	

Automating Tasks

In this lesson you will learn how to:

- ✔ *Find and replace text and formatting.*
- ✔ *Automate insertion of frequently used text.*
- ✔ *Automate text formatting.*
- ✔ *Check spelling and grammar.*
- ✔ *Find word substitutes with the thesaurus.*
- ✔ *Create and run a macro.*
- ✔ *Change capitalization within a document.*

ESTIMATED TIME
40 min.

Microsoft Word is full of features that help speed up your word processing. For example, instead of hunting line-by-line for a misspelled name in a document, you can use the *Find And Replace* feature to quickly locate all occurrences. If you frequently use a company name or address, you can use *AutoText* to create a shortcut to inserting the text. With *AutoFormat* options, you can instantly update list styles and turn Internet addresses into hyperlinks. The *Spelling and Grammar Checker* is speedy and thorough, and it often identifies errors you might otherwise overlook. Finally, Word *macros*, mini-programs you create, can help automate repetitive tasks.

In this lesson, you use all of these features to edit a document Impact Public Relations has written for its client, Pacific Books. The document describes an upcoming book fair sponsored by Pacific Books. You refine the language and formatting and add a few more details. When you finish editing, you create a macro that checks spelling and grammar, and then saves and prints the document.

More Buttons

important

The default toolbar setting in Microsoft Word 2000 displays both the Standard and Formatting toolbars in one row, at the top of the document window, just below the menu bar. This gives you maximum workspace. While working through the exercises in this book, toolbar buttons you need may not initially be visible. If a toolbar button is not visible, click one of the two More Buttons drop-down arrows on the toolbar to locate the button you need. When you select a new toolbar button, it is automatically added to the visible portion of the toolbar, replacing one that is not used as often.

If you have not yet installed this book's practice files, refer to "Using the Microsoft Word 2000 Step by Step CD-ROM," earlier in this book.

Start Word and open a practice file

In this exercise, you start Word, open a practice file, and then save it with a new name.

1. On the Windows taskbar, click the Start button.

   The Start menu appears.
2. On the Start menu, point to Programs, and then click Microsoft Word.

   Microsoft Word 2000 opens.
3. On the Standard toolbar, click the Open button.

   The Open dialog box appears.
4. Click the Look In drop-down arrow, and then select your hard disk.
5. In the list of folders, double-click the Word 2000 SBS Practice folder, and then double-click the Lesson06 folder.
6. In the file list, double-click the 06A file to open it.

   The document opens in the document window.
7. On the File menu, click Save As.

   The Save As dialog box appears.
8. Be sure that the Lesson06 folder appears in the Save In box.
9. In the File Name box, select the text, and then type **Book Fair 06**
10. Click Save.

Open

Display formatting marks

To make it easier to edit your document, you can display formatting marks such as paragraph marks and space marks on your screen.

Show/Hide ¶

- If formatting marks are not currently displayed, on the Standard toolbar, click the Show/Hide ¶ button.

Finding and Replacing Text

In the document you're creating for Pacific Books, you want to change some phrases that appear throughout. You can use the *Find And Replace* feature to quickly locate and, if you want, replace all occurrences of a certain word or phrase. You can change every occurrence of it all at once, or you can accept or reject each change individually.

When you click More to expand the Find And Replace dialog box, you can be very specific about your search. If you want to search for whole words, so the search doesn't stop on a word that might only contain your search word (stopping on *discovery*, for example, when you want it to find *disco*), you select Find Whole Words Only. If you want to find a phrase that matches a certain capitalization exactly, you select Match Case. You can also find all forms of a word, such as various tenses of a verb.

tip

After selecting additional search options with the Find And Replace dialog box expanded, click Less. This will return the dialog box to a smaller size and keep it from covering too much of the document.

Find and replace text

If you are not working through this lesson sequentially, before proceeding to the next step, open the 06A file in the Lesson06 folder, and save it as Book Fair 06.

In this exercise, you use the Replace command to locate the occurrences of the word *stagings* in the document and replace all but one of them with the word *scenes*.

1. On the Edit menu, click Replace.

   The Find And Replace dialog box appears, with the Replace tab selected.
2. In the Find What box, type **stagings**
3. In the Replace With box, delete any text, and type **scenes**
4. Click More.

   The Find And Replace dialog box expands to show additional options.
5. In the Search Options area, be sure that All appears in the Search box. If it doesn't, click the Search box drop-down arrow, and then click All.

   The entire document will be searched, rather than just the section above or the section below the insertion point.

   Your screen should look similar to the following illustration.

Click this button to return to a short Find And Replace dialog box.

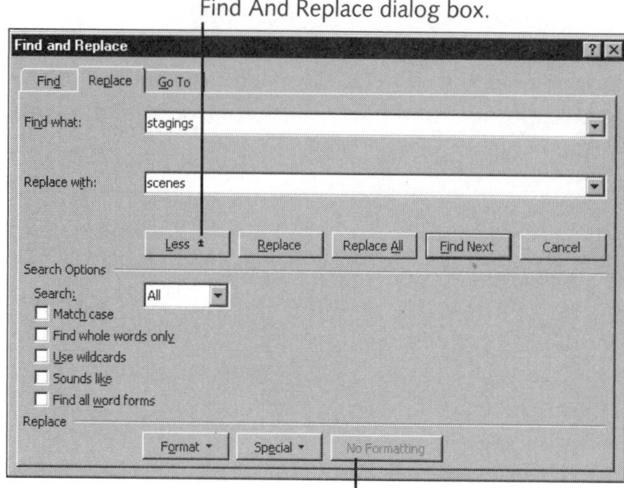

You can click No Formatting to disable finding or replacing formatting.

6. Click Find Next to locate the first occurrence of the word. Click Less to shorten the dialog box if necessary.

   The first instance of *stagings* is located and selected. This is the one place you want to keep the word as it is, so you won't replace this one.

If you want to replace every occurrence of a word, click Replace All, rather than Find Next, when you begin your search.

7. Click Find Next to move to the next occurrence of *stagings*.

   The next occurrence of the word is located in a heading.

8. Click Replace.

   The word *stagings* is replaced, and a message is displayed that Word has finished searching the document.

9. In the message box, click OK, and leave the Find And Replace dialog box open.

Finding and Replacing Formatting

Using the Format button in the Find And Replace dialog box, you can search your document for specific fonts, bold and italic type, highlighted text, tabs, or template styles. With the Special button, you can also find and replace special characters, such as paragraph marks, numbers, and symbols, as well as hard page breaks and comment marks.

The Format and Special buttons can be used together to find certain types of text. In the next exercise, you use both buttons to find italic numerals.

tip

When you want to resume looking for text, and not formatting, place the insertion point in the Find What box, and then click No Formatting. To eliminate formatting options from your replacement text, place the insertion point in the Replace With box, and then click No Formatting.

Find an italic numeral

If you are not working through this lesson sequentially, before proceeding to the next step, open the 06B file in the Lesson06 folder, and save it as Book Fair 06.

In this two-part exercise, you use the Find And Replace dialog box to find a numeral formatted in italic type, and then you replace it with regular type.

1. If the Find And Replace dialog box is not open from the preceding exercise, on the Edit menu, click Replace.

   The Find And Replace dialog box appears, with the Replace tab selected.
2. In the Find What and Replace With boxes, delete any text.
3. Click in the Find What box.
4. In the Find area, click Format, and then click Font.

   The Find Font dialog box appears.
5. In the Font Style list, click Italic, and click OK.

   In the Find And Replace dialog box, the type of formatting you want to search for is displayed under the Find What box.
6. In the Find area, click Special, and then click Any Digit.

   The character code for numerals (^#) is inserted in the Find What box. You are now ready to find numerals with italic formatting.

Remove the italic formatting

In the second part of this exercise, you remove the italic formatting of a numeral.

1. Click in the Replace With box.
2. In the Replace area, click Format, and then click Font.

   The Replace Font dialog box appears.

3. In the Font Style list, click Regular, and click OK.

   In the Find And Replace dialog box, the replacement formatting is designated as Not Bold, Not Italic. This description appears under the Replace With box.

4. In the Search Options area, be sure All is displayed in the Search box, and then click Less to make the dialog box smaller.

5. Click Find Next.

   The first italic numeral—the 5 in 50 percent—is selected.

6. Click Replace.

   The italic 5 is replaced with a 5 in regular type, and the 0 is selected.

7. Click Replace again.

   The italic 0 is replaced with a 0 in regular type.

8. When the search is finished, click OK, and then click Close.

   The Find And Replace dialog box closes.

tip

In the Find And Replace dialog box, you can use key combinations, called shortcut keys, to apply formatting to characters and paragraphs. For example, to find italic formatting, instead of using the Format button and menu, you can type Ctrl+I in the Find What box. For more about shortcut keys, refer to Microsoft Word Help.

Navigating Your Documents

Skill in using the basic navigational features of Word will add to your editing efficiency. Here are some quick ways to move around in your documents.

Using the keyboard

To Move Here	Do This
Start of a document	Press Ctrl+Home.
End of a document	Press Ctrl+End.
Previous page	Press Ctrl+Page Up.
Next page	Press Ctrl+Page Down.
Previous screen	Press Page Up.
Next screen	Press Page Down.

Using scroll arrows

To Scroll	Do This
Up or down by one line	Click the up or down scroll arrow.
Up or down one screen	Click above or below the scroll box.
To a specific page	Drag the scroll box.
Left or right	Click the left or right scroll arrow.
Left, beyond the margin, in Normal view	Press Shift, and click the left scroll arrow.

Using Select Browse Object

Select Browse Object

Word includes a browse feature, called *Select Browse Object*, that gives you an alternative way to find items in your document. You may want to browse your document to see each table, read all the comments, or see a certain heading level to check for style consistency. Or you may want to browse by page and move quickly to the preceding or next page.

Next Page

The Select Browse Object button appears at the bottom of the vertical scroll bar. Its default is Browse By Page. On the vertical scroll bar, click the Next Page and Previous Page buttons to browse page by page.

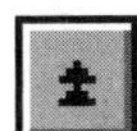

Previous Page

To select a different browse object, click the Select Browse Object button, and click one of the icons on the menu to select it as the current browse object. Objects include tables, headings, find and replace, comments, footnotes, the Go To feature, and others.

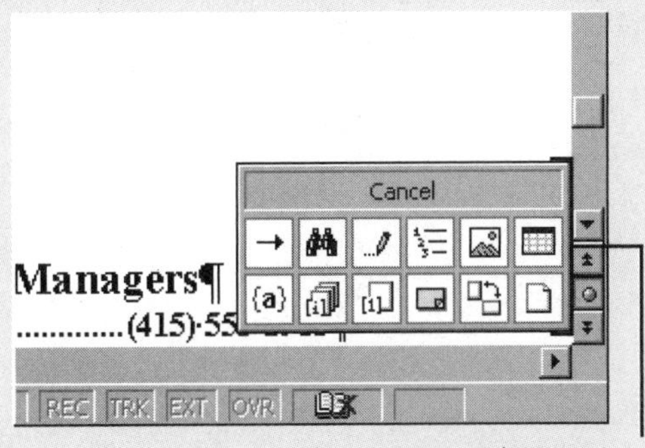

Select Browse Object menu

When you select a new browse object, the Previous and Next buttons find the previous or next instance of that object. For example, if the object is

continued

continued

a table, the buttons look for the previous table or next table in the document. If you want these buttons to resume their default behavior of Next Page and Previous Page, select the Browse By Page icon from the menu when you're finished browsing by other objects.

Using the Go To Feature

Use the Go To feature to quickly move to a certain page. To use Go To, on the Edit menu, click Go To. Enter the page number you want to go to, and then click Go To. The specified page is displayed on your screen. You can also browse for specific objects by selecting an item in the Go To What list and then using the Next and Previous buttons on the Go To tab. A quick way to display the Go To tab is to double-click the page area on the left side of the status bar.

Using Shortcuts with Frequently Used Text

The Word AutoText feature allows you to use shortcuts to insert frequently used names, phrases, words, and other characters in your documents. The AutoText command on the Insert menu expands to list a range of default entries, such as common salutations, attention lines, and headers or footers, that you can insert into your document just by selecting them from the submenu.

You can also add to this list of AutoText entries. When you add an entry, you assign it to a menu and can give it a short name. Thereafter, when you type the short name in a document and then press F3, the AutoText is inserted. In addition to words, you can store formatting, numbers, symbols, and graphics.

If you are not working through this lesson sequentially, before proceeding to the next step, open the 06C file in the Lesson06 folder, and save it as Book Fair 06.

In the following three-part exercise, you create two new AutoText entries and then insert them into the Book Fair 06 document.

Create an AutoText entry

In this exercise, you create an AutoText entry for the address of your client, Pacific Books.

1. In Book Fair 06, press Ctrl+End to move the insertion point to the end of the document.
2. In the last row of the table of addresses, select the Seattle address, *41 S. Marion St.* Don't include the end-of-cell marker in your selection.

You can also press Alt+F3 to open the Create AutoText dialog box.

3. On the Insert menu, point to AutoText, and then click New.

   The Create AutoText dialog box appears, displaying the text you selected.
4. Replace the existing text by typing **ad**, which is short for *address*.
5. Click OK.

Create a second AutoText entry

In this exercise, you create an AutoText entry for the store hours of Pacific Books.

1. In the document, in the table row for the Seattle address, select *10-10 daily*.
2. On the Insert menu, point to AutoText, and then click New.

   The Create AutoText dialog box appears, displaying the text you selected.
3. Replace the existing text by typing **hr**, which is short for *hours*.
4. Click OK.

Insert the AutoText entries

In this exercise, you type new text into the document and insert your new AutoText entries, the Seattle address and the hours for Pacific Books.

1. Press Page Up to go to page 2 of Book Fair 06, and then scroll to the heading *Festival Entry Forms and Book List*.
2. Click in the second sentence, after *Pacific Books*; type a comma, press the Spacebar, and then type **ad**
3. Press F3.

   The bookstore address is inserted.
4. At the end of the address, type a comma, press the Spacebar, and then type **open** and then press the Spacebar.
5. Type **hr** and Press F3.

   The bookstore hours are inserted after the word *open*.

   Your screen should look similar to the following illustration.

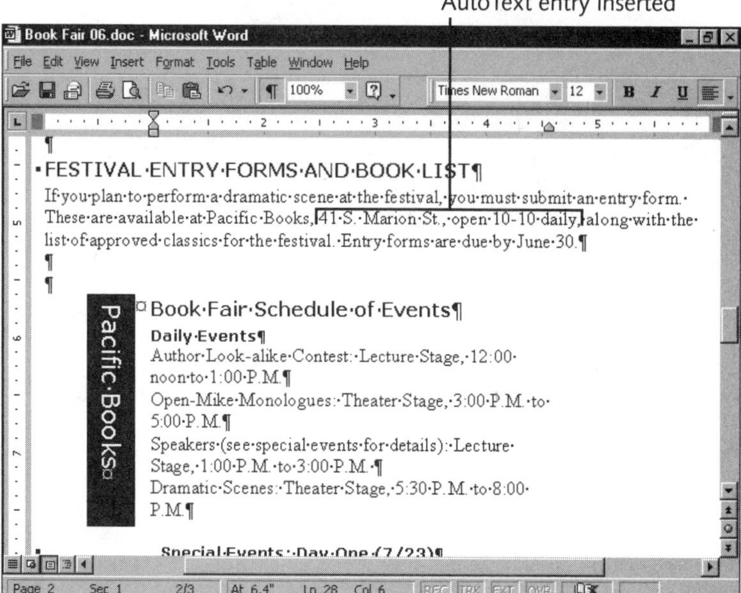

6. Click Save.

tip

Another way to insert the entry is to type the first four characters of the AutoText phrase in your document. A ScreenTip is displayed with the full phrase. If you want to insert the full phrase, press either F3 or Enter. If the ScreenTip doesn't appear, on the Insert menu, point to AutoText, and then click AutoText. The AutoCorrect dialog box appears. On the AutoText tab, select the Show AutoComplete Tip For AutoText And Dates check box.

Adding and Deleting AutoText Entries

To view or edit AutoText entries, on the Insert menu, point to AutoText, and then click AutoText. The AutoCorrect dialog box appears with the AutoText tab selected. You can see and edit all of your AutoText entries from this dialog box.

Your screen should look similar to the following illustration.

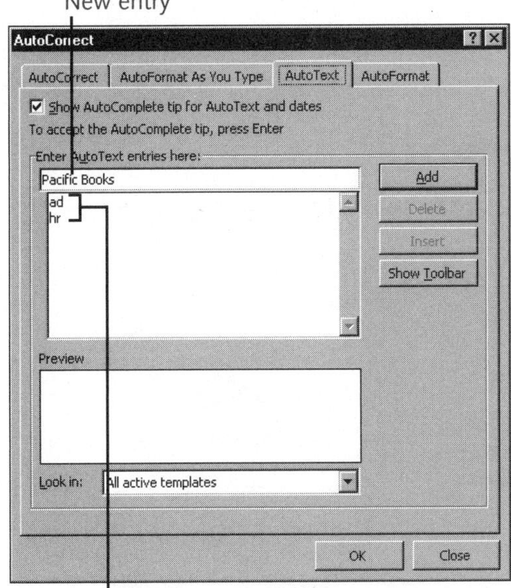

The full text of a selected entry appears in the Preview window. To add an entry, type new text in the text box, and then click Add. When you click Show Toolbar, the dialog box closes, and the AutoText toolbar is displayed in your document window. On the toolbar, you can click All Entries to see categories of your AutoText entries, and click any entry to insert it into your document. The same list is displayed when you point to AutoText on the Insert menu.

Automating Text Formatting

You can use the *AutoFormat* command to apply different types of text formatting all at once. For example, if a document has been styled with straight quotation marks (" ") rather than curved (“ ”), you can select an AutoFormat option that will convert all of the quotation marks to curved (“smart” quotes). Or AutoFormat can correct extra lines or indentation in numbered and bulleted lists. You can also review each AutoFormat change and choose to accept or reject it.

If you want the formatting to be applied as you work, you can use the AutoFormat As You Type option. If you select this option, Word converts a character right after you type it—you don't have to use the AutoFormat command. For example, you can select options that convert an Internet address to a hyperlink after you finish typing it or automatically turn characters to superscript (for example, the *st* in *1st*).

If you are not working through this lesson sequentially, before proceeding to the next step, open the 06D file in the Lesson06 folder, and save it as Book Fair 06.

In the following exercises, you view the available AutoFormat options and select some formatting to be applied automatically as you type.

View AutoFormat options

In this exercise, you view the formatting options that will be applied to your document.

1. On the Format menu, click AutoFormat.

   The AutoFormat dialog box appears.
2. In the AutoFormat dialog box, click Options.

   The AutoCorrect dialog box appears with the AutoFormat tab selected.

   The types of formatting that will be applied to your document are selected in the Apply area.
3. Because you don't want to apply formatting right now, click Cancel in both the AutoCorrect and AutoFormat dialog boxes.

Select options to be formatted as you type

In this exercise, you use AutoFormat As You Type to apply formatting as you work.

1. On the Tools menu, click AutoCorrect, and then click the AutoFormat As You Type tab.
2. In the Replace As You Type area, be sure the following three options are selected:

   "Straight Quotes" With “Smart Quotes”

   Ordinals (1st) With Superscript

   Symbol Characters (--) With Symbols (—)

   You can leave any other options selected.
3. Click OK.

Apply formatting as you type

In this exercise, you type new text and see formatting applied as you work.

1. In the Book Fair 06 document, click at the end of the last sentence under the heading *FESTIVAL ENTRY FORMS AND BOOK LIST*, and then press Enter twice.

The insertion point is positioned before the second paragraph mark below the text.

2. Type **Note: The festival book list--drawn**

An em dash is a long dash symbol used to set off a phrase in a sentence.

3. Press the Spacebar.

   The two hyphens you typed are automatically replaced by the em dash symbol.

4. Type **up by scholars and store personnel--may omit a classic you have in mind.**

   The hyphens are again replaced by the em dash.

5. Type **Submit your book suggestions by June 1st to the Seattle store's "Book List" box**.

6. Press the Spacebar.

   The *st* you typed for the ordinal number becomes superscript, and the quote marks are curved rather than straight.

   Your screen should look similar to the following illustration.

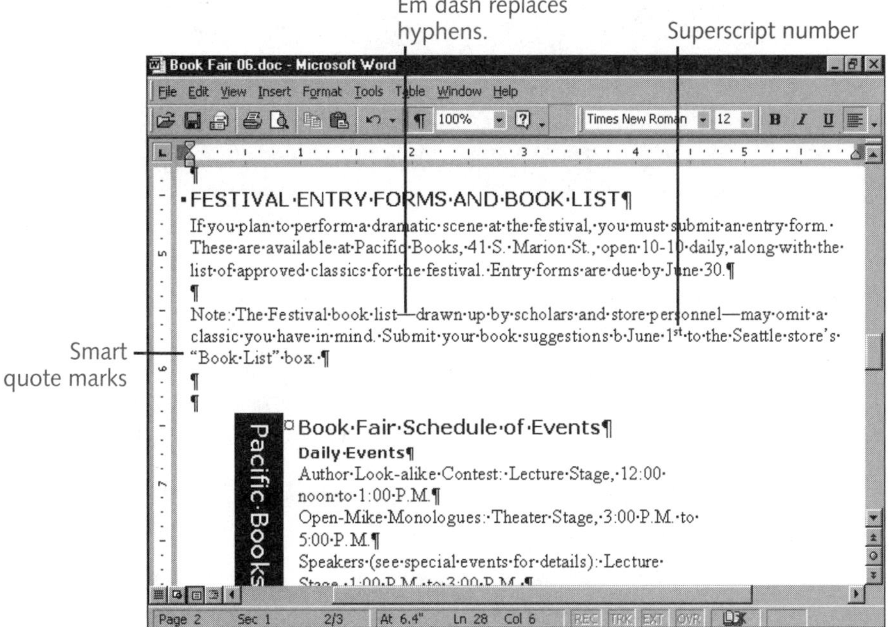

7. Click Save.

Checking Spelling and Grammar

The *Spelling and Grammar Checker* finds misspelled words and words that aren't in the Word dictionary. It identifies possible grammatical errors, makes suggestions for correcting them, and finds writing that is nonstandard. If you want to check spelling only, on the Tools menu, click Options. On the Spelling & Grammar tab, in the Grammar area, clear the Check Grammar With Spelling check box.

On the Spelling & Grammar tab, you can specify spelling and grammar checking as you type. Then, if you type a word that isn't recognized in the custom dictionary, it will be underlined with a wavy red line. A grammatical error is underlined with a wavy green line. To specify spelling and grammar checking as you type, on the Spelling & Grammar tab, select the Check Spelling As You Type and Check Grammar As You Type check boxes. To disable these features, clear the check boxes for the two options.

tip

If you want to hide spelling and grammar underlines only temporarily, leave these options selected, but also select the options Hide Spelling Errors In This Document and Hide Grammatical Errors In This Document. On the Spelling & Grammar tab, you can also select types of text you want the Spelling and Grammar Checker to ignore, including uppercase words, words with numbers, and Internet and file addresses.

To select options specifically for the grammar check, on the Spelling & Grammar tab, click Settings, and select your grammar setting preferences in the Grammar Settings dialog box. A spelling and grammar check begins where the insertion point is placed in the document. The document is checked from that point to the end, and then you are asked if you want to search from the top of the document to the insertion point.

Responding to the Spelling and Grammar Checker

When you start a spelling and grammar check, the Spelling And Grammar dialog box appears and gives you a range of options for responding to questionable or wrong spellings and grammar. Misspellings are selected in red; grammatical errors are selected in green. To accept a suggestion, in the Suggestions list, select the word or phrase you want, and click Change. If the change you want isn't suggested, type the change in the Not In Dictionary text area. Change All changes every instance of a spelling or phrase. To add a word to the custom dictionary, click Add, and the word will be left as currently spelled and added to the dictionary.

To ignore Spelling and Grammar Checker suggestions, click Ignore. Once you've chosen to ignore a word or phrase, the Spelling and Grammar Checker will ignore that instance of the word or phrase in the document. Ignore All skips all instances of the word or phrase in a document.

If you are not working through this lesson sequentially, before proceeding to the next step, open the 06E file in the Lesson06 folder, and save it as Book Fair 06.

To add a frequently misspelled word to your AutoCorrect entries, in the Spelling And Grammar dialog box, click AutoCorrect. This corrects the current misspelling and adds the word to AutoCorrect. In the future, the misspelling will be corrected right after you type it.

Select options on the Spelling & Grammar tab

In this exercise, you display the Spelling & Grammar tab and select options before starting the spelling and grammar check.

1. On the Tools menu, click Options.

   The Options dialog box appears.
2. Click the Spelling & Grammar tab.
3. In the Spelling area, be sure these options are selected:

   Always Suggest Corrections

   Ignore Words In UPPERCASE
4. In the Custom Dictionary list, be sure Custom.dic is displayed.
5. In the Grammar area, be sure these options are selected:

   Check Grammar With Spelling

   Writing Style: Standard
6. Click Settings, and be sure these grammatical options are selected:

   Hyphenated And Compound Words

   Subject-Verb Agreement
7. In the Grammar Settings dialog box, click OK, and in the Options dialog box, click OK.

Start a spelling and grammar check

In this two-part exercise, you begin the proofing check at the beginning of the document.

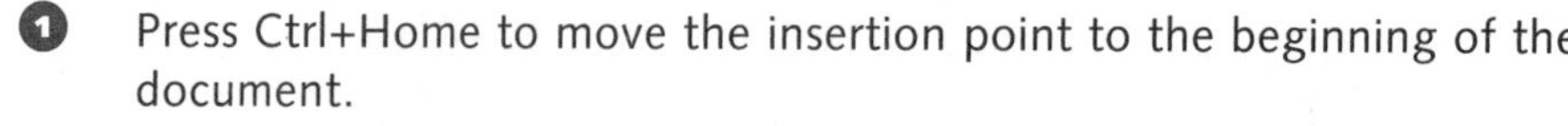

1. Press Ctrl+Home to move the insertion point to the beginning of the document.

Spelling And Grammar

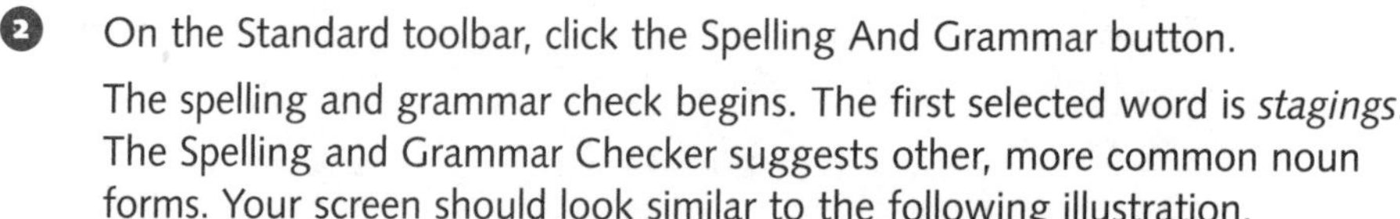

2. On the Standard toolbar, click the Spelling And Grammar button.

   The spelling and grammar check begins. The first selected word is *stagings*. The Spelling and Grammar Checker suggests other, more common noun forms. Your screen should look similar to the following illustration.

You can also press F7 to initiate the spelling and grammar check.

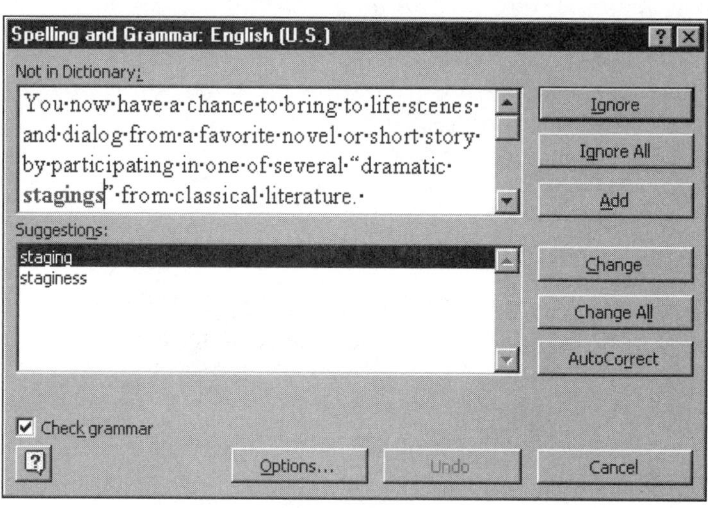

Respond to suggestions

In this exercise, you decide to ignore the suggested change to *stagings* and continue the proofing check.

1. Click Ignore to leave *stagings* as it is, and continue checking.

   A grammatical error, *you likes*, is selected and the correct verb form is suggested.
2. Click Change.

   The correct word, *like*, is inserted.
3. The word *wilingness* is selected, and alternatives are suggested.
4. Click AutoCorrect.

   The spelling is corrected in your document, and the misspelled word is added to your AutoCorrect entries.
5. For the remaining errors identified by the spelling check, do the following.

The problem	The solution
The Word dictionary spells *sagelike* differently.	You could click Add to put this spelling in the dictionary, but you decide to use a more common word. Select *sagelike* in the Not In Dictionary window, type **wise**, and then click Change.
The word *or* is repeated.	Click Delete.
An extra space occurs between *author* and *trivia*.	Click Change to apply the correction.
Some proper names aren't in the dictionary.	Click Add for all of these. Once in the dictionary, they won't appear in the spelling check again.
Hard-cover has a hyphen.	To accept the suggestion *hardcover*, click Change.

tip

If you want to run a completely fresh proofing check on your document, on the Tools menu, click Options, and then click the Spelling & Grammar tab. In the Grammar area, click Recheck Document. If a message box appears, telling you that the operation will reset the Spelling and Grammar Checker, click Yes. Now any questionable words you specified to be ignored earlier will again be identified.

6. When the spelling and grammar check is complete, click OK.

Replacing Words Using the Thesaurus

Word's *Thesaurus* helps you add precision and variety to your writing. It offers alternatives for words you've chosen in your draft documents, but with which you might not be quite satisfied. You can also look up words that stem from the synonyms the Thesaurus has suggested. By expanding your search, you might get even closer to the exact meaning you are looking for.

Look up a better word

In this exercise, you use the Thesaurus to find a more fitting word than *colorful* to describe Pacific Books.

If you are not working through this lesson sequentially, before proceeding to the next step, open the 06F file in the Lesson06 folder, and save it as Book Fair 06.

1. Press Ctrl+F to open the Find And Replace dialog box.
2. In the Find What box, type **colorful**

   If necessary, click More, and then in the Find area, click No Formatting. This removes any formatting options from your search specifications.
3. Click Find Next.

   The only instance of the word is in the phrase *this colorful bookstore*. If you get the message that your document was searched but the word was not found, click More, and be sure that All is selected under Search.
4. Click Cancel to end the search.
5. With the word *colorful* still selected, on the Tools menu, point to Language, and then click Thesaurus.

   The Thesaurus dialog box appears.

   Your screen should look similar to the following illustration.

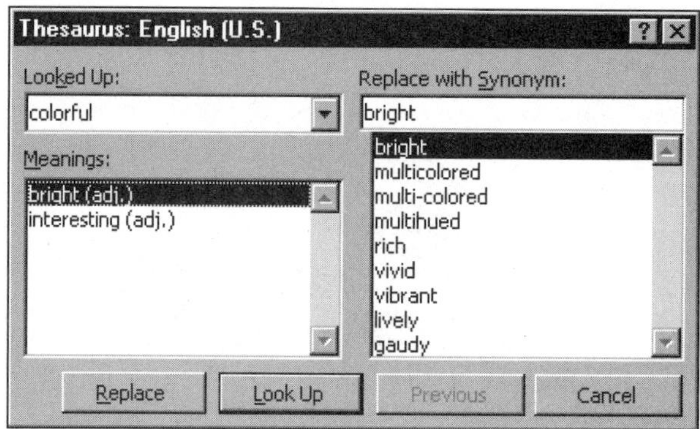

6. In the Replace With Synonym list, select *vivid*, and then click Look Up.

   A new list of synonyms for *vivid* appears. These are closer to what you want to say, but you don't see one that's exactly right.
7. In the Replace With Synonym box, type **resourceful** and then click Look Up.
8. In the new list of synonyms, select *inventive*, and then click Replace.

   Inventive replaces *colorful* in the document.

Making Tasks Easier with Macros

A *macro* is a small program that performs routine tasks. You click one command to run the macro, and it carries out several commands for you. For example, you can create a macro that saves and prints your document or finds and replaces bold or italic type. Using macros, you can execute everyday commands quickly and eliminate repetitive actions.

Macros are written in the programming language Microsoft Visual Basic for Applications (VBA). But you don't have to know this language to record a macro; the Word *macro recorder* automates the process for you. Using the macro recorder, you simply record the tasks you want in the macro, and the recorder translates the steps into VBA. You simply turn on the recorder, specify a name for the macro and whether you want a toolbar button or keyboard command to run it, and then perform the tasks you want the macro to carry out.

Another way to open the Macros dialog box is to press Alt+F8.

If you don't create a toolbar button or key combination to run the macro, you can run it from the Macros dialog box. To open this dialog box, on the Tools menu, point to Macro, and then click Macros. In the Macro Name list in the Macros dialog box, select the macro, and then click Run. The Macros dialog box also contains other options for your macros, such as editing and deleting.

More complex macros require some editing in the *Visual Basic Editor*, which you open from the Macros dialog box. You'll view this feature in an exercise later in the lesson.

Recording a macro

If you are not working through this lesson sequentially, before proceeding to the next step, open the 06G file in the Lesson06 folder, and save it as Book Fair 06.

When the macro recorder is on, your actions are turned into Visual Basic code as you step through tasks. You can record almost any Word action, but you cannot record text selections using your mouse—you must select text using the keyboard. You can still use the mouse to choose commands and click toolbar buttons, however.

In the following exercises, you record a macro for tasks that are routinely performed after a document is created. These are checking spelling and grammar, saving, and then printing the document.

> **tip**
>
> If your computer is not connected to a printer, you can still record the first two parts of the following macro: running a spelling and grammar check, and saving the document.

Start the macro recorder

You can also double-click the REC button on the status bar to display the Record Macro dialog box. Double-click the REC button again if you want to stop recording.

For a demonstration of how to record a macro, in the Multimedia folder on the Microsoft Word 2000 Step by Step CD-ROM, double-click StartMacro.

In the following exercises, with Book Fair 06 open, you record a macro that will check grammar and spelling, save the document, and then print it.

1. On the Tools menu, point to Macro, and then click Record New Macro.

   The Record Macro dialog box appears.

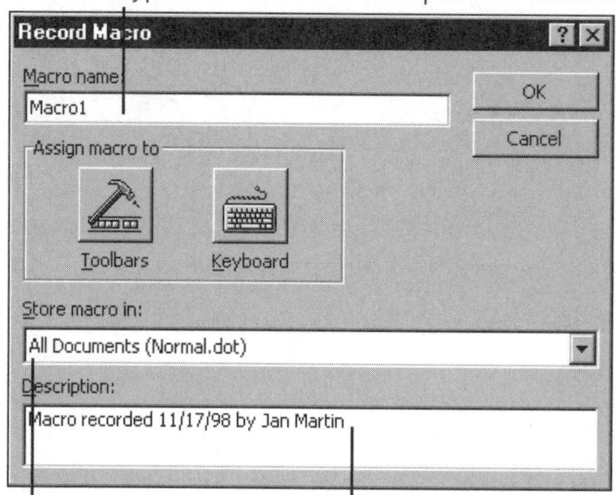
Type a new name here to replace the default name.
Record Macro
Macro name:
Macro1
OK
Cancel
Assign macro to
Toolbars
Keyboard
Store macro in:
All Documents (Normal.dot)
Description:
Macro recorded 11/17/98 by Jan Martin
By default, the macro is stored in the Normal.dot template so it can be used with all Word documents.
You can type additional information here.

2. In the Macro Name box, type **SpellSavePrint** (use a descriptive name so that later you will know what the macro does).
3. In the Assign Macro To area, click Toolbars.

   The Customize dialog box appears.
4. Click the Commands tab.

   Your screen should look similar to the following illustration.

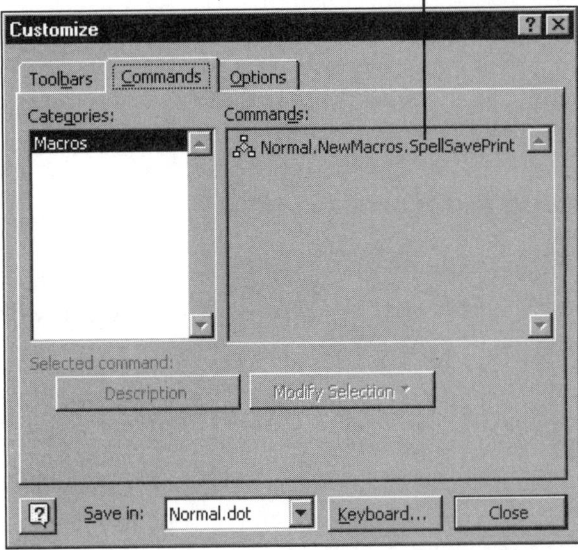

5. In the Commands list, select Normal.NewMacros.SpellSavePrint—the name of the macro you are about to record—and then drag it to the Standard toolbar.

   The macro appears as a long button on the toolbar.

> **tip**
>
> If you want to have a macro button icon on the toolbar, but not the macro's whole name, right-click the new button, and select Default Style from the menu. This leaves the macro icon but deletes the macro name from the button.

6. In the Customize dialog box, click Close.

   The mouse pointer now has a cassette tape image attached, and the Stop Recording toolbar appears. You're now ready to start recording.

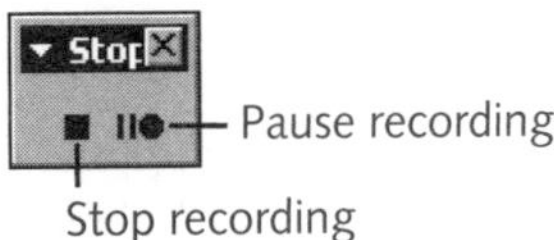

Record the spelling and grammar check

Spelling And Grammar

1. On the Standard toolbar, click the Spelling And Grammar button.
2. When the spelling and grammar check is complete, click OK.

   The spelling and grammar check is recorded as the first part of the macro, and the recorder remains running.

Record saving a document

Save

- On the Standard toolbar, click Save.

  The *save document* part of your macro is now recorded. The macro recorder is still running.

Record printing from the Print button

Print

1. Be sure your printer is on. On the Standard toolbar, click the Print button.

   While your document is printing, the cassette tape pointer is displayed and the Recording toolbar disappears. The toolbar reappears after the document has printed.

Stop Recording

2. On the Recording toolbar, click the Stop Recording button.

   The recording of the macro is complete.

tip

While recording a macro, you can click the Pause Recording button at any time to temporarily stop recording. You can resume recording where you left off by clicking the Pause Recording button again. When you pause recording, the cassette tape mouse pointer disappears. It reappears when you resume recording.

Run the macro

In this exercise, you run the macro with Book Fair 06.

1. Be sure your printer is turned on.
2. On the Standard toolbar, click the SpellSavePrint macro button you created.

   The Spelling And Grammar Checker runs, the document is saved, and then it is printed.

Editing a macro

Using the *Visual Basic Editor*, you can display the code used to run the macro, and then you can modify it. This kind of editing requires knowledge of the Visual Basic for Applications language. In the Editor, the Standard toolbar changes to include many buttons related to macro editing.

View the Editor

In this exercise, you view the Visual Basic Editor to gain familiarity with it and then switch back to the document window.

1. On the Tools menu, point to Macro, and then click Macros.

   The Macros dialog box appears.

2. In the Macro Name list, select the macro SpellSavePrint, and then click Edit.

   The Visual Basic Editor window opens.

   Your screen should look similar to the following illustration.

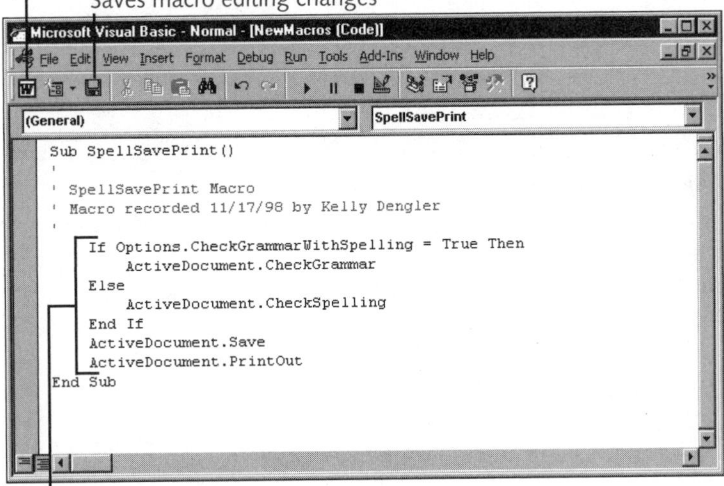

This is the programming code for your macro.

3. To close the Visual Basic Editor, on the Visual Basic Editor File menu, click Close And Return To Microsoft Word.

Delete a macro

In this exercise, you delete the macro created in the previous exercises.

1. On the Tools menu, point to Macro, and then click Macros.

   The Macros dialog box appears.
2. In the Macro Name list, select the macro SpellSavePrint, and then click Delete.
3. Click Yes when you are prompted.
4. Click Close to close the Macros dialog box.

Delete the macro toolbar button

In this exercise, you delete the macro button you created in a previous exercise.

- With the Alt key depressed, drag the SpellSavePrint macro button off the toolbar.

  The button is deleted from the toolbar.

One Step Further Changing Capitalization with the Change Case Command

If you are not working through this lesson sequentially, before proceeding to the next step, open the 06G file in the Lesson06 folder, and save it as Book Fair 06.

When you are nearly finished with a document, you might notice inconsistency in capitalization style. For example, you might want headings to be in title case, which capitalizes only the initial letter of each word in the heading, but you find that some headings are currently in all capitals. The *Change Case* command can be used to make the headings consistent without requiring retyping. When you change a heading from all caps to title case, you may have to change an initial capital to lowercase for some types of words, such as articles, prepositions, and conjunctions.

Change a heading to title case

In this exercise, you change the all-caps heading in Book Fair 06 to title case. Then you edit the heading to lowercase the conjunction *and*.

Next Page

1. Click the Next Page button to display page 2 of Book Fair 06.

2. Scroll down and select the heading *FESTIVAL ENTRY FORMS AND BOOK LIST*.
3. On the Format menu, click Change Case.

   The Change Case dialog box appears.

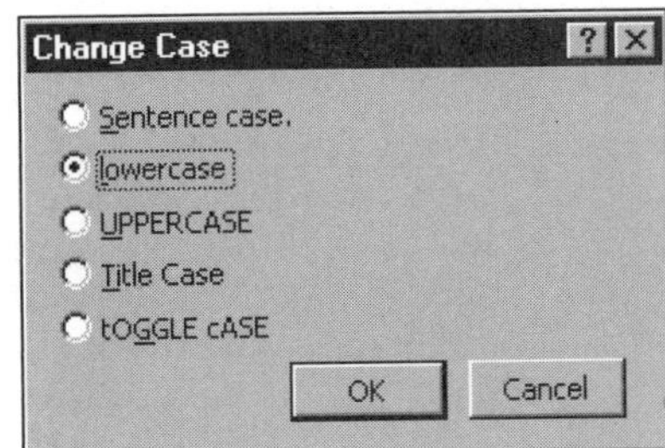

4. Click the Title Case option, and click OK.

   The heading is changed to title case capitalization.
5. In the heading, select the *A* in *And*, and type **a**

tip

If you want to change the capitalization in several headings, use the Change Case dialog box to change the first heading, and then select the second heading in the document, and press F4. This key repeats any command that immediately preceded it. You can quickly change numerous headings in this way.

Finish the lesson

Save

1. On the Standard toolbar, click the Save button.

   Changes made to Book Fair 06 are saved.
2. On the File menu, click Close.
3. On the File menu, click Exit.

Lesson 6 Quick Reference

To	Do this
Find and replace text	On the Edit menu, click Replace. In the Find What box, type the text you're searching for, and then in the Replace With box, type the text to replace it with. Click Find Next to find the first instance of the word. Click Replace to change the selected text, or click Find Next if you don't want to change the selected word. Click Replace All to change all instances of the word at once.
Find and replace formatting	On the Edit menu, click Replace. Click More, and then in the Replace area, click the Format and Special buttons to select types of formatting and special characters to find and replace.
Create AutoText entries	Select the text you want for the entry. On the Insert menu, point to AutoText and click New. Type a name to assign to the entry. Click OK.
Insert the AutoText entries	Type the assigned name for the entry, and then press F3.
Add and delete AutoText entries	To add an entry, select the text in your document. On the Insert menu, point to AutoText, and then click AutoText. In the AutoCorrect dialog box, click Add. Or in the Enter AutoText Entries Here box, type an entry, and click Add. To delete an entry, select an entry on the AutoText tab and then click Delete.

Lesson 6 Quick Reference

To	Do this	Button
Use AutoFormat	On the Format menu, click AutoFormat; click Options, and then select formatting options on the AutoFormat tab.	
Use AutoFormat As You Type	On the Tools menu, click AutoCorrect. In the AutoCorrect dialog box, click the AutoFormat As You Type tab and select options.	
Check spelling and grammar	On the Standard toolbar, click the Spelling And Grammar button.	ABC
Use the Thesaurus to replace a word	On the Tools menu, point to Language, and then click Thesaurus. Replace a word with synonyms, or use the Look Up feature.	
Create a macro	On the Tools menu, point to Macro, and then click Record New Macro. Use the Macro Recording toolbar to record the macro.	
Run a macro	Click the toolbar button or press the key combination you created for the macro. Or on the Tools menu, point to Macro, and then click Macros. Select the macro in the dialog box, and click Run.	
Use the Change Case command to change capitalization	Select the text you want to change. On the Format menu, click Change Case. In the Change Case dialog box, select the desired option.	

Formatting Pages and Working with Styles and Themes

In this lesson you will learn how to:

- ✔ *Change page margins.*
- ✔ *Insert and remove page numbers.*
- ✔ *Apply styles and themes.*
- ✔ *Manage styles using the Style Organizer.*
- ✔ *Create headers and footers.*
- ✔ *Insert footnotes.*

ESTIMATED TIME **40 min.**

In earlier lessons, you learned about applying formatting to individual words and paragraph selections. For more comprehensive formatting of your document you can use styles and themes.

A *style* is a collection of format settings that can be applied to text. For example, you might want all of the headings in a document to be in a 16-point font with bold and italic formatting. Applying a style with those attributes saves time and helps reduce formatting errors. *Themes* are styles applied to an entire document that not only format text, but change the appearance of the page, applying background patterns, for example. Microsoft Word 2000 provides more than 30 attractive themes to choose from.

In this lesson, you work with the overall format of the Pacific Books book fair announcement by changing margins, working with page numbers, and applying a theme. You also create, modify, and apply styles for both characters and paragraphs. Finally, you organize styles and insert headers, footers and footnotes.

important

The default toolbar setting in Microsoft Word 2000 displays both the Standard and Formatting toolbars in one row at the top of the document window, just below the menu bar. This gives you maximum workspace. While working through the exercises in this book, toolbar buttons you need may not initially be visible. If a toolbar button is not visible, click one of the two More Buttons drop-down arrows on the toolbar to locate the button you need. When you select a new toolbar button, it is automatically added to the visible portion of the toolbar, replacing one that is not used as often.

More Buttons

If you have not yet installed the this book's practice files, refer to "Using the Microsoft Word 2000 Step by Step CD-ROM," earlier in this book.

Start Word and open a practice file

In this exercise, you start Word, open a practice file, and then save it with a new name.

1. On the Windows taskbar, click the Start button.
   The Start menu appears.
2. On the Start menu, point to Programs, and then click Microsoft Word.
   Microsoft Word 2000 opens.
3. On the Standard toolbar, click the Open button.
   The Open dialog box appears.

Open

4. Click the Look In drop-down arrow, and then select your hard disk.
5. In the list of folders, double-click the Word 2000 SBS Practice folder, and then double-click the Lesson07 folder.
6. In the file list, double-click the 07A file to open it.
   The document opens in the document window.
7. On the File menu, click Save As.
   The Save As dialog box appears.
8. Be sure the Lesson07 folder appears in the Save In box.
9. In the File Name box, select the text, and then type **Book Fair 07**
10. Click Save.

Display formatting marks

To make it easier to edit your document, you can display formatting marks such as paragraph marks and space marks on your screen.

Show/Hide ¶

- If formatting marks are not currently displayed, on the Standard toolbar, click the Show/Hide ¶ button.

Working with Page Setup

Every document page in Word has *margins*—the space between the text and the edge of the paper. Margins help ensure that text isn't printed off the page, and they help to display your document in an orderly and pleasing way. Word default margins can easily be adjusted to accommodate letterhead or decorative stationery, which would require a wider top margin.

If you are not working through this lesson sequentially, before proceeding to the next step, open the 07A file in the Lesson07 folder, and save it as Book Fair 07.

You can change the left, right, top, or bottom margins of an entire document, a single page, or a paragraph. The default margins in Word are 1 inch at the top and bottom of a page, and 1.25 inches on the left and right. You can also reset the default margins to be applied to each new document you create.

Change margins

In this exercise, you change the margin settings on the book fair announcement for your client Pacific Books.

1. On the File menu, click Page Setup.

   The Page Setup dialog box appears.
2. Click the Margins tab.
3. In the Top box, select the text, type **.75** and then press Tab.
4. In the Bottom box, type **.75** and then press Tab.
5. In the Left box, type **1** and then press Tab.
6. In the Right box, select the text, and then type **1**

   In the Preview area, you can see how your text will appear on a page.

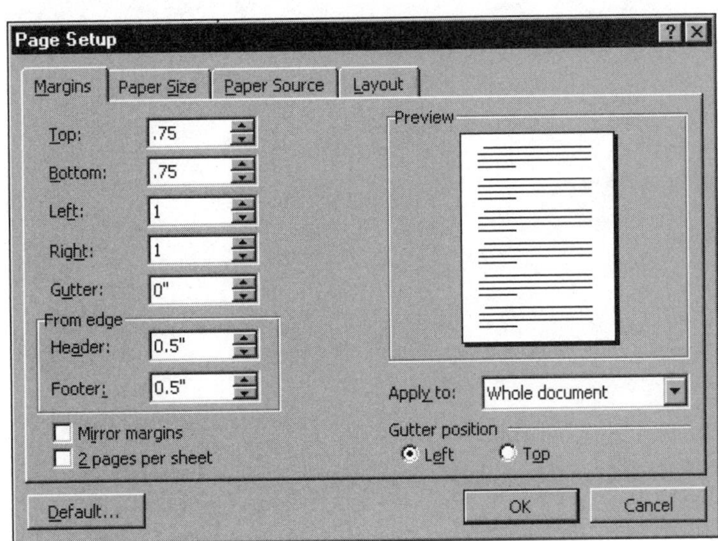

7. Click OK.

   The margins are adjusted.

Additional Options for Page Settings

Set default margins

You can change the margins in a single document, and you can define new default margins for all new documents you create in Word. The preceding exercise illustrated how to change margins for the current document. To change the default margins, follow these steps:

1. On the File menu, click Page Setup, and then change the margin settings.
2. Click Default.
3. Click Yes when you are prompted.

Changing Page Orientation

In Word, you can select one of two printing orientations—*portrait* or *landscape*. In portrait orientation, documents are printed lengthwise (taller than they are wide), and in landscape orientation, documents are printed widthwise (wider than they are tall).

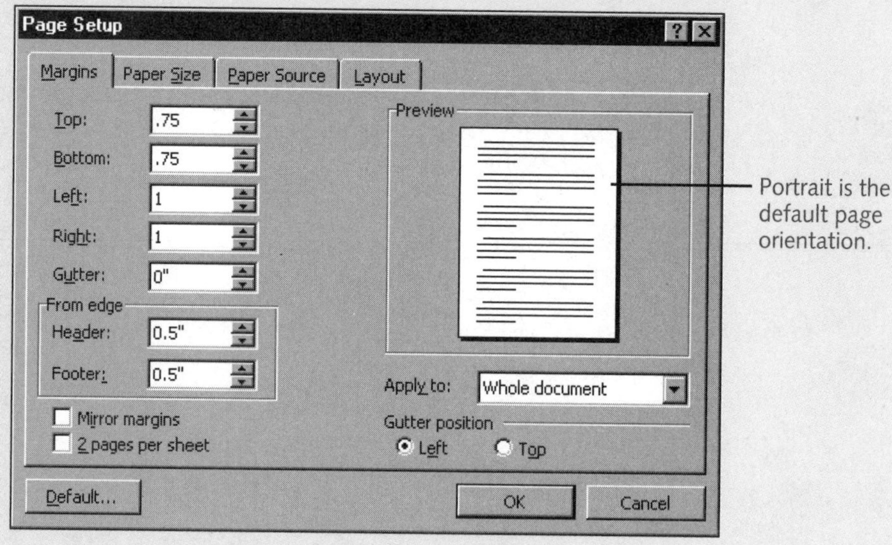

To change from portrait to landscape orientation, follow these steps:

1. On the File menu, click Page Setup.
2. In the Page Setup dialog box, click the Paper Size tab. In the Orientation area, click Landscape.

   Your screen should look similar to the following illustration.

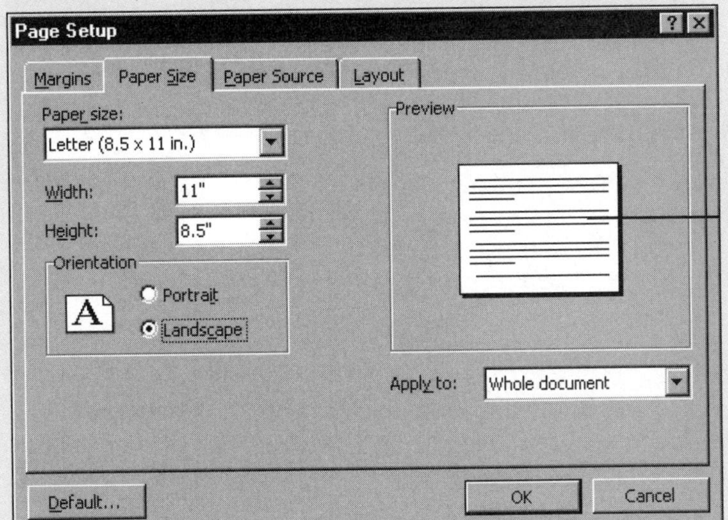

Change paper size

You can print your documents on any size paper your printer will accommodate. To change the paper size, follow these steps:

1. On the File menu, click Page Setup. In the Page Setup dialog box, click the Paper Size tab.
2. In the Paper Size list, select a paper size. To specify a customized paper size, in the Paper Size list, select Custom Size, and in the Width and Height boxes, select the text and type the paper dimensions. Click OK.

Add paragraph line numbering

You can number each paragraph of a document, or even each line, as in legal documents. To apply line numbers, follow these steps:

1. On the File menu, click Page Setup.
2. In the Page Setup dialog box, click the Layout tab, and then click Line Numbers.
3. Select the Add Line Numbering check box, and click OK.
4. Click OK to close the Page Setup dialog box.

Inserting Page Numbers

If you are not working through this lesson sequentially, before proceeding to the next step, open the 07B file in the Lesson07 folder, and save it as Book Fair 07.

You can set up your Word document for automatic page numbering in several page-numbering formats. If you insert or delete document pages, Word renumbers the entire document. Page numbers are printed either at the top of a page (in the *header*) or at the bottom of the page (in the *footer*). Headers and footers are blocks of text at the top and bottom of the page that contain information such as page number, company name, document, author, date, and so on. You'll learn more about headers and footers later in this lesson.

Insert page numbers

In this exercise, you add page numbers to the bottom of each page of your document.

1. On the Insert menu, click Page Numbers.

   The Page Numbers dialog box appears.
2. In the Position box, be sure that Bottom Of Page (Footer) is displayed.
3. In the Alignment area, click the drop-down arrow, and select Left.

   Your screen should look similar to the following illustration.

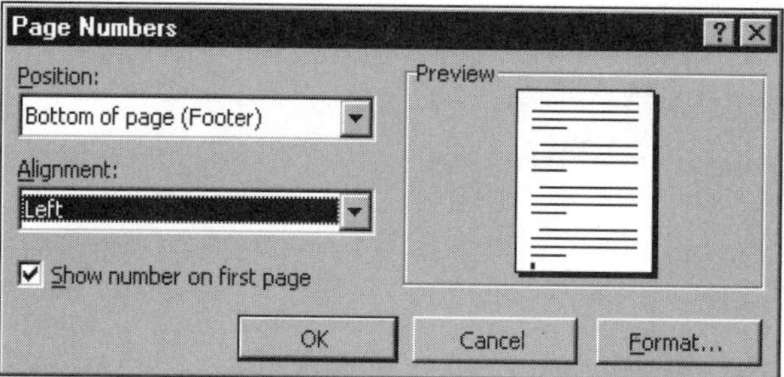

4. Click OK.

   Page numbers are inserted into the document.
5. Scroll down to the end of page 1 and view the page number.

important

To view page numbers, headers, and footers, you must be in Print Layout view. To change to Print Layout view, on the View menu, click Print Layout.

Remove page numbers

In this exercise, you remove the page numbers from your document.

1. On the View menu, click Header And Footer.

   The Header And Footer toolbar appears.

2. On the Header And Footer toolbar, click the Switch Between Header And Footer button.

   Switch Between Header And Footer

   The Page Footer editing pane opens.

3. In the Page 1 footer editing pane, position the pointer on the page number. When the pointer becomes a four-headed arrow, click the page number.

   The page number and the surrounding frame are selected.

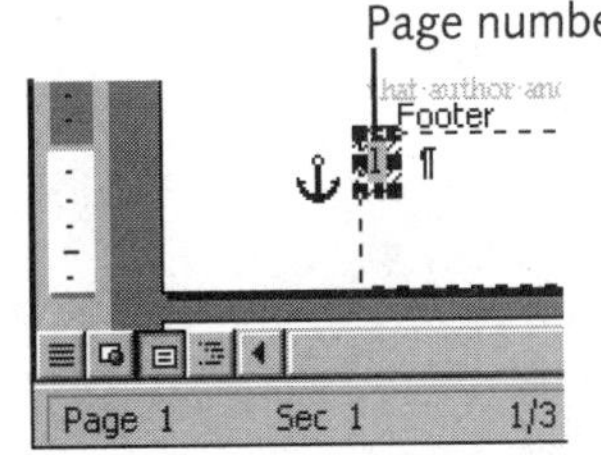

Cut

4. On the Standard toolbar, click the Cut button.

   All the page numbers in your document are deleted.

5. On the Header And Footer toolbar, click the Close button.

Applying Themes to Documents

You can change the entire look of a document by applying a *theme*. Themes coordinate the look of your document by changing the background image, headings, text, and bullets. Themes also format hyperlinks, which makes them useful when creating Web pages. Your final document will have a unified look based on the theme you select. For example, the Blends theme uses a gradual blue-to-white background with matching text design elements. The Blueprint theme applies background that looks like graph paper, and text design elements that match that background. Themes are very useful in designing Web pages, reports, and presentations. Word 2000 provides over 30 different theme choices.

For a demonstration of how to apply a theme to a document, in the Multimedia folder on the Microsoft Word 2000 Step by Step CD-ROM, double-click ApplyTheme.

Apply a theme to a document

In this exercise, you apply a theme to the Book Fair 07 document, preparing to convert it into a newsletter.

If you are not working through this lesson sequentially, before proceeding to the next step, open the 07B file in the Lesson07 folder, and save it as Book Fair 07.

1. On the Format menu, click Theme.

   The Theme dialog box appears.
2. In the Choose A Theme list, scroll down and click Citrus Punch.
3. Click OK.

   The document is completely reformatted with the Citrus Punch theme and is displayed in the Web Layout view.

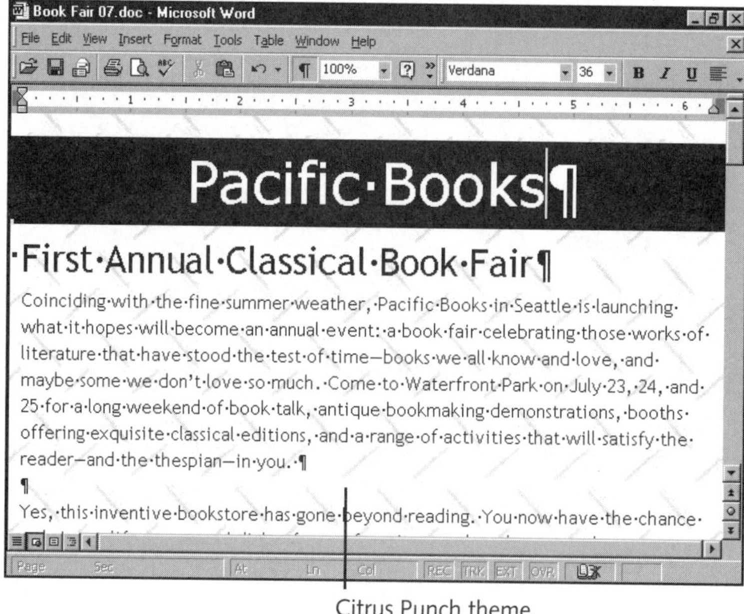

Citrus Punch theme applied to document

Applying Styles to Documents

You can apply a group of formatting attributes to your document all at once using *styles*. *Character styles* format words and lines of text, while *paragraph styles* format entire paragraphs and include indenting, tabs, and line spacing. One style, for example, might specify a 16-point font, bold, underlined, and centered. If you want a portion of your text to display all of these attributes, you can apply a style rather than applying each attribute individually. You can also create a new style based on an existing style if you want to change or eliminate attributes associated with the original style.

All new documents are associated with the Normal (default) style. The Normal style includes the default font style, font size, and alignment. When Word is installed, the default Normal style is 12-point Times New Roman, aligned left. You can choose from many other styles in Word, such as Heading 1, which changes text to 16-point Arial, bold, aligned left. You can also create a new style or modify an existing style by giving it a new name. Once you apply a modified style, all the text in your document that is formatted in that style is updated. This helps make formatting changes in your document a snap.

Apply a character style

If you are not working through this lesson sequentially, before proceeding to the next step, open the 07C file in the Lesson07 folder, and save it as Book Fair07.

In this exercise, you start working with styles by applying a standard Word style to a heading in the Book Fair 07 document.

1. Press Ctrl+End to move the insertion point to the end of the document.
2. Scroll up the page and select the text *Summer Lecture Series.*
3. View the style in the Style box at the far left of the Formatting toolbar.

   This text is formatted in the Normal style.
4. On the Formatting toolbar, click the Style drop-down arrow.
5. In the Style list, select Heading 3.

   The text is formatted in the Heading 3 style.
6. Click anywhere outside of the selected text to cancel the selection.

Create a character style

In this exercise, you create a new style based on the Heading 1 style.

1. On the Format menu, click Style.

   The Style dialog box appears.
2. In the Style dialog box, click New.

   The New Style dialog box appears.
3. In the Name box, type **Pacific Books 1**
4. In the Based On list, click Heading 1.

   Your screen should look similar to the following illustration.

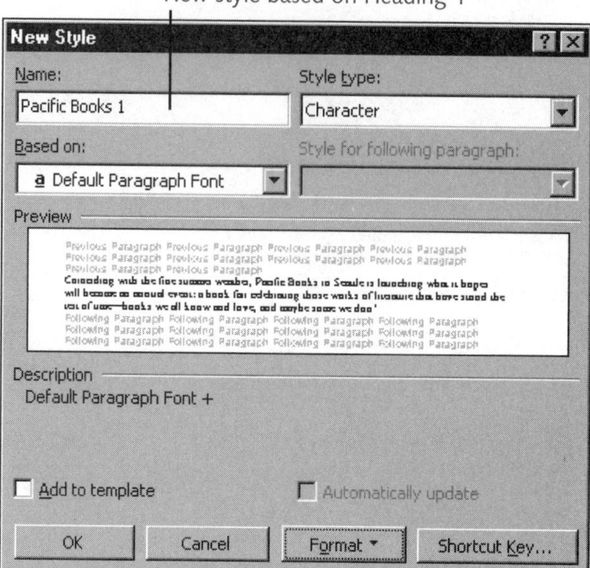

5. Click Format, and then click Font.

   The Font dialog box appears.
6. In the Font Style list, click Bold; in the Size list, click 20; and click OK.
7. In the New Style dialog box, click OK.
8. In the Style dialog box, click Close.

Apply the new style

In this exercise, you apply the style you just created to change a heading in the book fair document.

1. Press Ctrl+Home to move the insertion point to the beginning of the document, and in the first paragraph, select the text *First Annual Classical Book Fair*.
2. On the Formatting toolbar, click the Style drop-down arrow.
3. In the Style list, click **Pacific Books 1**

   The text is formatted in the style Pacific Books 1.
4. Scroll down to the middle of page 1, select the text *Contests*, and then apply the Pacific Books 1 style by following steps 2 and 3 above.

Applying Paragraph Styles to Documents

Paragraph styles are the same as character styles except that they include paragraph formatting such as indents, alignment, and tabs. You can also apply paragraph formatting commands, such as Keep Lines Together, in a paragraph style.

Create a style with paragraph attributes

In this exercise, you create a new style for Pacific Books 2 based on Heading 5.

1. On the Format menu, click Style.

   The Style dialog box appears.
2. Click New.

   The New Style dialog box appears.
3. In the Name box, type **Pacific Books 2**
4. In the Based On list, click Heading 5.
5. Click Format, and then click Paragraph.

   The Paragraph dialog box appears.
6. In the Spacing area, in the Before box, select the text, type **6**, and then press Tab.
7. In the After box, type **6** and click OK.
8. In the New Style dialog box, click OK.

Apply the new paragraph style

In this exercise, you apply the paragraph style you just created to a table heading.

1. Press Ctrl+End to move the insertion point to the end of the document.
2. Scroll up to display the table and select the first row containing the text *Pacific Books Branch Locations*.
3. On the Formatting toolbar, click the Style drop-down arrow.
4. In the Style list, click Pacific Books 2.
5. Click anywhere outside of the selected text to cancel the selection.

   The heading is formatted in the Pacific Books 2 style.

Modifying Styles

You can modify a style that you have created and already applied to text. When you modify a style, the text in your document associated with that style is automatically updated to reflect the changes.

Reformat a paragraph style

In this exercise, you modify the paragraph style you created and applied to the table heading earlier in the lesson.

1. On the Format menu, click Style.
   The Style dialog box appears.
2. In the Styles list, select Pacific Books 2.
3. In the Style dialog box, click Modify.
   The Modify Style dialog box appears.
4. Click Format, and then click Font.
   The Font dialog box appears.
5. In the Font Style list, click Bold, and in the Size list, click 14.
6. Click OK.
   The Font dialog box closes.
7. In the Modify Style dialog box, select the Automatically Update check box.
   Any text with this style will be updated automatically.
8. Click OK, and in the Style dialog box, click Close.
   The text with Pacific Books 2 style is updated.

Using the Style Area

You can change your document window to include an area that displays the style names applied to all the text in your document. This feature is called the *Style Area.* It is especially useful in verifying that your styles are applied correctly —especially if many similar styles are used in your document. Your document must be in the Normal or Outline view to display the Style Area.

Display the Style Area

1. On the View menu, click Normal.
   The document is changed to the Normal view.
2. On the Tools menu, click Options.
   The Options dialog box appears.
3. Click the View tab.
4. In the Outline And Normal Options area, select the number in the Style Area Width box, and type **1**

5. Click OK.

   The Options dialog box is closed, and the Style Area appears on your screen.

The Style Area width should be just wide enough to view the style names.

6. Press Ctrl+Home, and then scroll through the document to view the styles applied in this document.

Hide the Style Area

In this exercise, you use the Options dialog box to hide the Style Area.

1. On the Tools menu, click Options.

   The Options dialog box appears.
2. On the View tab, in the Outline And Normal Options area, select the text in the Style Area Width box, and type **0**
3. Click OK.

   The Options dialog box closes.
4. On the View menu, click Print Layout.

   The document is displayed in the Print Layout view.

Delete a Style in a Document

You can delete styles that you have created but no longer need.

1. On the Format menu, click Style.

   The Style dialog box appears.
2. Click Organizer.

   The Organizer dialog box appears.
3. On the Styles tab, in the In *filename* list on the left side of the dialog box, scroll down and select a style you created and want to delete.
4. Click Delete.
5. Click Yes when you are prompted.
6. Click Close.

Creating Headers and Footers

If you are not working through this lesson sequentially, before proceeding to the next step, open the 07D file in the Lesson07 folder, and save it as Book Fair 07.

Headers and footers contain information that is printed at the top or bottom of the page. Common information in headers and footers includes page numbers, document title, date, author, and company name. You can also copy and paste text from a document into a header or footer. This is useful when you want to display a logo or letterhead at the top of each page, or reference information such as an address in a footer.

The Header And Footer toolbar is used to create headers and footers. You can also use this toolbar to insert header and footer entries using the AutoText feature. To learn more about AutoText, see Lesson 6, "Automating Tasks."

> **tip**
>
> To view headers and footers in your document, be sure you've selected Print Layout view. To switch to Print Layout view, on the View menu, click Print Layout.

Create a header using text from a document

In this exercise, you select the Pacific Books logo and insert it in a header.

1. Be sure you are in Print Layout view.
2. Press Ctrl+Home to move the insertion point to the top of the document.
3. Select the Pacific Books logo in the first line of the document.

Copy

4. On the Standard toolbar, click the Copy button.

   The Pacific Books logo is copied to the Clipboard.
5. On the View menu, click Header And Footer.

   The Header And Footer toolbar appears, and the insertion point is in the Header editing pane.

Show Next

6. On the Header And Footer toolbar, click the Show Next button.

   The header on page 2 is displayed.

Paste

7. On the Standard toolbar, click the Paste button.

   The Pacific Books logo is pasted into the Header editing pane.
8. On the Header And Footer toolbar, click the Close button.

   The Header And Footer toolbar closes.

Managing Headers and Footers

If you are not working through this lesson sequentially, before proceeding to the next step, open the 07l file in the Lesson07 folder, and save it as Book Fair 07.

Often, you don't want to display the header on the first page of your document —especially if the first page is a title page, or, as in this case, when the header consists of information already displayed on the first page. You can set Word to suppress the first page header, causing headers to be printed only on the second and subsequent pages.

When you set up headers and footers, you can customize them with AutoText entries that have been created especially for headers and footers. For example, you can insert an AutoText entry (a shortcut for inserting frequently used text) that inserts the author's name, the page number, and the date.

Once the headers and footers are created, you can view them in Print Layout view and make changes before printing the document.

Suppress the first page header

In this exercise, you suppress the first page header.

Page Setup

1. On the View menu, click Header And Footer.

   The Header And Footer toolbar appears.
2. On the Header And Footer toolbar, click the Page Setup button.

   The Page Setup dialog box appears.
3. In the Page Setup dialog box, click the Layout tab.
4. In the Headers And Footers area, select the Different First Page check box, and click OK.

   The First Page Header editing pane appears. Leave it blank.
5. On the Header And Footer toolbar, click the Close button.

   The first page header is suppressed.

Create a footer using AutoText entries

In this exercise, you insert a footer into your document using an AutoText entry.

Switch Between Header And Footer

Show Next

1. On the View menu, click Header And Footer.

   The Header And Footer toolbar appears, and the insertion point is in the Header editing pane.
2. On the Header And Footer toolbar, click the Switch Between Header And Footer button.

   The First Page Footer editing pane appears. Leave it blank.
3. On the Header And Footer toolbar, click the Show Next button.

   The Footer editing pane for the second page is displayed.

4. Click Insert AutoText, and then select Page X of Y.

   The text *Page 2 of 4* is displayed in the footer.

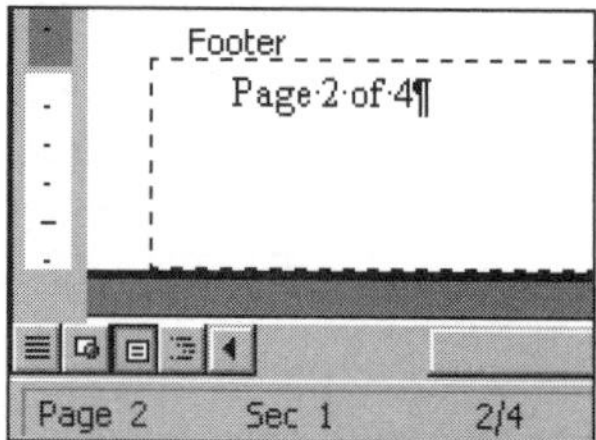

5. On the Header And Footer toolbar, click the Close button.

Preview headers and footers

You can preview all the headers and footers in Print Preview. In this exercise, you scan the entire document to view the layout of the headers and footers.

Print Preview

Multiple Pages

1. On the Standard toolbar, click the Print Preview button.

   The document is displayed in Print Preview.

2. On the Print Preview toolbar, click the Multiple Pages button, move the pointer across the first two boxes in each row to select them, and then click.

   Your screen should look similar to the following illustration. Note that the header margin does not line up with the first page margin.

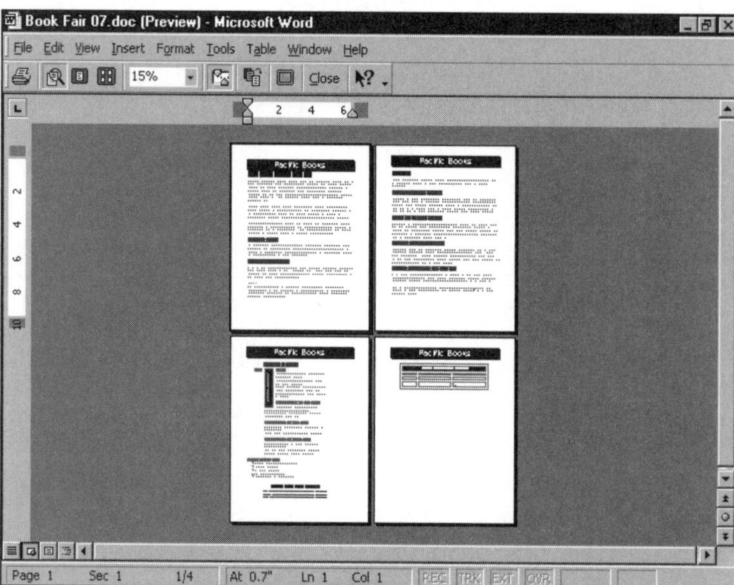

3. On the Print Preview toolbar, click the Close button.

Modify the headers and footers margin area

In this exercise, you adjust the distance between the edge of the page and the top of the header to align with the first page margin.

1. On the File menu, click Page Setup.

   The Page Setup dialog box appears.
2. Click the Margins tab.
3. In the Front Edge area, in the Header box, select the text, and type **.75**
4. Click OK.
5. On the Standard toolbar, click the Print Preview button.

   The Print Preview window opens. Note the change in the header alignment.
6. On the Print Preview toolbar, click the Close button.

Print Preview

Customize the footers

You can add information to customize the headers and footers in your documents. In this exercise, you add a reference to Pacific Books in the footer.

1. On the View menu, click Header And Footer.

   The Header And Footer toolbar appears.
2. On the Header And Footer toolbar, click the Switch Between Header And Footer button.
3. On the Header And Footer toolbar, click the Show Next button.
4. Press the End key to move the insertion point to the end of the line, and press Tab twice.
5. Type **Submitted by Impact Public Relations**
6. Select the text of the footer, and on the Formatting toolbar, click the Bold button.

   The Footer text is now formatted in bold.
7. On the Header And Footer toolbar, click the Close button.

Switch Between Header And Footer

Show Next

Bold

Additional Header and Footer Options

Create alternating headers and footers

You can create headers and footers that alternate on odd and even pages. This allows you to vary the text displayed in headers and footers.

1. On the View menu, click Header And Footer.

   The Header And Footer toolbar appears.

Page Setup

2. Click the Page Setup button.

   The Page Setup dialog box appears.
3. In the Headers And Footers area, select the Different Odd And Even check box, and click OK.

Switch

4. On the Header And Footer toolbar, click the Switch Between Header And Footer button.

   The first odd page footer is displayed.

Show Next

5. On the Header And Footer toolbar, click the Show Next button.

   The even page footer is displayed.
6. Type the information for the footer.
7. On the Header And Footer toolbar, click the Switch Between Header And Footer button, and repeat steps 5 and 6 to work with the even page header. If you want the same information in both the odd and even headers, enter the same information in the Even Page Header editing pane.

Remove headers and footers

You can remove headers and footers by deleting the text. To remove headers and footers, follow these steps.

1. On the View menu, click Header And Footer.

   The Header And Footer toolbar appears.
2. Display the header or footer that you want to remove.
3. Select the text in the header or footer, and press Delete.

   The text is removed.
4. On the Header And Footer toolbar, click the Close button.

One Step Further Inserting Footnotes

If you are not working through this lesson sequentially, before proceeding to the next step, open the 07J file in the Lesson07 folder, and save it as Book Fair 07.

You can also add information to the bottom of the page using *footnotes*. Footnotes are used when you want to reference text in your document with a note appearing at the bottom of the page containing the reference. Insert footnotes while in Normal view, and then switch to Print Layout to view them.

Insert a footnote

1. On the View menu, click Normal.
2. Click after the heading *Summer Lecture Series* near the bottom of page 3.

   Your screen should look similar to the following illustration.

A footnote will be inserted here.

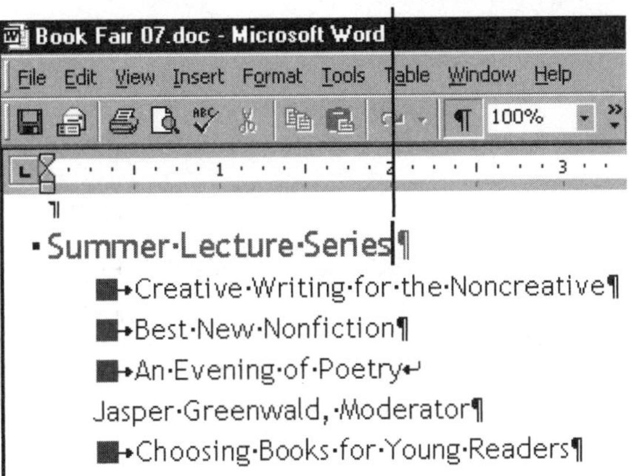

3. On the Insert menu, click Footnote.

   The Footnote And Endnote dialog box appears.
4. Click OK.

   The Footnote editing pane opens.

5. In the Footnote editing pane, type **Schedules for the lecture series are available by calling the Seattle store.**

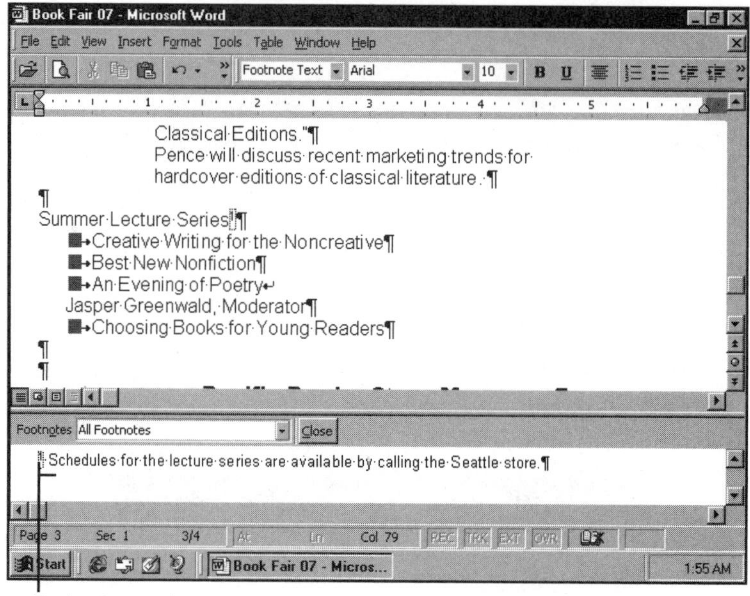

Footnote number 1

6. On the Footnote editing pane, click Close.
7. On the View menu, click Print Layout.

   The footnote is displayed.

Finish the lesson

Save

1. On the Standard toolbar, click Save.

   Changes to Book Fair 07 are saved.
2. On the File menu, click Close.
3. On the File menu, click Exit.

Lesson 7 Quick Reference

To	Do this	Button
Change margins	On the File menu, click Page Setup, and then click the Margins tab. Enter the new margin settings. Click OK.	
Insert page numbers	On the Insert menu, click Page Numbers. In the Page Numbers dialog box, in the Position list, select a position. In the Alignment list, select an alignment, and click OK.	
Remove page numbers from a footer	On the View menu, click Header And Footer. On the Header And Footer toolbar, click the Switch Between Header And Footer button. In the Page Footer editing pane, position the pointer on the page number. When the pointer becomes a four-headed arrow, click the page number. Press Delete. Click Close.	
Apply a theme to a document	On the Format menu, click Theme. In the Theme dialog box, in the Choose A Theme list, select a theme. Click OK.	
Create a character style	On the Format menu, click Style. In the Style dialog box, click New. In the New Style dialog box, in the Name box, type the new style name. In the Based On list, select the style to base the new style on. Click Format, and select an option. Select attributes for the new style, click OK, and close all open dialog boxes.	

Lesson 7 Quick Reference

To	Do this
Create a paragraph style	On the Format menu, click Style. In the Style dialog box, click New. In the New Style dialog box, in the Name box, type the name of the new style. In the Based On list, click the style the new style will be based on. Click Format, and then click Paragraph. In the Paragraph dialog box, select attributes for the new style, click OK, and close all open dialog boxes.
Reformat a paragraph style	On the Format menu, click Style. In the Style dialog box, in the Styles list, select a style, and then click Modify. In the Modify Style dialog box, click Format and select attributes, and then select the Automatically Update check box. Click OK, and in the Style dialog box, click OK.
Apply a style	Select the text to be formatted. On the Formatting toolbar, click the Style drop-down arrow. In the Style list, select a style.
Display the Style Area	On the View menu, click Normal. On the Tools menu, click Options. In the Options dialog box, click the View tab, and in the Outline And Normal Options area, select the text in the Style Area Width box, type **1**, and click OK.
Hide the Style Area	On the Tools menu, click Options. In the Options dialog box, click the View tab, and in the Outline And Normal Options area, select the text in the Style Area Width box, type **0**, and click OK.

Lesson 7 Quick Reference

To	Do this	Button
Create a header using text from the document	Be sure you are in the Print Layout view. Select the text for the header. On the Standard toolbar, click the Copy button. On the View menu, click Header And Footer. The First Page Header editing pane appears. On the Standard toolbar, click the Paste button. On the Header And Footer toolbar, click the Close button.	
Suppress the first page header	On the View menu, click Header And Footer. On the Header And Footer toolbar, click the Page Setup button. In the Page Setup dialog box, click the Layout tab. In the Headers And Footers area, select the Different First Page check box, and click OK. The First Page Header editing pane appears. Leave it blank. On the Header And Footer toolbar, click the Close button.	
Preview headers and footers	On the Standard toolbar, click the Print Preview button. On the Print Preview toolbar, click the Multiple Pages button, and drag to display the entire document. On the Print Preview toolbar, click the Close button.	
Modify the headers and footers margin area	On the File menu, click Page Setup. In the Page Setup dialog box, click the Margins tab. In the From Edge area, in the Header box, select the text, and type the new header width. Click OK.	

Lesson 7 Quick Reference

To	Do this
Insert a footnote	On the View menu, click Normal. Position the insertion point where you want the footnote marker. On the Insert menu, click Footnote. In the Footnote And Endnote dialog box, click OK. In the Footnote editing pane, type the footnote text. Click Close.

Using Templates and Forms

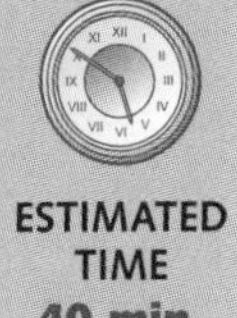

ESTIMATED TIME
40 min.

In this lesson you will learn how to:

- ✔ *Design a fax cover sheet using a template.*
- ✔ *Save a document as a template.*
- ✔ *Design a template for an electronic form.*
- ✔ *Protect an electronic form.*
- ✔ *Fill out and do calculations in an electronic form.*
- ✔ *Add Help content to a form.*

All documents created in Microsoft Word are based on *templates.* A template is a special kind of document that provides basic tools and text for shaping a final document. Templates can contain text, styles, glossary items, macros, and menu and key assignments.

A template saves you time by providing a basic format to start with. You can use the same template with as many documents as you wish. If you add some styles to a document as you work, you can save that document as a new template and base subsequent documents on it. Word includes a variety of templates, and you can modify these according to your needs. Templates can also be customized for certain types of documents, such as reports and resumes.

Another handy document type is an *electronic form,* such as a survey or time sheet, that users can fill out on their computers or print. Electronic forms are versatile; they can be used over a network or corporate intranet, or—after being converted to a Web format—published on the Internet. Forms are usually designed to contain very specific information, so it's useful to create templates for specific types of forms.

In this lesson, you create templates to speed up some of the administrative tasks at Impact Public Relations. You first create a fax cover sheet based on a Word template, and then you modify some styles and save the cover sheet as a new template. You also design a template for an electronic invoice form. Using the template, you fill out an invoice, include calculations in it, and add Help content.

More Buttons

important

The default toolbar setting in Microsoft Word 2000 displays both the Standard and Formatting toolbars in one row, at the top of the document window, just below the menu bar. This gives you maximum workspace. While working through the exercises in this book, toolbar buttons you need may not initially be visible. If a toolbar button is not visible, click one of the two More Buttons drop-down arrows on the toolbar to locate the button you need. When you select a new toolbar button, it is automatically added to the visible portion of the toolbar, replacing one that is not used as often.

Using Templates and Wizards

When you create a document using the New command on the File menu, you select a template on which to base your document. Template types range from a blank document—which is based on the *Normal* template and contains styles for a few headings, the body text, and paragraph style—to professional letters, memos, faxes, resumes, brochures, reports, and Web pages. When you select one of these templates, a new document opens that contains the styles in the template you chose. If you choose a memo template, for example, the document is styled and laid out in memo format. It includes placeholder text that you replace with your own text.

Word wizards also help automate the creation of documents. A *wizard* is a miniature application that does most of the work of creating a letter, Web page, report, and so on. The wizard presents you with a series of dialog boxes in which to select options and specify text. Then the wizard applies your choices to the document. In contrast, a template allows you to work directly in the document and doesn't restrict you to certain options.

If you have not yet installed this book's practice files, refer to "Using the Microsoft Word 2000 Step by Step CD-ROM," earlier in this book.

Impact Public Relations has done work for its client, Pacific Books, that ranges from market research to designing a Web site. It's now time to send a bill. In the following exercise, you create a fax cover sheet that you and others in your firm can quickly fill out and use when faxing invoices to Pacific Books. You base this fax document on an already designed Word template.

Start Word and create a fax cover sheet

In this exercise, you start Word and create a fax cover sheet.

1. On the Windows taskbar, click the Start button.

   The Start menu appears.

2. On the Start menu, point to Programs, and then click Microsoft Word.

   Microsoft Word 2000 opens.

3. On the File menu, click New.

   The New dialog box appears.

4. Click the Letters & Faxes tab, and then double-click the icon representing the Professional Fax template.

   A new document based on this template is opened.

When you want to choose the template for a new document, you must use the New command on the File menu rather than the New button on the Standard toolbar.

Adjust the magnification

In this exercise, you adjust the magnification of your document.

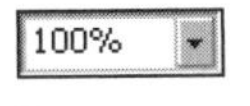

Zoom

- On the Standard toolbar, click the Zoom drop-down arrow, and then click Page Width.

  Your screen should look similar to the following illustration.

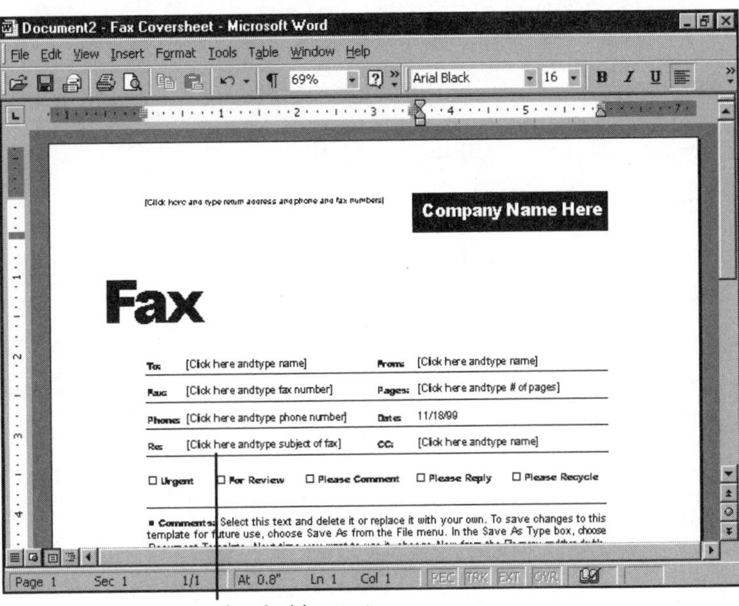

Display formatting marks

To make it easier to edit your document, you can display formatting marks such as paragraph marks and space marks on your screen.

Show/Hide ¶

- If formatting marks are not currently displayed, on the Standard toolbar, click the Show/Hide ¶ button.

Enter text in a fax document

In this exercise, you type your own text in place of placeholder text.

1. Click to select the text in the small print at the top of the document, and then type **18 Hunter St., San Francisco, CA 94117**
2. Press Enter, and then type **Phone: (415) 555-3984. Fax: (415) 555-3985**
3. In the upper-right corner of the document, select the text *Company Name Here*, and then type **Impact Public Relations**

   Don't press Enter after typing this text.
4. In the To line, click the placeholder text to select the line, and then type **V.J. Bernstein, Accounting, Pacific Books**
5. In the From line, click the placeholder text to select the line, and then type **Rebecca Smith**
6. For each of the remaining text lines except the CC line, click the placeholder text to select the line, and then type the following.

In this line	Type this text
Fax:	(206) 555-0066
Pages:	1
Phone:	(206) 555-3453
Re:	Invoice #10001

Leave the CC line blank. Note that the current date is automatically inserted.

Your screen should look similar to the following illustration.

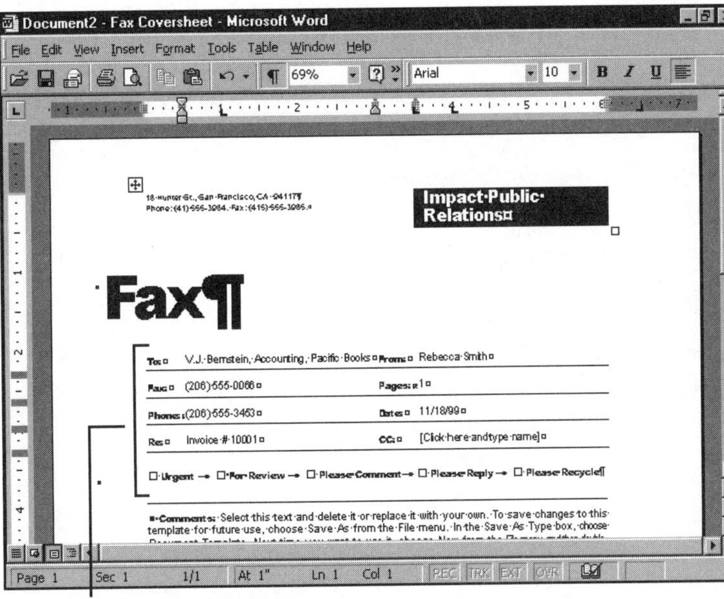

7. Select the text after *Comments*, and type **Here's the initial invoice for our company's services to date. Please contact Rebecca Smith with any questions. Thank you.**

Save a fax cover sheet

In this exercise, you save and name the new document as Fax Cover Sheet 08.

Save

1. On the Standard toolbar, click the Save button.

   The Save As dialog box appears.
2. Be sure the Lesson08 folder (within the Word 2000 SBS Practice folder) appears in the Save In box.
3. In the File Name box, select the text, and then type **Fax Cover Sheet 08**
4. Click Save.

Modify the document formatting

In this exercise, you alter the document heading in Fax Cover Sheet 08 and one of the cover sheet's elements.

If the Font Size button is not visible, on the Formatting toolbar, click the More Buttons drop-down arrow to locate the button.

1. In the row of options for attention, select the word *Urgent*, and then type **Invoice**

   The word *Invoice* replaces the word *Urgent* as an item to select.
2. Double-click the Invoice check box.

   A check mark is inserted in the box.
3. Select the heading *Fax*, including its ending paragraph mark.
4. On the Formatting toolbar, click the Font Size drop-down arrow, and then click 36.

   The heading is reduced from 54 points to 36 points.
5. On the Standard toolbar, click the Save button.

Save

Send an Instant Fax

The *Fax Wizard* creates a cover sheet and instantly faxes any document you specify. You can also send a cover sheet with a note, or print out a copy to send from a separate fax machine. To use the wizard, open the document that you want to fax. On the File menu, point to Send To, and then click Fax Recipient. The Fax Wizard appears and presents you with options.

Saving Documents as Templates

If you are not working through this lesson sequentially, before proceeding to the next step, open the 08A file in the Lesson08 folder, and save it as Fax Cover Sheet 08.

You'll be sending invoices to the Pacific Books accounting department regularly, so you can use this new fax cover sheet as the basis for future faxes. To do so, you will save the document as a template, but first you edit it to make it more general, because details will change from fax to fax. When you save a document as a template, the *.doc* filename extension changes to a *.dot* extension.

Edit the document

In this exercise, you add placeholder text to the fax cover sheet template created in the previous exercise.

1. In the Re line, select the number *10001*, and then type **[Number goes here]**

2. In the Pages line, select number *1*, and then type **[Number of pages goes here]**
3. Don't change the document date; it is updated automatically when you open a new document based on this template.
4. In the Comments area, select the text, and then type **[Remarks about the fax go here]**

Save the document as a template

In this exercise, you save Fax Cover Sheet 08 as a fax template.

1. On the File menu, click Save As.

   The Save As dialog box appears.
2. In the File Name box, type **Fax Template 08**
3. Click the Save As Type drop-down arrow, and then select Document Template (*.dot).

   The folder in the Save In box automatically changes to Templates.
4. Click Save.

   Your new template has a .dot filename extension and is stored in the Templates folder on your computer. When you create a new document with the New command on the File menu, this template will be available on the General tab.
5. On the File menu, click Close.

tip

To distinguish document files from template files, it's helpful to be able to see file extensions in filenames. Documents end with the .doc extension while templates end with a .dot extension. To display file extensions in Windows 98, open Windows Explorer, click View, and then click Folder Options. In the Folder Options dialog box, click the View tab. In the Advanced Settings list, clear the Hide File Extensions For Known File Types check box. Click OK. In Windows 95, open Windows Explorer, click the View menu, and then click Options. In the Options dialog box, click the View tab. Clear the check box for the Hide MS-DOS File Extensions For File Types That Are Registered option, and click OK. In Windows 2000, open Windows 2000 Explorer, click the View menu, and then Click Options. In the Options dialog box, click the View tab, and then clear the Hide File Extensions For Known File Types check box. Click OK.

Using Electronic Forms

Electronic forms are useful for gathering survey information or providing a design for frequently used documents, such as invoices and order forms. *Fields* in electronic forms are areas where users can enter a response to a prompt or question on the form. They are designed for specific types of data, such as numbers and addresses. A field might contain a drop-down list of options or a check box the user can select. You can design a field to perform calculations, too.

For details about saving a document as a Web page and publishing it to the Internet, see Lesson 11, "Designing Web Pages," and Lesson 12, "Editing and Publishing Web Pages."

If your company has an intranet, you can also make electronic forms available for employees or other users to fill out online. Moreover, if you want to place an electronic form, such as a survey or entry form, on your company's Web site, you can save the form as a Web page and publish it to the Internet.

In the following exercises, you use what you have learned about templates to create a template for an electronic invoice form. Employees will use this template whenever they need an invoice document for certain types of billing. The template provides the design and the fields needed for the invoice, so employees don't have to recreate these every time they need to fill out and send an invoice.

Creating an Electronic Form

To build an electronic form, you first create a template and specify the types of fields you want to include. You insert blank tables to arrange the fields. Then you protect the form so that others can fill it out as a document but cannot make any changes to its original text or formatting.

For the following exercises, on the View menu, click Print Layout. Click the Zoom drop-down arrow and select Page Width.

At Impact Public Relations, you want to provide an electronic invoice form that your employees can fill out on their computers for a variety of clients.

Create a template for the form

In this exercise, you create a template for an electronic form by saving an existing document as a template.

Open

1. On the Standard toolbar, click the Open button.

   The Open dialog box appears.
2. Click the Look In drop-down arrow, and then select your hard disk.
3. In the list of folders, double-click the Word 2000 SBS Practice folder, and then double-click the Lesson08 folder.

4. Be sure the Files Of Type list displays Word Documents (*.doc), and then in the file list, double-click the 08B file to open it. This document is an early version of an invoice.
5. On the File menu, click Save As.

   The Save As dialog box appears.
6. In the Save As dialog box, in the File Name box, select the text, and then type **Form Template 08**
7. Click the Save As Type drop-down arrow, and then select Document Template (*.dot).

   The folder in the Save In box changes to Templates.
8. Click Save.

   Your new template is stored in the Templates folder.

> **tip**
>
> To create a template starting with a blank document, on the File menu, click New. On the General tab, click the icon representing the Blank Document template. In the Create New area, select the Template option, and click OK.

Adding Tables to an Electronic Form

For more information about using and formatting tables in Word, see Lesson 5, "Mastering Indents, Tabs, and Tables."

Blank tables make a convenient starting point when you create electronic forms because the ready-made grid design gives you a place to insert text and fields. The grid format also helps you retain columns of text even when you delete or add new text.

When you insert a table, Word outlines the table and its cells with borders. You can change the look of the borders or eliminate them altogether with the Borders And Shading command on the Format menu. If you work with formatting marks displayed (using the Show/Hide ¶ button on the Standard toolbar), you'll see end-of-cell marks in the tables you create. The marks are at the end of every table cell, and end-of-row marks appear at the end of every table row. These function in the same way as paragraph marks within a document.

Display the Forms toolbar

The Forms toolbar includes all the buttons you need to create forms.

- Right-click anywhere on any toolbar, and then in the list of toolbars, click Forms.

  The Forms toolbar appears. To move the toolbar, drag its title bar. To place the toolbar above the document with other toolbars, double-click the title bar.
  Your screen should look similar to the following illustration.

Forms toolbar

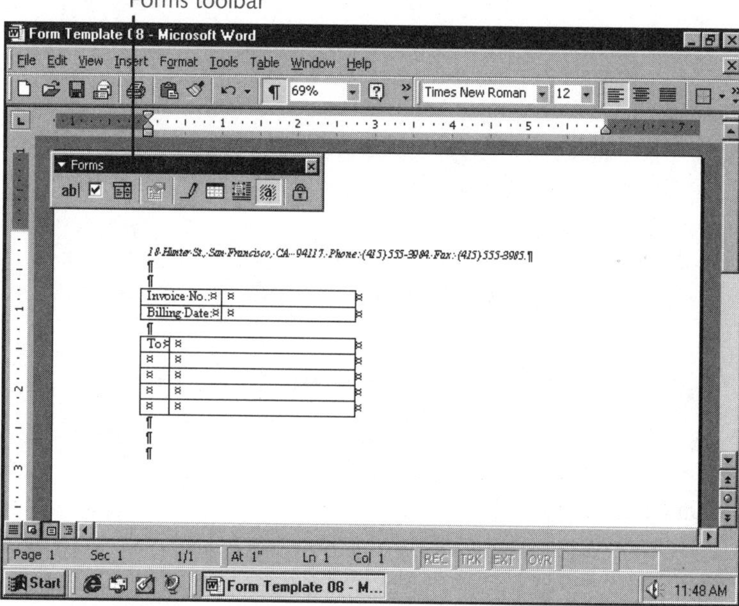

Insert a blank table

In this exercise, you insert a blank table into Form Template 08.

1. Click below the second table, and then press Enter.

   The insertion point moves to two lines below the table.

Insert Table

2. On the Forms toolbar, click the Insert Table button to display the grid.

If you need more room to expand the grid, move the Forms toolbar toward the center of the window, and then click the Insert Table button again.

3. Click in the upper-left square and drag across the grid to select five rows down by six columns across, and then release the mouse button.

   An empty table containing five rows and six columns is inserted.

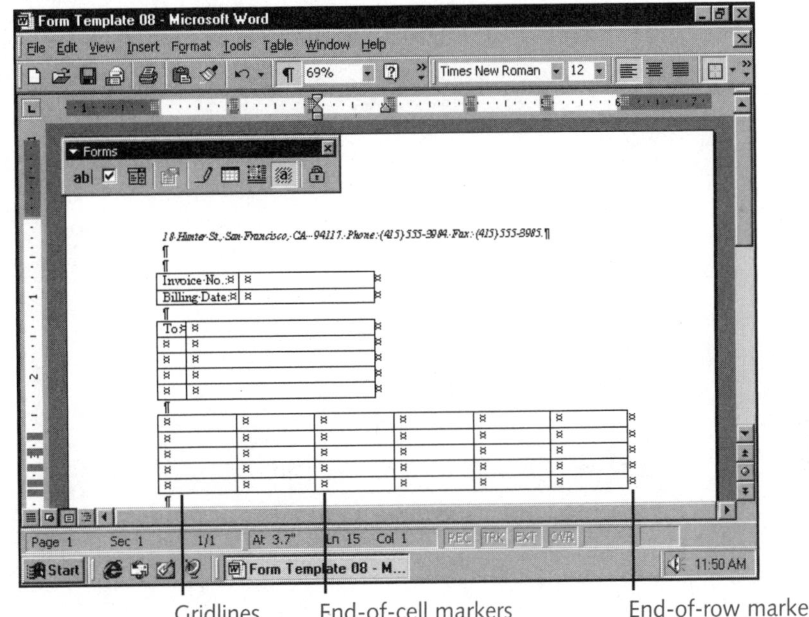

Gridlines End-of-cell markers End-of-row markers

Add text to the table

In this exercise, you type headings into the table.

- In the top row of the newly created table, press Tab to move from cell to cell as you type these headings:

  Date of Service

  Description

  Hours

  Flat Rate

  Hourly Rate

  Totals

Your screen should look similar to the following illustration.

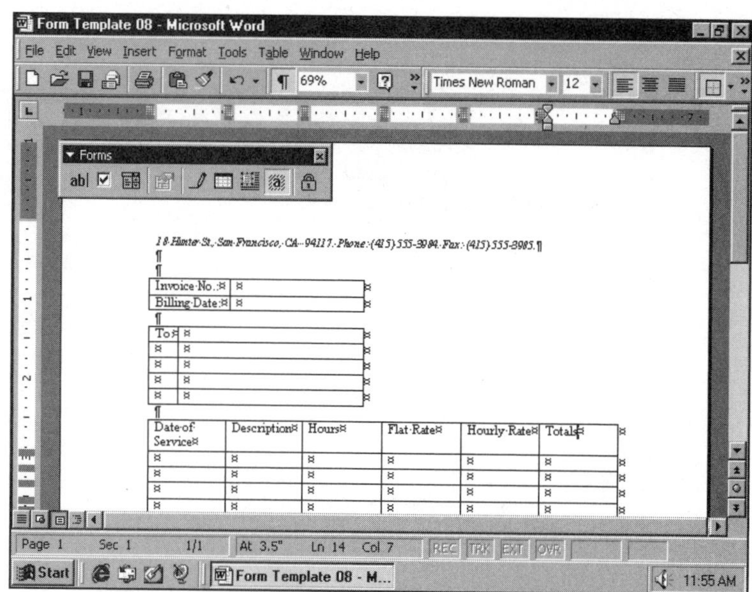

Using Cell References in Tables

Microsoft Excel uses the same system of referencing table cells.

Each cell in a table has an address, or *reference*, that identifies its location in the table by a column letter and a row number. The following illustration shows the cell references for a 3 x 4 table.

	A	B	C	D
1	A1	B1	C1	D1
2	A2	B2	C2	D2
3	A3	B3	C3	D3

The letters across the top are the column letters, and the numbers along the left side are the row numbers. To refer to a cell using a reference, list column letter first, and then row number. For example, the reference for the second cell in the second column would be B2. Use this method of cell referencing when you want a program to manipulate table data or do calculations on the data.

Cell references are used in the following tasks to quickly tell you which cell to insert a field into. Note that even though a cell might contain a heading label, it still counts as a cell in cell referencing.

If you are not working through this lesson sequentially, before proceeding to the next step, open the 08B file in the Lesson08 folder, and save it as Form Template 08.

Inserting Fields and Controls

Electronic forms contain *labels* that tell the user what information is desired, along with *blank cells* that are filled in by the user. For the blank cells, you create fields that determine what kind of characters can be entered in the cell. A field might require text or numbers of limited or unlimited length. You can design the field to insert some information automatically, such as the current date. You can also insert controls into the fields if you want the user to select from a list of options (created with a drop-down list box control) or put an *X* in a check box (created with a check box control). You use the Text Form Field Options dialog box to specify the characteristics of each field.

For a demonstration of how to insert a text field, in the Multimedia folder on the Microsoft Word 2000 Step by Step CD-ROM, double-click InsertTextField.

Insert a text field

In this exercise, you create a text field in which a user can type an invoice number.

Text Form Field

You can also click the Form Field Options button on the Forms toolbar to display the Text Form Field Options dialog box.

1. If necessary, scroll up, and in the top table, click in cell B1 (second column, first row).
2. On the Forms toolbar, click the Text Form Field button.

   Five small circles appear in the cell. This is the text field.
3. Double-click the text field.

   The Text Form Field Options dialog box appears.

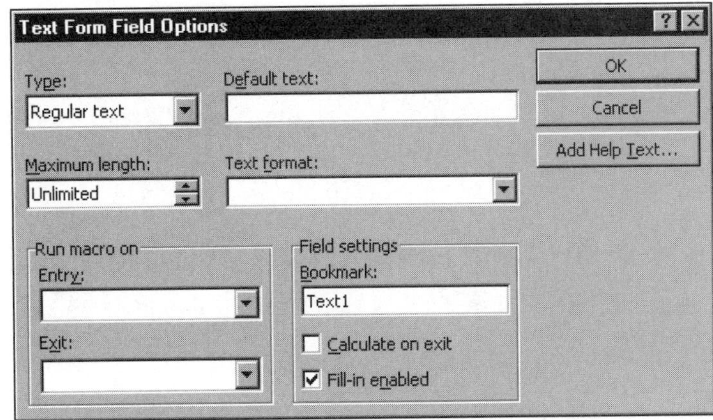

4. Click the Type drop-down arrow, and then select Number.
5. In the Maximum Length box, click the up arrow until the number 5 is displayed.

   The user is limited to using five digits in this field.

6. Click OK.

   In the table, no change to the field is apparent.

7. Click in cell B2 (second column, second row).

> **tip**
>
> In addition to the simple forms you can create by using the controls on the Forms toolbar, you can create other more powerful forms. See Microsoft Word Help for details about adding controls with the Control Toolbox. See Microsoft Word Help and Lesson 11, "Creating and Designing a Web Page," for details about controls added with the Web Tools toolbar.

Insert a date field

In this exercise, you insert a date field into the electronic form.

Text Form Field

1. On the Forms toolbar, click the Text Form Field button.
2. Double-click the text field.

   The Text Form Field Options dialog box appears.

3. Click the Type drop-down arrow, and then select Current Date.
4. Click the Date Format drop-down arrow, and select MMMM d, yyyy, the third list item from the top.
5. Leave the Maximum Length selection as Unlimited, and click OK to close the Text Form Field Options dialog box and return to the form.

   When a user types in a date on the invoice, the field formats the date to read as month, day, and year.

Save

6. On the Standard toolbar, click the Save button.

Insert fields for a name and address

In this exercise, you insert text fields for the client's name and address.

1. In the second table, click in cell B1.
2. On the Forms toolbar, click the Text Form Field button.

   The Text Form Field Options dialog box appears.

3. Double-click the text field.

   Because the user will type in a client's name in this field, you want the default selections of Regular Text (for Type) and Unlimited (for Maximum Length), so you make no changes.

4. Click OK to return to the form.
5. Click in cell B2, and then click the Text Form Field button on the Forms toolbar again.
6. Click in cell B3, and create the same type of field as in cells B1 and B2.

   You have a total of three rows of text fields in the second column.

   Your screen should look similar to the following illustration.

You can also use the Copy and Paste buttons to copy a text field and paste it into other cells.

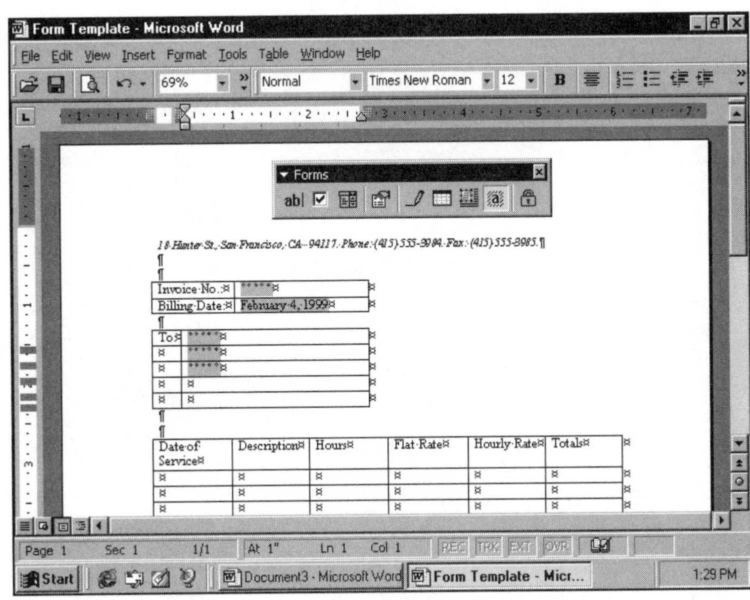

The user will type a client's address into the last two text fields you created.

Insert a check box field and label

You want to be able to specify whether you're billing a client online, by fax, or by mail, so in this exercise you create a check box field in the table.

1. In the second table, click in cell A5.
2. On the Forms toolbar, click the Check Box Form Field button.

   A check box is inserted in the cell.
3. Select the check box, and on the Formatting toolbar, click the Align Right button.

   The check box moves to the right side of the cell.

Check Box Form Field

Align Right

4. Press Tab to move the insertion point to cell, B5, and then type **Electronic Billing**

Save

5. On the Standard toolbar, click the Save button.

Insert a drop-down list

In this exercise, you insert a drop-down list with the types of jobs your company performs.

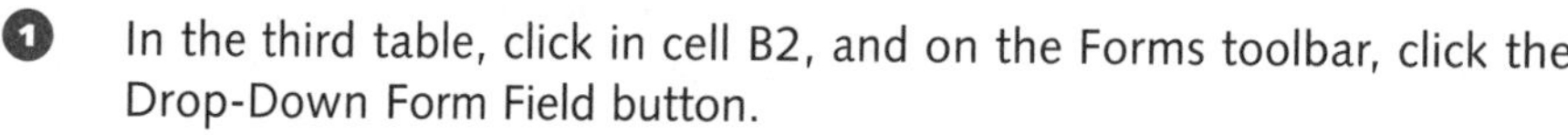

Drop-Down Form Field

1. In the third table, click in cell B2, and on the Forms toolbar, click the Drop-Down Form Field button.

   The field is inserted, and appears as an empty, shaded bar in the cell.
2. Double-click the field.

   The Drop-Down Form Field Options dialog box appears.
3. In the Drop-Down Item box, type **Market Research** and then click Add.

   Market Research appears in the Items In Drop-Down List box to the right.
4. Type **Project Planning** and then click Add.
5. Type **Web Site Design** and then click Add.
6. Click OK.

   Your screen should look similar to the following illustration.

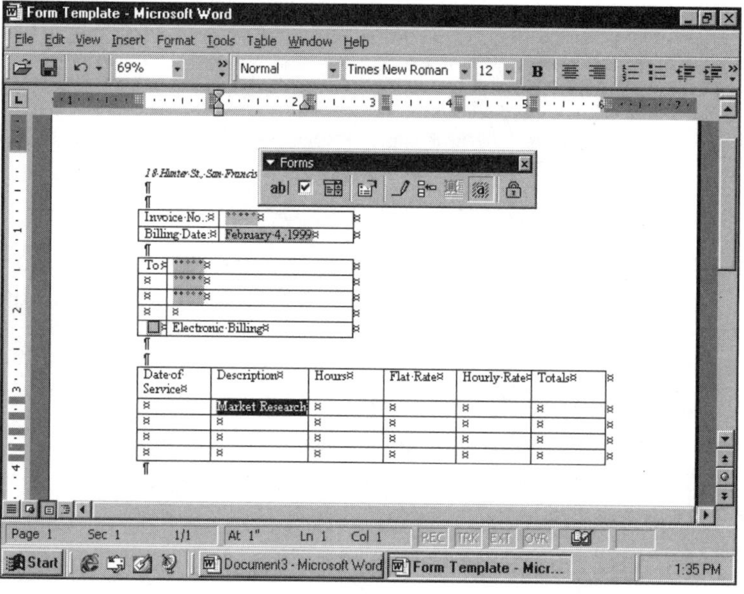

Save

7. On the Standard toolbar, click the Save button.

Copy the drop-down list to another cell

In this exercise, you copy the drop-down list field into an additional cell.

Copy

Paste

1. If the drop-down list field you just inserted is not selected, select it, and then, on the Standard toolbar, click the Copy button.

   The drop-down list items are copied to the Windows Clipboard.

2. Click in cell B3, and then, on the Standard toolbar, click the Paste button.

   The drop-down list is copied to the cell.

Add more text fields and labels

In this exercise, you add the remaining text fields to the table created in the previous exercises.

Text Form Field

1. In the third table, click in cell A2, and then click the Text Form Field button.

   A text field is inserted. Rather than specify this as a date field, you want to give users the flexibility to type in date ranges, so you leave this text field as it is.

2. Click in cell C3, and on the Forms toolbar, click the Text Form Field button.

   A text field is inserted.

3. Double-click the field to open the Text Form Field Options dialog box, click the Type drop-down arrow, select Number, and click OK.
4. Click in cell D2, and on the Forms toolbar, click the Text Form Field button. Then double-click the field.

   The Text Form Field Options dialog box appears.

5. Click the Type drop-down arrow, and then select Number. Click the Number Format drop-down arrow, and then select $#,##0.00;($#,##0.00), the fifth number format list item from the top. Click OK.
6. In cell E3, insert the same kind of number text field that you created in steps 4 and 5. You can also copy and paste the text field created in those steps.

7. In cell B5, type **Total Due:**

   Your screen should look similar to the following illustration.

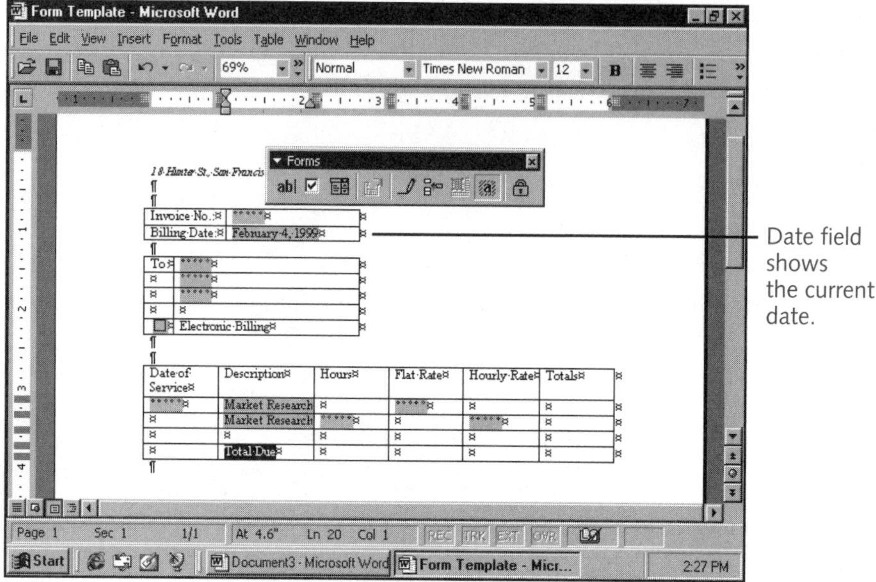

Date field shows the current date.

Save

8. On the Standard toolbar, click the Save button.

   Changes to your form are saved.

Inserting Calculation Fields

Though Word is not a spreadsheet program, you can use it to perform simple calculations. To create a calculation field, you specify a text field as a calculation and give it an *expression*, a formula that carries out the calculation.

Expressions rely on certain built-in Word functions, such as SUM and PRODUCT, to do addition, multiplication, subtraction, percentages, and so on. Expressions use *cell references* to find the table data to include in the calculation. In the next series of exercises, you'll format three fields in your template as calculation fields using functions for addition and multiplication.

If you are not working through this lesson sequentially, before proceeding to the next step, open the 08C file in Lesson08 folder, and save it as Form Template 08.

tip

For calculations beyond simple addition, subtraction, or multiplication, use Microsoft Excel. See Lesson 16, "Connecting with Other Microsoft Office 2000 Programs," for details about importing data from Microsoft Excel into a Word document.

Insert calculation fields

In this exercise, you insert fields in the Totals column and format them to calculate the sum or the product of the numbers in related table cells.

Text Form Field

1. Click in cell F2. On the Forms toolbar, click the Text Form Field button to insert a text field, and then double-click the field.

   The Text Form Field Options dialog box appears.
2. Click the Type drop-down arrow, and then select Calculation.

   The text box next to Type changes to an Expression box with an equal sign in it.
3. In the Expression box, next to the equal sign, type **SUM(LEFT)**
4. Click the Number Format drop-down arrow, select $#,##0.00;($#,##0.00, and click OK.

   The field in cell F2 now appears as $0.00.
5. Click in cell F3. On the Forms toolbar, click the Text Form Field button to insert a field, and then double-click the field.

   The Text Form Field Options dialog box appears.
6. In the Text Form Field Options dialog box, in the Type box, select Calculation.
7. In the Expression box, next to the equal sign, type **PRODUCT(C3,E3)**

   The two numbers in the referenced cells are multiplied.
8. Click the Number Format drop-down arrow, select $#,##0.00;($#,##0.00), and click OK.

   The field in cell F3 appears as $0.00.
9. Click in cell F5, and on the Forms toolbar, click the Text Form Field button. Double-click the field.

   The Text Form Field Options dialog box appears.

10. In the Text Form Field Options dialog box, click the Type drop-down arrow, and then select Calculation.
11. In the Expression box, next to the equal sign, type **SUM(ABOVE)**

    The numbers in the column above the cell are added.
12. Click OK.

    The field in cell F5 appears as $0.00.

    Your screen should look similar to the following illustration.

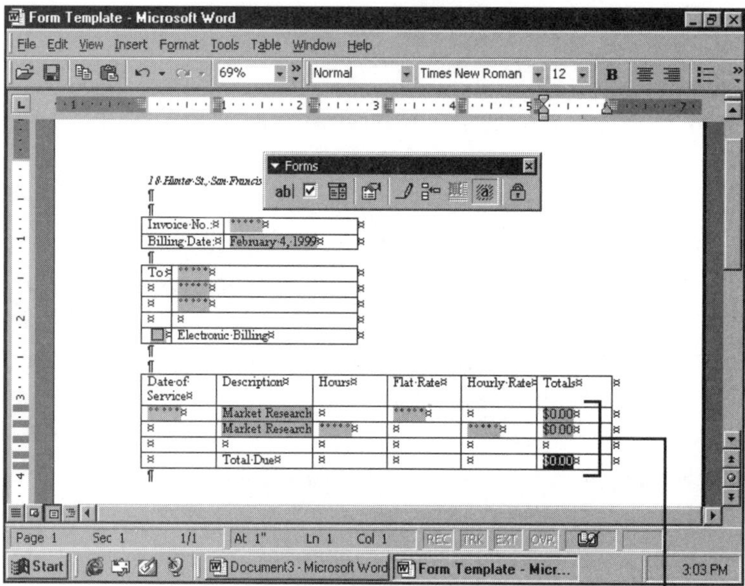

Calculation fields

tip

Form Field Shading

To format your form for easier reading, you can hide the shading behind the fields. On the Forms toolbar, click the Form Field Shading button. If you have hidden table borders but still see dotted lines bordering the table, they won't show in a printed document. However, if you want to remove them, on the Tools menu, click Options, and click the View tab. In the Print And Web Layout Options area, clear the Text Boundaries check box.

Protecting Electronic Forms

To protect forms from being altered when users fill them out electronically, you use the Protect Form button on the Forms toolbar.

When you create a form, by default, it is unprotected so that you can insert fields and text labels. However, you can turn form protection on as you work, to test your controls. For example, to see the drop-down list that you added to the form earlier in this lesson, you would temporarily protect the form by clicking the Protect Form button. Then you would click the control to expand the list. To continue editing the form, click the Protect Form button again.

When users create documents using the form template, they have the option of unprotecting the document. If you don't want users to be able to alter the form, you can protect it by assigning it a password. Only a user knowing the password could alter the fields or structure of the form. To assign a password, on the Tools menu, click Protect Document. In the Protect Document dialog box, select the type of document protection you want, and then assign a password.

If you are not working through this lesson sequentially, before proceeding to the next step, open the 08D file in the Lesson08 folder, and save it as Form Template 08.

There are some situations in which users need to be able to unprotect the form. For example, fields that are designated as calculations cannot be clicked by a user, and the calculations cannot be carried out, unless the form is unprotected. In this case, the user unprotects the form, does the calculations, and leaves the form unprotected.

Protect the form

In this exercise, you protect the form so that users can type only into cells where there are fields.

Protect Form

- On the Forms toolbar, click the Protect Form button to protect the form.

Hide the Forms toolbar

- On the Forms toolbar, click Close.

Save and close the form

Save

1. On the Standard toolbar, click the Save button.
2. On the File menu, click Close.

Filling Out Electronic Forms

Now that you have completed this template for an electronic form, you can base a new Word document on it.

Create a new form document

In this exercise, you create a new invoice based on Form Template 08. This will be an invoice to Pacific Books.

1. On the File menu, click New.
2. On the General tab, click the icon representing Form Template 08.

   In the Create New area, be sure that the Document option is selected.
3. Click OK.

Fill out the electronic form

If you are not working through this lesson sequentially, before proceeding to the next step, open the 08E file in the Lesson08 folder, and save it as Form Invoice 08.

Use Tab to move from field to field as you type text into the invoice. Because the form is protected, you won't be able to move to cells that do not contain fields.

1. In the Invoice No. field, type **10001**
2. Press Tab to move to the To field.
3. In the To field, type **Pacific Books**
4. Press Tab, and in the next two fields, type

   41 S. Marion St.

   Seattle, WA 98104
5. Select the Electronic Billing check box.
6. In Date Of Service box, type **March 1-31**
7. In the Description column, click the first cell containing *Market Research*.

   The drop-down list is displayed.

Your screen should look similar to the following illustration.

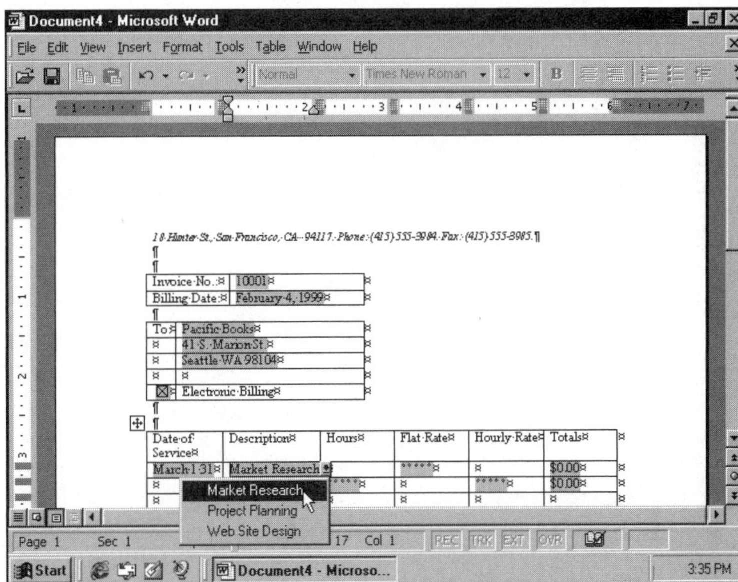

8 In the Description list, select Market Research.

9 Click in the Flat Rate field, and then type **500**

10 Press Tab. In the second drop-down list in the Description column, click the drop-down arrow, and then click Web Site Design.

11 Press Tab. In the Hours field, on the Web Site Design row, type **70**

12 Press Tab. In the Hourly Rate field, type **50**

Save the form

In this exercise, you save your new form.

1 On the File menu, click Save.

The Save As dialog box appears.

2 Be sure the Lesson08 folder (within the Word 2000 SBS Practice folder) appears in the Save In box.

3 In the File Name box, select the text, and type **Form Invoice 08**

4 Click Save.

All of the information you typed into the form is saved. Your original form template for the invoice remains unchanged.

Calculate table values

In this exercise, you calculate table values to get your final figures. Before you can complete the calculations, you must unprotect the document and leave it unprotected.

1. On the Tools menu, click Unprotect Document.
2. Position the pointer over the top of the Totals column, and wait for the pointer to turn into a black, down-pointing arrow. Then click.

   The Totals column is selected.

Another way to calculate is to select each result cell individually and press F9.

3. Press the F9 key.

   All the calculations are completed in the Totals column. They show $500.00 for Market Research; $3,500.00 for Web Site Design; and $4,000.00 as the Total Due.

> **important**
>
> Don't reprotect the document, because reprotecting it will return the fields to their original state, and you will lose the data you entered and calculated.

Hide formatting marks

Show/Hide ¶

- To see your form without the end-of-cell and end-of-row marks, on the Standard toolbar, click the Show/Hide ¶ button to hide formatting marks.

Save and close your completed form

Save

- On the Standard toolbar, click the Save button, and on the File menu, click Close to close the invoice.

One Step Further: Adding Help Content to a Form

To help a user fill out an electronic form, you can provide explanations for any of the fields you've created. The Help text appears as a message in the status bar. In this exercise, you create a message that appears on the status bar when a user clicks the drop-down list in a form that's based on Form Template 08.

Open the form template

In this exercise, you display Form Template 08.

Open

This exercise uses a file created in previous exercises. In order to complete this exercise, you must first create Form Template 08.

1. On the Standard toolbar, click the Open button.
2. Click the Look In drop-down arrow, and then select your hard disk.
3. In the file list, double-click Windows, double-click Application Data, double-click Microsoft, and then double-click Templates.
4. At the bottom of the Open dialog box, click the Files Of Type drop-down arrow, and then click Document Templates (*.dot).

   The templates in the folder are displayed.
5. Double-click the Form Template 08 template.

   Form Template 08 is displayed.

tip

If you are unable to locate the template, on the Tools menu, click Options, and then click the File Locations tab. In the File Types list, double-click User Templates. The Modify Location dialog box appears, and in the Folder Name list, the full path to your Templates folder is shown. Note this path, and click OK in this dialog box and then in the Options dialog box. On the Standard toolbar, click Open, and double-click the folders to follow the path to your Templates folder.

Unprotect the form

Because you will be modifying a field by adding Help information to it, you need to unprotect the template.

1. Right-click any toolbar, and then click Forms to display the Forms toolbar.

Protect Form

2. Click the Protect Form button.

   The form can now be modified.

Add Help information to a field

1. Double-click the first field in the Description column.
2. In the Drop-Down Form Field Options dialog box, click Add Help Text.
3. In the Form Field Help Text dialog box, be sure that the Status Bar tab is selected.
4. Select the Type Your Own option.
5. In the text box, type **Web site design applies to work done on content as well as on design.**

   Your screen should look similar to the following illustration.

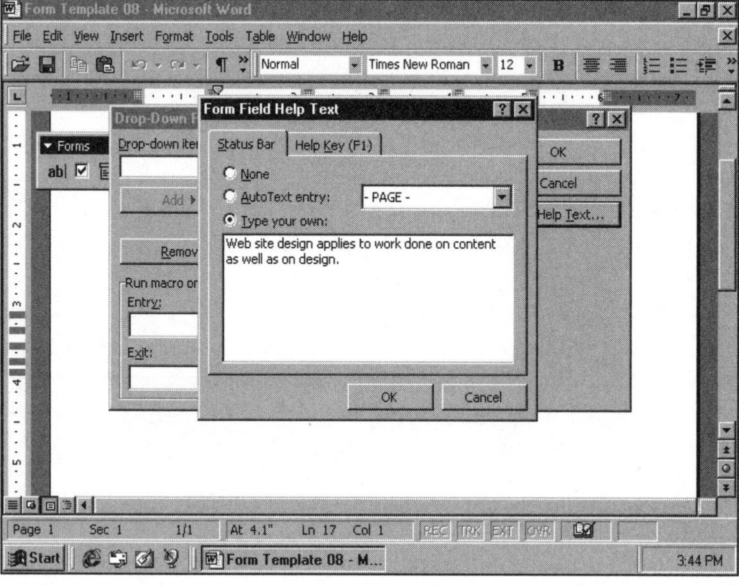

This message will appear in the status bar when the user clicks the drop-down list. If you want this message to also appear when a user clicks the second drop-down list in the form, repeat steps 1 through 5 for that field.

6. Click OK to return to the Drop-Down Form Field Options dialog box.
7. Click OK to return to the form.
8. On the Forms toolbar, click the Protect Form button.
9. In the form, click the first drop-down list to see the Help text.

   The list expands, and the Help text you added appears in the status bar.

Finish the lesson

Save

1. On the Standard toolbar, click the Save button.

   Changes to Form Template 08 are saved.
2. On the File menu, click Close.
3. If you want to quit Word for now, on the File menu, click Exit.

Lesson 8 Quick Reference

To	Do this
Create a fax document using a template	On the File menu, click New. On the Letters & Faxes tab, double-click a fax template. Enter text and modify formatting in the fax document, and then click Save.
Save a document as a template	On the File menu, click Save As. Type a new name in the File Name box, and select Document Template (*.dot) in the Save As Type box. Click Save.
Create a template for an electronic form	To create a template from an existing document, follow the procedure for saving a document as a template. To create a new template, on the File menu, click New. On the General tab, click Blank Document, and in the Create New area, select the Template option. Click OK.
Display the Forms toolbar	Right-click any toolbar, and then click Forms.

Lesson 8 Quick Reference

To	Do this	Button
Insert a blank table on a form	On the Forms toolbar, click the Insert Table button, and then in the grid, drag to select the number of columns and rows for the table.	
Insert a text field	On the Forms toolbar, click the Text Form Field button. Double-click the text field. Specify the options you want in the Text Form Field Options dialog box, and click OK.	ab|
Insert a check box	On the Forms toolbar, click the Check Box Form Field button.	
Insert a drop-down list field	On the Forms toolbar, click the Drop-Down Form Field button. Double-click the drop-down form field. Specify the desired options in the Drop-Down Form Field Options dialog box, and click OK.	
Insert a calculation field	Insert a text field, and then double-click the field. In the Text Form Field Options dialog box, click the Type drop-down arrow, and then select Calculation. Enter a formula in the Expression box, and specify a number format.	
Show or hide form shading	On the Forms toolbar, click the Form Field Shading button.	a
Turn form protection on or off	On the Forms toolbar, click the Protect Form button.	
Fill out an electronic form	On the File menu, click New, and then select the form template you created. In the Create New area, be sure the Document option is selected, and click OK.	

Lesson 8 Quick Reference

To	Do this
Make calculations in a form document	Select the column where you want the results, and then press F9. Or select each cell where you want a result, and press F9.
Add Help content to a form	Unprotect the form template, and then double-click the field you want to add Help text to. In the Form Field Options dialog box, click Add Help Text. Select the Type Your Own option, and then type the Help text you want to appear when the field is clicked.

PART

2

Review & Practice

You will review and practice how to:

- ✔ *Modify a document and save it as a template.*
- ✔ *Create a document using the new template and AutoText entries.*
- ✔ *Create, apply, and modify document styles.*
- ✔ *Design an electronic form.*

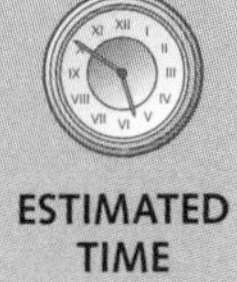

ESTIMATED TIME **30 min.**

Before you move on to Part 3, which covers advanced editing techniques such as merging documents and designing Web pages, you can practice the skills you learned in Part 2 by working through this Review & Practice section. You modify an existing document, save it as a template, create a document based on the template, and add AutoText entries. You work with various styles in your document. Then you design a template for an electronic form and add tables and calculation fields to it.

Scenario

At Impact Public Relations, you want a basic template for internal memos. You plan to use this template for a memo about upcoming employee evaluations. You also want a template for the employee evaluation form.

Step 1: Modify a Document and Save it as a Template

A memo you created earlier provides a good starting point for a new standard management memo, so you decide to modify and save it as a memo template.

1. Open file RP02A, and in the *Re* line, delete the existing text and type **[Subject]**
2. Under the horizontal line, delete the heading and type **[Heading]**
3. Delete the text under the heading, but not the last paragraph mark.
4. Save the document as a template, name it Management Memo RP2, and close it.

For more information about	See
Saving a document as a template	Lesson 8

Step 2: Create a Document from the Template

Now that you have a new memo template, you can use it to create a memo to employees concerning the upcoming employee evaluations.

1. Create a new document based on the Management Memo RP2 template, and save it as Employee Evaluations Memo.
2. In the *Re* line, type **Biannual Employee Evaluations**
3. Type **Evaluating Your Coworkers** as the heading.
4. Create AutoText entries for the phrases: *Impact Public Relations* and *employee evaluations*.
5. Select the text, and using the AutoText entries you just created, type:

   At Impact Public Relations, we take employee evaluations seriously. When you fill out an employee evaluation form, remember these points:

   Be open and fair.

   In the form, take full advantage of the Comments section.

   Allot yourself adequate time to fill out the form. Employee evaluations compete with other work, but they strengthen Impact Public Relations.

For more information about	See
Using templates and wizards	Lesson 8
Creating and inserting AutoText entries	Lesson 6

Step 3: Create, Modify, and Apply Styles

You want to change some of the styles in your memo and then you want to save the style changes for future use.

1. In the memo, create a new heading style called Memo Heading 1, based on the Heading 1 style. Change the font to bold and italic, and the font size to 14 points. For the paragraph style, add 6 points of space after the heading.
2. Apply the new style to the heading *Evaluating Your Co-workers*.
3. In the last paragraph of the memo, set a left indent at the 1-inch ruler mark and a right indent at the 5.5-inch ruler mark. Apply a bullet to the last paragraph, and change the bullet symbol to arrows.
4. With the bulleted text selected, create a new style called Memo Bullet, based on the Closing style.
5. Apply the Memo Bullet style to the last three memo paragraphs.
6. Modify the Memo Bullet style by adding three points of space before and after the bullet.
7. Save your changes, and close the memo.

For more information about	See
Creating bulleted and numbered lists	Lesson 5
Setting custom indents with the ruler	Lesson 5
Using styles	Lesson 7
Modifying styles	Lesson 7

Step 4: Create an Electronic Form

You want to make it easy for employees to fill out their coworker evaluations, so you create an electronic form.

1. Create a template based on the Blank Document template.
2. Insert a table with two columns and eight rows.
3. Below the table, press Enter, and on the new line, type **Comments:**
4. In the table cells A1, A2, and A3, respectively, type these labels:

   Name:

   Position:

   Date:
5. In cells B1 and B3, insert a text field.

6. Specify the text field in cell B3 as a Date type, and select a date format.
7. In cell B2, insert a drop-down list, and type these items in the list:

   Graphic Designer

   Writer

   Content Editor

   Support Technician
8. In cells A5 through A7, respectively, type these labels:

   Overall Improvement

   Attitude

   Progress Toward Goals

For more information about	See
Working with tables	Lesson 5
Adding tables to an electronic form	Lesson 8
Inserting fields and controls	Lesson 8

Step 5: Insert Calculation Fields into an Electronic Form

You want to make it easy to tally results of the employee evaluations, so you add calculation fields to your electronic form.

1. In the form, in each cell in the range B5 through B7, insert a text field specified as a Number type with a 0.00 format and a maximum length of four.
2. Add a row to the bottom of the table.
3. In cell A9, type **Total Rating**
4. In cell B9, insert a calculation field with the expression =SUM(ABOVE) and a Number format of 0.00.
5. Resize column A to about two inches on the ruler.
6. Add a row to the top of the table, merge the table cells for the row, and type **Performance Rating**
7. Style the heading as Heading 2, and then center it.
8. AutoFormat the table, turn off form field shading, and protect the document.
9. Save the template as Form Template RP2.

For more information about	See
Inserting calculation fields	Lesson 8
Protecting electronic forms	Lesson 8

Finish the Review & Practice

Follow these steps if you want to continue to the next lesson.

- On the File menu, click Close.

Follow these steps if you want to quit Microsoft Word for now.

1. On the File menu, click Exit.
2. If a message appears asking whether you want to save changes, click Yes.

PART 3

Developing Advanced Editing Techniques

LESSON

9

Mail Merging

In this lesson you will learn how to:

- ✔ *Create a main document for a mail merge.*
- ✔ *Create a data source for a mail merge.*
- ✔ *Merge a data source with a main document.*
- ✔ *Use an existing data source for a mail merge.*
- ✔ *Address an envelope for a mail merge.*
- ✔ *Filter records to be merged.*

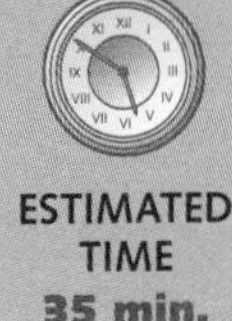

ESTIMATED TIME
35 min.

*Mail merg*ing is a useful Microsoft Word tool that can help you quickly and efficiently reach a wide audience in a personalized way. When you want to communicate organization news, for example, or new offerings of your company, merging a form letter with a mailing list can save considerable time and effort.

In this lesson, as a partner at Impact Public Relations, you use mail merge to create a letter to send to all of the contacts of your client, Pacific Books. You create a *main document* (a form letter in this case) and a *data source* (a mailing list), and then you merge the two to produce a *new document*—a file of individually addressed letters. You also learn how to attach an existing data source (one already created) to a main document, merge the information, and create mailing envelopes.

More Buttons

> **important**
>
> The default toolbar setting in Microsoft Word 2000 displays both the Formatting and Standard toolbars in one row at the top of the document window, just below the menu bar. This gives you maximum workspace. While working through the exercises in this book, toolbar buttons you need may not initially be visible. If a toolbar button is not visible, click one of the two More Buttons drop-down arrows on the toolbar to locate the button you need. When you select a new toolbar button, it is automatically added to the visible portion of the toolbar, replacing one that is not used as often.

Start Word and open a new document

In this exercise, you start Word and open a new document.

1. On the Windows taskbar, click the Start button.

   The Start menu appears.
2. On the Start menu, point to Programs, and then click Microsoft Word.

   Microsoft Word 2000 opens
3. On the Standard toolbar, click the New Blank Document button.

   A new blank document opens.

New Blank Document

Display formatting marks

To make it easier to edit your document, you can display formatting marks such as paragraph marks on your screen.

Show/Hide ¶

- If formatting marks are not currently displayed, on the Standard toolbar, click the Show/Hide ¶ button.

Mail Merging: The Basics

Mail merging involves taking information from one document (the main document) and combining it with information from another document (the data source) to create a *new document*, which contains information from both.

The main document is a Word document containing *boilerplate* text and *field names*. Boilerplate text is the text that will be the same in each of the copies of the main document that result from the merge. The field names are placeholders for information from the data source. They specify where that information will be placed in the document. For example, a field name might be *company*. Wherever that field is placed in the main document, a company name will be pulled from the data source and inserted into the new document during the merge.

The new document displays the information from the data source and the main document. If, for example, your main document is a one-page letter and your data source contains 25 names, your new document will be 25 pages long and will include a personalized letter to each of the 25 people in the data source.

Before you print your document, it's a good idea to check for errors. If you notice an error in the new document, or something else you want to change, close the new document without saving it, go back to either the data source or the main document, edit it, and merge again. This check could eliminate a wasted print job.

Performing Mail Merges

A mail merge has three steps.

- Creating the main document
- Setting up the data source
- Merging the data source with the main document

In the following exercises, you complete these three steps using the Word Mail Merge Helper to create a mailing to the contacts of your client, Pacific Books.

important

In order to produce all of the necessary elements of a mail merge, you must complete, in sequence, all of the exercises in this lesson from "Create a Main Document" through "Save and Close the Main Document."

Create a main document

In this exercise, you create a main document for a mail merge.

New Blank Document

1. If you don't have a blank document open, on the Standard toolbar, click the New Blank Document button.

   A new blank document is displayed in the Word window.

2. On the Tools menu, click Mail Merge.

   The Mail Merge Helper dialog box appears.

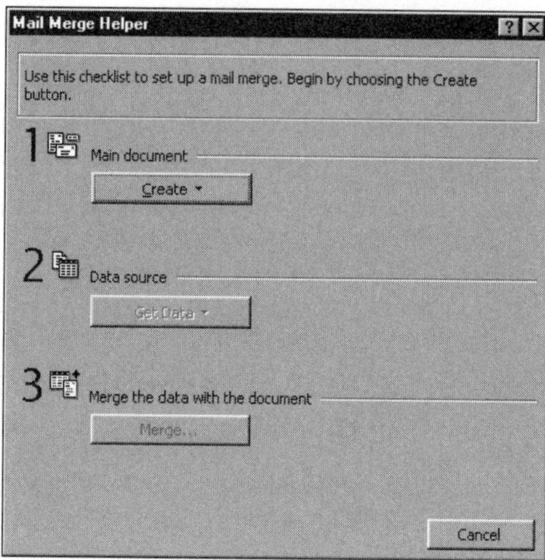

3. Click Create, click Form Letters, and then click Active Window.

   The blank document is now the main document for the merge.

4. In the Mail Merge Helper dialog box, click Close.

   The Mail Merge toolbar is displayed in the Word window.

Creating a Data Source

The data source contains all of the individualized information that ends up in a merged document. This information is organized into sets, or *data records,* for each entity in the data source—a specific customer, for example. The data record includes information such as name, company, account number, address, state, postal code, and so on. Pieces of information in a data source are called *fields.*

Each field name is identified in the header row of the data source. Each field name must be unique and can have up to 40 characters. Letters, numbers, and the underscore character can be used, but not spaces. The first character of a field must be a letter.

Select the data source field names

In this exercise, you create a new data source by defining the field names.

Mail Merge Helper

1. On the Mail Merge toolbar, click the Mail Merge Helper button.

   The Mail Merge Helper dialog box appears.

2. Click Get Data.

   The Data Source options are displayed.

3. Click Create Data Source.

   The Create Data Source dialog box appears, showing a list of suggested fields for the data source. You can select or delete fields from the list.

4. In the Field Names In Header Row list, select Address2, and click Remove Field Name.

   The field is removed from the data source.

5. In the same way, remove each of the following field names:

   Country

   HomePhone

   WorkPhone

6. In the Field Name box, type **Branch**

   The text you type replaces the text already in the box.

7. Click Add Field Name.

   The field Branch is added to the data source.

8. Click OK.

   The Save As dialog box appears.

Save the data source

In this exercise, you save the data source as a file on your hard disk.

1. Be sure that the Lesson09 folder (within the Word 2000 SBS Practice folder) appears in the Save In box.
2. Click in the File Name box and type **Pacific Books Data**
3. Click Save.

   The Microsoft Word dialog box appears.

Entering Data Records

Once you have created and saved a data source, you can add records using the Data Form dialog box. The Data Form dialog box displays the fields in the form, making it easy to enter information. Once you complete the form, you click either the Add New button to add another record or the OK button if you are finished. You can create as many records as you need.

Add records to the data source

In this exercise, you enter the name, company, address, and store branch for the first person on your list.

1. In the Microsoft Word dialog box, click Edit Data Source.

   The Data Form dialog box appears.

2. Type the following information in the form next to the text fields listed below on the left. Press Enter to move to the next field.

Title	**Ms.**
FirstName	**Nina**
LastName	**Valerio**
JobTitle	**General Manager**
Company	**Pacific Books**
Address1	**155 Sashume St.**
City	**San Francisco**
St	**CA**
Postal Code	**94104**
Branch	**San Francisco**

Completed data form

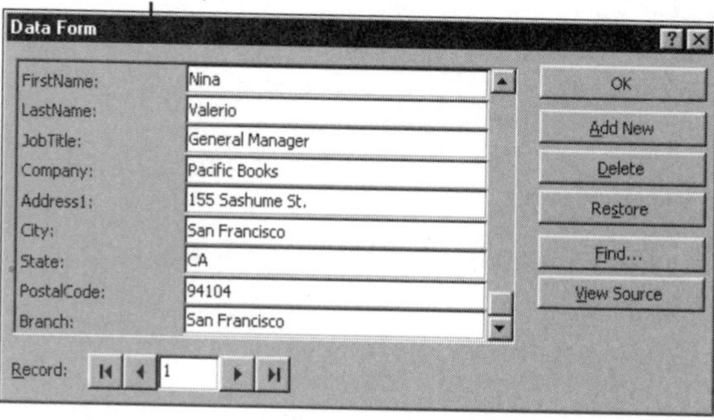

3. In the Data Form dialog box, click Add New, or press Enter.

   The record is added to the data source, and a new blank record form is displayed.

4. Add the data records for the following people.

   You will leave the Job Title field blank in one record. By default, Word will skip blank fields by closing up the space in the merged document, so blank fields in a record do not affect merges. Remember to click Add New each time you complete a record, except after record 4, when you click OK.

Record 2	
Title	**Mr.**
FirstName	**R.A.**
LastName	**Hiatt**
JobTitle	**Store Manager**
Company	**Pacific Books**
Address1	**2226 Shattuck Ave.**
City	**Berkeley**
St	**CA**
Postal Code	**92701**
Branch	**Berkeley**

Record 3	
Title	**Ms.**
FirstName	**Francis**
LastName	**Lockwood**
JobTitle	
Company	**Pacific Books**
Address1	**89 Rain Way**
City	**Portland**
St	**OR**
Postal Code	**97219**
Branch	**Portland**

Record 4	
Title	**Ms.**
FirstName	**Erica**
LastName	**Thomas**
JobTitle	**Store Manager**
Company	**Pacific Books**
Address1	**41 S. Marion**
City	**Seattle**
St	**WA**
Postal Code	**98104**
Branch	**Seattle**

5. In the Data Form dialog box, click OK.

   The main document is displayed.

Preparing the Main Document

The next step in a mail merge is to prepare the main document. This includes naming and saving the main document, attaching the data source to the main document, inserting the field names, and entering the text of the document.

Save the main document and attach the data source

In this exercise, you save the main document and attach the data source.

Save

1. On the Standard toolbar, click the Save button.

   The Save As dialog box appears.
2. Be sure that the Lesson09 folder (within the Word 2000 SBS Practice folder) appears in the Save In box.
3. In the File Name box, type **Pacific Books Main** and click Save.

   The data source is now attached to the main document.

Inserting Field Names in the Main Document

By inserting field names into the main document, you specify where you want the information from the data source to appear in the document. Field names are enclosed in angle brackets (<< >>) in the main document.

Insert a date

In this exercise, you insert the date into the document.

1. Be sure that the insertion point is at the top of the document.
2. On the Insert menu, click Date And Time.

   The Date And Time dialog box appears.
3. In the Available Formats area, select the third date format from the top of the list.
4. Select the Update Automatically check box.

   The date field will automatically display the current date each time you open this document.
5. Click OK, and press Enter three times.

   The date and two blank lines are inserted into the document.

Insert a title, first name, and last name

In this exercise, you insert fields to create the first line of an address block in the main document.

1. On the Mail Merge toolbar, click the Insert Merge Field button.

   A list of all the fields from the data source is displayed.

List shows all of the data source fields.

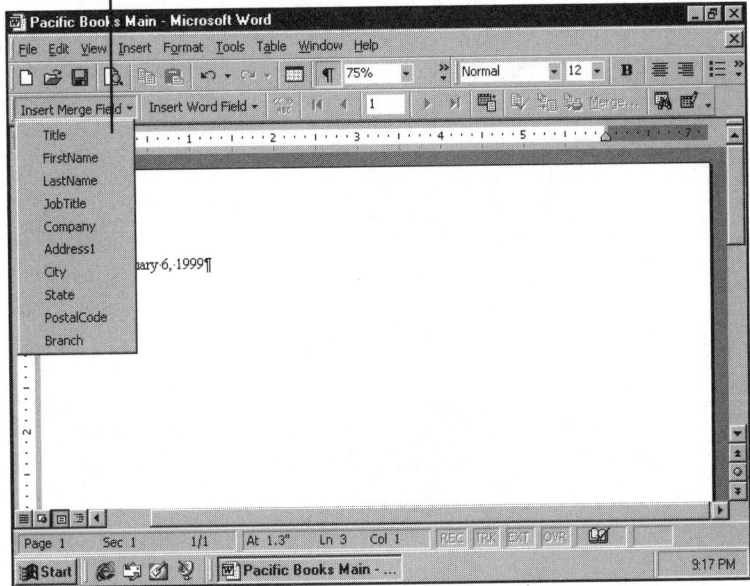

2. Click Title, and press the Spacebar.

   The merge field Title is inserted into the main document, and a space is inserted after the field.

3. On the Mail Merge toolbar, click the Insert Merge Field button, click FirstName, and then press the Spacebar.

4. On the Mail Merge toolbar, click the Insert Merge Field button, click LastName, and then press Enter.

   The first line of the main document is complete.

   Your screen should look similar to the following illustration.

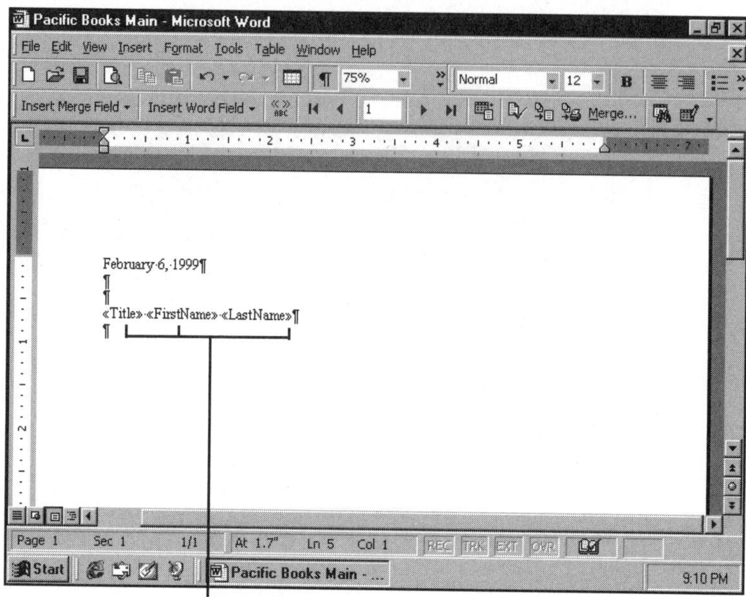

Document with fields inserted

Insert a company name, job title, and address

In this exercise, you insert fields to complete an address block in the main document.

1. On the Mail Merge toolbar, click the Insert Merge Field button.

   A list of all the fields from the data source is displayed.

2. Click Job Title, and press Enter.

   The merge field Job Title is inserted into the main document.

3. On the Mail Merge toolbar, click the Insert Merge Field button, click Company, and then press Enter.
4. On the Mail Merge toolbar, click the Insert Merge Field button, click Address1, and then press Enter.
5. On the Mail Merge toolbar, click the Insert Merge Field button, and then click City.

6. Type a comma, and press the Spacebar.
7. On the Mail Merge toolbar, click the Insert Merge Field button, click State, and then press the Spacebar.
8. On the Mail Merge toolbar, click the Insert Merge Field button, click Postal Code, and then press Enter three times.

   The address block is complete.

Create a salutation

In this exercise, you create a salutation for your letter.

1. Type **Dear** and press the Spacebar.
2. On the Mail Merge toolbar, click the Insert Merge Field button, click Title, and then press the Spacebar.
3. On the Mail Merge toolbar, click the Insert Merge Field button, and then click LastName.
4. Type a colon, and press Enter twice.

   Your screen should look similar to the following illustration.

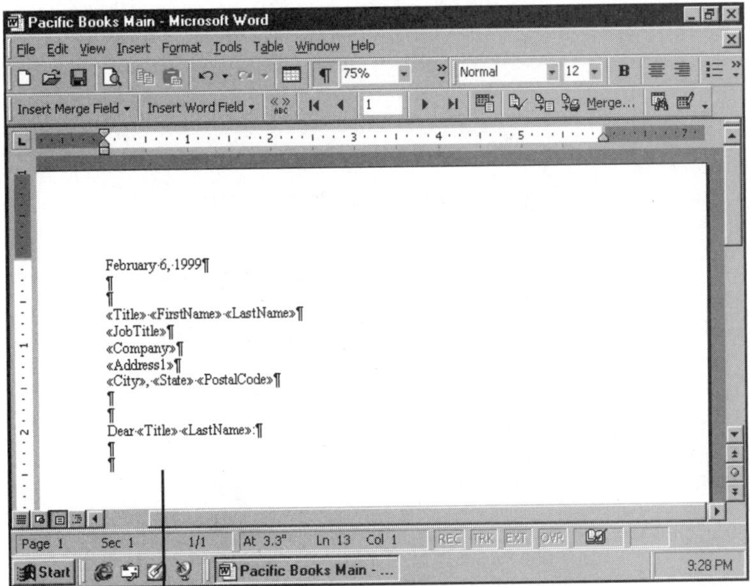

Document with additional text fields inserted

Type the body of a letter

You can use merge fields within the body of a letter. In this exercise, you type the body of the letter and insert a field.

1. Type **Thank you for selecting Impact Public Relations to create your upcoming public relations campaign. We have created your logo to be used at the**
2. Press the Spacebar, and on the Mail Merge toolbar, click the Insert Merge Field button, click Branch, and then press the Spacebar.
3. Type **location.** and press Enter twice.

   Your screen should look similar to the following illustration.

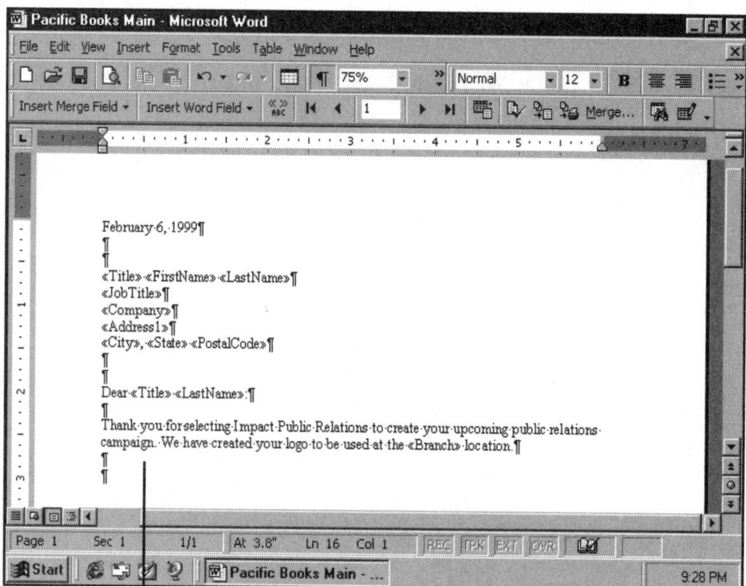

Body of the letter

Insert text from another file

In this exercise, you insert the contents of another file into the main document.

1. Type **Here is a sample of the logo for your approval.**
2. Press Enter twice.

3. On the Insert menu, click File.
4. Be sure that the Lesson09 folder (within the Word 2000 SBS Practice folder) appears in the Look In box.
5. Double-click the 09A file.

   The Pacific Books logo is inserted into the document.

Finish the letter

In this exercise, you finish and save the letter.

1. Press Ctrl+End to move the insertion point to the end of the document, press Enter twice, and then type **Please let me know if you have any questions regarding your campaign.**
2. Press Enter twice.
3. Type **Sincerely,** and then press Enter three times.
4. Type **Rebecca Smith**
5. On the Standard toolbar, click the Save button.

Save

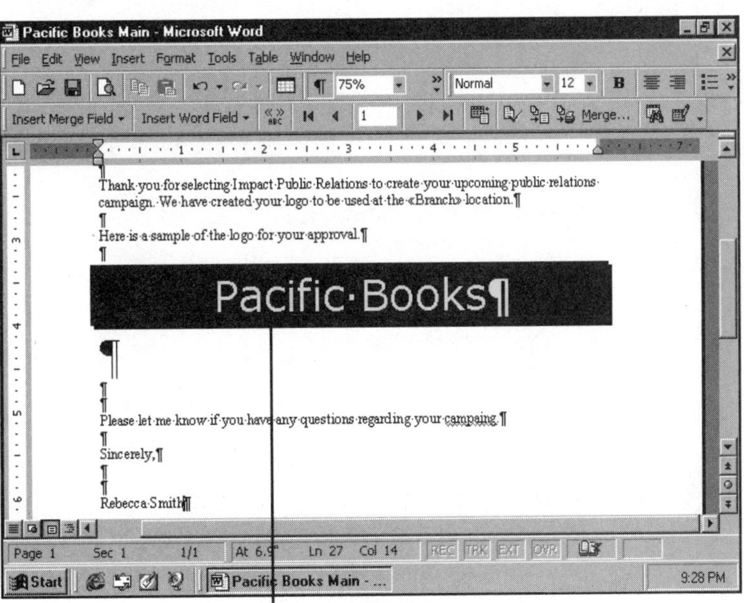

Letter with logo inserted

Completing the Mail Merge

Once you have inserted the data source fields and prepared the main document, you are ready to finish the mail merge. This process combines the main document with the data source and creates a new document with all the merged information, or directly prints the merged information. There are three buttons on the Mail Merge toolbar to help you complete a merge.

Check For Errors

- The Check For Errors button checks the main document for errors before you merge to print.

Merge To Printer

- The Merge To Printer button processes the merge and immediately sends the results to the printer.

Merge To New Document

- The Merge To New Document button merges the main document and the data source and creates a new document with the resulting information. You can view the merged document to check the formatting, spacing, page layout, and other details. This is the procedure you follow in this lesson.

Merge information into a new file

In this exercise, you merge the main document and data source to a new document.

- On the Mail Merge toolbar click the Merge To New Document button. A new document called Form Letters1 is created with the merged information.

View and edit the letters

- Scroll through the document Form Letters1 to check for errors.

Print the merged letters

In this exercise, you print the mailing. If you don't have a printer connected to your computer, skip to the next exercise.

Print

- On the Standard toolbar, click the Print button.

Close the merged document file

In this exercise, you close the merged document.

1. On the File menu, click Close.
2. Click No when you are prompted to save the file.

   You don't need to save this file since you can quickly create another one from the main document, Pacific Books Main.

Save and close the main document

In this exercise, you save and close the main document, Pacific Books Main.

1. Be sure Pacific Books Main is the active document. If not, be sure you have closed the Form Letters1 document.
2. On the Standard toolbar, click the Save button.
3. On the File menu, click Close.
4. Click Yes to save the Pacific Books Data file, if you are prompted.

Save

Attaching an Existing Data Source

The file Pacific Books Data used in this exercise was created in earlier exercises of this lesson. You must complete those exercises before proceeding.

You can attach an existing data source document to another main document and create additional merges. For example, you could create envelopes for the letters you produced in the preceding exercises. To do this, create a new main document, attach the already created data source, and then merge it to an envelope. You can also use data sources from other Microsoft programs such as Microsoft Access and Microsoft Excel.

Attach an existing data source

In this exercise, you create a new main document and attach an existing data source.

New Blank Document

You can also select Mailing Labels or Catalog instead of Envelopes.

1. On the Standard toolbar, click the New Blank Document button.

   A new blank document opens in the document window.
2. On the Tools menu, click Mail Merge.

   The Mail Merge Helper dialog box appears.
3. Click Create, click Envelopes, and then click Active Window.

   The file is now a main document for a merge.
4. In the Mail Merge Helper dialog box, click Get Data, and then click Open Data Source.

   The Open Data Source dialog box appears.

5. Double-click Pacific Books Data
6. Click Set Up Main Document.

   The Envelope Options dialog box appears.
7. Click OK.

   The Envelope Address dialog box appears.

Using Data from Other Programs as Data Sources in Word

Data sources are created using basic database concepts. Because of this standardization, you can use data sources from other programs for Word mail merges. The most commonly used program for such merges is Microsoft Access, a database management program. You can also set up a database in Microsoft Excel and use it as a data source in a Word merge. Microsoft Exchange, Schedule+, and Outlook are three other programs from which you can import information to be used as data sources in a Word merge.

Import a file to use as a data source in a Word merge

If you are using a source from Outlook, the Personal Address Book, or Schedule+ Contacts, click Use Address Book and select the program containing your data source. The data source will be converted to a Word source.

To use a file from another program as a data source in a Word merge, follow the steps below.

1. Open or create a main document and display the Mail Merge Helper dialog box. For more information, see "Creating a Main Document," earlier in this lesson.
2. In the Mail Merge Helper dialog box, click Get Data, and click Open Data Source.

   The Open Data Source dialog box appears.
3. In the Files Of Type area, select All Files.
4. Locate the file to import.
5. Double-click the file to be used as the data source.
6. Click Edit Main Document to add fields from the imported data source.
7. On the Mail Merge toolbar, click the Insert Merge Field button, and insert the fields you want in the main document.
8. Complete the main document, and on the Mail Merge toolbar, click the Merge To New Document button to finish the merge.

Use an envelope as a main document

In this exercise, you set up an envelope as the main document.

1. In the Envelope Address dialog box, click Insert Merge Field.
   The list of fields from the data source is displayed.
2. Click Title, and then press the Spacebar.
3. Click Insert Merge Field, click FirstName, and then press the Spacebar.
4. Click Insert Merge Field, click Last Name, and then press Enter.
5. Click Insert Merge Field, click Company, and then press Enter.
6. Click Insert Merge Field, click Address1, and then press Enter.
7. Click Insert Merge Field, click City, type a comma, and then press the Spacebar.
8. Click Insert Merge Field, click State, and then press the Spacebar.
9. Click Insert Merge Field, and then click PostalCode.
   Your screen should look similar to the following illustration.

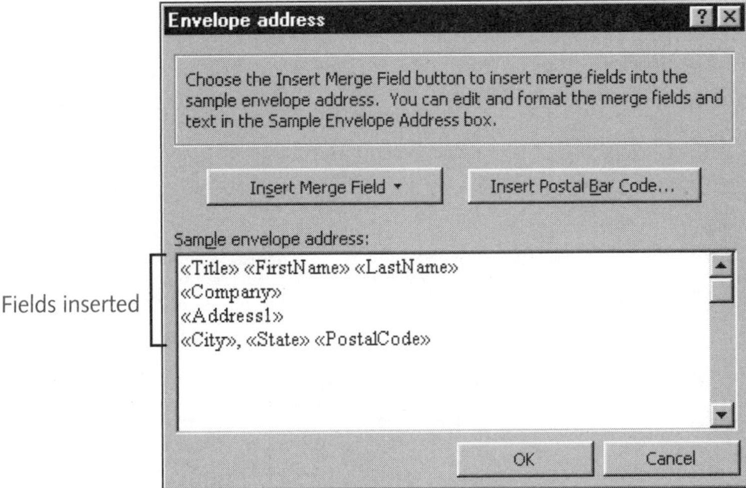

10. Click OK, and then click Close.
    The main document is displayed.

Finish the envelope

In this exercise, you add return address information and save the document.

1. Be sure that the main document is displayed and that the insertion point is at the top of the document.
2. Type **Pacific Books** and then press Enter.
3. Type **155 Sashume St**. and then press Enter.
4. Type **San Francisco, CA 94104**

Save

5. On the Standard toolbar, click the Save button.

   The Save As dialog box appears.
6. In the Save In box, be sure the Lesson09 folder (within the Word 2000 SBS Practice folder) is displayed.
7. In the File Name box, type **Pacific Books Envelope** and click Save.

Complete the merge for an envelope

In this exercise, you merge the main document and data source to a create envelopes.

Merge To New Document

1. On the Mail Merge toolbar, click the Merge To New Document button.

   The main document and data source are merged to create an envelope for each letter produced in the preceding merge.

Print Preview

2. On the Standard toolbar, click the Print Preview button, and view the envelopes.
3. On the Print Preview toolbar, click the Close button.
4. To print the envelopes, be sure the envelopes are properly loaded into the printer.

Print

5. On the Standard toolbar, click the Print button.
6. On the File menu, click Close, and click No when you are prompted to save the file.

   The Pacific Books Envelopes document is displayed.
7. On the File menu, click Close, and then click Yes to save any changes to the Pacific Books Envelopes document.

One Step Further: Filtering Data Records Before Merging

Files used in this exercise were created in earlier exercises in this lesson. In order to complete the following exercise, you must first create those files.

You can filter a merge by selecting data records that meet a certain criterion—all records carrying a particular postal code, for example. You can select up to six filters for a merge, using the Query Options dialog box.

Define a record query

In this exercise, you define a record query for a merge.

Open

1. On the Standard toolbar, click the Open button.
2. Be sure the Lesson09 folder (within the Word 2000 SBS Practice folder) is displayed in the Look In box.
3. Double-click Pacific Books Main.

   The main document, Pacific Books Main, and the data source, Pacific Books Data, are available for a merge.

To view the data source, on the Mail Merge toolbar, click the Mail Merge Helper button.

4. On the Mail Merge toolbar, click the Mail Merge Helper button.

   The Mail Merge Helper dialog box appears.
5. Click Merge.

   The Merge dialog box appears.

Mail Merge Helper

6. Click Query Options.

   The Query Options dialog box appears.
7. Click the Field drop-down arrow, and then select State.

   The insertion point moves to the Compare To box.
8. In the Compare To box, type **CA** and click OK.

   The Mail Merge Helper dialog box appears.
9. Click Merge.

   The merge is completed; two records matching the query are found.
10. On the File menu, click Close, and then click No when you are prompted to save the file.

Save

11. On the Standard toolbar, click the Save button.

    The main document is saved with the new query options.

Clear a query selection

The Mail Merge Helper remembers your filter queries from one merge to the next. If you later want to merge all records, therefore, you need to clear the query from the Helper. In this exercise, you clear a query in a merge.

Mail Merge Helper

1. On the Mail Merge toolbar, click the Mail Merge Helper button.
   The Mail Merge Helper dialog box appears.
2. Click Query Options.
   The Query Options dialog box appears.
3. Click Clear All.
   The query selection is removed.
4. Click OK.
   The Mail Merge Helper dialog box appears.
5. Click Close.

Finish the lesson

Save

1. On the Standard toolbar, click the Save button.
   Changes to Pacific Books Main are saved.
2. On the File menu, click Close.
3. On the File menu, click Exit.

Lesson 9 Quick Reference

To	Do this
Create a main document	Be sure the document you want to use as a main document is open. On the Tools menu, click Mail Merge. In the Mail Merge Helper dialog box, click Create, click one of the available options, and then click Active Window. In the Mail Merge Helper dialog box, click Close.

Lesson 9 Quick Reference

To	Do this	Button
Create and save a data source	Be sure the document you want to use as the main document is open. On the Tools menu, click Mail Merge. Click Get Data, and then click Create Data Source. Select the fields to delete from the list of fields provided, and click Remove Field Name. In the Field Name box, type the name of a field to add, and then click Add Field Name. Click OK. Click in the File Name box, type the file name, and then click Save.	
Add records to a data source	Be sure the document you want to use as the main document is open and you have attached a data source. On the Tools menu, click Mail Merge. Click Edit Data Source, type the information in the first field, and press Enter to move to the next field or fields. Click Add New to add another record, or click OK if you are finished adding records.	
Insert a date	On the Insert menu, click Date And Time. Select the date format. In the Date And Time dialog box, select the Update Automatically check box. Click OK.	
Insert a merge field	Be sure the document you want to use as the main document is open. On the Mail Merge toolbar, click the Insert Merge Field button, and then click the field to insert.	
Insert the contents of another file	On the Insert menu, click File. Double-click the file you want to insert.	
Merge information into a new file	Be sure the document you want to use as the main document is open. On the Mail Merge toolbar, click the Merge To New Document button.	

Lesson 9 Quick Reference

To	Do this	Button
Print merged letters	Be sure your printer is turned on, and on the Standard toolbar, click the Print button.	
Close a merged document file	On the File menu, click Close. Click No when you are prompted to save the file.	
Define a record query	Open a main document and data source, and then, on the Mail Merge toolbar, click the Mail Merge Helper button. Click Merge, and then click Query Options. Click the Field drop-down arrow, and select the field to query. In the Compare To box, type the query, and click OK. Click Merge.	
Clear a query selection	On the Mail Merge toolbar, click the Mail Merge Helper button. Click Query Options, click Clear All, and then click OK. Click Close.	

Enhancing Documents with Columns and Art

In this lesson you will learn how to:

- ✔ *Reformat text into multiple columns.*
- ✔ *Adjust the flow of text from column to column.*
- ✔ *Create and position text boxes.*
- ✔ *Insert, format, and reposition clip art and AutoShapes.*
- ✔ *Create and modify graphics using the Drawing toolbar.*
- ✔ *Create a self-mailing newsletter and merge it to mailing labels.*

ESTIMATED TIME **25 min.**

Varying column formats, inserting graphics, creating art, and adding text effects can help add interest and impact to your documents. With easy-to-use tools in Microsoft Word 2000, you can quickly convert a basic text document into a lively and colorful flyer, brochure, newsletter, or Web page.

In this lesson, you create a newsletter for your client, Pacific Books, that tells all about an upcoming book fair. You take a basic text document and add visual interest to it by formatting it into columns and adjusting the column widths and text flow. Then you enhance your newsletter with text boxes, drop caps, and clip art. You insert an *AutoShape,* which is a graphic shape that can contain text, and you use *WordArt,* a tool to create special effects with text. Finally, you turn your finished newsletter into a self-mailer, complete with mailing labels.

important

More Buttons

The default toolbar setting in Microsoft Word 2000 displays both the Standard and Formatting toolbars in one row, at the top of the document window, just below the menu bar. This gives you maximum workspace. While working through the exercises in this book, toolbar buttons you need may not initially be visible. If a toolbar button is not visible, click one of the two More Buttons drop-down arrows on the toolbar to locate the button you need. When you select a new toolbar button, it is automatically added to the visible portion of the toolbar, replacing one that is not used often.

Start Word and open a practice file

In this exercise, you start Word, open a practice file, and then save it with a new name.

1. On the Windows taskbar, click the Start button.
   The Start menu appears.
2. On the Start menu, point to Programs, and then click Microsoft Word.
   Microsoft Word 2000 opens.
3. On the Standard toolbar, click the Open button.
   The Open dialog box appears.

Open

4. Click the Look In drop-down arrow, and then select your hard disk.
5. In the list of folders, double-click the Word 2000 SBS Practice folder, and then double-click the Lesson10 folder.
6. In the file list, double-click the 10A file to open it.
   The document opens in the document window.
7. On the File menu, click Save As.
   The Save As dialog box appears.
8. Be sure that the Lesson10 folder appears in the Save In box.
9. In the File Name box, type **Book Fair 10**
10. Click Save.

Display formatting marks

To make it easier to edit your document, you can display formatting marks such as paragraph marks and space marks on your screen.

Show/Hide ¶

- If the formatting marks are not currently displayed, on the Standard toolbar, click the Show/Hide ¶ button.

Creating Columns

With Microsoft Word you can create a document with newspaper-style, or *snaking*, columns in which the text flows from the bottom of one column to the top of the next. You can also set column breaks to force headings or text to the top of the next column to achieve special effects, or eliminate problematic text flow. You can start a new document with defined columns, or you can take a previously created document and change it from the default one-column setting to a format of up to 12 columns. If you don't like the way your document looks, you can change the number of columns, the column width, or the space between columns to achieve your desired results.

> **tip**
> Documents must be in Print Layout view to see the column settings. To switch to Print Layout view, on the View menu, click Print Layout.

If you are not working through this lesson sequentially, before proceeding to the next step, open the 10A file in the Lesson10 folder, and save it as Book Fair 10.

Reformat a document to multiple columns

In this exercise, you begin to create a newsletter by converting a document into a multiple-column format.

Columns

- On the Standard toolbar, click the Columns button, and then click 2 Columns.

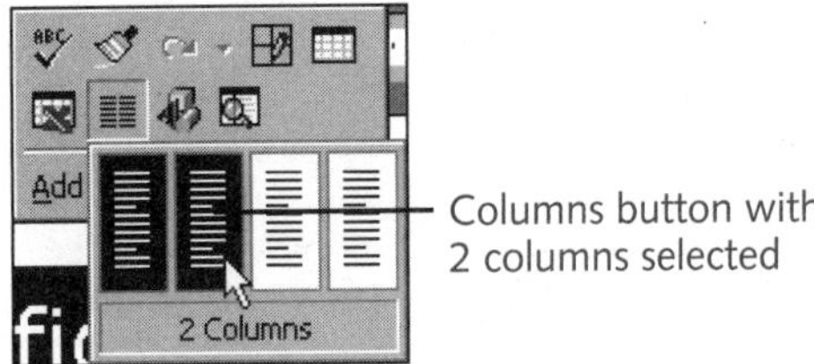

The entire document is converted to two columns.

Varying Columns Within a Document

Once you choose a column format for your document, you're not limited to that format for the entire document. You can vary the number of columns and other formatting throughout the document. For example, you might format the top of a page in one column, creating a heading across the page, and then format the remainder of the page in two columns. You can either select the text and then specify the new formatting for that section, or you can add a *section break*. A section break appears in your document as a double dotted line. It does not appear in a printed copy. You can insert a section break using the Break command on the Insert menu.

To select an entire paragraph along with its ending paragraph mark, quickly triple-click anywhere in that paragraph.

Create a newsletter heading

In this exercise, you create a heading for your newsletter by switching to a one-column format.

Columns

1. Press Ctrl+Home to move the insertion point to the beginning of the document, and select the text *Pacific Books*—including the ending paragraph mark—at the top of the document.
2. On the Standard toolbar, click the Columns button, and then click 1 Column.

   The text is expanded across the entire page, creating a heading for the newsletter. A section break is automatically inserted after the ending paragraph mark.
3. Click anywhere outside of the selected text to cancel the selection.

Changing Column Width and Spacing Between Columns

When the document was formatted into two columns, the appropriate column width as well as the spacing between the columns were automatically applied by Word based on the margin settings and number of columns selected. Column width and the spacing between the columns are interdependent; if you change the column width, the spacing between the columns is automatically adjusted, and vice versa. You can change the column width or spacing between the columns to change the layout of a document.

Modify column width

In this exercise, you decrease the width of the columns that are formatted in 2-column format and increase the spacing between the columns.

1. Click anywhere in the text that is formatted in two columns, and on the Format menu, click Columns.

   The Columns dialog box appears.
2. Select the Equal Column Width check box.

3. In the Width box, select the text, and type **2.75**
4. Press Tab.

   The selection in the Spacing box changes to 1".

   Your screen should look similar to the following illustration.

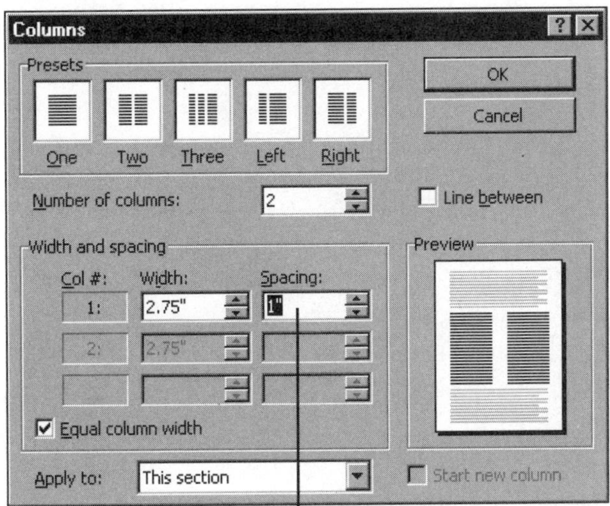

Spacing between columns will be 1".

5. Click OK.

Inserting Column Breaks

When you change the layout of a document from one column to two or more columns, the text is rarely laid out exactly as you want it. Typical layout problems include:

- A heading or first line of a paragraph appears at the bottom of one column, while the following paragraph text appears at the top of the next column or page. The lone heading or line is known as an *orphan*.
- The last line of a paragraph appears at the top of a new column or page. The single line is known as a *widow*.

You fix text flow problems by inserting *column breaks*. A column break forces the text up or down the column depending on where the break is inserted. For example, if a heading appears at the bottom of the first column in a document, you can apply a column break immediately before the heading to force the heading to the top of the second column. You can also use a column break to force a heading appearing at the bottom of the last column on a page to the top of the first column on the next page.

You can also force text to a new page by inserting a *next page break*. A next page break inserts a section break on the page where the insertion point is currently flashing, and moves the text after the break to a new section on the next page. With a next page section break, you actually break the connection between the first section and the new section. Once this connection is broken, there may be some properties of the first section that you need to redefine in the new section if you want them repeated—for example, a header in the top margin of each page.

Insert a column break

In this exercise, you insert a column break to keep a paragraph together.

1. Scroll down to the end of page 1, and click before the heading *Contests,* the last heading on the page in the second column.
2. On the Insert menu, click Break.

   The Break dialog box appears.
3. Select the Column Break option, and click OK.

   The heading *Contests* is moved to the top of the first column on the next page.

Insert a next page break

In this exercise, you insert a next page column break to force text to a new page.

1. Scroll down to the end of page 2, and click before the heading *Schedule of Events,* the last heading on the page in the second column.

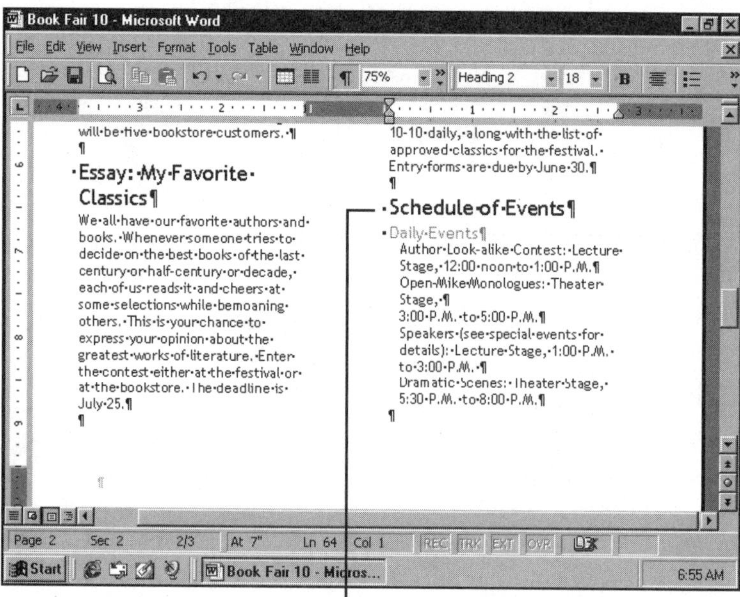

Click the insertion point here.

2. On the Insert menu, click Break.

   The Break dialog box appears.

3. In the Section Break Types area, click Next Page, and click OK.

   The text after the insertion point is moved to a new page.

Creating a Different Number of Columns in Each Section

With section breaks inserted in your document, you can easily change the number of columns in each section. To change the number of columns for a particular section, position the insertion point at the top of the desired section and select the appropriate number of columns.

Reformat a section

In this exercise, you reformat the columns in a section of the document.

1. Be sure the insertion point is still positioned before the heading *Schedule of Events*.

Columns

2. On the Standard toolbar, click the Columns button, and then click 1 Column.

   All of the text in the section is reformatted to one column, and the other sections remain unchanged.

Previewing the Layout

As you adjust your columns of text, you will probably want to view the document to see the overall affect. With Print Preview you can get a quick overview of your entire document.

Preview the newsletter

In this exercise, you view the layout of a document in Print Preview.

1. Press Ctrl+Home to move the insertion point to the top of the document.

Print Preview

2. On the Standard toolbar, click the Print Preview button.

   Notice that there is no header on the last page because the page was formatted using a next page break, which broke the connection between the original section and the new one.

   Your screen should look similar to the following illustration.

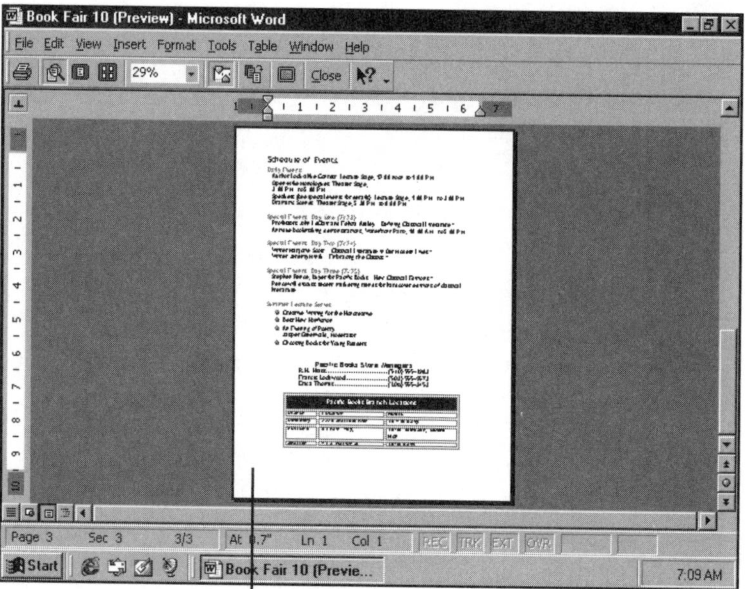

Page 3 in Print Preview shows 1-column formatting.

3. On the Print Preview toolbar, click the Close button.

Creating and Placing Text Boxes

If you are not working through this lesson sequentially, before proceeding to the next step, open the 10B file in the Lesson10 folder, and save it as Book Fair 10.

A text box places a frame around a block of text. You can then position the text box anywhere in a document, and wrap the surrounding text around it. When you use *wordwrap*, the text shifts on the page so that it fits around an object. If you resize the text box, the surrounding text will again adjust to wrap around it.

The frame and the inside of the text box can be reformatted without affecting the surrounding text. You can either create a text box and type text within it, or cut and paste existing text into it.

Create a text box frame

In this exercise, you create a text box frame.

1. Press Ctrl+End to move the insertion point to the end of the document.
2. Scroll up and click anywhere in the table containing the Pacific Books branch locations.

3. On the Table menu, point to Select, and then click Table.

   The table containing the Pacific Books branch locations is selected.

   Your screen should look similar to the following illustration.

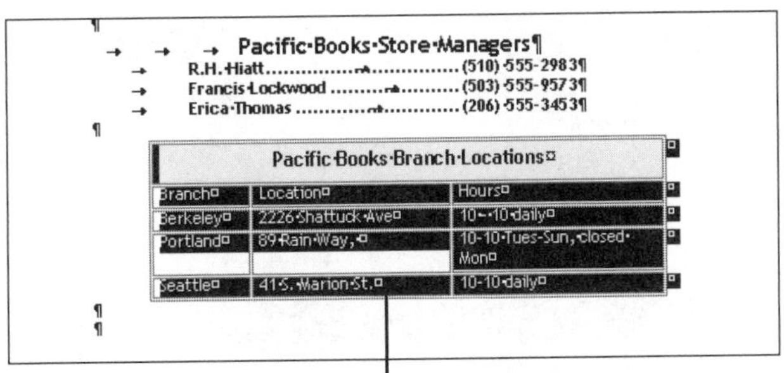

Table is selected

Cut

4. On the Standard toolbar, click the Cut button.

   The text is placed on the Clipboard.

5. On the Insert menu, click Text Box.

   The pointer changes to a plus sign.

6. Drag to create a rectangle 5 inches wide by 2 inches high.

   A blank text box and the Text Box toolbar appear.

   Your screen should look similar to the following illustration.

Text Box toolbar

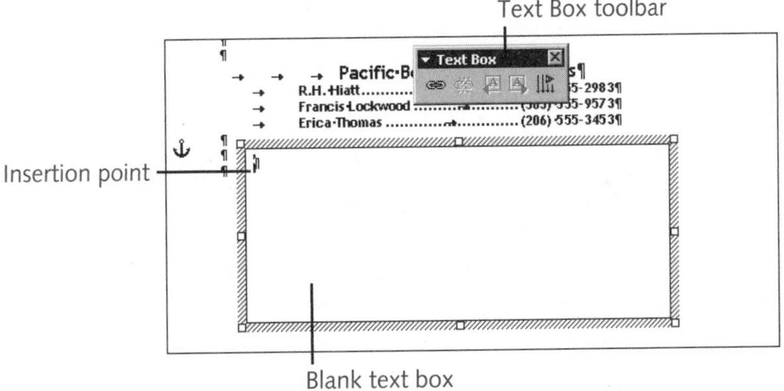

Insertion point

Blank text box

Paste

7. On the Standard toolbar, click the Paste button.

   The text from the Clipboard is pasted into the text box.

   Your screen should look similar to the following illustration.

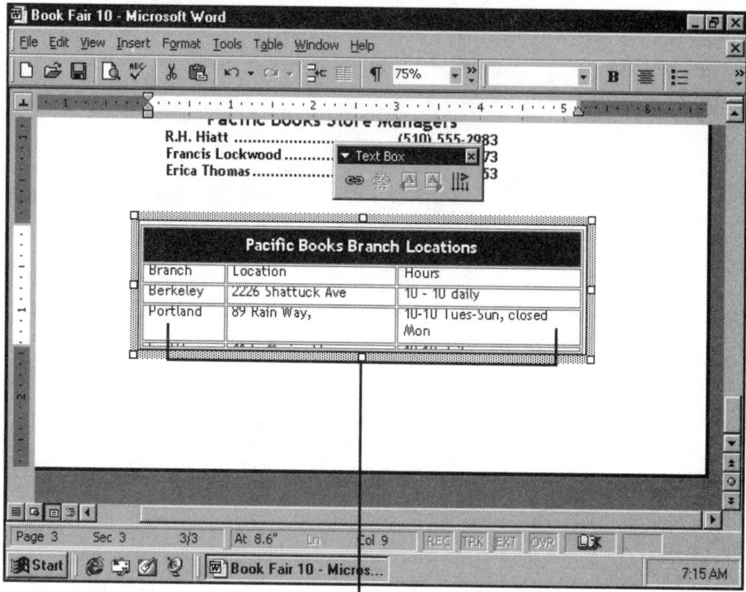

Text from Clipboard is pasted into the text box.

Size a text box

In this exercise, you resize the text box so that it better fits the size of the table.

1. Position the pointer over the bottom-middle sizing handle, which is the square box on the border.

   The pointer changes to a two-headed arrow.

2. Drag the sizing handle up to just below the last row in the table that contains the location information for the Seattle branch.

   The text box is resized to fit the table.

3. Click anywhere outside of the text box to view the result.

   Your screen should look similar to the following illustration.

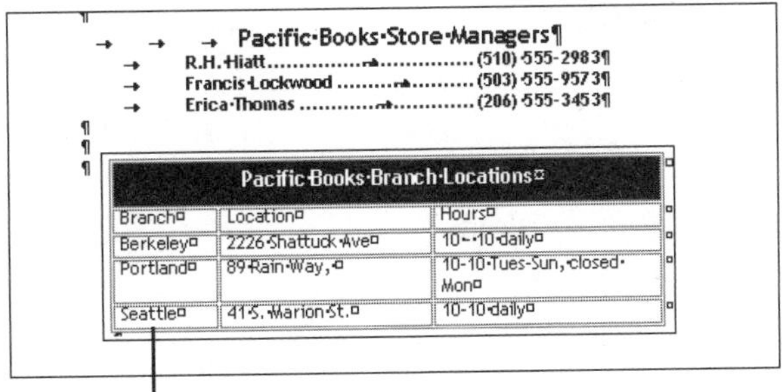

Pacific Books Store Managers

R.H. Hiatt .... (510) 555-2983

Francis Lockwood .... (503) 555-9573

Erica Thomas .... (206) 555-3453

Pacific Books Branch Locations		
Branch	Location	Hours
Berkeley	2226 Shattuck Ave	10 - 10 daily
Portland	89 Rain Way,	10-10 Tues-Sun, closed Mon
Seattle	41 S. Marion St.	10-10 daily

Resized text box

Move a text box

In this exercise, you reposition the text box.

1. Click the text box frame.

   The sizing handles are displayed.

2. Position the pointer anywhere on the text box frame, except on a sizing handle, to display the four-headed arrow.

3. Slowly drag the box up to page 2, and drop it when the text box is centered in the page below the heading *Author Look-alike Contests*.

   Your screen should look similar to the following illustration.

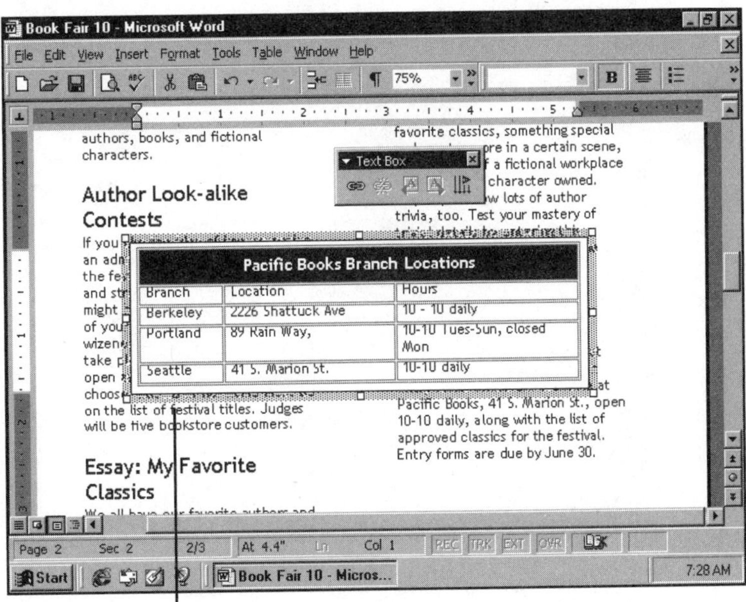

Text box in new position before text is wrapped

Use wordwrapping

In this exercise, you wrap existing text around the text box.

1. With the text box still selected, on the Format menu, click Text Box.
   The Format Text Box dialog box appears.
2. Click the Layout tab.
3. In the Wrapping Style area, click Square.
4. Click OK.
   The surrounding text is wrapped around the text box.

Format a text box

In this exercise, you format the text box with a colored border.

1. Double-click the border of the text box.
   The Format Text Box dialog box appears.
2. In the Format Text Box dialog box, click the Colors And Lines tab.
3. In the Line area, click the Color drop-down arrow, and select Dark Blue.
4. In the Line area, click the Style drop-down arrow, and select 3 pt.
5. Click OK, and then click anywhere outside of the text box to cancel the selection.
   Your screen should look similar to the following illustration.

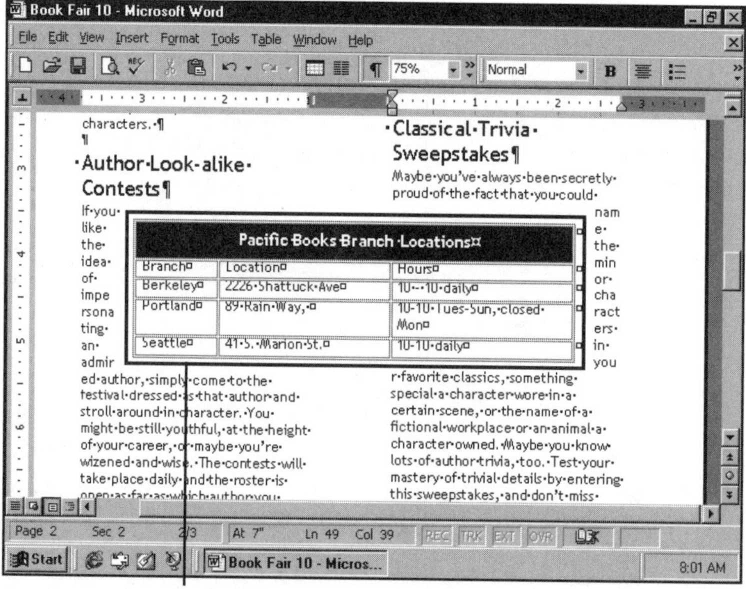

Text box in new position with text wrapped around it

Applying Drop Caps

Another special effect for enhancing your documents is *drop caps*. When you apply a drop cap to the first character of a paragraph, it adds visual interest and directs the reader's eye to the beginning of the section. The remaining text is aligned with the top of the drop cap character, creating the dropped effect. You control how many lines to drop a character; the more lines that are selected, the larger the character will be. A frame is created around a drop cap character so that the drop cap can be moved or deleted.

Insert a drop cap

If you are not working through this lesson sequentially, before proceeding to the next step, open the 10C file in the Lesson10 folder, and save it as Book Fair 10.

In this exercise, you enhance your newsletter by using a drop cap.

1. Press Ctrl+Home to move the insertion point to the beginning of the document, and click anywhere in the first paragraph beginning with the word *Coinciding*.
2. On the Format menu, click Drop Cap.

   The Drop Cap dialog box appears.
3. In the Position area, click Dropped.
4. In the Lines To Drop box, type **3**
5. Click OK.

   The C in *Coinciding* is now formatted as a drop cap.

Working with the Word Clip Gallery

Word provides a selection of graphics, or *clip art*, that you can use to liven up your documents. When you install Microsoft Word 2000, some graphics are loaded onto your hard disk. The Office 2000 CD-ROM contains additional graphics you can use. You can also insert graphics imported from other programs and locations. Some graphics file types require the installation of a specific graphics filter before the graphic can be imported into Word. The most popular graphics file types that do not require a special filter in Word include Enhanced Metafile (.emf), Joint Photographic Experts Group (.jpg), Windows Bitmap (.bmp), and Windows Metafile (.wmf) graphics. These file types can be easily imported from other programs and locations for use in Word.

Insert clip art

If you are not working through this lesson sequentially, before proceeding to the next step, open the 10D file in the Lesson10 folder, and save it as Book Fair 10.

In this exercise, you insert a piece of clip art into your document from the Word Clip Gallery.

1. Press Ctrl+End to move the insertion point to the end of the document.
2. On the Insert menu, point to Picture, and then click ClipArt.

   The Insert ClipArt dialog box appears.
3. Click in the Search For Clips box, type **Books** and then press Enter.
4. Click the first graphic in the top row.

   The Insert Clip options are displayed.

   Your screen should look similar to the following illustration.

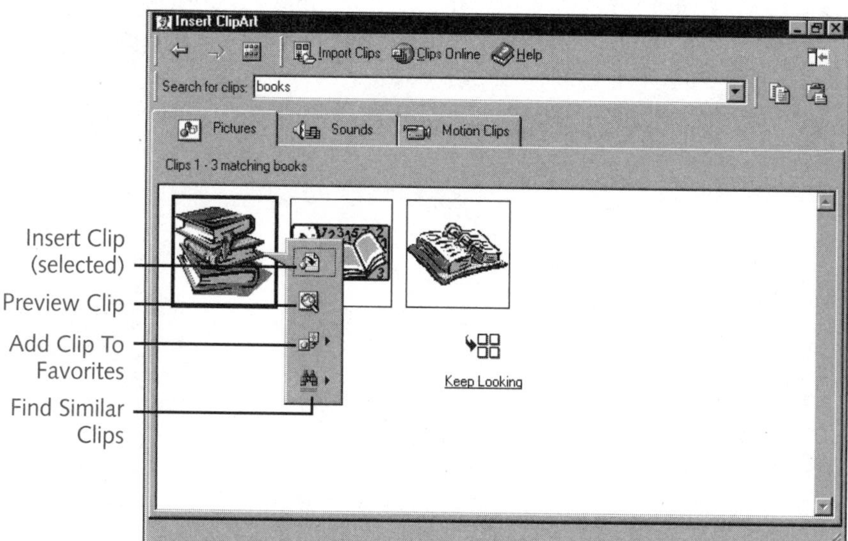

5. Click Insert Clip.
6. Close the Insert ClipArt dialog box.

   The graphic is inserted into the document.

Resize a graphic

In this exercise, you resize the graphic inserted in the previous exercise.

1. Double-click the graphic.

   The Format Picture dialog box appears.
2. Click the Size tab.

3. In the Height box, select the text, type **1.5** and then press Tab.
4. In the Width box, select the text, and type **1.5**
5. Click OK, and then click anywhere outside of the selected graphic to cancel the selection.

   The graphic is resized.

Cut and paste to move a graphic

In this exercise, you move a graphic to a new location in the document using the Cut and Paste buttons.

1. Click the graphic.

   The sizing handles appear.
2. On the Standard toolbar, click the Cut button.

   The graphic is removed from the document and placed on the Clipboard.

Cut

3. Press Ctrl+Home to move the insertion point to the beginning of the document, and then scroll down and click before the heading *Costumes* in the second column.
4. On the Standard toolbar, click the Paste button.

   The graphic is pasted back into the document.

Paste

5. Press Enter.

   The heading *Costumes* is moved down one line.

Creating Graphics with the Drawing Toolbar

Using the Drawing toolbar, you can create and format many different kinds of graphics, such as lines, arrows, stars, banners, and *callouts* (text used to call attention to pictures and graphics). You can also modify existing graphics by changing the line size or line color, or by adding a shadow or 3-D effect. When you use the WordArt button on the Drawing toolbar, you can add a special effect to text. You can add a shadow to the text; skew, rotate, and stretch the text; and you can even fit text into a predefined shape.

If you are not working through this lesson sequentially, before proceeding to the next step, open the 10E file in the Lesson10 folder, and save it as Book Fair 10.

Display the Drawing toolbar

In this exercise, you display the Drawing toolbar.

- On the Standard toolbar, click the Drawing button.

  The Drawing toolbar appears at the bottom of the Word window.

Drawing

Draw a line in a document

In this exercise, you draw a straight line in your document to begin a decorative element.

1. On page 3, click before the paragraph mark above the heading *Summer Lecture Series*.

Line

2. On the Drawing toolbar, click the Line button.

   The pointer changes to a plus sign.

3. Using the horizontal ruler at the top of the window as a guide, drag a line on the page from the 1-inch mark to the 5.5-inch mark.

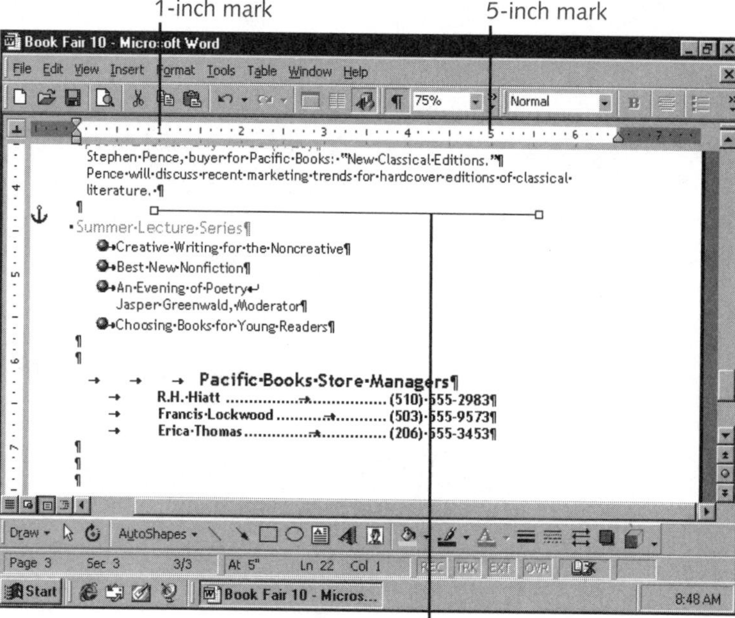

4. Click anywhere away from the line to cancel the selection.

Modify a line

In this exercise, you change the thickness and color of the line you inserted into the document in the previous exercise.

1. Click anywhere on the line.

   The sizing handles appear at each end of the line, indicating that the line is selected.

Line Style

Line Color

2. On the Drawing toolbar, click the Line Style button, and then click 4½ pt.

   The line thickness is changed to 4.5 points.

3. On the Drawing toolbar, click the Line Color drop-down arrow, and then click Dark Blue.

   The line color is changed to dark blue.

4. Click anywhere away from the line to cancel the selection.

Insert an AutoShape

In this exercise, you insert an AutoShape into the document.

1. Press Ctrl+End to move the insertion point to the end of the document.
2. On the Drawing toolbar, click the AutoShapes drop-down arrow, and point to Stars And Banners.

   Your screen should look similar to the following illustration.

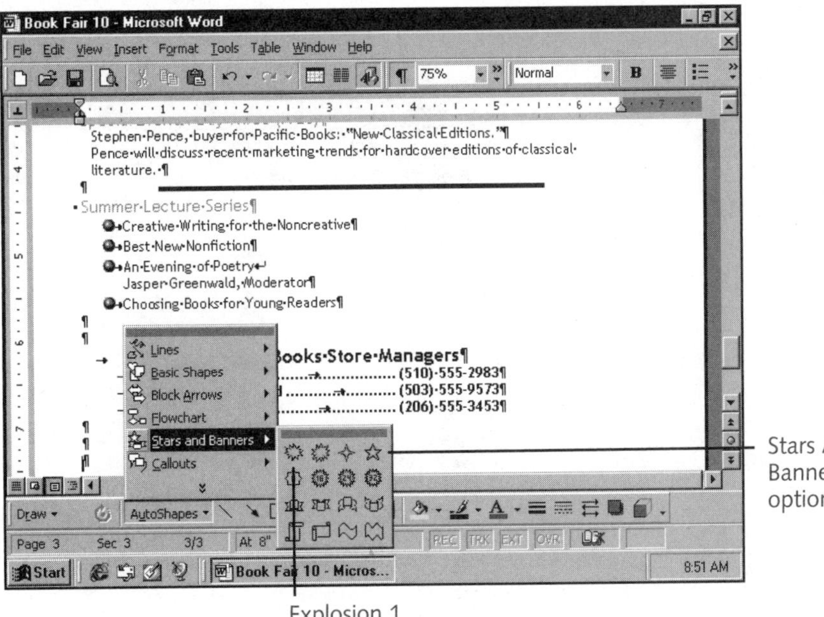

3. Click the Explosion 1 shape.
4. Click a blank area of the document.

   The AutoShape is inserted into the document.

5. Drag the lower-right sizing handle to enlarge the AutoShape.

   Your screen should look similar to the following illustration.

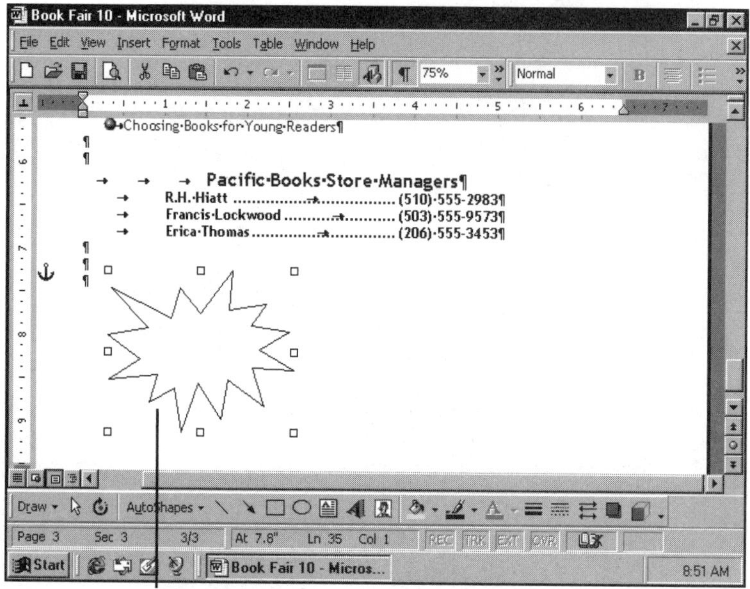

Resized AutoShape

Add text to an AutoShape

In this exercise, you add text promoting the book fair to the AutoShape.

1. Right-click anywhere near the center of the AutoShape.

   The AutoShape shortcut menu appears.

2. On the AutoShape shortcut menu, click Add Text.

   The insertion point is placed inside the AutoShape, and the Text Box toolbar is displayed.

Bold

Center

3. On the Formatting toolbar, click the Bold and Center buttons, and then type **All books 10 percent off during the book fair!**

4. Click anywhere outside of the AutoShape to cancel the selection.

Move an AutoShape

In this exercise, you reposition the AutoShape.

You can resize the AutoShape to display all the text.

1. Click the AutoShape.

   The frame and sizing handles are displayed.

2. Hover the pointer anywhere on the AutoShape frame, except on a sizing handle, to display the four-headed arrow.
3. Drag the AutoShape up page 3, and position it in the blank space to the right of the Summer Lecture Series information.
4. Click anywhere outside of the AutoShape to cancel the selection.

   Your screen should look similar to the following illustration.

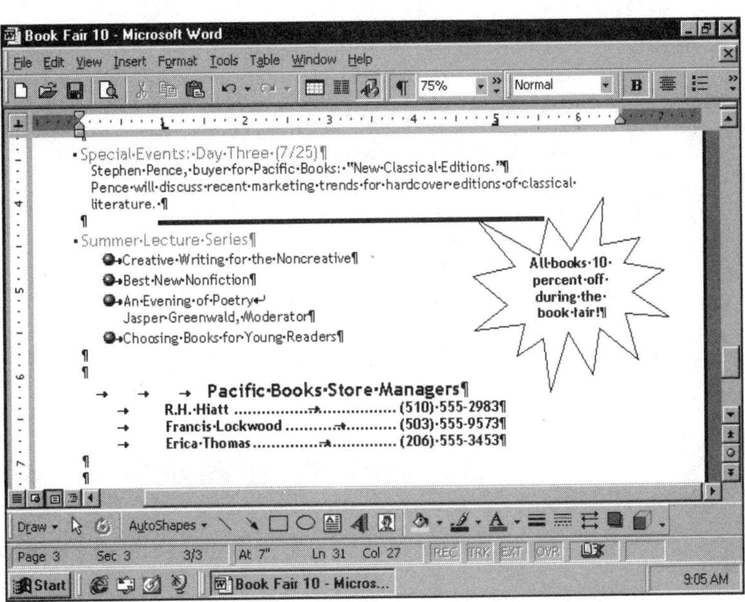

Insert a WordArt drawing object

In this exercise, you insert and reposition a WordArt drawing object in your document.

1. Press Ctrl+End to move the insertion point to the end of the document.
2. On the Drawing toolbar, click the Insert WordArt button.

   The WordArt Gallery dialog box appears.

Insert WordArt

3. In the Select A WordArt Style area, click the third button from the left on the top row.

   Your screen should look similar to the following illustration.

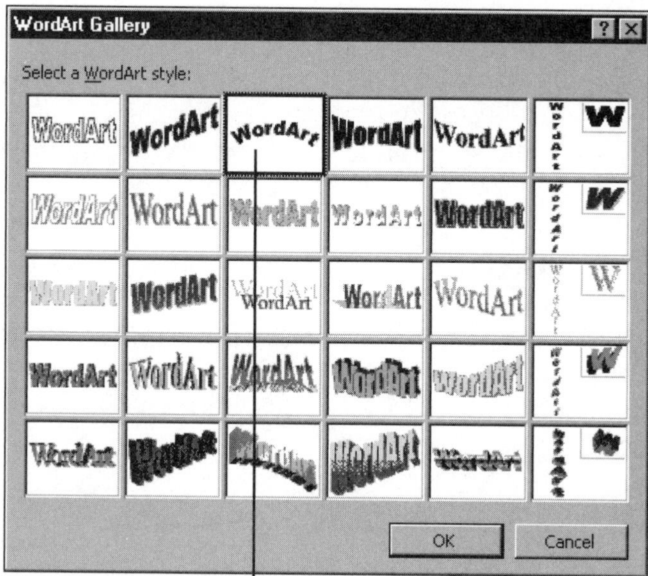

WordArt style selected

4. Click OK.

   The Edit WordArt Text dialog box appears.
5. Click the Font drop-down arrow, and select Book Antiqua.
6. Click the Size drop-down arrow, and select 16.
7. Select the text in the Text box, type **Pacific Books** and click OK.

   The WordArt object is displayed in the center of your page and the WordArt toolbar appears.
8. Drag the WordArt graphic directly below the Pacific Books store managers information.

Adding 3-D Effects and Color to Graphics

If you are not working through this lesson sequentially, before proceeding to the next step, open the 10F file in the Lesson10 folder, and save it as Book Fair 10.

After you insert a graphic, you can add three-dimensional (3-D) effects and colors to it. Both effects are applied using the Drawing toolbar.

Apply color and a 3-D effect

In this exercise, you apply color and a 3-D effect to an AutoShape graphic.

1. On page 3, select the Explosion 1 AutoShape.
2. On the Drawing toolbar, click the 3-D button.

   The 3-D options are displayed.
3. Click 3-D Style 2.

   The graphic is displayed in 3-D.

   Your screen should look similar to the following illustration.

3-D

If the Drawing toolbar is not displayed, on the Standard toolbar, click the Drawing button.

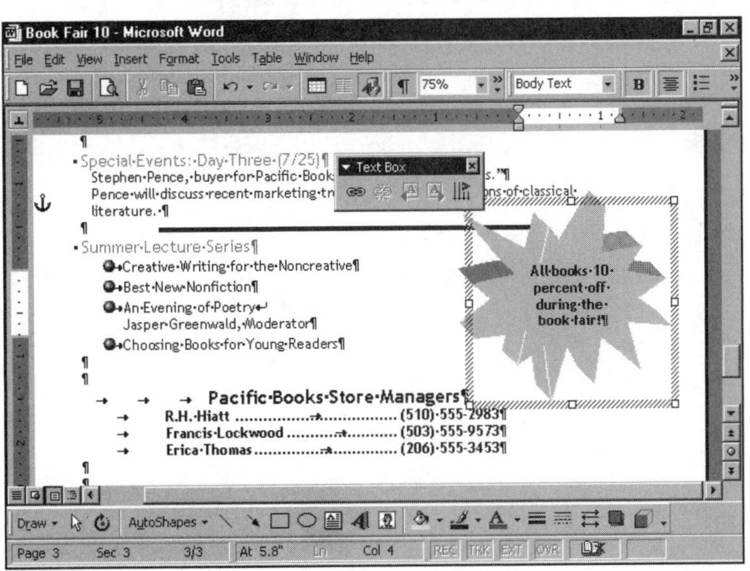

4. On the Drawing toolbar, click the Fill Color drop-down arrow, and select Dark Blue.
5. Select the text in the AutoShape.

Fill Color

Font Color

6. On the Drawing toolbar, click the Font Color drop-down arrow, and select Gold.

   Your screen should look similar to the following illustration.

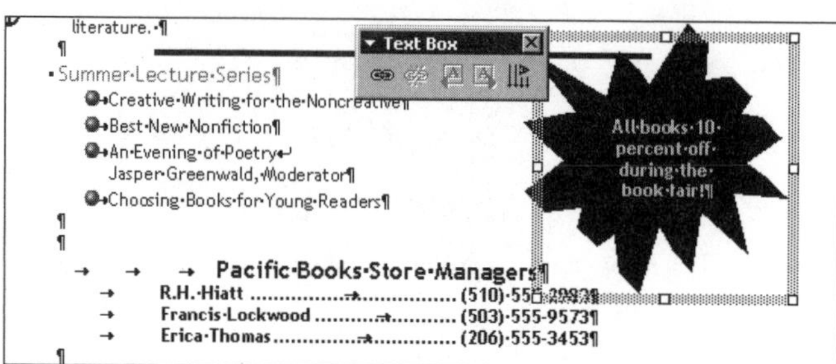

7. Click anywhere outside of the selected text to cancel the selection.

Change the orientation of a shape

In this exercise, you change the orientation of the 3-D AutoShape.

1. On page 3 of the document, select the Explosion 1 AutoShape.
2. On the Drawing toolbar, click the 3-D button.

   The 3-D options are displayed.

3-D

3. Click the 3-D Settings button.

   The 3-D Settings toolbar is displayed.

Tilt Left

4. Click the Tilt Left button five times.

   The graphic is rotated with each click.
5. Click anywhere outside of the selected graphic to cancel the selection.
6. Close the 3-D Settings toolbar.

Delete a graphic

In this exercise, you delete a graphic from your document.

1. Scroll to the bottom of page 3, and click the WordArt graphic that reads *Pacific Books*.

   The graphic frame and WordArt toolbar appear.
2. Press the Delete key.

   The graphic is deleted.

One Step Further: Creating a Self-Mailing Newsletter

Once your newsletter is complete, you will probably want to prepare it for distribution. If you plan to mail it, you can either print the newsletter and insert it into envelopes, or before printing, you can prepare it as a *self-mailer*. A self-mailer reserves one panel as an address window, which includes your return address and space for a mailing label. Because this newsletter is three pages long, the back side of the second sheet of 8.5 x 11-inch paper can be used for address information. The newsletter can then be folded in half, sealed, stamped, and mailed.

Add a return address

If you are not working through this lesson sequentially, before proceeding to the next step, open the 10G file in the Lesson10 folder, and save it as Book Fair 10.

In this exercise, you add a return address to your newsletter.

1. Press Ctrl+End to move the insertion point to the end of the document, and then press Enter repeatedly to move to the next page.
2. Scroll to the 5.5-inch mark on the vertical ruler, double-click to activate Click And Type, and then type the following return address.

   Pacific Books

   41 S. Marion

   Seattle, WA 98104

Create mailing labels

In this exercise, you create mailing labels for your newsletter.

New Blank Document

1. On the Standard toolbar, click the New Blank Document button to create a new document.
2. On the Tools menu, click Mail Merge.

   The Mail Merge dialog box appears.
3. Click Create, click Mailing Labels, and then click Active Window.
4. Click Get Data, and then click Open Data Source.
5. In the Lesson10 folder within the Word 2000 SBS Practice folder, double-click 10H, and then click Set Up Main Document.

   The Label Options dialog box appears.
6. In the Product Number list, scroll down and select 5161-Address.

7. Click OK.

   The Create Labels dialog box appears.
8. Click Insert Merge Field, select F_Name, and then press the Spacebar.
9. Click Insert Merge Field, select L_Name, and then press Enter.
10. Click Insert Merge Field, select Address, and then press Enter.
11. Click Insert Merge Field, select City, type a comma, and then press the Spacebar.
12. Click Insert Merge Field, select State, and then press the Spacebar.
13. Click Insert Merge Field, select Postal_Code, click OK, and then click Close.

    The main document is displayed with the label information.

Finish the mailing labels

For more information about mail merging, see Lesson 9, "Mail Merging."

In this exercise, you save the main document with the label information and merge the document to create a mailing for the newsletter.

Save

Merge To New Document

1. On the Standard toolbar, click the Save button.
2. Be sure the Lesson10 folder is displayed.
3. In the File Name box, type **Newsletter Labels**
4. Click Save.
5. On the Mail Merge toolbar, click the Merge To New Document button.

Close the merged document

In this exercise, you close the merged document.

1. On the File menu, click Close.
2. Click No when you are prompted to save the file.

   You do not need to save this file because you can quickly create another one from the main document called Newsletter Labels.

Finish the lesson

1. On the Standard toolbar, click the Save button.

   Changes to Book Fair 10 are saved.
2. On the File menu, click Close.
3. On the File menu, click Exit.

Lesson 10 Quick Reference

To	Do this	Button
Create columns	On the Standard toolbar, click the Columns button, and select the number of columns.	
Modify column width	On the Format menu, click Columns, and select the Equal Column Width check box. In the Width text box, select the width size, and type the new width size. Click OK.	
Insert a column break	On the Insert menu, click Break. Select the Column Break check box, and click OK.	
Insert a next page break	On the Insert menu, click Break. Select the Next Page check box, and click OK.	
Preview a document's layout	On the Standard toolbar, click the Print Preview button.	
Create a text box	On the Insert menu, click Text Box. Drag to create a box.	
Resize a text box	Select the inserted text box and drag one of the sizing handles.	
Move the text box	Select the text box and then position the pointer anywhere on its frame except on a sizing handle. When the four-headed pointer appears, drag the box to the new location.	
Wrap text around a text box	Select the text box. On the Format menu, click Text Box, and then click the Layout tab. In the Wrapping Style area, select an option. Click OK.	
Format a text box	Double-click the border of the text box to display the Format Text Box dialog box. Click the Colors And Lines tab. Select line color, line size, and any other formatting options. Click OK.	

Lesson 10 Quick Reference

To	Do this	Button
Insert a drop cap	Click in front of the character to which you want to apply the drop cap. On the Format menu, click Drop Cap. In the Position list, select the Dropped option. In the Lines To Drop box, type the number of lines to drop. Click OK.	
Insert clip art	On the Insert menu, point to Picture, and then click ClipArt. Click the graphic to insert, and then click Insert Clip. Click Close.	
Cut and paste to move a graphic	Click the graphic. On the Standard toolbar, click the Cut button. Click a new location. On the Standard toolbar, click the Paste button.	 
Size a graphic	Double-click a graphic. In the Format Picture dialog box, click the Size tab. Change the height and width. Click OK.	
Display the Drawing toolbar	On the Standard toolbar, click the Drawing button.	
Draw a line	On the Drawing toolbar, click the Line button. Drag to create a line.	
Insert an AutoShape	On the Drawing toolbar, click the AutoShapes button. Point to an AutoShape option and click the AutoShape type. Click a blank area of the document.	
Add text to an AutoShape	Position the pointer anywhere on the AutoShape, and right-click. Click Add Text, and then type text.	
Insert WordArt	On the Drawing toolbar, click the Insert WordArt button. Click a WordArt style, and click OK. Click the Font drop-down arrow, and select a font. Click the Size drop-down arrow, and select a font size. Select the text in the text box, and enter your own text. Click OK.	
Create a 3-D shape	Select the AutoShape to apply a 3-D effect. On the Drawing toolbar, click the 3-D button. Click a 3-D style to use.	

Designing Web Pages

In this lesson you will learn how to:

- ✔ *Save a Word document as a Web page.*
- ✔ *Design a Web page.*
- ✔ *View a Web page in a Web browser.*
- ✔ *Add controls to a Web page.*
- ✔ *Submit information to the Internet.*
- ✔ *Create a bookmark hyperlink.*
- ✔ *Add a background sound to a Web page.*

ESTIMATED TIME **40 min.**

With the growing interest in Web sites on the Internet, you may find that your job requires Web authoring skills too. New Web authoring tools in Microsoft Word 2000 make it easier than ever to create a single Web page—or an entire Web site. You can quickly create all-new Web pages or convert existing documents to Web format.

With the new *Web Tools* toolbar, you can add Web page controls such as text and list boxes and then modify them to fit your needs. Also, you can give your Web page color and character by applying one of the many design themes in Word 2000.

New! 2000

As you work on your Web page design, the new *Web Layout* view gives you an idea of how the design elements will look in a Web browser. For a more precise view, the new *Web Page Preview* command opens your browser and displays your page—without connecting to the Internet. For speed and simplicity when designing Web pages, you can choose one of a number of new Web page templates or the Web Page Wizard. With these new tools, you start with a predesigned page and simply fill in your own content.

At Impact Public Relations, you produce content for both print and electronic media. For example, you created a contest entry form for your client Pacific Books that can be printed and filled in by hand. Now you want to modify it for use on the Pacific Books Web site by adding online controls, such as text boxes, and design features that make it effective online. In this lesson, you convert the entry form document to a Web page, adding a picture, a theme, other design elements, and controls in which users will type information.

More Buttons

important

The default toolbar setting in Microsoft Word 2000 displays both the Standard and Formatting toolbars in one row at the top of the document window, just below the menu bar. This gives you maximum workspace. While working through the exercises in this book, toolbar buttons you need may not initially be visible. If a toolbar button is not visible, click one of the two More Buttons drop-down arrows on the toolbar to locate the button you need. When you select a new toolbar button, it is automatically added to the visible portion of the toolbar, replacing one that is not used as often.

Start Word and open a practice file

In this exercise, you start Word and open a practice file.

1. On the Windows taskbar, click the Start button.
   The Start menu appears.
2. On the Start menu, point to Programs, and then click Microsoft Word.
   Microsoft Word 2000 opens.
3. On the Standard toolbar, click the Open button.
   The Open dialog box appears.

Open

4. Click the Look In drop-down arrow, and then select your hard disk.
5. In the list of folders, double-click the Word 2000 SBS Practice folder, and then double-click the Lesson11 folder.
6. In the file list, double-click the 11A file to open it.
   The document opens in the document window.

Saving Documents as Web Pages

In Word, you can save a document as a Web page, preserving much of its formatting in the Web page version while retaining the original formatting in the Word document. When a document is saved as a Web page, it is converted to *Hypertext Markup Language* (HTML) format. This format allows the file to be displayed by a *browser*, such as Microsoft Internet Explorer, on the World Wide Web.

To save a document as a Web page, you use the new Save As Web Page command on the File menu. Once a document has been saved, its file name extension changes from .doc to .htm, and the document view changes to Web Layout view. The New Blank Document button on the Standard toolbar changes to the New Web Page button.

Web browsers do not support certain types of document formatting, such as decorative borders and multiple text columns. If your document contains formatting that isn't supported by your browser, a message appears when you try to save the document as a Web page. The message lists the unsupported formatting and tells you how the current formatting will be changed. If you proceed to save the document as a Web page, the alternative formatting is applied. For example, if a document heading has a fill color with shading around the border, the heading will have just a single-line border in the Web page version.

For some types of documents, a new folder is created after the document is saved as a Web page. For example, if the document contains graphics, the graphics are stored in files that are separate from the Web page, and these files are located in the new folder. The new folder is automatically named, based on the name of the Web page, and it is in the same file location as the Web page. The Web page and its supporting folder must be in the same file location to ensure that all the elements of the Web page will be displayed.

At Impact Public Relations, you've created a contest entry form for your client's book fair. Now you will convert the document to Web page format so you can display it on the client's Web site and add features to it that make it usable and attractive online.

tip

When you open a Web page from Windows Explorer, the page opens in your browser window. To edit the page, you need to display it in Word. To switch to Word from Microsoft Internet Explorer or from any browser, on the browser's File menu, click Edit With Microsoft Word For Windows. To open a Web page from within Word, follow the usual procedure for opening a file: on the Standard toolbar, click the Open button, and select the Web page to open.

Save a document as a Web page

In addition to the Entry Form 11 Web file, Word 2000 creates a folder containing all of the associated Web pages and supporting files.

In this exercise, you save file 11A as a Web page and then rename it.

1. On the File menu, click Save As Web Page.

   The Save As dialog box appears. In the File Name box, the 12A file now has an .htm filename extension, and in the Save As Type box, the file type is now Web Page.
2. Be sure that the Lesson11 folder appears in the Save In box.
3. In the File Name box, select the text, and then type **Entry Form 11**
4. Click Save.

   The document is saved as a Web page, and the view in the Word window changes from Print Layout view to Web Layout view.

   Your screen should look similar to the following illustration.

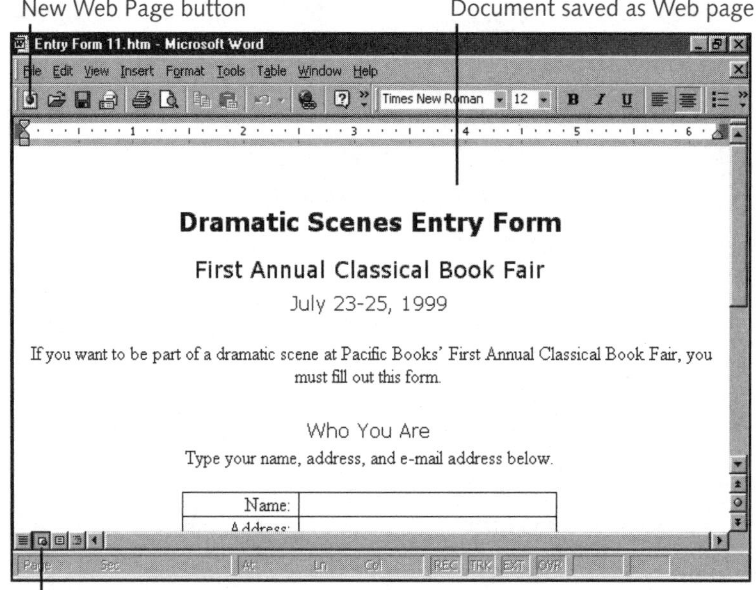

When you save a document as a Web page, you can choose to publish it directly to the Web. This is discussed in Lesson 12, "Editing and Publishing Web Pages."

tip

You can customize Word so that all new documents automatically open in Web Layout view and default to a Web page, or .htm, file type when you save a new document. On the Tools menu, click Options. In the Options dialog box, click the Save tab. In the Save Word Files As list, select Web Page (*.htm, *.html), and click OK.

Display nonprinting characters

To make it easier to edit your document, you can display nonprinting characters, such as paragraph marks and space marks, on your screen.

Show/Hide ¶

- If nonprinting characters are not currently displayed, on the Standard toolbar, click the Show/Hide ¶ button.

Designing Web Pages

To help you design a Web page or document, Word 2000 includes design themes that you can apply with one simple command. To set off a heading or other section of a Web page, you can insert a horizontal line that is styled to fit your theme. You can also alter font colors in the theme. Another way to make a Web page attractive is to insert a graphic using a picture from the Clip Gallery.

In Word, you design a Web page in Web Layout view. This view displays your page in HTML format and gives you a good idea of how the page will look in a Web browser. To actually see your page in a browser, use the Web Page Preview command as you work. This command opens your Web browser and displays the current Web page. You can then resume designing the page in Word.

To use the Web Page Preview command, you don't have to be connected to the Internet. However, you must have a Web browser, such as Internet Explorer, installed on your computer. This lesson uses the Microsoft Internet Explorer Web browser.

tip

As discussed earlier in this lesson, some Word formatting is not supported in Web browsers. To avoid using formatting that isn't supported by your browser, on the Tools menu, click Options. In the Options dialog box, on the General tab, click the Web Options button. Select the Disable Features Not Supported By option, and then select the type of browser that you use.

Using Web Page Templates and the Web Page Wizard

The exercises in this lesson help you build a Web page that's been converted from a Word document. However, there are several other ways you can create a Web page in Word 2000. If you want to start with a page that already has heading styles, hyperlinks, and page layout, you can use one of the new Web page templates. These range from a simple page with very basic formatting, to a page with left-aligned or right-aligned text columns and space for art, to a table of contents page with hyperlinks.

If you want to create an entire Web site, as well as get help with designing your Web pages, you can use the *Web Page Wizard*. The wizard gives you choices for page layout, navigation, and design. You can add your own pages or templates to the site, and the wizard helps you organize them and choose a theme. Then you can embellish and change the pages as you wish.

You can also start with a new, blank page that you design from scratch, with no built-in styles or design.

Create a Web page using a template

1. On the File menu, click New.

   The New dialog box appears.
2. Click the Web Pages tab.
3. On the Web Pages tab, click the type of Web page you want, and click OK.

   The selected Web page is displayed.
4. Fill in the Web page with your own content, and then save your new page.

Create a Web page or site using the Web Page Wizard

1. On the File menu, click New.

   The New dialog box appears.
2. Click the Web Pages tab.
3. On the Web Pages tab, click the Web Page Wizard icon, and then click OK.

   The first screen in the wizard appears.
4. Complete the steps in the wizard to create a new page or Web site.

Start with a blank Web page

1. On the File menu, click New.

   The New dialog box appears.

2. Click the General tab.
3. On the General tab, click the Web Page icon, and then click OK.
   A blank page appears in Web Layout view.
4. Design the Web page, and then save it.

If you are not working through this lesson sequentially, before proceeding to the next step, open the 11B file in the Lesson 11 folder, and save it as Entry Form 11.

In the following exercises, you make design changes to the Entry Form 11 Web page to enhance its appearance online. The original document already had centered text and tables; you apply a theme, change font colors, insert a decorative horizontal line, and add a graphic. You also use the Web Page Preview command as you work to preview your page in a Web browser.

Apply a theme

In this exercise, you apply a theme to the Web page.

New! 2000

1. On the Format menu, click Theme.
   The Theme dialog box appears.
2. In the Choose A Theme list, scroll down and select Poetic.
   In the Sample area, a preview of the theme is displayed.
   If a message appears, asking you to click Install in order to see the theme preview, insert the Microsoft Office 2000 CD and then click Install.
   Your screen should look similar to the following illustration.

For more about using themes in Word documents, see Lesson 7, "Formatting Pages and Working with Styles and Themes."

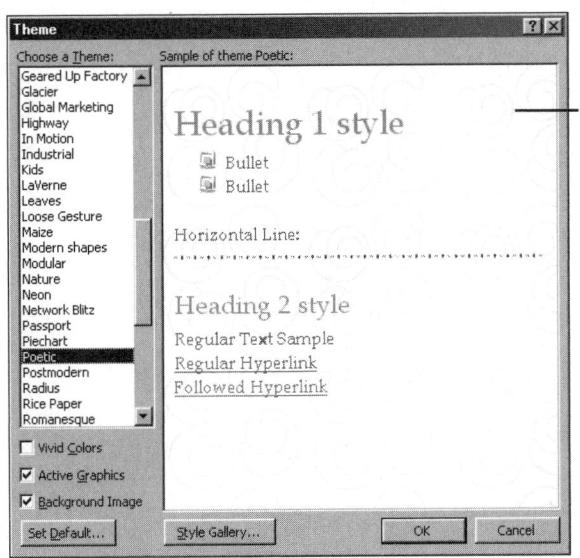

Theme sample shows background design, font styles, picture bullets, colors, and a horizontal line.

3. Click OK to apply the theme to the page.

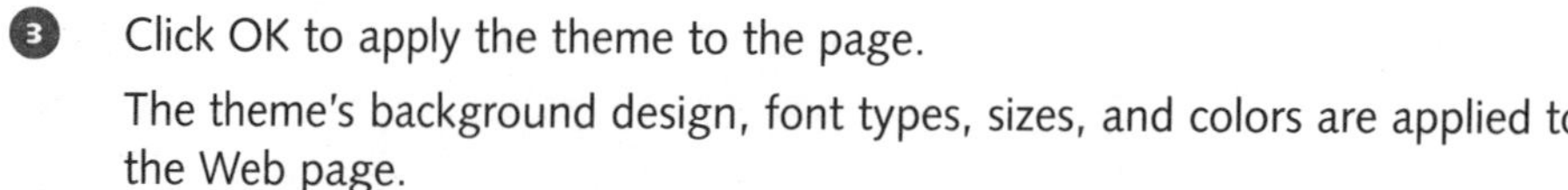

The theme's background design, font types, sizes, and colors are applied to the Web page.

Save

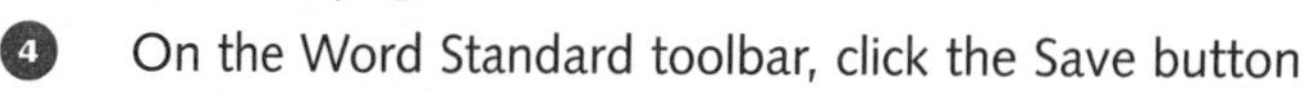

4. On the Word Standard toolbar, click the Save button.

Change heading colors

In this exercise, you continue to fine-tune the entry form by changing the headings to a darker color.

1. On the Web page, drag to select the first three headings, from *Dramatic Scenes Entry Form* through *July 23-25, 1999*. You can include ending paragraph marks in the selection.

Font Color

If the Font Color button is not visible, on the Formatting toolbar, click the More Buttons drop-down arrow to locate the button.

2. On the Formatting toolbar, point to the Font Color drop-down arrow.

   The Font Color palette is displayed.
3. Click Dark Blue.
4. Click anywhere outside of the selection to cancel it.

   The three headings now appear in dark blue.
5. Select the heading *Who You Are*, and then press the F4 key.

   Your last command is repeated, changing the heading color to dark blue.
6. Select the heading *Your Scene*, and then press F4.

   All the headings in your entry form are now dark blue.

Add a horizontal line

In this exercise, you add a horizontal line to emphasize the heading.

1. Scroll to the top of the page, and then click before the paragraph mark directly under the heading *July 23-25, 1999*.
2. Right-click any toolbar, and then click Tables And Borders.

   The Tables And Borders toolbar appears.

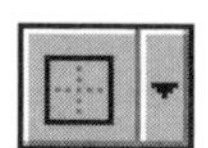

Outside Border

3. Click the Outside Border drop-down arrow to display the border options.

   If you don't see the Outside Border ScreenTip on the toolbar, the most recent border you applied from this toolbar will be named in the ScreenTip. Click the drop-down arrow next to it.

Horizontal Line

4. Click Horizontal Line.

   A decorative line in the style of the Poetic theme is inserted.

   Your screen should look similar to the following illustration.

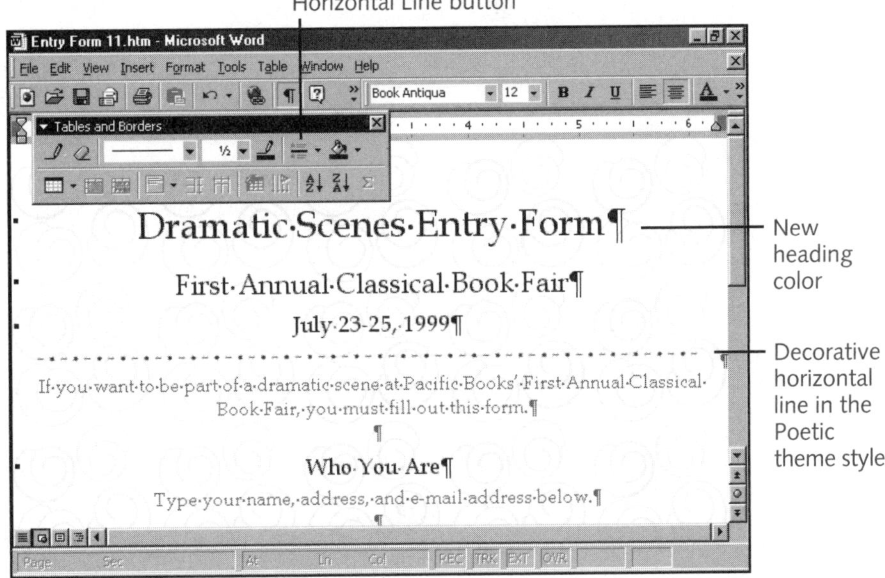

Save

5. On the Standard toolbar, click the Save button.
6. Right-click any toolbar, and then click Tables And Borders.

   The Tables And Borders toolbar closes.

Insert a picture

In this exercise, you add a picture from the Clip Gallery to your page.

1. Click before the paragraph mark above the first heading on the Web page.
2. On the Insert menu, point to Picture, and then click ClipArt.

   The Insert ClipArt dialog box appears.
3. In the Search For Clips box, click to select the text, type **drama** and then press Enter.

   A clip or clips that match the search keyword are displayed.
4. Click the first clip in the top row (its ScreenTip is Theatrical Productions, and it shows smiling and frowning masks).

   A shortcut menu is displayed.

Insert Clip

5. On the menu, click the Insert Clip button, and then close the Insert ClipArt dialog box.

   The picture is displayed at the top of the Web page. At its current size, it takes up a large portion of the window.

Resize a picture

In this exercise, you reduce the size of the picture so that it takes up only a small part of the page.

1. On the Web page, click the inserted picture.

   The picture is selected, surrounded by a border with sizing handles in the four corners, and the Picture toolbar appears.

   Your screen should look similar to the following illustration.

2. Point to a sizing handle in any corner of the picture and, when the pointer changes to a double-headed arrow, drag the corner inward diagonally until the selection border is about 1-inch square.
3. Release the mouse button, and then click outside the selection to cancel it.

   The picture is resized. (You may have to scroll to see the picture.)
4. Close the Picture toolbar.

   Your screen should look similar to the following illustration.

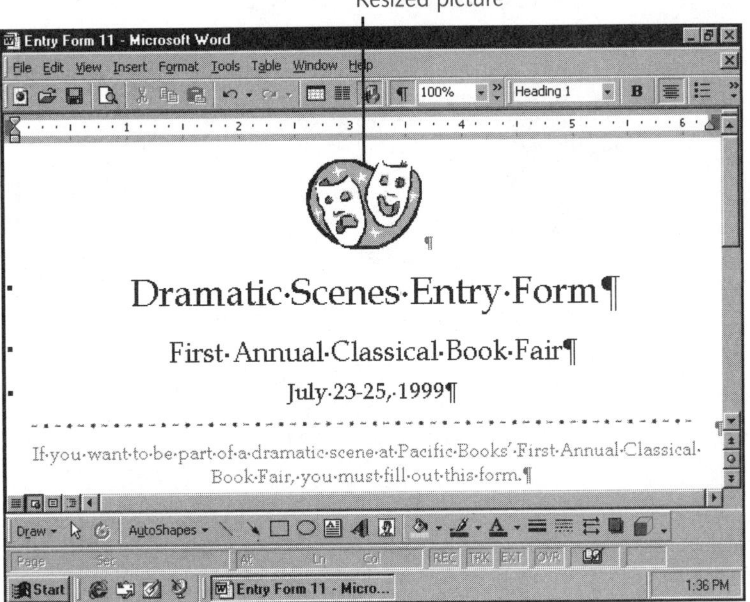

Preview changes in the browser

In this exercise, you view your Web page in the browser to see how the theme, inserted graphic, new font color, and horizontal line look.

1. On the File menu, click Web Page Preview.

   Your browser window opens and displays the current Web page. The browser applies a temporary, descriptive name to the Web page, *Dramatic Scenes Entry Form*, which appears in the browser's title bar.

   Your screen should look similar to the following illustration.

Web page previewed in the Web browser

2. To resume your editing in Word, close the browser window.

   The Word window becomes active.

Save

3. On the Standard toolbar in Word, click Save to save changes to Entry Form 11.

> **tip**
>
> If you are using Microsoft Internet Explorer 5.0, you can leave the browser window open and switch to Word from within the browser. To switch to Word, on the File menu in the browser, click Edit With Microsoft Word For Windows. The Word window containing the Web page becomes the active window. The next time you click the Web Page Preview command in Word, the browser window becomes active and displays your latest changes.

Adding Controls to Web Pages

Using the new Word 2000 Web Tools toolbar, you can add controls such as text boxes, option buttons, and drop-down lists to a Web page. These controls are designed for a Web page, or HTML, file format. For each control, you can set properties, such as width of the control, its label, and the total number of characters a user can type.

After you insert a control using the Web Tools toolbar, the Design Mode button is activated and is displayed as a floating button on your screen. When the Design Mode button is activated, you can apply properties to the control, such as width and character limit. When the Design Mode button is not activated, you cannot design the control, but you can use it. For example, you can type text into a text box. When you click the floating Design Mode button to turn it off, the floating button disappears, but the button is still available on the Web tools toolbar. To activate the Design Mode button, click the button on the Web tools toolbar.

On Entry Form 11, you want to include several text boxes and other controls so that users can type information on the form. In the following exercises, you use the Web Tools toolbar to insert these controls.

Using Text Box Controls

For a discussion about controls you can use in electronic forms, see Lesson 8, "Using Templates and Forms."

A text box is one of the most common Web page controls. It is an empty box in which a user types information, such as a name and address. Among the properties you can set for the text box are character limit for the name, and the width and height of the box.

> **tip**
>
> Some Web page controls require *scripts*, types of computer code, to make them function. For example, you might want to include a counter-type control in your Web page that keeps track of the number of visitors to the page. Such a control requires Web scripting. Microsoft Word 2000 provides the Microsoft Script Editor, which you can open from the Web Tools toolbar, as a tool for scripting. For more information about scripting in Word, open Microsoft Word Help, and search using the keywords *creating scripts.*

Add a text box

If you are not working through this lesson sequentially, before proceeding to the next step, open the 11C file in the Lesson11 folder, and save it as Entry Form 11.

In this exercise, you add a text box to a table in Entry Form 11.

1. Right-click any toolbar, and then click Web Tools.

   The Web Tools toolbar appears.

2. On the Web page, scroll to the table under the *Who You Are* heading, and click in the empty cell in the Name row.

Text Box

3. On the Web Tools toolbar, click the Text Box button.

   A text box control is inserted, and section lines appear at the top and bottom of the table, designating it as a form.

   Your screen should look similar to the following illustration.

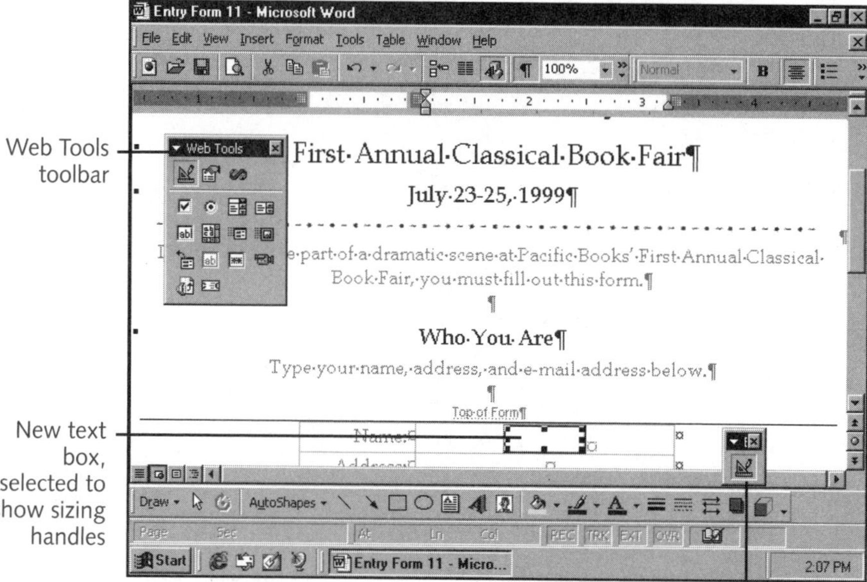

You can also open the Properties dialog box by right-clicking the control and then selecting Properties from the shortcut menu.

4. Double-click inside the text box.

   The Properties dialog box appears.

Properties dialog box for the new text box

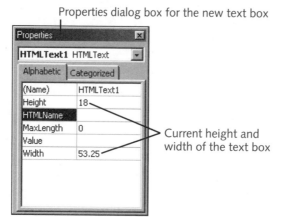

Properties

HTMLText1 HTMLText

Alphabetic | Categorized

(Name)	HTMLText1
Height	18
HTMLName	
MaxLength	0
Value	
Width	53.25

Current height and width of the text box

You can also increase the size of the control by dragging its handles.

5. In the Width row, select the number, type **80.25** and press Enter.

   The text box on your Web page widens to reflect the new measurement.
6. Leave the MaxLength number at 0 so that a user isn't limited to typing a certain number of characters in the box.
7. Close the Properties dialog box.

> **tip**
>
> To learn more about what form controls you can use on a Web page and the properties you can set for them, open Microsoft Word Help, and search by using the phrase *Form controls you can use on a Web page.*

Add more text boxes

In this exercise, you copy the text box you just inserted and paste it into the Address and E-mail rows. Then you create a new text box for the Zip Code row.

1. Be sure the text box you inserted in the last exercise is selected (shows the sizing handles), and then right-click it.

   A shortcut menu appears.
2. Click Copy.
3. Click in the empty cell in the Address row, right-click, and on the shortcut menu that appears, click Paste.

   A text box is pasted into the Address row.
4. Click in the empty cell of the E-mail row (the last row in the table), and press F4 to repeat the most recent action.

   A text box is pasted into the E-mail row.
5. Click in the empty cell in the Zip Code row, and on the Web Tools toolbar, click the Text Box button.

   A text box is inserted in the Zip Code row.

Text Box

6. Double-click the text box.

   The Properties dialog box appears.
7. In the Properties dialog box, in the MaxLength row, select the number, and then type **10**
8. In the Width row, select the number, type **60** and press Enter.

   The text box in Entry Form 11 expands to the new width.
9. Close the Properties dialog box, and click outside of the new text box to cancel the selection.

Your screen should look similar to the following illustration.

Save

10. On the Standard toolbar, click the Save button.

Align text boxes in the table

In this exercise, you align the text boxes on the left side of the column.

1. In the table, move the pointer over the top of the right column until you see a black, down-pointing arrow, and then click.

   The column is selected.

Align Left

2. On the Formatting toolbar, click the Align Left button.

   All of the text boxes align to the left side of the column.

3. Click outside the selection to cancel it.

Remove the table border

In this exercise, you turn off the table border so that when your page is viewed in a browser, the controls in the table aren't surrounded by gridlines.

1. Click inside the table.
2. On the Table menu, point to Select, and then click Table.

   The table is selected.

3. On the Format menu, click Borders And Shading.

   The Borders And Shading dialog box appears.

4. On the Borders tab, in the Setting area, click None.

   In the Preview area, the sample text is shown without borders.

5. Click OK.

6. On the Web page, click outside of the selection to cancel it.

   In the browser, the text boxes and labels will appear without gridlines, though you still see gridlines when the page is viewed in Word.

Preview controls in a browser

In this exercise, you view and test the new controls in your Web browser.

1. On the File menu, click Web Page Preview.

   Your browser displays the current version of Entry Form 11.

2. In the browser, scroll down to the new text boxes.

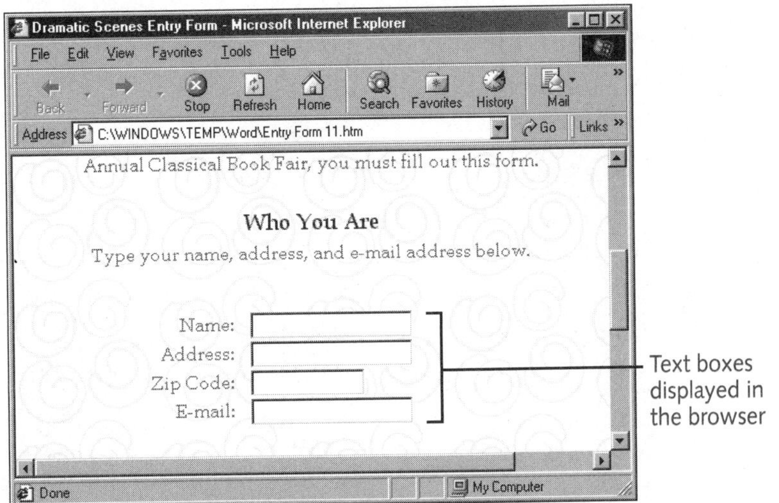

3. In the browser, in the Address box, type your address.

   If the address you type is longer than the text box, the text scrolls horizontally to accommodate the full address.

4. In the Zip Code box, type any ten-character zip code (include a hyphen, which counts as one character, after the first five numbers), and then try to type an eleventh number.

   You are limited to 10 characters, as specified when you designed the text box.

5. Close the browser window.

   The Word window is the active window.

Save

6. On the Standard toolbar in Word, click the Save button.

   Changes to Entry Form 11 are saved.

Add a text area control

In this exercise, you add a final text box, in which users can type a book title, and you add a text area control so that users can write a scene description. A text area control includes scroll bars and a large area for text.

1. In the Web page, scroll to the table below the heading *Your Scene.*
2. Click in the empty cell in the Book Title row.

Text Box

3. On the Web Tools toolbar, click the Text Box button.

   A text box is inserted, and section lines appear above and below the table, designating the area as a form.
4. Double-click the text box.

   The Properties dialog box appears.
5. In the Width row, select the number, type **100.50** and press Enter.

   The text box in the Web page is widened.
6. If necessary, drag the Properties dialog box down so you can see the Web Tools toolbar.
7. On the Web page, click in the empty cell in the Description row.

Text Area

8. On the Web Tools toolbar, click the Text Area button.

   A text area box is inserted.
9. In the Properties dialog box, in the Rows row, select the number, type **6** and then press Enter.

   The text area is sized to contain six rows of text. If the user types more than six rows of text, the text area control will scroll to accommodate the additional lines.
10. In the Width row, select the number, type **144.75** and press Enter.

    The text area control widens.
11. Close the Properties dialog box.

Align the controls

In this exercise, you align the controls and remove the table border.

Left Align

1. In the table under *Your Scene*, select the right column.
2. On the Formatting toolbar, click the Left Align button.
   The text boxes are aligned.
3. Select the table, and on the Format menu, click Borders And Shading.
   The Borders And Shading dialog box appears.
4. On the Borders tab, in the Setting area, click None, and then click OK.
   The table will now appear without borders when it is viewed in a browser.
5. On the Standard toolbar, click the Save button.

Gathering Information on the Internet

If your Web page is designed, like Entry Form 11, to gather information from a user, you need to include a *Submit control*. On the form, the control appears as a Submit button. When a user fills out the form and clicks the Submit button, the information is forwarded to another address on the Internet so that you, as the owner of the page, can process it. The Submit button appears at the end of the form so that the user can click it after filling in the form.

To make a Submit control functional, you need to specify an Internet mail address to which the information on the form can be sent. You specify the address as a property for the Submit control. The address goes in the Action row of the Properties dialog box. For more information about the Submit control, open Microsoft Help, and search using the phrase *Form controls you can use on a Web page*.

In the following exercise, you add a Submit control to your Web page and give it a label. However, the control would need additional information, as specified above, in order to actually work on the Internet.

Add a Submit button

In this exercise, you insert and label a Submit control.

Submit

1. Scroll to the bottom of Entry Form 11, and position the insertion point before the first paragraph mark under the last paragraph.
2. On the Web Tools toolbar, click the Submit button.
   A Submit control is inserted into the entry form, and section lines appear above and below the control, designating the control as a form.

3. Double-click the Submit control.

   The Properties dialog box appears.

4. In the Properties dialog box, in the Caption row, select the text, type **Submit Your Form** and press Enter.

   The control in the Web page displays this label.

5. Close the Properties dialog box.

6. On the File menu, click Web Page Preview.

   The browser window opens.

7. Scroll to view the new text area and Submit control.

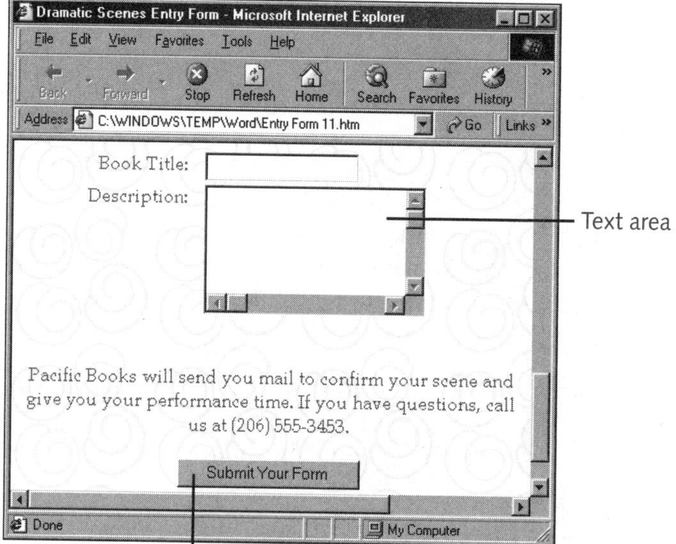

Submit control, which sends form data

8. Close the browser window.

Save

9. On the Standard toolbar in Word, click the Save button.

   Changes to Entry Form 11 are saved.

Exit Design Mode

10. On the Web Tools toolbar, click the Exit Design Mode button.

    The Design Mode is turned off.

11. On the Web Tools toolbar, click the Close button.

    The Web Tools toolbar closes.

Inserting a Bookmark Hyperlink

For information about creating hyperlinks to other Web pages, see Lesson 12, "Editing and Publishing Web Pages."

If you're familiar with the Internet, you probably know about *hyperlinks.* A hyperlink is text or a graphic that, when clicked, takes you to another Internet address, often within the current Web site. Hyperlinks make it possible to *navigate* the Web site—that is, move from page to page.

A certain kind of hyperlink, called a *bookmark,* enables you to jump between sections of a single Web page. This kind of link lets a user move quickly to a section of the page without scrolling. When you create a long Web page, it might be simpler to create links to sections of the page rather than dividing up the sections into individual Web pages and linking all of them.

In Word, you create bookmark hyperlinks by using the Insert Hyperlink dialog box. In the dialog box, when you click the Bookmark button, the sections of your document are displayed by heading. A plus sign by a heading means that there are subheadings beneath it. If you want to create a link to one of the subheadings, click the plus sign to expand the heading, and select the desired subheading.

Create a hyperlink

If you are not working through this lesson sequentially, before proceeding to the next step, open the 11D file in the Lesson11 folder, and save it as Entry Form 11.

In this exercise, you create a bookmark hyperlink that jumps to the top of the page.

1. In Entry Form 11, click before the paragraph mark at the bottom of the Web page.
2. On the Standard toolbar, click the Insert Hyperlink button.

   The Insert Hyperlink dialog box appears.

Insert Hyperlink

3. In the Insert Hyperlink dialog box, click the Bookmark button.

   The Select Place In Document dialog box appears.

   Your screen should look similar to the following illustration.

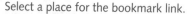

You can also press Ctrl+K to display the Insert Hyperlink dialog box.

For a demonstration of how to create a hyperlink in the Multimedia folder on the Microsoft Word 2000 Step by Step CD-ROM, double-click CreateHyperlink.

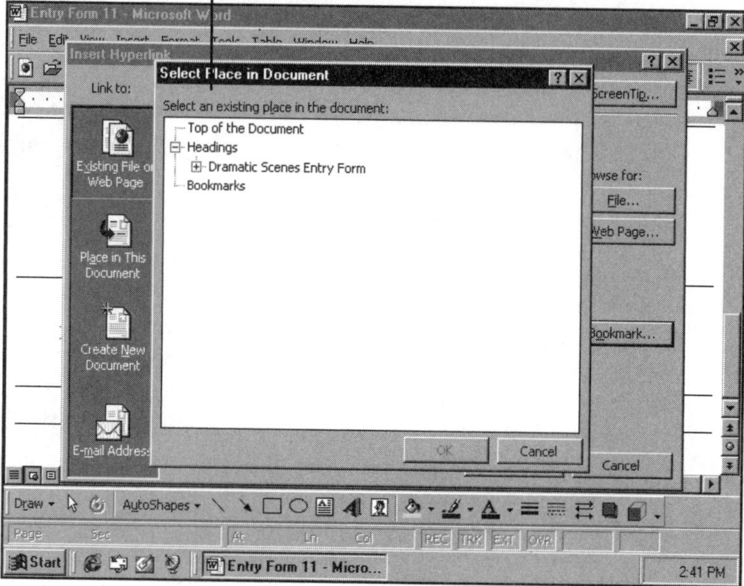

4. Click Top Of The Document, and click OK.

   In the Insert Hyperlink dialog box, in the Type The File Or Web Page Name box, the link for your bookmark appears as *#Top of the Document*.

5. In the Text To Display box, select the text, and then type **Top of Page**

6. Click the ScreenTip button.

   The Set Hyperlink ScreenTip dialog box appears.

7. In the Set Hyperlink ScreenTip dialog box, type **Return to the top of the entry form.**

   The ScreenTip will appear when you point to the hyperlink in the browser.

8. In the Set Hyperlink ScreenTip dialog box, click OK, and then in the Insert Hyperlink dialog box, click OK.

   The hyperlink *Top of Page* appears at the bottom of Entry Form 11.

9. On Entry Form 11, click the *Top of Page* hyperlink.

   The insertion point moves to the top of the page.

Save

10. On the Standard toolbar, click the Save button.

One Step Further: Adding a Background Sound

To turn off formatting marks in Word, click the Show/Hide ¶ button on the Standard toolbar.

If you are not working through this lesson sequentially, before proceeding to the next step, open the 11E file in the Lesson11 folder, and save it as Entry Form 11.

To add some fun to your Web page, you can include a *background sound* that plays whenever a user opens or returns to the page. To hear the sound, users must have a sound card installed and a browser that supports the sound file format. In this lesson, you will add a sound file with a .wav file format.

When you add the sound, you have the option of setting it to play several times or only once. Keep in mind that if you set it to the Infinite setting, the user will have no way to turn off the sound while visiting your Web page.

If you're displaying formatting marks, such as paragraph marks, in your Web page, the sound file you insert appears as a series of periods. These won't be visible in a Web browser.

Add a background sound

In this exercise, you add a background sound to Entry Form 11.

1. With Entry Form 11 displayed in the Word window, right-click any toolbar, and then click Web Tools.

   The Web Tools toolbar appears.

Sound

2. On the Web Tools toolbar, click the Sound button.

   The Background Sound dialog box appears.

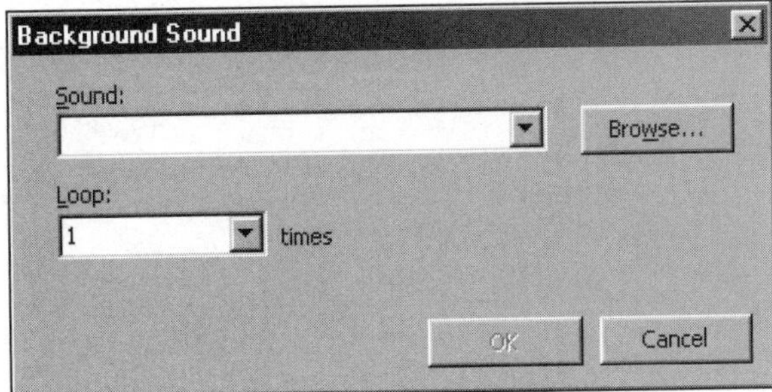

3. In the Background Sound dialog box, click Browse.

   The File Open dialog box appears, displaying sound files from the Media folder within Windows 98.

If you do not see the Tada.wav file, choose any other .wav file in the Media folder.

4. Double-click the Tada.wav. file

   The complete path to this file's location appears in the Background Sound dialog box.
5. In the Loop list, be sure that 1 is selected, and click OK.

   The sound plays, and a series of periods representing the sound control is inserted at the top of your Web page. The series of periods won't be visible in the Web browser.
6. Close the Web Tools toolbar.
7. On the File menu, click Web Page Preview.

   Your browser window appears, displaying the Web page, and the sound plays.
8. Close the browser window.

Finish the lesson

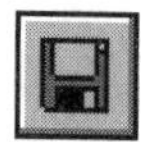

Save

1. On the Standard toolbar, click the Save button.

   Changes to Entry Form 11 are saved.
2. On the File menu, click Close.
3. On the File menu, click Exit.

Lesson 11 Quick Reference

To	Do this	Button
Save a document as a Web page	On the File menu, click Save As Web Page.	
Apply a theme	On the Format menu, click Theme, select a theme from the Choose A Theme dialog box, and click OK.	
Add a horizontal line	On the Tables And Borders toolbar, click the Outside Border drop-down arrow, and then click Horizontal Line.	
Change text colors	Select the text. On the Formatting toolbar, click the Font Color drop-down arrow to display the color palette, and then click the color of your choice.	

Lesson 11 Quick Reference

To	Do this	Button
Insert a picture from the Clip Gallery	On the Insert menu, point to Picture,and click Clip Art. Use keywords to search for the art. Click the desired image to display a menu of ClipArt buttons, and then click the Insert Clip button.	
Resize a picture	Click the picture to select it, and drag a sizing handle to resize the picture.	
Preview your page in a Web browser	On the File menu, click Web Page Preview.	
Add a text box control	Place the insertion point where you want the control. On the Web Tools toolbar, click the Text Box button.	
Set properties for a control	On the Web Tools toolbar, be sure the Design Mode button is activated. Double-click the control to display the Properties dialog box, and then specify the desired properties.	
Add a text area control	Place the insertion point where you want to insert the control. On the Web Tools toolbar, click the Text Area button.	
Add a Submit button	Place the insertion point where you want to insert the button. On the Web Tools toolbar, click the Submit button.	
Insert a bookmark hyperlink	On the Standard toolbar, click the Insert Hyperlink button. In the Insert Hyperlink dialog box, click Bookmark, and then select an area of the page to create a link to.	
Add a background sound	Position the insertion point on the Web page. On the Web Tools toolbar, click the Sound button. In the Background Sound dialog box, click Browse. Select a sound file from the Media folder in Windows 98. In the Background Sound dialog box, click OK.	

Editing and Publishing Web Pages

In this lesson you will learn how to:

- ✔ *Organize Web pages using frames.*
- ✔ *Add header and table of contents frames.*
- ✔ *Create and test Web page hyperlinks.*
- ✔ *Publish a Web page to a Web server.*
- ✔ *Use multiple themes in a frames page.*

ESTIMATED TIME
35 min.

New! 2000

The design of your Web pages often determines how effective you and your business will be in the electronic marketplace. To help you build more powerful and appealing Web pages, Microsoft Word 2000 provides a number of organizing and editing tools. Using the new *frames* feature, you can divide up a Web page into separate horizontal and vertical sections that can be designed and edited independently. One frame might include scrolling text, another might run a video, and a third could contain a table of contents with hyperlinks. The new *Frames* toolbar in Word 2000 makes it easy to add and modify frames. You can use Word 2000 themes to unify the look of the frames or to create constrast, and you can quickly add and edit hyperlinks.

Microsoft Office 2000 also enables you to publish a completed Web page directly to a server on the World Wide Web, using the *Web folders* feature. Publishing a Web page means you place the page and its supporting files on a Web server. To use the publishing features, you must have a network connection to a Web server.

If you have not yet installed this book's practice files, refer to "Using the Microsoft Word 2000 Step by Step CD-ROM," earlier in this book.

At Impact Public Relations, you are creating a Web page for your client Pacific Books. The material you use to create the Web page was originally written and designed to be used in a print document. Now you want to adapt it for use online. You insert frames for a heading and table of contents, create and edit hyperlinks, and apply themes to individual frames of the Web page.

Start Word and open a practice file

In this exercise, you start Word and open a practice file.

1. On the Windows taskbar, click the Start button.

   The Start menu appears.
2. On the Start menu, point to Programs, and then click Microsoft Word.

   Microsoft Word 2000 opens.
3. On the Standard toolbar, click the Open button.

   The Open dialog box appears.

Open

4. Click the Look In drop-down arrow, and then select your hard disk.
5. In the list of folders, double-click the Word 2000 SBS Practice folder, and then double-click the Lesson12 folder.
6. In the file list, double-click the 12A file to open it.

   The document opens in the document window.

Save a document as a Web page

For a discussion about saving documents as Web pages, see Lesson 11, "Designing Web Pages."

In this exercise, you save the 12A document as a Web page.

1. On the File menu, click Save As Web Page.

   The Save As dialog box appears. In the File Name box, the 12A file now has an .htm filename extension, and in the Save As Type box, the file type is now Web Page.
2. Be sure that the Lesson12 folder appears in the Save In box.
3. In the File Name box, select the text, and type **Book Fair 12**
4. Click Save.

   The document is saved as a Web page, and the Word window changes from Print Layout view to Web Layout view.

Display nonprinting characters

To make it easier to edit your document, you can display nonprinting characters, such as paragraph marks and space marks, on your screen.

Show/Hide ¶

- If formatting marks are not currently displayed, on the Standard toolbar, click the Show/Hide ¶ button.

Organizing Web Pages Using Frames

New! 2000

For more information about frames, see Microsoft online Help. Search using the phrase "Frames: What they are and how they work."

In Word 2000 you use frames—vertical and horizontal areas—to organize the elements of your Web pages, maximize the amount of important information on the page, make the design more interesting, and improve navigation. For example, to keep the page heading in view while the user scrolls through the page, you can insert a header frame. You also might add a video or colorful graphic to another frame, and to help users navigate the page or move quickly to other pages, you could add a table of contents frame.

When you include frames in a Web page, you are actually creating several Web pages that are bound together by a single *frames page*. The individual frames, or Web pages, exist as separate files, but the larger frames page allows you to display all the frames, and their contents, together. An existing Web page becomes a frames page when you first insert a frame into it.

Using the Frames toolbar, you can insert horizontal frames, vertical frames, and a table of contents frame. You can add frames within frames to create more horizontal and vertical spaces, if you want. The Frame Properties button on the Frames toolbar gives you options for displaying frame borders or turning them off, changing border width, and hiding or showing scroll bars. You can easily delete a frame you don't want by using the Delete Frame button.

In the following exercises, you insert a header frame into Book Fair 12, creating a new frames page. You create a heading in the horizontal frame and then insert a table of contents frame to help users navigate through the text.

Insert a header frame

In this exercise, you insert a header frame into Book Fair 12 for the Web page's heading.

1. Right-click any toolbar, and then click Frames.

   The Frames toolbar appears.
2. Drag the Frames toolbar up in the window and position it below the Standard and Formatting toolbars.
3. In Book Fair 12, click before the heading *First Annual Classical Book Fair.*
4. On the Frames toolbar, click the New Frame Above button.

A horizontal frame is inserted at the top of the page, and the title bar now says *Document2*. When you save this document, it will be a frames Web page that contains a collection of frames.

Your screen should look similar to the following illustration.

You can also create a frames page by displaying the Format menu, pointing to Frames, and then clicking New Frames Page.

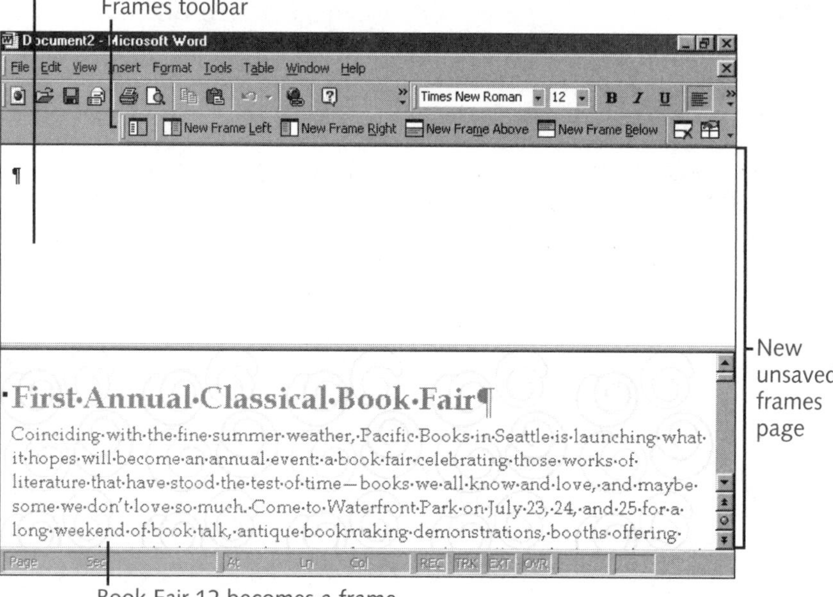

Create a heading

In this exercise, you apply a theme to the header frame, create the heading text, and then change its font size.

For more information about applying a theme to a Web page, see Lesson 11, "Designing Web Pages."

1. Click inside the new frame.
2. On the Format menu, click Theme.

   The Theme dialog box appears.
3. In the Choose A Theme list, click Poetic, and click OK.

   The Poetic theme is applied to the header frame.
4. Click in the header frame, and type **Pacific Books**

   If a message appears asking you to click Install, insert the Microsoft Office 2000 CD-ROM, and in the message box, click Install.
5. Select the new text, and on the Formatting toolbar, click the Style drop-down arrow, and then click Heading 1.

   The new text is styled as a Heading 1.

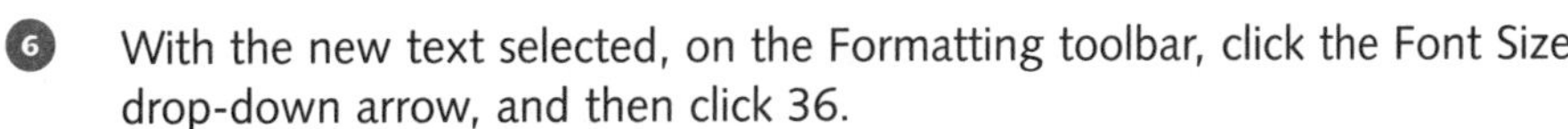

6. With the new text selected, on the Formatting toolbar, click the Font Size drop-down arrow, and then click 36.

   The new text enlarges to 36 points.

Center

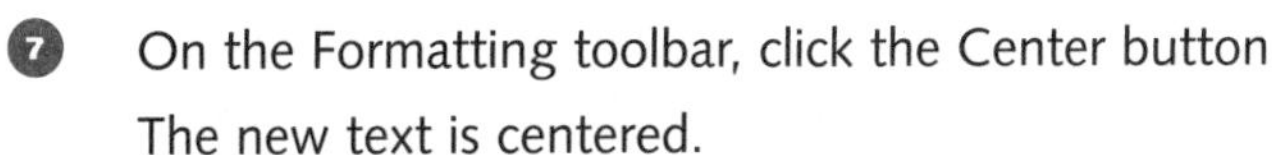

7. On the Formatting toolbar, click the Center button.

   The new text is centered.

8. Click anywhere outside of the selected text to cancel the selection.

Save the frames page

In this exercise, you save and name the new frames page.

Save

1. On the Standard toolbar, click the Save button.

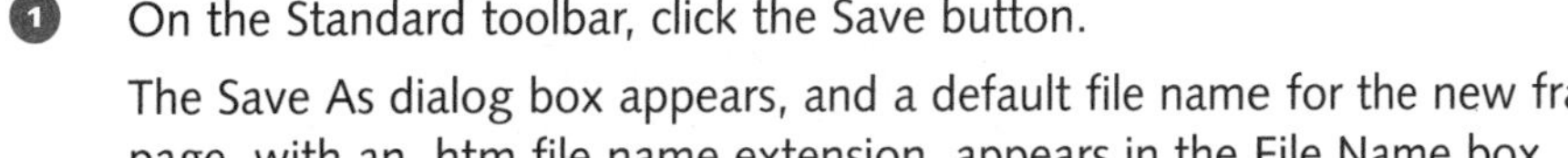

   The Save As dialog box appears, and a default file name for the new frames page, with an .htm file name extension, appears in the File Name box.

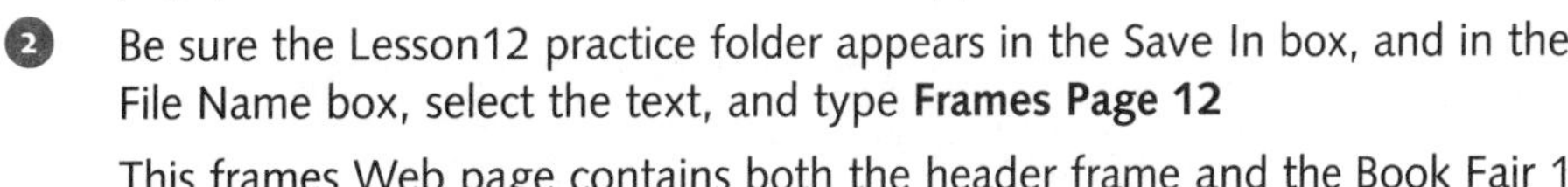

2. Be sure the Lesson12 practice folder appears in the Save In box, and in the File Name box, select the text, and type **Frames Page 12**

   This frames Web page contains both the header frame and the Book Fair 12 frame. When you save the frames page, the header frame is also given a file name, Pacific Books.htm, and is saved as a separate file.

3. Click Save.

   Your screen should look similar to the following illustration.

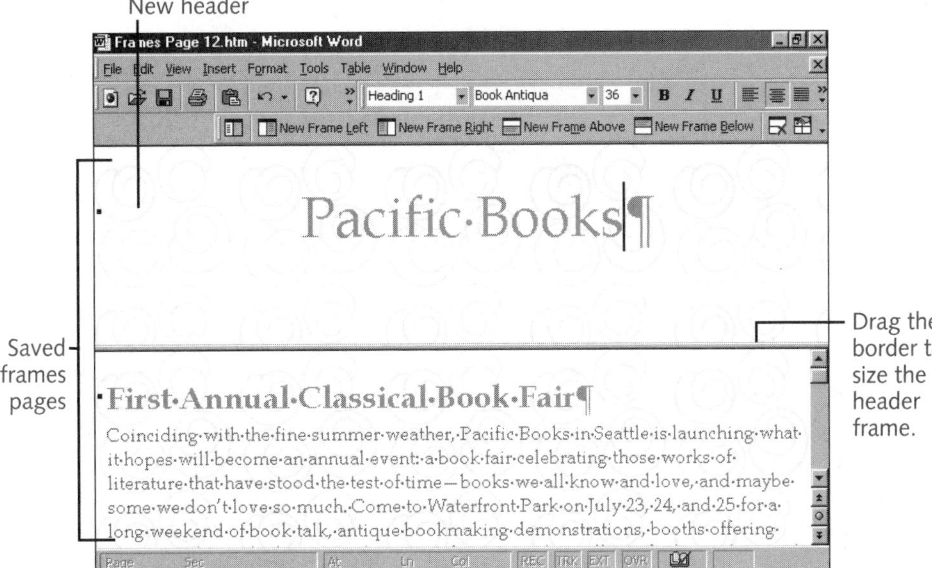

Editing/Publishing Web Pages 12

Size the header frame

You can also size frames in the Frame Properties dialog box. On the Frame tab, select a percentage, or type a measurement, and then select a number.

In this exercise, you size the header frame to fit the heading text.

- Point to the bottom border of the header frame, and when the pointer turns into a double-headed arrow, drag the border up until the frame is about 1.5 inches high.

Customize the frame borders

In this exercise, you change the color and size of the frame borders.

Frame Properties

1. On the Frames toolbar, click the Frame Properties button.

   The Frame Properties dialog box appears.
2. In the Frame Properties dialog box, click the Borders tab.

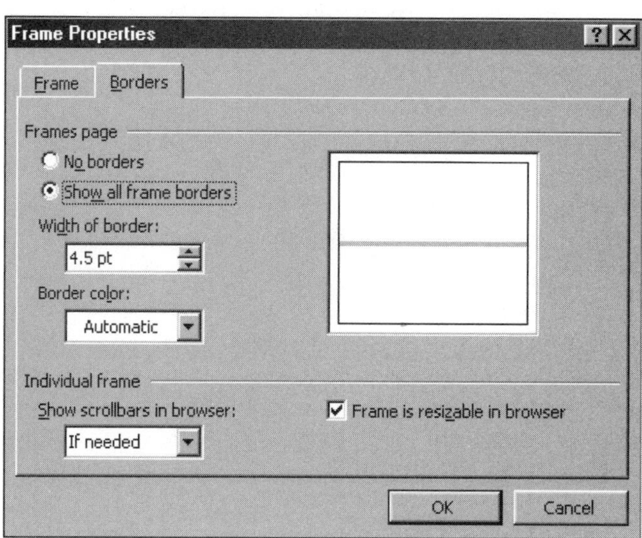

3. Click the Width Of Border up or down arrow to select 3 pt.
4. In the Border Color drop-down list, select Indigo.
5. In the Individual Frame area, in the Show Scrollbars In Browser drop-down list, be sure that If Needed is selected, and that the Frame Is Resizable In Browser check box is selected.

6. Click OK.

   In Frames Page 12, the bottom border of the header frame is narrower and its color is indigo.

Resized header frame with customized border

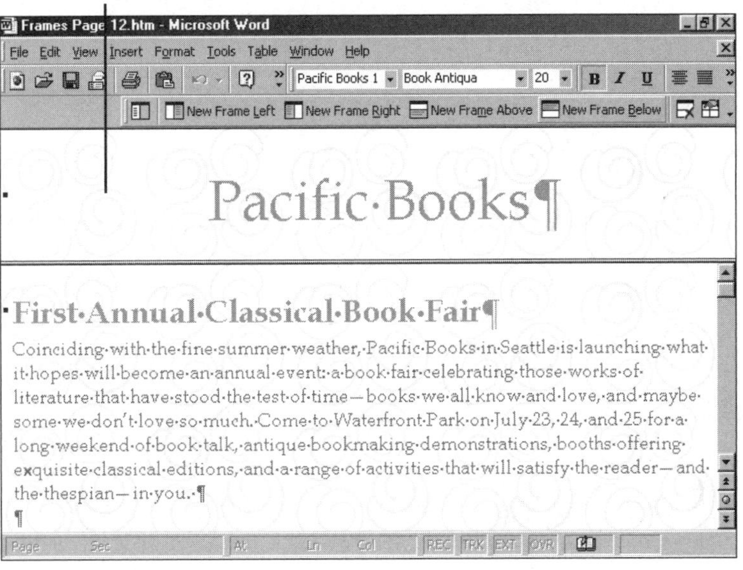

Frames Page 12.htm - Microsoft Word
File Edit View Insert Format Tools Table Window Help
Pacific Books 1
Book Antiqua
20
New Frame Left
New Frame Right
New Frame Above
New Frame Below
Pacific·Books¶
·First·Annual·Classical·Book·Fair¶
Coinciding·with·the·fine·summer·weather,·Pacific·Books·in·Seattle·is·launching·what·it·hopes·will·become·an·annual·event:·a·book·fair·celebrating·those·works·of·literature·that·have·stood·the·test·of·time—books·we·all·know·and·love,·and·maybe·some·we·don't·love·so·much.·Come·to·Waterfront·Park·on·July·23,·24,·and·25·for·a·long·weekend·of·book·talk,·antique·bookmaking·demonstrations,·booths·offering·exquisite·classical·editions,·and·a·range·of·activities·that·will·satisfy·the·reader—and·the·thespian—in·you.·¶
¶

Save

7. On the Standard toolbar, click the Save button.

> **tip**
>
> As you work on your Web page, you can view it at any time in your Web browser. You don't need to be connected to the Internet to open the browser, but you do need to have the browser program installed on your computer. To view your Web page in the browser, on the Word File menu, click Web Page Preview. The browser window opens and displays the current Web page. If you are using Microsoft Internet Explorer 5, you can switch back to Word from the browser. On the File menu of the browser, click Edit With Microsoft Word For Windows. The browser is minimized, and the Word window becomes active.

Inserting a Table of Contents Frame

You can make it easy for readers to navigate through your Web page by including a table of contents. Using the Table Of Contents In Frame button on the Frames toolbar, you can design a page so that a table of contents appears in a vertical frame on the left side of the page, and the sections it links to appear in a frame on the right. When you insert a table of contents frame, the table of contents is automatically constructed based on the headings and subheadings in your document, and it contains hyperlinks to those headings in the main text body.

After you insert the table of contents frame, you will see some HTML text that's formatted to be hidden. The text has a dotted underline at the top of the frame. This is the link to Book Fair 12, the file that appears in the right frame. The hidden text is visible because you are displaying nonprinting characters. It won't be shown in a Web browser or when you click the Show/Hide ¶ button on the Standard toolbar.

Insert a table of contents frame

In this exercise, you use the Frames toolbar to insert a table of contents frame into Frames Page 12.

1. In Frames Page 12, click before the heading *First Annual Classical Book Fair.*
2. On the Frames toolbar, click the Table Of Contents In Frame button.

Table Of Contents In Frame

   A table of contents is inserted on the left side of Frames Page 12.

   Your screen should look similar to the following illustration.

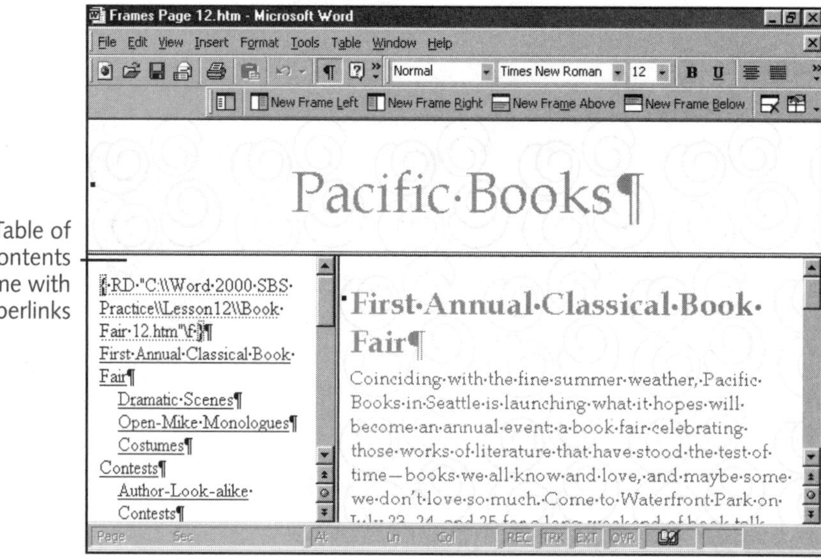

Save

3. On the Standard toolbar, click the Save button.

   The table of contents frame is saved as a separate Web page called FirstAnn.htm. It is saved in the Lesson12 practice folder.
4. Scroll through the table of contents frame to see how it looks. If you'd like more space to view the hyperlinks, drag the frame's right border to the right.
5. Right-click any toolbar, and click Frames to close the Frames toolbar. Drag frames as necessary to close any gaps.

Editing a Table of Contents Frame

Because the hyperlinks in the table of contents were created automatically, you should review them to make sure they appear and link the way you want. If you discover that some hyperlinks aren't on the right level in the table of contents hierarchy, you might have to restyle some headings in the main text body of the page. If you see hyperlinks that you don't want, convert those styles in the text body to a non-heading style, such as Normal, and the unwanted hyperlinks will disappear from the table of contents. After changing the styles, use the Update Field command to refresh the table of contents and see the results of your changes.

In the following exercises, you test hyperlinks in the table of contents. Then you remove hyperlinks and fix a hyperlink that is on the wrong level. Finally, you add a theme to the table of contents to make it consistent with the rest of the page.

Test the hyperlinks

In this exercise, you test a couple of the new hyperlinks in Frames Page 12.

1. In the table of contents frame, click the *Dramatic Scenes* hyperlink.

   The text in the right frame, Book Fair 12, jumps to the *Dramatic Scenes* heading, and the table of contents hyperlink changes color to show that you have clicked it. The Web toolbar is also displayed.
2. In the table of contents frame, click the *Schedule of Events* hyperlink.

   The text in the right frame jumps to the *Schedule of Events* heading, and the table of contents hyperlink changes color.

Remove hyperlinks

In this exercise, you remove hyperlinks from the table of contents by changing a character style in the Book Fair 12 frame.

1. In the table of contents frame, scroll to the *Pacific Books Branch Locations* hyperlink.

   Several hyperlinks appear below it, showing the hours of the Portland bookstore.

2. Click the *Pacific Books Branch Location* hyperlink.

   This section is displayed in the text in the right frame.

3. In the right frame, under the heading *Pacific Books Branch Locations*, click the word *Berkeley*, and then look at the Style box on the Formatting toolbar.

   The Style box shows that this text is styled as Normal.

4. In the right frame, in the second address of the section, click the word *Portland*, and then look at the Style box on the Formatting toolbar.

   The Style box shows that this text is styled as Heading 8. Because of its heading style, the information was automatically included as a hyperlink in the table of contents frame.

5. In the right frame, select all the text in the Portland section, from *Portland* through *closed Mon.*, and include the ending paragraph mark.

   Your screen should look similar to the following illustration.

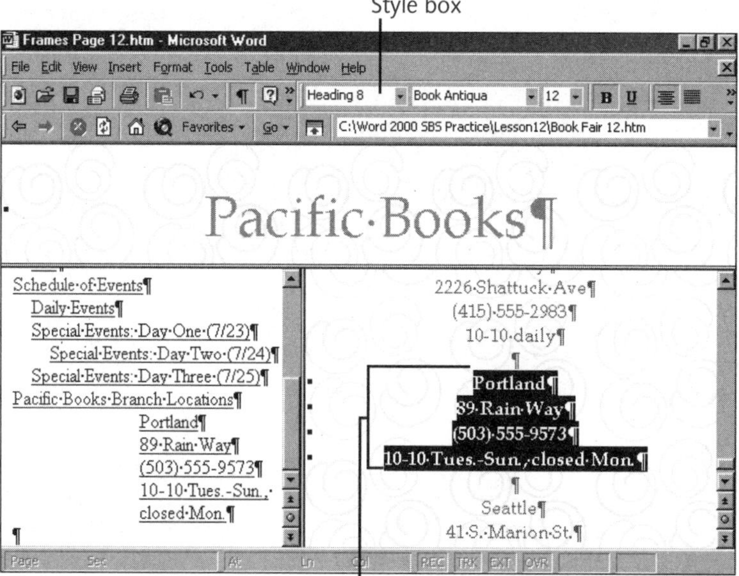

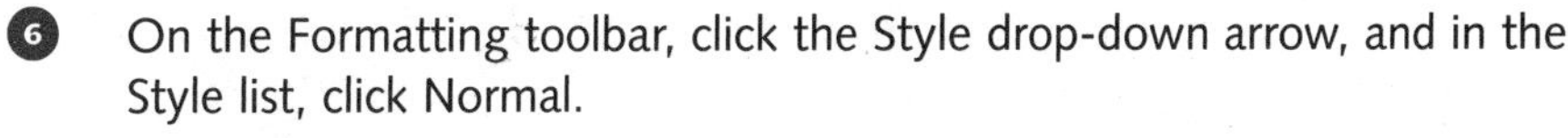

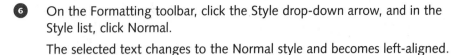

6. On the Formatting toolbar, click the Style drop-down arrow, and in the Style list, click Normal.

   The selected text changes to the Normal style and becomes left-aligned.

Center

7. On the Formatting toolbar, click the Center button.

   The text is centered.

8. Point to the table of contents, and click away from any hyperlinks to position the insertion point in any text in the frame.

9. Right-click, and on the shortcut menu, click Update Field.

   The table of contents is updated.

10. In the table of contents frame, scroll to the *Pacific Books Branch Locations* hyperlink and note that the hyperlinks for the Portland address and hours no longer appear.

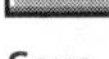

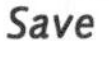

Save

11. Click Save.

Change the indentation of a hyperlink

In this exercise, you change a heading style in the text of the right frame to make a hyperlink in the table of contents appear on the correct level.

1. In the table of contents, look at the hyperlinked subheadings under *Schedule of Events*.

   One of the hyperlinks, *Special Events Day Two (7/24)*, is on a lower level (further indented) than the others.

2. Click the hyperlink *Special Events Day One (7/23).*

   The text in the right frame jumps to this section, and the insertion point appears in the heading *Special Events Day One (7/23),* in the right frame.

3. On the Formatting toolbar, look at the Style box.

   The heading is styled as Heading 2.

4. In the right frame, scroll as necessary, and click the heading *Special Events Day Two (7/24).*

   On the Formatting toolbar, in the Style box, the heading style is shown as Heading 3.

   Your screen should look similar to the following illustration.

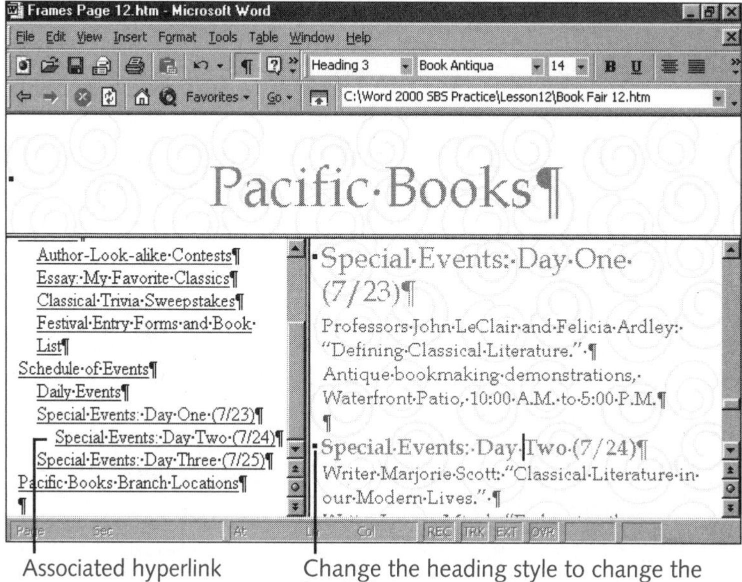

Associated hyperlink

Change the heading style to change the level of the associated hyperlink.

5. With the insertion point still in the heading *Special Events: Day Two (7/24),* on the Formatting toolbar, click the Style drop-down arrow to display styles, and then click Heading 2.

   The heading *Special Events Day Two (7/24)* changes to a Heading 2 style and is now the same size as related headings.

6. Point to the table of contents, and click away from any hyperlinks to position the insertion point in any text in the frame.

7. Right-click, and on the shortcut menu, click Update Field.

   The table of contents is updated, and the hyperlink *Special Events Day Two (7/24)* now appears on the same level as the *Special Events: Day One* and *Special Events: Day Three* hyperlinks.

Save

8. On the Standard toolbar, click the Save button.

Add a theme to the table of contents

In this exercise, you make the design of the table of contents frame consistent with the other frames by applying the same theme to it.

1. Click in the table of contents.
2. On the Format menu, click Theme.

   The Theme dialog box appears.
3. In the Choose A Theme list, click Poetic, and click OK.

   The Poetic theme is applied to the table of contents frame.
4. On the Standard toolbar, click the Save button.

Adding Hyperlinks to a Web Page

To learn about hyperlinks called bookmarks, see Lesson 11, "Designing Web Pages."

A *hyperlink* is the text or a graphic that users click to go from one location in a file to another, to jump to an Internet or intranet site, move within a Web site, or link to another Web site. You can create hyperlinks anywhere in your Web page for instant navigation to other pages.

When you insert a table of contents frame, hyperlinks are created that link to each heading in the page in which you inserted the frame. You can include additional hyperlinks in the table of contents or in any other frame on the page, and you can format existing text to turn it into a hyperlink. The new hyperlinks can link to any of the other frames in your frames page, to a Web page that opens separately from the frames page, or to another Web site.

In the following exercises, you create a new hyperlink in the table of contents that links to a Web page about contest prizes, which you specify to be displayed in the right frame. In the table of contents, you click the new hyperlink and display the contest prizes page in the right frame. Then you create a link in the contest prizes page that redisplays your book fair page, Book Fair 12, in the right frame.

Add a hyperlink to the table of contents

In this exercise, you add a hyperlink that jumps to a Web page about contest prizes.

1. In the table of contents frame, click before the *Schedule of Events* hyperlink.
2. Press Enter to create a new blank line in the table of contents, and click before the new paragraph mark.

Insert Hyperlink

3. On the Standard toolbar, click the Insert Hyperlink button.

   The Insert Hyperlink dialog box appears.

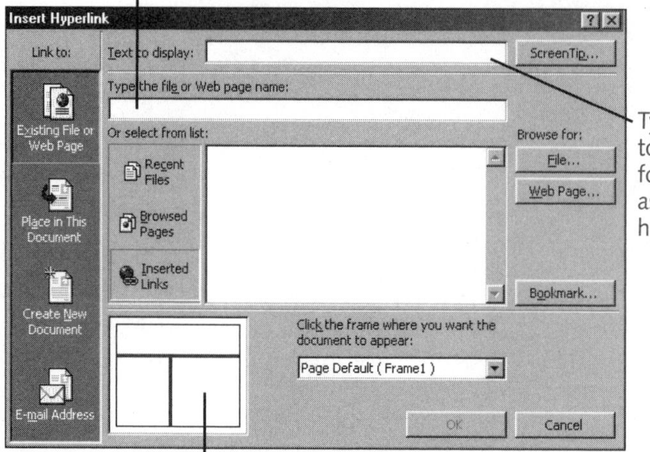

4. In the Text To Display box, type **Contest Prizes**
5. In the Type The File Or Web Page Name box, type **12B.htm**
6. Click the ScreenTip button.

   The Set Hyperlink ScreenTip dialog box appears.
7. In the Set Hyperlink ScreenTip dialog box, type **Find out what bookishly exciting prizes await you.**

   When you point to the *Contest Prizes* hyperlink in the table of contents frame, this ScreenTip will appear.
8. Click OK to close the Set Hyperlink ScreenTip dialog box.
9. In the Insert Hyperlink dialog box, in the frame diagram in the lower-left corner, click the frame on the right.

   The right frame in the diagram is selected. In the Click The Frame Where You Want The Document To Appear drop-down list, the selection changes to Frame 1—the number of the selected frame. Now the new hyperlink will open a page in this frame.
10. Click OK.

    In the table of contents frame, the new hyperlink, *Contest Prizes,* appears above the *Schedule of Events* hyperlink.
11. On the Standard toolbar, click the Save button.

Save

Test the new hyperlink

In this exercise, you view the new ScreenTip and test the link.

1. In the table of contents, point to *Contest Prizes*.

   The ScreenTip you created appears.

2. Click the *Contest Prizes* hyperlink.

   In the right frame, a new page with the heading *Contest Prizes* appears. On the Web toolbar, the path to the new file location is displayed.

   Your screen should look similar to the following illustration.

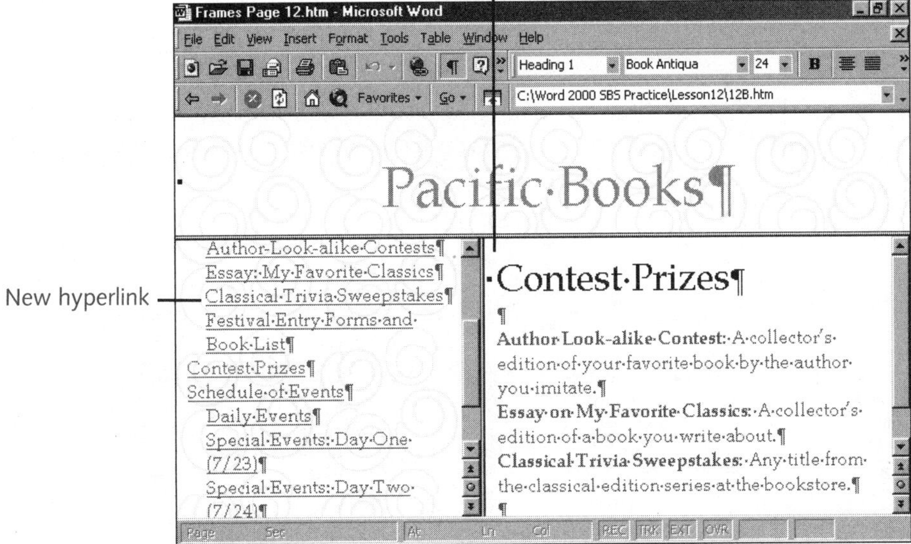

Back

3. On the Web toolbar, click the Back button.

   Book Fair 12, the previous page, is again displayed in the right frame.

Create a hyperlink from existing text

In this exercise, you format existing text in the contest prizes page as a hyperlink that will always display the Book Fair 12 page.

1. In the table of contents frame, click the Contest Prizes hyperlink again.

   The contest prizes page is displayed in the right frame.

2. In the right frame, in the last paragraph of the contest prizes page, select the word *here*, and then right-click.

   A shortcut menu appears.

3. On the shortcut menu, click Hyperlink.

   The Insert Hyperlink dialog box appears.

4. In the Text To Display box, the text you selected on the Contest Prizes page—the word *here*—is displayed. This word will be formatted as the hyperlink.

5. In the Type The File Or Web Page Name, type **Book Fair 12.htm**

   This is the name of the page about the book fair.

6. Click ScreenTip.

   The Set Hyperlink ScreenTip dialog box appears.

7. In the ScreenTip Text box, type **Go to the book fair page.**

8. Click OK.

   The Set Hyperlink ScreenTip dialog box closes.

9. In the Insert Hyperlink dialog box, in the frames diagram, select the right frame.

   In the Click The Frame Where You Want The Document To Appear box, the selection changes to Frame 1. The hyperlink you're creating will display the book fair page in this frame.

10. Click OK.

    On the Contest Prizes page, *here* appears as a hyperlink.

    Your screen should look similar to the following illustration.

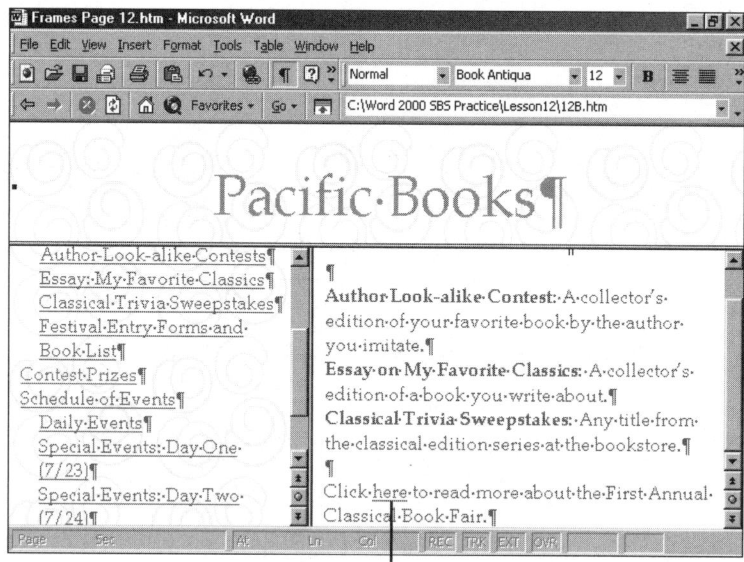

Hyperlink created from existing text

Save

11. On the Standard toolbar, click the Save button.

tip

To edit an existing hyperlink, select the hyperlink and right-click. On the shortcut menu, point to Hyperlink, and then click Edit Hyperlink. This displays the Insert Hyperlink dialog box, in which you can make changes to the link. To remove a hyperlink from a frame other than the table of contents frame, such as a link you have created from existing text on the Web page, right-click the link you want to remove. On the shortcut menu, point to Hyperlink, and then click Remove Hyperlink.

Test the new hyperlink

In this exercise, you view the ScreenTip for the *here* hyperlink, and then you test the link.

1. In the Contest Prizes page, point to the *here* hyperlink.

   The ScreenTip you created appears.

2. Click the *here* hyperlink.

   In the right frame of Frames Page 12, the book fair page appears with its main heading, *First Annual Classical Book Fair*, at the top.

Publishing a Web Page

Microsoft Office 2000 enables you to publish your Web pages to a Web server using *Web folders*. A Web server is a computer that is maintained by a system administrator or Internet service provider that responds from a user's browser. A Web folder is a shortcut to a Web server.

To use Web folders, your computer must have a network connection to a Web server. Using this server connection, you can create, copy, save, and manage files and folders on that server through the Web Folders shortcut on the Places bar. A network connection to a Web server is required for direct publication to the Web from within Microsoft Office. If your computer isn't connected to a Web server, you can't use the Web Folders feature and must save your Web documents on your computer or local area network until they can be published to your Web server using a separate Web publishing or Internet file transfer program.

The Web folders shortcut appears on the Places bar even if you don't have a network connection to a Web server.

(continued)

continued

To save a Web page to a Web folder, you use the Save As Web Page command on the File menu in Word. This command will transfer your Web page along with all its related pages and supporting files so that all the graphics and frames in your page will be displayed. If you just want to save the Web page and supporting files to a location on your computer until you can publish them to a server, the Save As Web Page command will transfer all your supporting files to the local folder that you specify.

Publish a Web page

1. In Word, open the Web page you want to publish.
2. On the File menu, click Save As Web Page.
3. In the Save As dialog box, on the Places Bar, click Web Folders.

   The Web folders file list is displayed.
4. In the Web Folders list, select the Web folder to which you want to publish the Web page, and then click Save.

   The Save As dialog box closes. A copy of the Web page is now published to a Web server.

Once you have published a Web page, you can edit it offline through Web folders. You can then synchronize the local changes with the server version. For more information about synchronizing files, open Microsoft Word Help, and search using the phrase *Working offline with folders and files on Web servers*. For more information about publishing Web pages, search using the phrase *About Web Folders*.

One Step Further: Using Multiple Themes in a Frames Page

Exercises in this section use files created in previous exercises in this lesson. Before proceeding to the next step, complete all exercises beginning with "Organizing Web Pages Using Frames."

Since a frames page consists of several Web pages that appear together, you can apply different themes to the frames page to give more variety to the page design.

In Frames Page 12, created in this lesson, you applied a consistent theme. In these exercises, you apply a different theme to the book fair frame, Book Fair 12, and insert some picture bullets in the design of the new theme.

Apply a new theme

In this exercise, you apply a new theme to the book fair frame in Frames Page 12.

1. Click in the right frame of Frames Page 12.
2. On the Format menu, click Theme.

   The Theme dialog box appears.
3. In the Choose A Theme list, click Expedition, and click OK.

   The Expedition theme is applied to the book fair frame.

Add picture bullets using the new theme

In this exercise, you add picture bullets to the table of contents frame in Frames Page 12.

1. In the table of contents frame, click the *Daily Events* hyperlink.
2. In the right frame, under the *Daily Events* heading, position the insertion point before the first word, *Author*.
3. On the Formatting toolbar, click the Bullets button

   A bullet in the design of the Expedition theme is inserted, and the text is indented.
4. Position the insertion point before the word *Open*, at the beginning of the next paragraph, and then press F4.

   A picture bullet is inserted.
5. Position the insertion point before the word *Speakers*, at the start of the next paragraph, and press F4.

   A picture bullet is inserted.

Bullets

If the Bullets button is not visible, on the Formatting toolbar, click the More Buttons drop-down arrow to locate the button.

6. Click before the word *Dramatic*, at the start of the last paragraph in the section, and press F4.

   A picture bullet is inserted.

   Your screen should look similar to the following illustration.

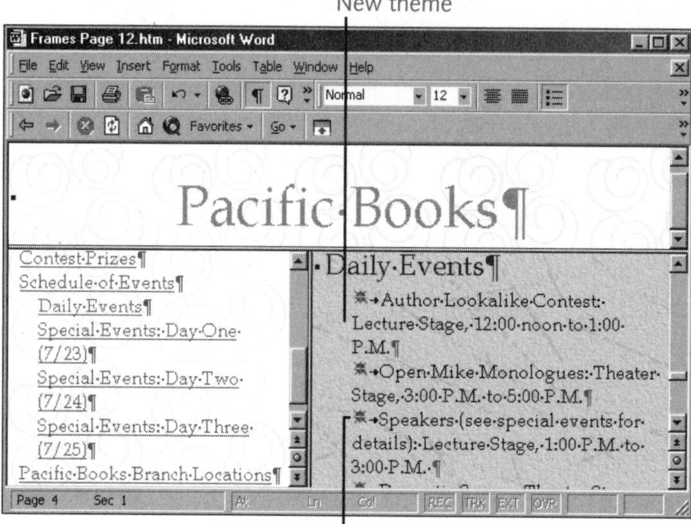

7. Position the insertion point before each paragraph under the *Special Events* headings, and press F4.

   Bullets are inserted before each remaining event in the Schedule of Events section.

Finish the lesson

Save

1. On the Standard toolbar, click Save.
2. On the File menu, click Close.
3. On the File menu, click Exit.

Lesson 12 Quick Reference

To	Do this	Button
Save a document as a Web page	On the File menu, click Save As Web Page.	
Insert a header frame and create a heading	On the Frames toolbar, click the New Frame Above button. Apply a theme and type the heading text. Drag the frame border to size the frame.	
Change frame properties	On the Frames toolbar, click the Frame Properties button. In the Frame Properties dialog box, select options for frame size and borders.	
Insert a table of contents frame	On the Frames toolbar, click the Table Of Contents In Frame button.	
Remove a hyperlink in the table of contents frame	In the main text body, select the text whose hyperlink you want to remove. On the Formatting toolbar, click the Style drop-down arrow, and change the style from a heading style to Normal. Place the insertion point in the table of contents frame, right-click, and on the shortcut menu, click Update Field.	
Change the level of a hyperlink in the table of contents	In the main text body, select the text whose hyperlink you want to change. On the Formatting toolbar, click the Style drop-down arrow, and change the style to the correct heading level. Place the insertion point in the table of contents frame, right-click, and on the shortcut menu, click Update Field.	
Add a hyperlink to the table of contents frame	Click in the table of contents. On the Standard toolbar, click the Insert Hyperlink button. In the Insert Hyperlink dialog box, type a name for the hyperlink, the file that the hyperlink will link to, and a ScreenTip. Click the frame you want the link to connect to.	

Lesson 12 Quick Reference

To	Do this
Create a hyperlink from existing text	Select the phrase you want to format as a hyperlink, and right-click. On the shortcut menu, click Hyperlink to display the Insert Hyperlink dialog box, and then give the hyperlink a name, a file to link to, and a ScreenTip. Click the frame you want the link to connect to.
Add a theme to a frame	Click the frame to which you want to apply a theme. On the Format menu, click Theme, select a theme, and click OK.

PART

3

Review & Practice

You will review and practice how to:

- ✔ *Create a main document and perform a mail merge.*
- ✔ *Format text with columns, art, and a text box.*
- ✔ *Save a document as a Web page and add a theme and an AutoShape.*
- ✔ *Add a table of contents frame and hyperlink to a Web page.*

ESTIMATED TIME **15 min.**

Before you move on to Part 4, which covers Word 2000 features that help teams collaborate on group projects, you can practice the skills you learned in Part 3 by working through this Review & Practice section. You create a main document, attach a data source, and then merge the data into the main document. Then you format a document with columns, a graphic, and a text box. Using a slightly different version of this document, you save it as a Web page, move the graphic, and add an AutoShape and theme. Finally, you insert a table of contents frame and create a bookmark hyperlink.

Scenario

As part of the work that Impact Public Relations is doing for its client Pacific Books, you need to send a cover letter to several speakers who are participating in an upcoming classical book fair. To prepare the letter, you create a main document form letter. Then you merge data from an existing table of speakers' names and addresses into the letter. The speaker biographies will be part of a printed newsletter and also part of a Web site. For the newsletter, you format the biographies with columns, art, and other design elements. For the Web site, you save a version of the biographies as a Web page, apply a theme, alter the art, and insert a table of contents frame and a hyperlink.

Step 1: Create a Main Document and Merge Data

In this step, you create a main document, attach an existing data source, and then perform a mail merge to insert names and addresses into the main document.

1. Create a main document based on a form letter, open the data source file RP03A, and then when you are prompted, click to edit the main document.
2. In the main document, insert the following merge fields: date, first name, last name, address, city, state, Zip Code, and country. Insert paragraphs, spaces, or commas, as needed, between the fields.
3. Create a salutation, inserting the merge fields for title and last name, and add a colon at the end.
4. In the body of the letter, type **Enclosed is a draft of your biography that we will include in a newsletter and on a Web site for Pacific Books. The newsletter and Web site give details about the bookstore's classical book fair, for which you'll be a speaker. Could you review the write-up and return changes to me by June 15?**
5. Type **Thank you**, sign the letter **Rebecca Smith, Impact Public Relations** and save the main document as **Main Letter RP3**.
6. Merge the letter with the data source to create a new form letters document.
7. Save the new document if you'd like, and then close it. Save changes to Main Letter RP3, and then close it.

For more information about	See
Merging a document with a data source	Lesson 9

Step 2: Create Columns and Insert Art and a Text Box

In this step, you format a document to be used in a newsletter for Pacific Books.

1. Open file RP03B, and save it as Speakers RP3.
2. Excluding the first heading and introductory paragraph, select the remaining text and format it into two columns.
3. In the section under the heading *Marjorie Scott*, select the last paragraph, which begins *"Get beyond the antiquated style"* and ends with the name *Marjorie Scott*, and create a text box for the text. Size the text box to 2.5 inches wide by 1.5 inches high.

4. Position the text box in the center of the page, and format it so the surrounding text wraps around it in a square. If the text box covers a nearby heading, move the text box farther up in the body text. Format it with a 2.25-point dotted black border.
5. Insert a horizontal line that sits below the single-column introductory paragraph and above the first section break.
6. In front of the paragraph mark at the top of the page, insert a clip art image that relates to books, and size it to 1 inch in height and width.
7. Save your changes and close the file.

For more information about	See
Creating columns	Lesson 10
Creating and placing text boxes	Lesson 10
Working with graphics	Lesson 10

Step 3: Convert a Document to a Web Page and Design the Page

In this step, you open a version of Speakers RP3 that is formatted in a single column and has no text box. You save it as a Web page.

1. Open RP03C, and save it as a Web page called Speakers Web Page RP3.
2. Position the insertion point in front of the horizontal line, press Enter three times, and move the graphic before the first new paragraph mark so that it now appears below the first paragraph. On the right side of the graphic, insert a callout-type AutoShape that points to the graphic and is about 1.5 inches high and 3.5 inches wide. In the AutoShape, paste the quote under the *Marjorie Scott* heading that begins, *"Get beyond the antiquated style."*
3. Apply the Bubbles theme to the Web page, and adjust the AutoShape as necessary to contain all of the text.
4. Preview the page in your browser. Return to the Word window, delete the blank line at the top of the page, and save changes.

For more information about	See
Saving a document as a Web page	Lessons 11 and 12
Working with graphics	Lesson 10
Creating graphics with the Drawing toolbar	Lesson 10
Designing a Web page	Lesson 11

Step 4: Insert a Table of Contents Frame and Hyperlink

In this exercise, you add a table of contents frame to the Web page, and then you create a bookmark hyperlink from existing text.

1. In Speakers Web Page RP3, insert a table of contents frame.
2. Position and size the AutoShape so it is in view.
3. In the fame on the right, under the heading *John LeClair and Felicia Ardley*, create a bookmark hyperlink from the text *new editions,* at the end of the paragraph. The hyperlink should jump to the *Stephen Pence* heading, above the last section of the Web page.

For more information about	See
Inserting a table of contents frame	Lesson 12
Creating a bookmark hyperlink	Lesson 11
Creating a hyperlink from existing text	Lesson 12

Finish the Review & Practice

Follow these steps if you want to continue to the next lesson.

1. On the File menu, click Close.
2. When a message appears, asking whether you want to save changes, click Yes, and save your new frames Web page.

Follow these steps if you want to quit Microsoft Word for now.

1. On the File menu, click Exit.
2. If a message appears, asking whether you want to save changes, click Yes.

PART 4

Collaborating Online

LESSON

13

Tracking Changes in Group Projects

In this lesson you will learn how to:

- ✔ *Track edits using revision marks.*
- ✔ *Highlight text for special attention.*
- ✔ *Insert and edit comments.*
- ✔ *Accept and reject edits.*
- ✔ *Protect documents for access and changes.*
- ✔ *Create and compare document versions.*
- ✔ *Schedule an online meeting to review a document.*

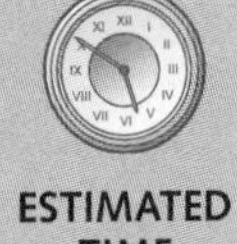

ESTIMATED TIME **35 min.**

When a number of people work together on a team project, they usually end up with one final report of their work. It's often the responsibility of the project leader to compile that document—and that's not always a simple task. Gathering and processing edits by numerous people on one document can be cumbersome, and it's easy to lose track of outstanding questions and who made what changes along the way.

Microsoft Word provides a number of convenient document editing tools to help manage and speed the process. With these tools, a project leader can easily gather input on a single copy of a document, keeping track of questions and comments from each editor while preserving the original document. Once the input is gathered, all proposed changes can be considered—all at one time, and in one place.

In this lesson, you learn how to track changes by individual reviewers, use the Reviewing toolbar to accept or reject edits, insert comments, highlight text, and compare a revised document with its original. You also learn how to use password protection to prevent or limit changes by reviewers.

Working on a project team at Impact Public Relations, you have submitted a document for review by team members. You and your project team members will use the document editing tools to develop the document further.

More Buttons

important

The default toolbar setting in Microsoft Word 2000 displays both the Standard and Formatting toolbars in one row, at the top of the document window, just below the menu bar. This gives you maximum workspace. While working through the exercises in this book, toolbar buttons you need may not initially be visible. If a toolbar button is not visible, click one of the two More Buttons drop-down arrows on the toolbar to locate the button you need. When you select a new toolbar button, it is automatically added to the visible portion of the toolbar, replacing one that is not used often.

Start Word and open a practice file

In this exercise, you start Word, open a practice file, and then save it with a new name.

1. On the Windows taskbar, click the Start button.
   The Start menu appears.
2. On the Start menu, point to Programs, and then click Microsoft Word.
   Microsoft Word 2000 opens.
3. On the Standard toolbar, click the Open button.
   The Open dialog box appears.

Open

4. Click the Look In drop-down arrow, and then select your hard disk.
5. In the list of folders, double-click the Word 2000 SBS Practice folder, and then double-click the Lesson13 folder.
6. In the file list, double-click the 13A file to open it.
   The document opens in the document window.
7. On the File menu, click Save As.
   The Save As dialog box appears.
8. Be sure that the Lesson13 folder appears in the Save In box.

9. In the File Name box, select the text, and type **Book Fair 13**
10. Click Save.

Display formatting marks

To make it easier to edit your document, you can display formatting marks such as paragraph marks and space marks on your screen.

Show/Hide ¶

- If formatting marks are not currently displayed, on the Standard toolbar, click the Show/Hide ¶ button.

Editing with Revision Marks

When several people review and edit a document in Word, the changes can be tracked using a feature called *revision marks*. These marks are similar to editing marks you'd use if you were editing on paper—but they have some big advantages. First, you can change your mind and reverse your edit if you want, without making the document messy or unreadable. Word can also capture the edits of numerous reviewers and keep track of each one's comments individually. By default, revision marks show the proposed changes as underlined text for additions and strike-through text for deletions. Revisions by different editors are shown in different colors. Word accommodates up to eight reviewers before colors are repeated.

Word also records the date, time, type of change, and name of editor for each edit to the document. So, if a color is repeated because there are more than eight reviewers, other data to distinguish the editor is still available.

When revision marks are displayed, vertical lines, called *change lines*, also appear in the margin, identifying lines containing changes. Changes to formatting can also be tracked.

All changes are really only proposed changes until they are accepted or rejected by someone, so the original document is preserved throughout the process. You learn more about accepting and rejecting changes later in this lesson.

If you are not working through this lesson sequentially, before proceeding to the next step, open the 13A file in the Lesson13 folder, and save it as Book Fair 13.

Turn on Track Changes while editing

In this exercise, you set Word to track changes in a document.

1. On the Tools menu, point to Track Changes, and then click Highlight Changes.

   The Highlight Changes dialog box appears.

2. Select the Track Changes While Editing and Highlight Changes On Screen check boxes, and click OK.

Select revision options

In this exercise, you set Word to track formatting changes in a document.

1. On the Tools menu, point to Track Changes, and then click Highlight Changes.

   The Highlight Changes dialog box appears.
2. Click Options.

   The Track Changes dialog box appears.
3. In the Changed Formatting area, click the Mark drop-down arrow, and select Double Underline.

   Formatting changes will now be indicated by a double underline.
4. Click OK.
5. In the Highlight Changes dialog box, click OK.

Use revision marks

In this exercise, you edit a document using revision marks.

1. In the Book Fair 13 document, scroll to the bottom of page 2.
2. In the paragraph under the heading *Festival Entry Forms and Book List*, select the text *June 30*.
3. Type **July 1**

   The deleted text appears with a line drawn through it (a strikethrough), and the new text appears underlined. Changes also appear in color.

   Your screen should look similar to the following illustration.

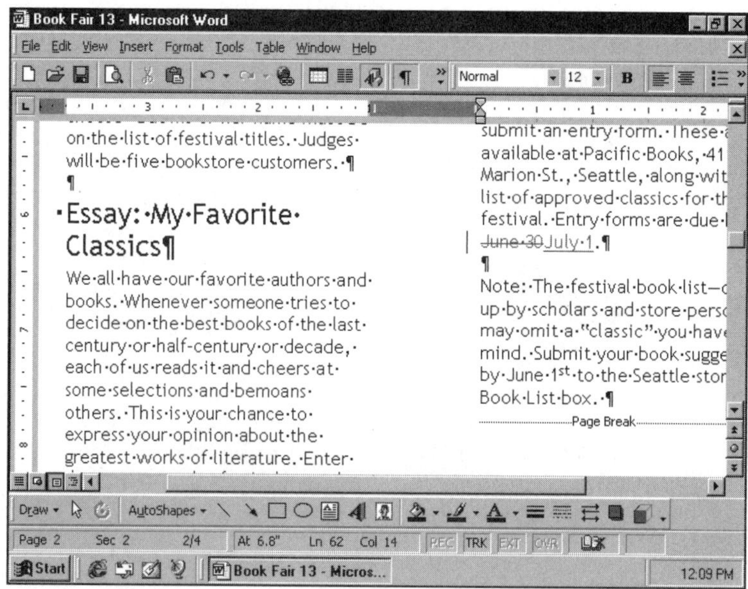

Italic

Bold

If the Italic and Bold buttons are not visible, on the Formatting toolbar, click the More Buttons drop-down arrow to locate the buttons.

4. Scroll down to the top of page 3, and select the heading *Schedule of Events*.
5. On the Formatting toolbar, click the Italic and Bold buttons.

   Click anywhere outside the selected text to cancel the selection. The formatted text appears with a double underline.

   Your screen should look similar to the following illustration.

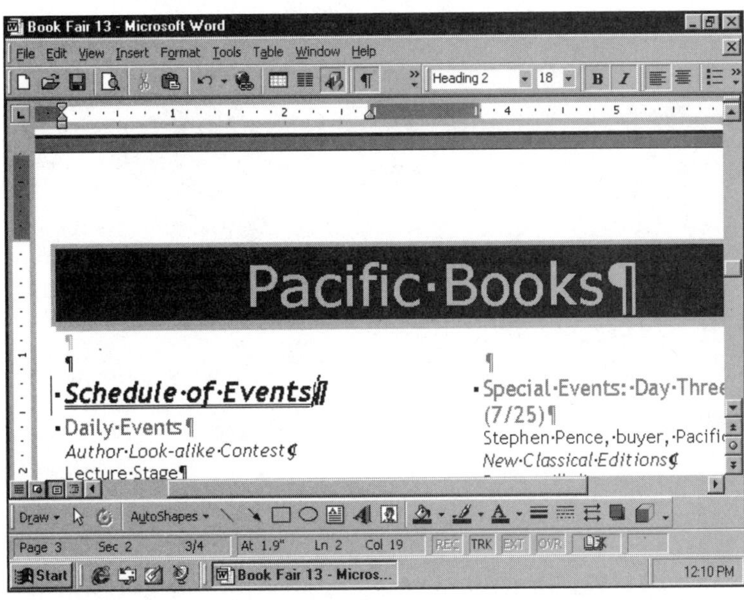

View revision information

In this exercise, you view the information about a change in the document.

- Position the mouse pointer over the reformatted text *Schedule of Events*. A ScreenTip appears, showing your name, the date, time, and type of change.

> **tip**
>
> If your name does not appear in the ScreenTip over the revised text, on the Tools menu, click Options, and then click the User Information tab. Fill in the boxes with your name and initials, and then click OK. The new information will appear in the ScreenTip when you position the mouse pointer over subsequent changes. If you share a computer with others, you can restore the user information after you've finished this lesson.

Turning Off Revision Mark Display

When a document contains extensive edits, it can be difficult to read when all of the revision marks are displayed on the screen. In this case, you might find it helpful to adjust your settings so that changes continue to be tracked, but revision marks are no longer displayed on the screen. When you select this option, revision marks will be seen only in Print Preview and on the printed document.

Turn off Highlight Changes On Screen

1. On the Tools menu, point to Track Changes, and then click Highlight Changes.
2. In the Highlight Changes dialog box, clear the Highlight Changes On Screen check box.
3. Click OK.

You can also choose to hide revision marks in the printed copy by following the same procedure as above, but clearing the Highlight Changes In Printed Copy check box.

Displaying Only Changed Lines

You can also set the Track Changes options to display just a vertical line in the margin indicating which lines were changed while the actual changes are hidden.

Display only changed lines

1. On the Tools menu, click Options, and then click the Track Changes tab.
2. In the Inserted Text area, click the Mark drop-down arrow, and then select None.
3. In the Deleted Text area, click the Mark drop-down arrow, and then select Hidden.
4. In the Changed Formatting area, click the Mark drop-down arrow and then select None.
5. In the Changed Lines area, click the Mark drop-down arrow, and be sure Outside Border is selected.
6. Click OK.

Highlighting Text for Special Attention

If you are not working through this lesson sequentially, before proceeding to the next step, open the 13B file in the Lesson13 folder, and save it as Book Fair 13.

When you work in a group project document, you might want to call the attention of subsequent reviewers to certain text. You can do this by highlighting the text in color. You might even want to use various highlight colors to mean different things. For example, you could use the default yellow highlight to tell the next reviewer that information needs to be confirmed, and green to indicate that further explanation needs to be inserted. Or you might want to choose one color to indicate your questions, while other colors could indicate other editors.

Highlight text

In this exercise, you highlight text to help your colleague review a document.

1. In the Book Fair 13 document, scroll to page 1, and in the first paragraph, under the heading *First Annual Classical Book Fair*, select the text *July 23, 24, and 25*.
2. On the Formatting toolbar, click the Highlight button.

   The selected text is highlighted in yellow—the default color.

Highlight

If the Highlight button is not visible, on the Formatting toolbar, click the More Buttons drop-down arrow to locate the button.

3. Scroll down to the bottom of page 2, and in the paragraph under the heading *Festival Entry Forms and Book List*, select the text *Entry forms are due by July 1*.
4. On the Formatting toolbar, click the Highlight drop-down arrow, and click Turquoise.

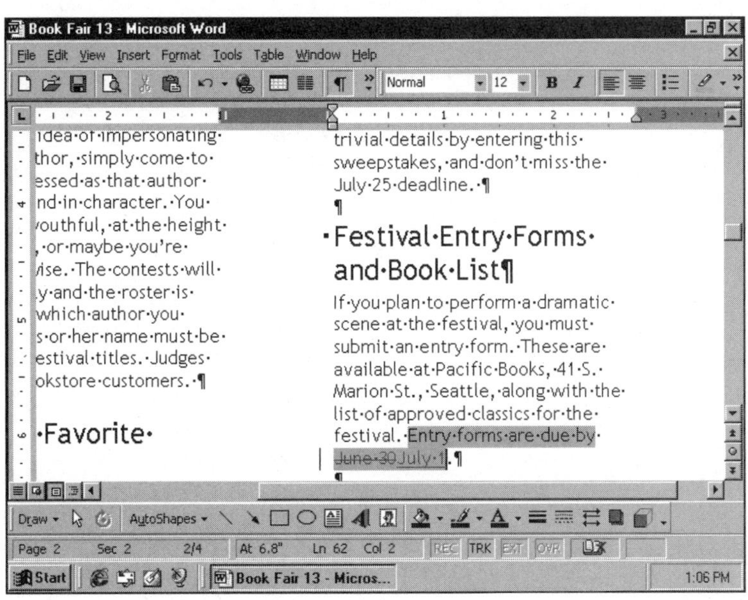

The sentence is highlighted in turquoise, and the Highlight button now shows turquoise as the highlight color.

Inserting Comments

While editing, reviewers often have questions or comments about the document that they'd like other team members to consider. The Word *Comments* feature helps reviewers communicate to the author, or subsequent reviewers, without actually typing the message within the body of the document. Instead, when a reviewer inserts a comment, his or her initials are inserted into the document along with a sequential reference number. Word obtains the reference initials from the User Information tab of the Options dialog box.

The initials, the reference number, and text the comment refers to are all highlighted. The text of the comment is entered in a comment pane that opens at the bottom of the document window. A number corresponding to the sequential number in the document appears next to the comment in the comment pane.

When you select Comments from the View menu or double-click a comment reference mark within the document, all the comments in the document are displayed in the comment pane at the bottom of the document. You can also position the pointer over a comment within the document and display a ScreenTip with the complete text of the comment.

Comments can be deleted from a document after issues have been resolved or before the document is finalized.

Insert a comment

If you are not working through this lesson sequentially, before proceeding to the next step, open the 13C file in the Lesson13 folder, and save it as Book Fair 13.

In this exercise, you insert a comment for the next reviewer of the Book Fair 13 document.

1. On page 2 of the Book Fair 13 document under the heading *Festival Entry Forms and Book List*, click after the word *Seattle*.
2. On the Insert menu, click Comment.

   A comment reference mark with your initials and a sequential number is inserted in the document. The comment pane is opened at the bottom of the Word window, and the insertion point is automatically positioned in it next to the new comment reference number.

3. Type **Please insert the hours of the Seattle branch**

   Your screen should look similar to the following illustration

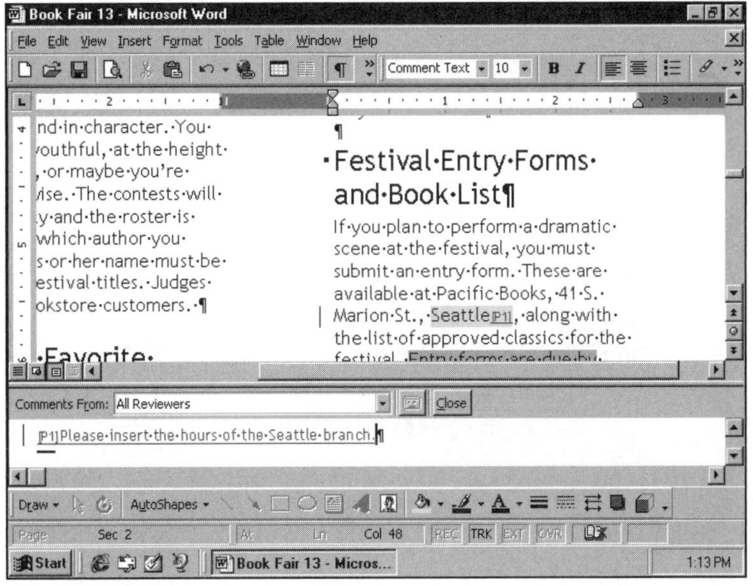

Save

4. In the comment pane, click Close.

   The comment pane closes.

5. On the Standard toolbar, click the Save button.

   Changes to Book Fair 13 are saved.

View a comment

In this exercise, you view a ScreenTip containing your comment.

- Position the pointer over the yellow highlighted text. A ScreenTip appears with your name and comment.

Edit a comment

In this exercise, you edit a comment.

1. Position the pointer over the comment reference mark, and double-click.

   The comment pane opens.
2. Press the End key to move the insertion point to the end of the comment, and type **(in parentheses)**
3. In the comment pane, click Close.

   The comment pane closes.

Save

4. On the Standard toolbar, click the Save button.

   Changes to the document are saved.
5. On the File menu, click Close.

Accepting and Rejecting Changes

Once you've gathered all the input from your team members, it's time to decide which edits to accept and which to reject. To *accept* a change is to accept the edit that has been made to a document. If you do not agree with a revision that has been made, you can *reject* that revision. When you reject a change, you revert to the original text or eliminate added text.

To assist you in reviewing an edited Word document, you can use the Word *Reviewing* toolbar. This toolbar makes it easy to quickly identify and consider all proposed changes—to accept or reject them; to add, revise, and delete comments; and to apply or remove highlighting. You can also use the toolbar to accept all changes at one time—without reviewing them individually. And you can use the Reviewing toolbar to save *versions* of a document, which you learn more about later in this lesson.

In the following exercises, you review revisions and accept and reject changes.

Display the Reviewing toolbar

If you are not working through this lesson sequentially, before proceeding to the next step, open the 13D file in the Lesson13 folder, and save it as Book Fair 13.

In this exercise, you display the Reviewing toolbar.

- On the View menu, point to Toolbars, and then click Reviewing.

  The Reviewing toolbar appears.

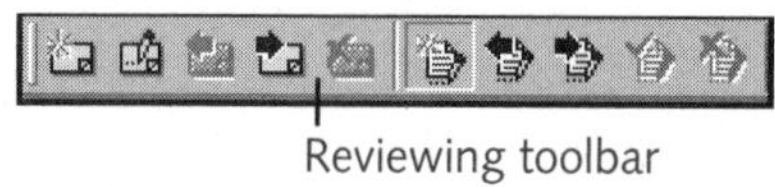

Reviewing toolbar

Read and then delete a comment

In this exercise, you read and then delete a comment.

1. Press Ctrl+Home to move the insertion point to the beginning of the document.

Next Change

2. On the Reviewing toolbar, click the Next Change button.

   The first revision in the document, which is a comment, is highlighted.
3. Position the pointer over the comment reference mark.

   A ScreenTip appears with the comment text.
4. Click the comment reference mark.

   The insertion point is positioned in front of the comment reference mark.

Delete Comment

5. On the Reviewing toolbar, click the Delete Comment button.
6. Press the Spacebar once, and type **(10-10 daily)**

   Revision marks are inserted and the new text appears underlined.

Accept a change

In this exercise, you accept a change.

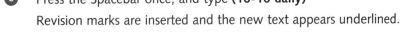

Accept Change

For deletions, the Accept Change command deletes the text, while the Reject Change command reinstates the text.

1. Press Ctrl+Home to move the insertion point to the beginning of the document.
2. On the Reviewing toolbar, click the Next Change button twice.

   The text, *June 30,* which appears with a horizontal line through it, is selected.
3. On the Reviewing toolbar, click the Accept Change button.

   The deletion is accepted, and the text is removed.

Undo an accepted change

In this exercise, you undo the accepted change made in the previous exercise.

Undo

- On the Standard toolbar, click the Undo button.

  The accepted change is undone, and the deleted text reappears with revision marks.

Reject changes

In this exercise, you use the Reviewing toolbar to reject changes.

Reject Change

Next Change

1. With the text *June 30* still highlighted, on the Reviewing toolbar, click the Reject Change button.

   The text, *June 30*, is reinstated in the document.
2. On the Reviewing toolbar, click the Next Change button, and then click the Reject Change button.

   The inserted text, *July 1*, is removed from the document.

Accept remaining changes

In this exercise, you accept the remaining changes.

1. On the Tools menu, point to Track Changes, and then click Accept Or Reject Changes.

   The Accept Or Reject Changes dialog box appears.
2. Click Accept All, and click Yes when you are prompted.
3. Click Close.

   The remaining revisions are accepted.

All passwords are case sensitive, which means they must be typed exactly as they were originally typed, using capital and lowercase letters.

Protecting Documents from Changes

Word provides several ways to protect your document from being changed by others who are reviewing it. For example, you can assign a password that prevents any changes except those that are tracked. This level of protection ensures that all changes made by other reviewers are flagged with revision marks allowing you to accept or reject them. You can also assign a password that allows others to add comments to the document, but not to make any changes.

Protect a document from untracked changes

If you are not working through this lesson sequentially, before proceeding to the next step, open the 13E file in the Lesson13 folder, and save it as Book Fair 13.

In this exercise, you protect your document so that reviewers can make changes, but all changes are tracked. That is, tracking cannot be turned off.

1. On the Tools menu, click Protect Document.

   The Protect Document dialog box appears.
2. In the Protect Document For area, be sure the Tracked Changes check box is selected.

3. In the Password box, type **password** and click OK.

   The Confirm Password dialog box appears.

4. In the Confirm Password dialog box, type **password** again, and click OK.
5. On the Standard toolbar, click the Save button.

Save

View password protection

In this exercise, you view the password protection you applied in the previous exercise.

1. On the Tools menu, point to Track Changes, and then click Highlight Changes.

   The Track Changes While Editing check box is selected and is shaded, which means no reviewer can turn off this option without knowing the password.

2. Click OK.

Unprotect a document

In this exercise, you unprotect the document so that others can turn off Track Changes While Editing without knowing the password.

1. On the Tools menu, click Unprotect Document.
2. In the Unprotect Document dialog box, type **password** and click OK.

   The password protection is removed, and Track Changes While Editing can now be turned on and off by reviewers.

Limiting Access by Using Passwords

If you want, you can require a user to enter a password to open a document. This type of protection limits access to the document to just those who have the password.

Require a password to open a document

1. On the Tools menu, click Options.
2. In the Options dialog box, click the Save tab.
3. In the File Sharing Options For *filename* area, type the password in the Password To Open box. You can also enter a password to modify the document.
4. If desired, select the Read-only Recommended check box. This option means users will not be able to change the document.

Creating Multiple Versions of a Document

Over the course of a major project, you might find it useful to save *versions*—or drafts—of a document as it appears in various stages of development. You might be required to produce interim reports, for example, or you might want to look back at an earlier draft to compare it with the current version of the document. Versions help you maintain a paper trail of how your document is evolving, which is useful in case you need to revise a newer version with information that was deleted from an older version. Once you've saved a document as a version, you can no longer change it. The document version feature of Word lets you save versions of your document and protects them from further revisions.

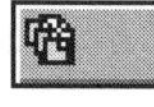

Versions

When you save a version of a document, Word displays the *File Versions* icon at the far right of the status bar. The first version of a document is called the *baseline* version.

When you compare versions of a document, changes between the documents are identified with revision marks. Word uses the same revision marks used in Tracking Changes to identify changes made between two documents.

tip

Version numbers should not be confused with document *revision* numbers. The revision number corresponds to the number of times a document is saved. When you save a Word document, the revision number is tracked on the Statistics tab of the Properties dialog box—accessed through the File menu. If you save your document frequently, the revision number can become quite large.

Save a version of a report

If you are not working through this lesson sequentially, before proceeding to the next step, open the 13F file in the Lesson13 folder, and save it as Book Fair 13.

In this exercise, you save a version of a document as a baseline draft.

1. On the File menu, click Versions.

   The Versions In Book Fair 13 dialog box appears.

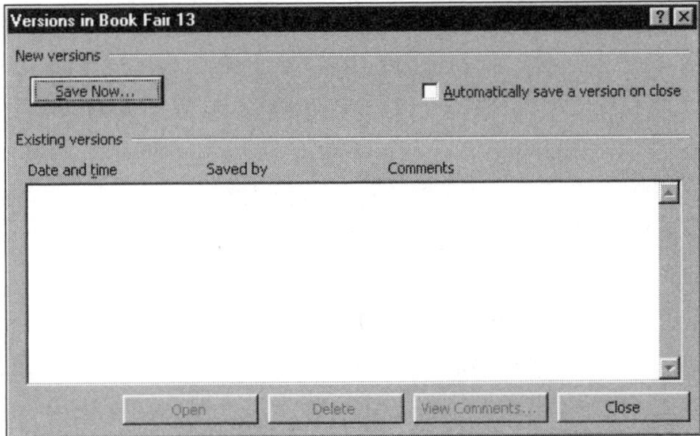

2. Click Save Now.

   The Save Version dialog box appears.

3. In the Comments On Version box, type **First Draft–Baseline Version**

4. Click OK.

   The dialog boxes close and the document is displayed.

View version details of a document

In this exercise, you view the version details of a document.

1. Double-click the File Versions icon at the far right of the status bar.

   The Versions In Book Fair 13 dialog box appears and shows the version information for the document.

   Your screen should look similar to the following illustration.

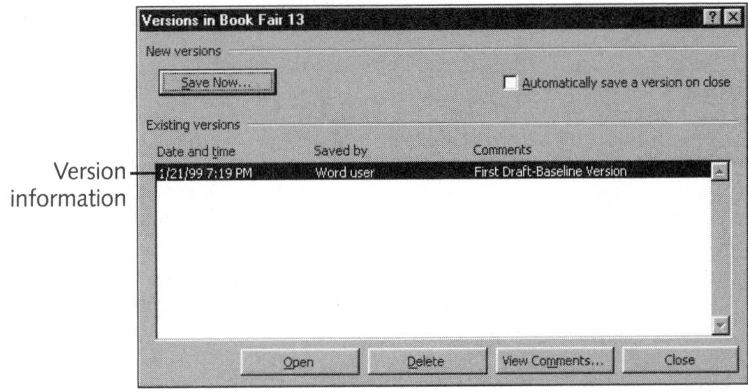

2. Click Close.

Modify and save another version of a document

In this exercise, you open a new copy of the Book Fair 13 document so you can make some revisions and then save it as a new version, which you compare with the baseline version.

Because you are archiving document versions, you cannot go back and modify a saved version of a document. To make changes to the document, you must save it with a new name. Only then will you be able to make changes to the document.

1. On the File menu, click Save As.

   The Save As dialog box appears.
2. In the File Name box, type **Book Fair 13 Revisions** and click Save.
3. On the first page of the document, under the heading *Dramatic Scenes*, select the text *with the willingness* and type **who are willing**

   The deleted text appears with a line drawn through it and the new text appears underlined.
4. On the File menu, click Versions.

   The Versions In Book Fair 13 Revisions dialog box appears.
5. Click Save Now.

   The Save Version dialog box appears.
6. In the Comments On Version box, type **Second Draft-Revisions** and click OK.

   The dialog boxes close and the document is displayed.

To compare an earlier version of the document with the current version, you must save the current version as a separate file.

Open a baseline version

In this exercise, you open the baseline version of the document.

1. Be sure the Book Fair 13 Revisions document is open. On the status bar, double-click the Versions icon.

   The Versions In Book Fair 13 Revisions dialog box appears.
2. In the Existing Versions box, select First Draft–Baseline Version, and click Open.

   The baseline version is opened in a new window, and Word displays the two documents tiled vertically.
3. Maximize the baseline version, which should be the document in the lower part of the window.

   This is the document as it appeared before any changes were made.
4. Click Close.

   The revised version remains on your screen.

Compare documents

In this exercise, you compare the baseline document to the second draft.

1. Maximize the revised version of the document.
2. On the Tools menu, point to Track Changes, and then click Compare Documents.

   The Select File To Compare With Current Document dialog box appears.
3. Be sure the Lesson13 folder appears in the Look In box.
4. Double-click Book Fair 13.
5. When you are prompted, click Yes.

   Word compares the baseline version to the second draft of the document.
6. At the top of page 1, note the revision marks indicating the differences in the two drafts.
7. Close the document without saving changes.

One Step Further Collaborating Online

If you're going to collaborate with coworkers on a group editing project, you're probably going to transfer files as e-mail attachments either over your company's intranet or over the Internet. But you can also collaborate online in real time with Microsoft NetMeeting, a product that comes with Microsoft Internet Explorer. You can initiate an online meeting from within any Microsoft Office application, or you can work directly within the NetMeeting program. When you start an online meeting from within an Office application, NetMeeting automatically starts in the background and allows you to begin sharing the contents of your file.

If you host an online meeting, at the beginning of the meeting, you are the only person who has control of the document, although all participants can see the Word document on their screens. You can allow participants to make changes to the document by turning on collaboration, and you can also turn off collaboration at any time. When collaboration is turned off, the other participants cannot make changes, but they can watch you work. When collaboration is turned on, each person in the online meeting can take turns editing and controlling the document.

The first time you initiate on online meeting, you select a directory server to connect to in the NetMeeting dialog box. You can either select from the Server name list or ask your system administrator for the name of a directory server to connect to.

Schedule a meeting

In this exercise, you schedule an online meeting to review a document with team members.

Open

1. On the Standard toolbar, click the Open button.

   The Open dialog box appears.
2. In the list of files, double-click the 13A file.
3. On the File menu, click Save As, and in the File Name box, type **Meeting** and then click Save.
4. On the Tools menu, point to Online Collaboration, and then click Schedule Meeting.

   The Microsoft NetMeeting window opens.
5. Click To.

   The Select Attendees And Resources dialog box appears.
6. Select the names of the people you want to invite to the meeting, click the Required button, and click OK.
7. Click in the Subject box, and type **Pacific Books Online Meeting**
8. Leave the Location box blank because this is an online meeting.
9. In the Start Time area, click the first drop-down arrow, select a date, click the second drop-down arrow, and then select a time.

   Your screen should look similar to the following illustration.

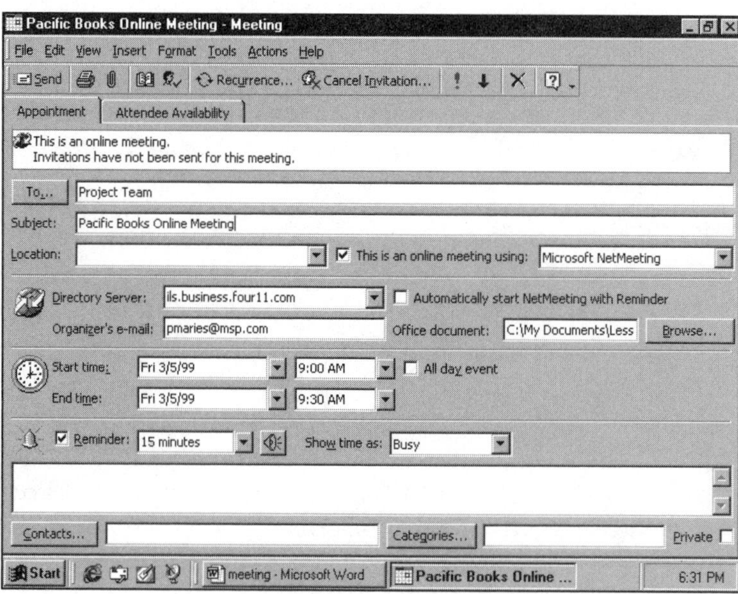

10. On the Outlook Standard toolbar, click the Send button.

    The invitation is sent to the recipients.

Finish the lesson

Save

1. On the Standard toolbar, click the Save button.

   Changes to Book Fair 13 are saved.
2. On the File menu, click Close.
3. On the File menu, click Exit.

Lesson 13 Quick Reference

To	Do this	Button
Track changes while editing	On the Tools menu, point to Track Changes, and then click Highlight Changes. Select the Track Changes While Editing and Highlight On Screen check boxes, and click OK.	
View revision information	In the Highlight Changes dialog box, be sure the Highlight Changes On Screen check box is selected. Place the pointer over the revised text to display a ScreenTip with the author's name, the date, time, and type of change.	
Highlight text	Select the text. On the Formatting toolbar, click the Highlight button. To change the highlight color, on the Formatting toolbar, click the Highlight drop-down arrow, and select a color from the palette.	
Insert a comment	Click where you want to insert a comment. On the Insert menu, click Comment. Or on the reviewing toolbar, click the Insert Comment button. Type a comment. Click Close to close the comment pane.	
View a comment	In the Highlight Changes dialog box, be sure the Highlight Changes On Screen check box is selected. Place the pointer over the comment reference marker. A ScreenTip displays the author's name and comment.	

Lesson 13 Quick Reference

To	Do this	Button
Edit a comment	Double-click the comment reference mark. Edit the comment text. Click Close to close the comment pane.	
Display the Reviewing toolbar	On the View menu, point to Toolbars, and then click Reviewing.	
Delete a comment	Select the comment reference mark of the comment you want to delete. On the Reviewing toolbar, click the Delete Comment button.	
Accept a change	Select the change you want to accept. On the Reviewing toolbar, click the Accept Change button.	
Undo an accepted change	Before completing any other edits, on the Standard toolbar, click the Undo button.	
Reject a change	Select the change you want to reject. On the Reviewing toolbar, click the Reject Change button.	
Accept remaining changes	On the Tools menu, point to Track Changes, and then click Accept Or Reject Changes. In the Accept Or Reject Changes dialog box, click Accept All, and click Yes when you are prompted. Click Close.	
Protect a document from untracked changes	On the Tools menu, click Protect Document. In the Protect Document dialog box, be sure that the Tracked Changes check box is selected. In the Password box, type a password, and click OK. In the Confirm Password dialog box, retype the password, and click OK.	
Unprotect a document	On the Tools menu, click Unprotect Document. In the Unprotect Document dialog box, type the password selected when the document was protected, and click OK.	
Save a version of a report	On the File menu, click Versions. Click Save Now. In the Comments On Version box, type the name of the version, and click OK.	

Lesson 13 Quick Reference

To	Do this	Button
View version information for a document	Double-click the File Versions icon at the far right of the status bar.	[button]
Modify and save a version of a report	On the File menu, click Save As. In the File Name box, type a different file name and click Save. In the document, make the desired changes. On the File menu, click Versions. Click Save Now. In the Comments On Version box, type the name of the version, and click OK.	
Open the baseline version of a document	On the status bar, double-click the File Versions icon. In the Existing Versions list, select the baseline version, and click Open.	
Compare documents	On the Tools menu, point to Track Changes, and then click Compare Documents. In the Select File To Compare With Current Document dialog box, double-click to open the document to compare.	
Schedule an online meeting to review a document	On the Tools menu, point to Online Collaboration, and then click Schedule Meeting. When the Microsoft NetMeeting window appears, click To. When the Select Attendees And Resources dialog box appears, select the names of invitees, click Required, and click OK. In the Subject box, type a descriptive topic. In the Start Time area, select a date and time. On the Outlook Standard toolbar, click the Send button.	

14

Using Outline View and Master Documents

In this lesson you will learn how to:

- ✔ *Use Outline view and the Outlining toolbar to reorganize a document.*
- ✔ *Expand and collapse headings.*
- ✔ *Promote and demote headings.*
- ✔ *Move a block of text using its outline heading.*
- ✔ *Create a subdocument from a master document.*
- ✔ *Use a bookmark to navigate a document.*

ESTIMATED TIME **35 min.**

Organizing a document is easy when you use Outline view and the Outlining toolbar in Microsoft Word 2000. Outline view lets you focus on the structure of your document by displaying the heading levels you choose, without displaying the body text under them. By concentrating on the heading structure of your document, you can see ways to rearrange it to improve organization and clarity. Working in Outline view, you can also move large blocks of text within a document just by moving headings. The Outlining toolbar appears when you view a document in Outline view and allows you to choose the heading levels you want to focus on.

When you are working with a document in Outline view, you can convert sections of the document into *subdocuments*. A subdocument is a separate file that is linked to its original, or *master*, document. The purpose of subdocuments is to allow various people to work on sections of a larger, master document all at one time. When team members have finished their work on the subdocuments, the edited subdocuments can then be converted back into the master document file.

Whereas Outline view gives you a quick structural picture of a long document, *bookmarks* help you navigate through a long document. A bookmark is an invisible tag that marks a specific place in a document and allows you to move quickly to that place. Instead of scrolling through pages of text to find a section, you can use a bookmark to go directly to the section you want.

In this lesson, you reorganize an outline describing a Web site that Impact Public Relations is creating for its client, Pacific Books. You also create a subdocument so that you and your business partner can work on different parts of the outline simultaneously. To help you quickly reach an important section of the outline, you add a bookmark to that area.

More Buttons

important

The default toolbar setting in Microsoft Word 2000 displays both the Standard and Formatting toolbars in one row at the top of the document window, just below the menu bar. This gives you maximum workspace. While working through the exercises in this book, toolbar buttons you need may not initially be visible. If a toolbar button is not visible, click one of the two More Buttons drop-down arrows on the toolbar to locate the button you need. When you select a new toolbar button, it is automatically added to the visible portion of the toolbar, replacing one that is not used often.

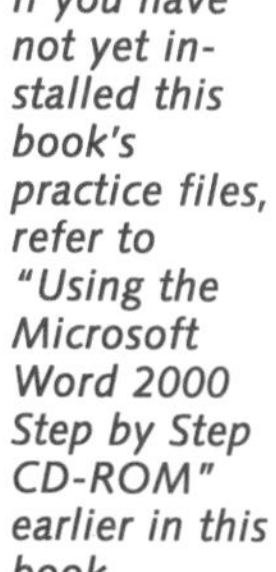

If you have not yet installed this book's practice files, refer to "Using the Microsoft Word 2000 Step by Step CD-ROM" earlier in this book.

Start Word and open a practice file

In this exercise, you start Word, open a practice file, and then save it under a new name.

1. On the Windows taskbar, click the Start button.
   The Start menu appears.
2. On the Start menu, point to Programs, and then click Microsoft Word.
   Microsoft Word 2000 opens.
3. On the Standard toolbar, click the Open button.
   The Open dialog box appears.

Open

4. Click the Look In drop-down arrow, and then select your hard disk.

5. In the list of folders, double-click the Word 2000 SBS Practice folder, and then double-click the Lesson14 folder.
6. In the file list, double-click the 14A file to open it.

   An outline document for a client's Web site opens.
7. On the File menu, click Save As.

   The Save As dialog box appears.
8. Be sure that the Lesson14 folder appears in the Save In box.
9. In the File Name box, select the text, and then type **Web Outline 14**
10. Click Save.

Using Outline View

The Web Outline 14 document was written in Print Layout view. To edit it, you need to switch to Outline view to get a clearer picture of the headings, subheadings, and overall structure. You switch to Outline view by using the View buttons at the left end of the horizontal scroll bar.

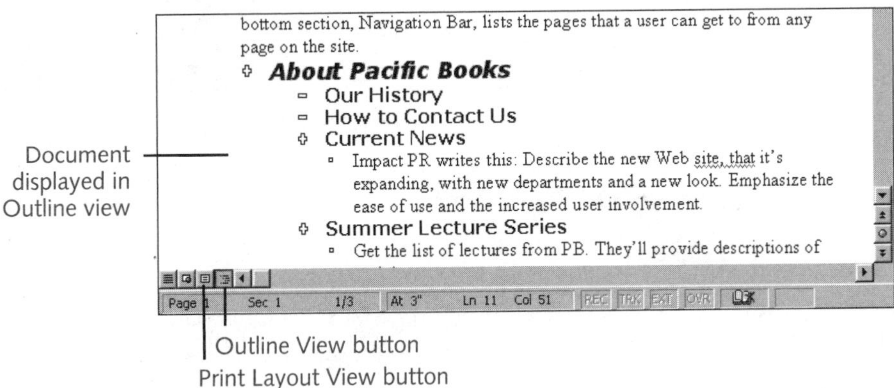

In Outline view, indentations show the hierarchy of headings in a document, with lower-level headings indented under higher-level headings. If a heading has subheadings or body text (any text not formatted as a heading) below it, a plus sign is displayed beside that heading. If no subheadings or body text are below a heading, a minus sign is displayed beside that heading. Body text, which is usually indented under the heading it follows, is marked with a small square adjacent to the text.

When a document is in Outline view, the Outlining toolbar is displayed below the Standard and Formatting toolbars. This toolbar gives quick access to the special functions of Outline view.

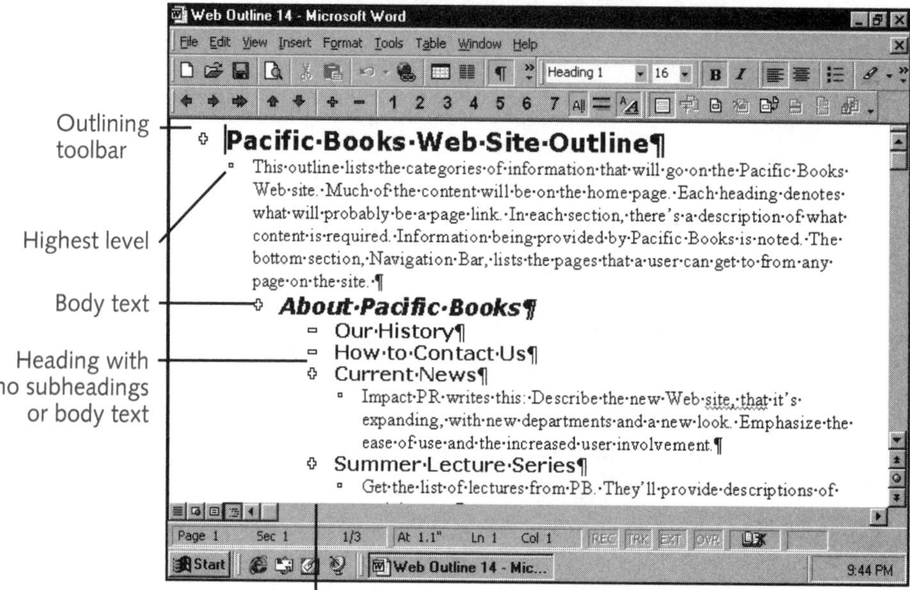

Switch to Outline view

In this exercise, you switch to Outline view.

Outline View

- On the left end of the horizontal scroll bar, click the Outline View button.
  Web Outline 14 is displayed in Outline view.

> **tip**
>
> If you don't see the correct formatting in your document headings when you switch to Outline view, on the Outlining toolbar, click the Show Formatting button to turn on the formatting.

Using the Outlining Toolbar

In Outline view, the Outlining toolbar appears below the other toolbars at the top of the window. The following table describes the buttons on the Outlining toolbar.

To	Use these buttons
Promote a heading	
Demote a heading	
Demote a heading to body text	
Move a heading and associated text and subheadings up one line	
Move a heading and associated text and subheadings down one line	
Expand a heading to show its subheadings and body text	 +
Collapse a heading to hide its subheadings and body text	 −
Show a specific heading level and levels above it	1 2 3 4 5 6 7
Show all heading levels	All
Show only the first line of body text in a paragraph (toggle this button to display all lines)	
Show the outline with formatting	
Display subdocument formatting	

tip

Outline view is similar to the Document Map view—both views help you see the structure of your document. Document Map view is most useful as a navigational tool, while Outline view helps you analyze and rearrange the document structure. For a discussion of Document Map view, see Lesson 2, "Working with Text."

Viewing Specific Levels of a Document Outline

By using Outline view when you are working in a long document, you can quickly see the organization of the document by heading levels. A heading is ranked by its style—for example, a first-level heading is Heading 1 style, a second-level heading is Heading 2 style, and so on. If you want to be sure of how a heading is styled, select the heading, and then look at the Style box on the Formatting toolbar to see the name of the heading style.

To get an overview of the document, for example, you can choose to display only the uppermost heading levels and hide subheadings and body text. The numbered heading level buttons on the Outlining toolbar allow you to select the level of headings you want to see.

View the first three heading levels

In this exercise, you use the Show Heading 3 button to review the document organization without viewing every heading level.

1. If necessary, press Ctrl+Home to move to the beginning of the document.
2. On the Outlining toolbar, click the Show Heading 3 button.
   The first three heading levels of Web Outline 14 are displayed.
   Your screen should look similar to the following illustration.

3

Show Heading 3

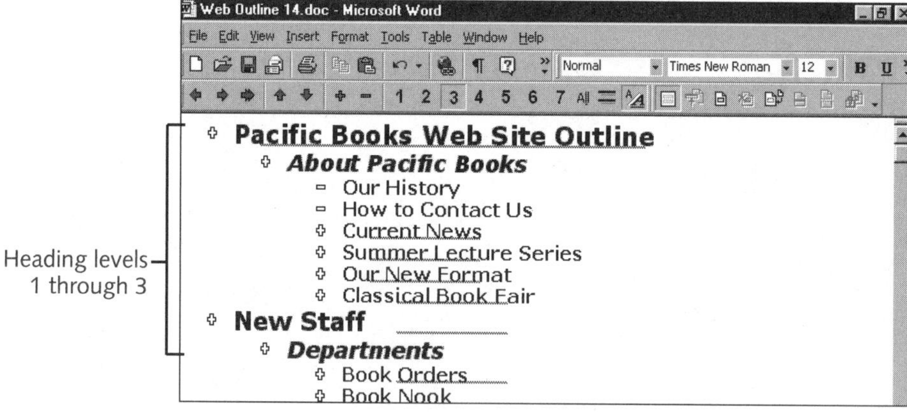

View all headings and body text

In this exercise, you expand the outline to see all the headings and body text again.

Show All Headings

- On the Outlining toolbar, click the Show All Headings button.

  All of the heading levels and body text are displayed.

View two heading levels

In this exercise, you reduce the outline to the first two heading levels.

Show Heading 2

- On the Outlining toolbar, click the Show Heading 2 button.

  The first two levels of the outline are displayed.

Body text expands after all subheadings are expanded.

Expanding and Collapsing Headings

Another way to focus on specific parts of the document for editing is to use the Expand and Collapse buttons on the Outlining toolbar. For example, if only certain heading levels of a document are displayed, you can *expand* just one section of the outline—displaying subheadings and body text in that section only—to analyze and revise its content. When you finish working on that section, you can *collapse* it again and expand a different section. By expanding and collapsing one section at a time, you keep the overall heading structure of your document in view while doing more detailed editing on a specific part, and you reduce the amount of scrolling you have to do. The Expand and Collapse buttons affect the section under the heading containing the insertion point.

Expand a heading

In this exercise, you expand every level within one section of the Web Outline 14 document.

1. Scroll so that the heading *New Staff* is at the top of the document window, and then click the second-level heading Departments.

Expand

2. On the Outlining toolbar, click the Expand button.

   The third-level subheadings under the *Departments* heading are displayed.
3. Click the Expand button two more times.

   The subheadings under the *Departments* section expand to the Heading 5 level. Note that the headings above and below this section remain collapsed.

To expand or collapse a heading, you can also double-click the plus sign to the left of that heading.

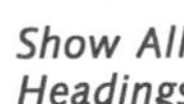

Your screen should look similar to the following illustration.

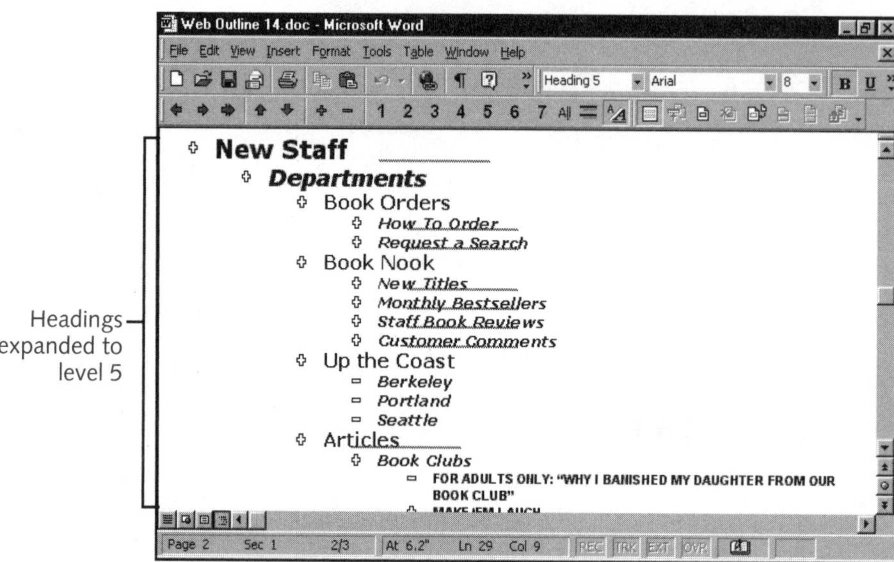

Headings expanded to level 5

Collapse a heading

In this exercise, you use the Collapse button to hide all the levels under the *Departments* subheading.

Collapse

- Be sure that the insertion point is still in the heading *Departments*, and on the Outlining toolbar, click the Collapse button three times.

  The subheadings under *Departments* collapse.

Promoting and Demoting Headings

If you want to change a heading level in a document, you can use buttons on the Outlining toolbar to *promote* or *demote* it. To promote a heading is to give it a higher level in the document, and to demote a heading is to give it a lower level. You can also promote body text to a heading level, and you can demote a heading to body text.

As you review document headings to see if they are at the correct level, use the Show First Line Only button on the Outlining toolbar to reduce the amount of body text in view. This allows you to see just the first line of body text under a heading as a reminder of the content below, while saving space for you to work with more heading levels on the screen.

Show only the first line of body text

In this exercise, you use the Show First Line Only button to reduce the amount of body text on the screen.

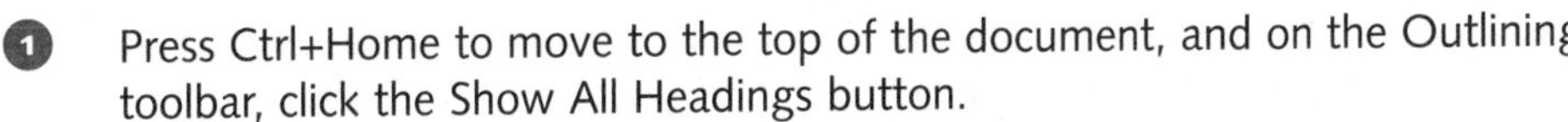

Show All Headings

1. Press Ctrl+Home to move to the top of the document, and on the Outlining toolbar, click the Show All Headings button.

   All headings and body text in the Web Outline 14 document are displayed.

2. On the Outlining toolbar, click the Show First Line Only button.

   Each paragraph of body text is reduced to one line.

Show First Line Only

Promote a heading

In this exercise, you promote a heading to modify the hierarchy in a section of the document.

1. In the Web Outline 14 document, click the heading *Current News*, which is in the section *About Pacific Books*.

Promote

2. On the Outlining toolbar, click the Promote button.

   The heading *Current News* is promoted from Heading 3 to Heading 2.

   Your screen should look similar to the following illustration.

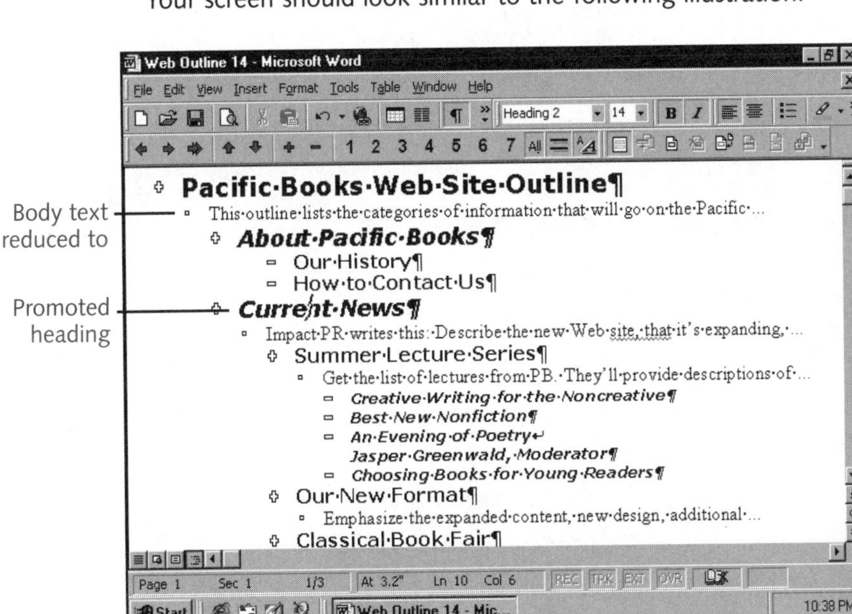

3. To reduce scrolling, point to the plus sign before *Current News* and double-click.

   The section is collapsed.

Demote a heading

In this exercise, you demote a heading by two levels, and then you demote another heading to body text.

Demote

When the pointer appears as a four-headed arrow, drag a plus or minus sign to the left to promote a heading or to the right to demote a heading.

1. Click the heading *New Staff* and then, on the Outlining toolbar, click the Demote button twice.

   The heading is demoted from Heading 1 to Heading 3.

   Your screen should look similar to the following illustration.

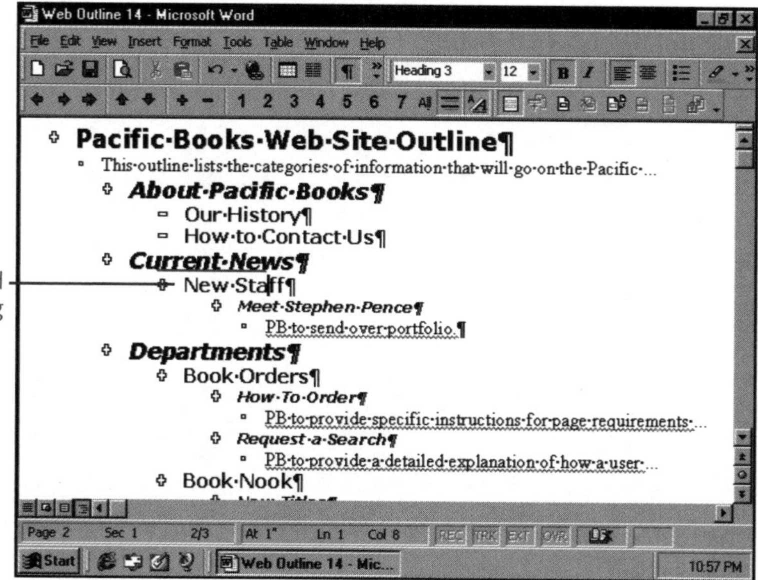

2. Scroll down to the subheading that begins *For Adults Only* (Heading 5).
3. Position the insertion point before the phrase *"Why I banished my daughter..."* and press Enter.

   This portion of the heading moves down to the next line.

Demote To Body Text

4. On the Outlining toolbar, click the Demote To Body Text button.

   The heading is demoted from Heading 5 to body text.
5. At the end of the heading *For Adults Only,* delete the colon.

   Your screen should look similar to the following illustration.

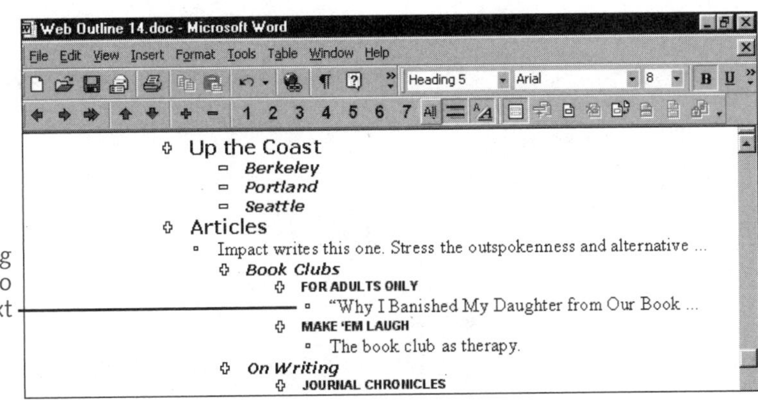

Heading demoted to body text

Save

6. On the Standard toolbar, click the Save button.
7. On the Outlining toolbar, click the Show First Line Only button again.

   All of the body text is displayed.

Show First Line Only

Moving Blocks of Text

If you are not working through this lesson sequentially, before proceeding to the next step, open the 14B file in the Lesson14 folder, and save it as Web Outline 14.

In Outline view, not only can you revise a document by promoting or demoting a heading, but you can also move blocks of text within the document by moving a heading. When you move a collapsed heading, all of the hidden subheadings and body text under it move, too. This makes moving text blocks simple: you don't have to select whole paragraphs or scroll to move them over long distances. Note, however, that this works only for collapsed headings—if you move an expanded heading, only the selected heading moves.

To move headings one line at a time, use the Move Up and Move Down buttons on the Outlining toolbar. You can also select and move more than one heading at a time.

Move blocks of text

In this exercise, you use the Move Up and Move Down buttons to move collapsed headings in the Web Outline 14 document.

Show Heading 3

1. On the Outlining toolbar, click the Show Heading 3 button.

   The headings in the outline expand to the third level heading.
2. Under the heading *Current News*, click the subheading *Our New Format*.
3. On the Outlining toolbar, click the Move Up button to move the heading above the heading *Summer Lecture Series*.
4. On the Outlining toolbar, click the Expand button.

   The body text that moved with the heading *Our New Format* is displayed.

Move Up

Expand

Your screen should look similar to the following illustration.

You can also drag the plus or minus sign to move a heading.

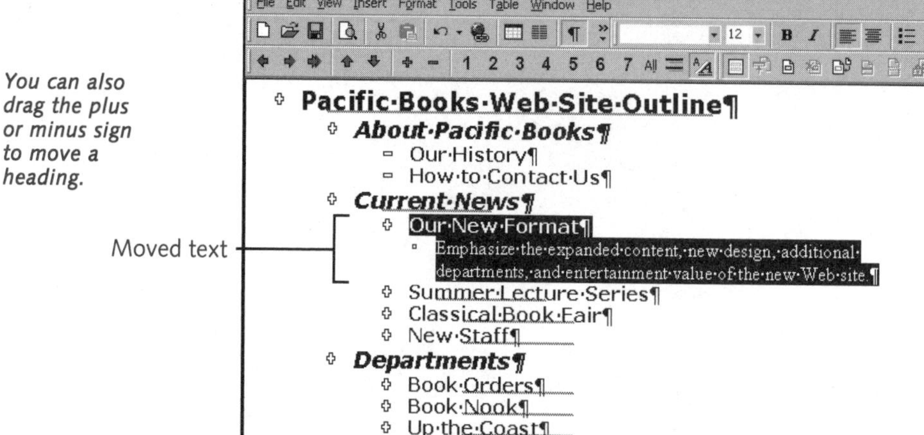

Move Down

Expand

Save

5. Click the heading *Summer Lecture Series.*
6. On the Outlining toolbar, click the Move Down button twice.

   The heading *Summer Lecture Series* is moved below the heading *New Staff.*
7. On the Outlining toolbar, click the Expand button twice.

   The entire block of moved text and subheadings under the heading *Summer Lecture Series* is displayed.
8. On the Standard toolbar, click the Save button.

Creating Subdocuments from a Master Document

If you want to work on a particular portion of a document while your partner works on another, you can create a *subdocument* for part of the document. A subdocument is a separate file that is linked to the larger, *master* document. By dividing up the original file into subdocuments, you enable several people to work on portions of the document at one time. When work on a subdocument is complete, you can open the subdocument within the master document, and all the latest changes to the subdocument are reflected in the master document. This means that you don't have to compare different versions of one file that has multiple authors or pass one document around for several people to work on at different times. When all subdocuments are finished, they can be converted back into part of the master document.

Using buttons on the Outlining toolbar, you can create subdocuments from any portion of a document, or you can insert an already existing file into the document as a subdocument. When you create or insert a subdocument, the document that contains the subdocument automatically becomes a master document, and a link between the subdocument and master document is created. If the subdocument was created from the master document, it is given a new file name. The subdocument is shown within the master document with section breaks above and below it.

When you first view a document in Outline view, the Master Document View button on the Outlining toolbar is activated. The view shows a subdocument that you create or insert surrounded by a box, and a small document icon appears in the upper-left corner of the box. To open the subdocument in a separate window, double-click the document icon. When a subdocument opens in its own window, the Outlining toolbar disappears from that window, the document is displayed in Print Layout view, and the Web toolbar appears.

In a master document, you may also see a padlock icon in the upper-left corner of a subdocument. This means that the subdocument is locked. For details about locked subdocuments, see "Locking and Unlocking Subdocuments," later in this lesson.

Your business partner at Impact Public Relations is going to complete the *Navigation Bar* section of the Web Outline 14 document. You decide to create a subdocument for your partner so the two of you can work on parts of Web Outline 14 at the same time.

If you are not working through this lesson sequentially, before proceeding to the next step, open the 14C file in the Lesson14 folder and save it as Web Outline 14.

Create a subdocument within the existing document

In this exercise, you display formatting marks and then create a subdocument in Web Outline 14. Web Outline 14 then becomes the master document.

1. On the Standard toolbar, click the Show/Hide button.

   Formatting marks, such as paragraph marks and section breaks, become visible in the document.

Show/Hide

2. On the Outlining toolbar, be sure that the Master Document View button is depressed.

3. Double-click the plus sign before the heading *Pacific Books Web Site Outline*.

   The subheadings under the heading collapse.

Master Document View

4. Point to the plus sign before the heading *Navigation Bar*. When the pointer turns into a four-headed arrow, click.

   The heading *Navigation Bar* and all of its subheadings are selected.

Create Subdocument

5. On the Outlining toolbar, click the Create Subdocument button.

   The selected text becomes a subdocument. Section breaks appear above and below the subdocument, a box shows around it, and a small document icon appears in its upper-left corner.

Your screen should look similar to the following illustration.

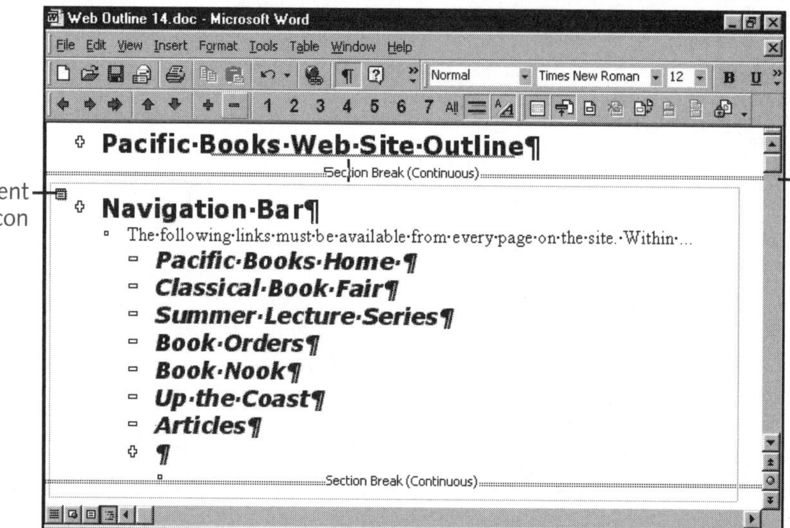

Save

6. On the Standard toolbar, click the Save button.

   Changes to the Web Outline 14 document are saved. The subdocument becomes a separate file named Navigation Bar.doc.

tip

To insert a separate file as a subdocument in a master document, in the master document, click the point at which you want to insert the subdocument. On the Outlining toolbar, click Insert Subdocument. In the Insert Subdocument dialog box, select the folder that contains the document you want to insert, and then double-click the file to insert it into the master document. If you have already created other subdocuments in the master document and collapsed them, on the Outlining toolbar, click Expand Subdocuments. This makes the Insert Subdocuments button available.

Collapsing Subdocuments to Display Hyperlinks

Rather than always displaying the text of subdocuments within the master document, you may prefer to see only the link to the subdocument file. You can do this by collapsing the subdocument within the master document. Instead of the subdocument's text, a hyperlink to the subdocument file is displayed. You can click the hyperlink to open and edit the subdocument in a separate window. In the new window, the Web toolbar is displayed, and its Back button is activated so that you can easily switch back to the master document. Changes made to the subdocument are reflected in the master document when you return to the master document and expand the subdocument again.

Collapse a subdocument

In this exercise, you collapse the subdocument you created in Web Outline 14 and view its hyperlink in the master document.

- On the Outlining toolbar, click the Collapse Subdocuments button.

  A hyperlink replaces the text in the subdocument.

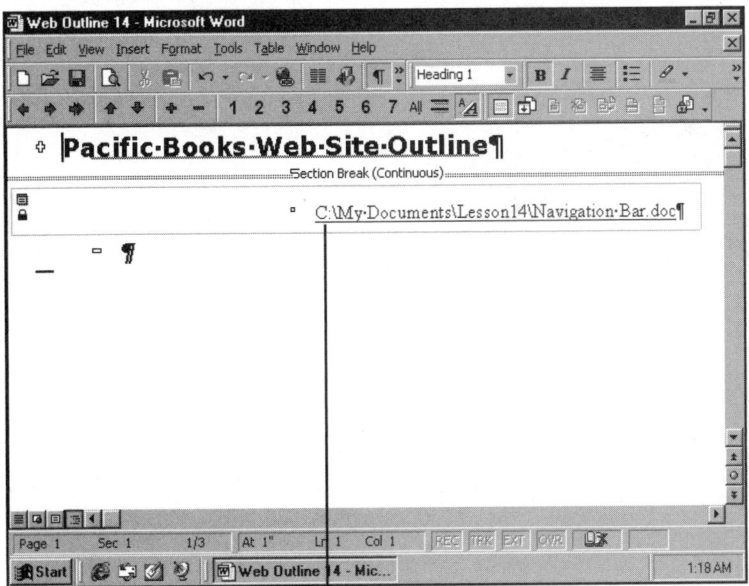

Hyperlink to new subdocument file

Locking and Unlocking Subdocuments

When a subdocument is locked, a padlock icon appears in the subdocument's upper-left corner, within the master document. A subdocument is locked in the following instances:

- When the subdocument is open in a separate window. Another user can make changes to the subdocument in the separate window, but no changes can be made to it within the master document until the separate window is closed, which unlocks the subdocument.
- When the subdocument has been protected by the Lock Document button on the Outlining toolbar. To lock a subdocument this way, click the subdocument within the master document, and on the Outlining toolbar, click Lock Document. No changes can be made to the subdocument either from within the master document or in a separate window. To unlock the subdocument, click the Lock Document button.
- When a subdocument is collapsed within the master document and there is a hyperlink for it. To unlock the subdocument, either click the hyperlink or click the Expand Subdocuments button on the Outlining toolbar.
- When a subdocument has been given limited access or is read-only. For an overview about these options, type "master documents" in the Office Assistant window or search the Index in the Microsoft Help file.

Open and edit a subdocument

In this exercise, you open the Navigation Bar subdocument and add text to it.

1. In the Web Outline 14 document, click the hyperlink for the subdocument, *C:\Word 2000 SBS Practice\Lesson14\Navigation Bar.doc*.

   The Navigation Bar subdocument opens in a separate window in Print Layout view. The new filename is displayed in the title bar, and a section break appears at the end of the document (you might have to scroll to see it).

Your screen should look similar to the following illustration.

Subdocument opened in a separate window

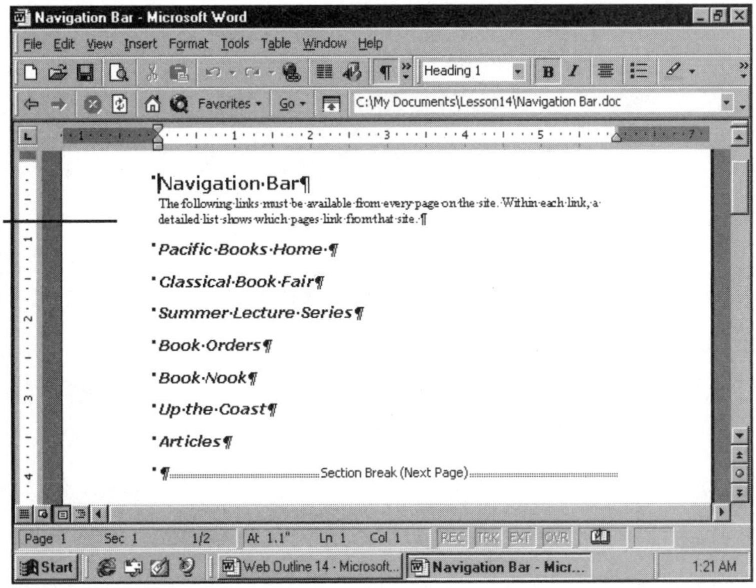

important

Be sure not to remove the section break within the subdocument. This break preserves the relationship between the subdocument and master document.

2. Click in front of the heading *Summer Lecture Series*, and press Enter.

   A new, blank line is inserted above the heading *Summer Lecture Series.*

3. In the new line, click in front of the paragraph mark.

If the Style box is not visible, on the Formatting toolbar, click the More Buttons drop-down arrow to locate the style button.

4. On the Formatting toolbar, click the Style drop-down arrow, and then click Normal.

   The paragraph mark changes to Normal style.

5. Type **This page links to the following Web pages:** and press Enter.

6. Type the following five lines, pressing Enter at the end of each line to create a paragraph break:

   Pacific Books Home

   Dramatic Scenes Entry Form

   Classic Trivia Sweepstakes

   Essay Contest

   Book List

Format the text

In this exercise, you format some of the new text so that the Web page names will be easier to read.

Font Color

Save

1. Select the five lines of text you typed in step 6 of the preceding exercise.
2. On the Formatting toolbar, click the Font Color drop-down arrow, and then click Dark Blue.
3. Click any area outside of the selected text.

   The text changes to dark blue.
4. On the Standard toolbar, click the Save button.
5. On the File menu, click Close to close the subdocument window.

Review the changes in the master document

In this exercise, you expand the Navigation Bar subdocument in the master document to see the changes you made.

Expand Subdocuments

- In the Web Outline 14 document, on the Outlining toolbar, click the Expand Subdocuments button.

  The subdocument is expanded within the master document, and the changes you made are shown.

  Your screen should look similar to the following illustration.

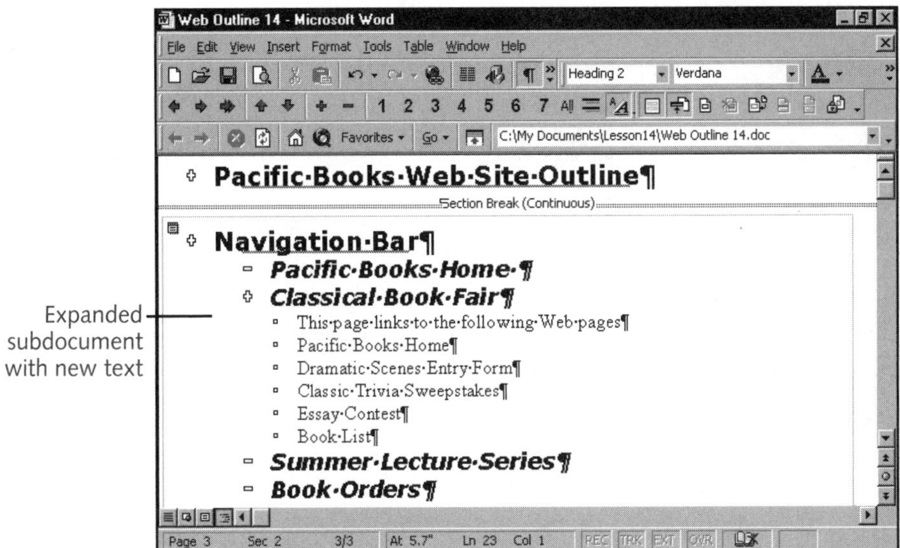

Converting a Subdocument into Part of the Master Document

When you finish editing a subdocument, you can convert the subdocument back into part of the master document. Before you can convert the subdocument, it must be unlocked. After you convert the subdocument, the subdocument file remains in its original location, and you can delete it.

Convert the subdocument

1. Open the master document.
2. If the document is not in Outline View, on the left end of the horizontal scroll bar, click the Outline View button.

   The document switches to Outline view, and the Outlining toolbar is displayed.
3. If the subdocument within the master document is collapsed, on the Outlining toolbar, click the Expand Subdocuments button.
4. In the subdocument, click the subdocument icon.

   The entire subdocument is selected.
5. On the Outlining toolbar, click the Remove Subdocument button.

   The subdocument icon disappears from the subdocument, and the box surrounding the subdocument is removed.
6. Save the master document.

   The subdocument is converted back into part of the master document.

One Step Further Navigating by Using Bookmarks

A *bookmark*, an invisible tag that marks a specific point in a document, allows you to move quickly to a particular place in a document. Instead of scrolling through pages of text to find a section of your document, you can go directly to the bookmark that tags the section you need. You can insert an unlimited number of bookmarks into a document.

To create a bookmark, you begin by placing the insertion point where you want the bookmark to go, or you select words, phrases, or entire paragraphs that you want to mark. Then, using the Bookmark command and dialog box, you give the selected location or text a bookmark name. Later, if a bookmark becomes unnecessary, you can delete it.

Because you frequently review and revise the content under the heading *Departments* in the Web Outline 14 document, you decide to create a bookmark at that heading to give you quick access to it.

Create a bookmark

If you are not working through this lesson sequentially, before proceeding to the next step, open the 14D file in the Lesson14 folder, and save it as Web Outline 14.

In this exercise, you create a bookmark for the *Departments* heading in the Web Outline 14 document.

1. On the Outlining toolbar, click Show All Headings.
2. Scroll down to the heading *Departments*, and then click directly in front of it.
3. On the Insert menu, click Bookmark.

   The Bookmark dialog box appears.
4. In the Bookmark Name box, type **departments**
5. Click Add.

   The Bookmark dialog box closes, and a bookmark named *departments* is assigned to the location of the insertion point.
6. On the Standard toolbar, click the Save button.
7. Press Ctrl+Home to move the insertion point to the beginning of the document.

You can include uppercase or lowercase letters in the bookmark name, but you cannot include spaces.

Save

Go to the bookmark location

In this exercise, you use the Go To feature to move to the *departments* bookmark that you created, and then you use an existing bookmark to navigate to another section of the document.

1. On the left side of the status bar, double-click the page number.

   The Find And Replace dialog box appears.

2. On the Go To tab, in the Go To What box, select Bookmark.

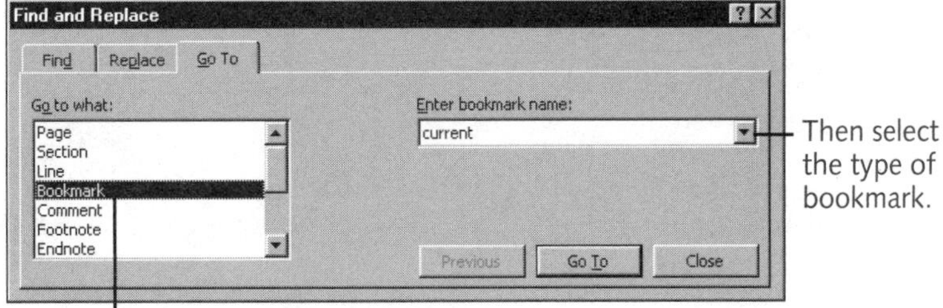

Then select the type of bookmark.

First select Bookmark.

3. Click the Enter Bookmark Name drop-down arrow.
4. In the Enter Bookmark Name list, select departments.
5. Click the Go To button.

   The insertion point jumps to the *Departments* heading, and the Find And Replace dialog box remains displayed. (Move the Find And Replace dialog box to view your document.)

6. In the Find And Replace dialog box, click the Enter Bookmark Name drop-down arrow, select current, and then click Go To.

   The insertion point moves to the *Current News* heading.

7. In the Find And Replace dialog box, click Close.

tip

You can create a bookmark that has a hyperlink. This type of link is often used to navigate through a Web page. For details on creating a bookmark hyperlink, see Lesson 11, "Designing Web Pages."

Finish the lesson

Save

1. On the Standard toolbar, click the Save button.

   Changes made to Web Outline 14 are saved.
2. On the File menu, click Close.
3. On the File menu, click Exit.

Lesson 14 Quick Reference

To	Do this	Button
Display a document in Outline view	On the left end of the horizontal scroll bar, click the Outline View button.	
Display specific heading levels	On the Outlining toolbar, click the heading level button that corresponds to the heading level you want to see in your document.	
Display subheadings and body text under a heading	Click the heading, and then on the Outlining toolbar, click the Expand button.	
Hide subheadings and body text under a heading	Click the heading, and then on the Outlining toolbar, click the Collapse button.	
Promote a heading	Click the heading, and on the Outlining toolbar, click the Promote button.	
Demote a heading	Click the heading, and on the Outlining toolbar, click the Demote button.	
Demote a heading to body text	Click the heading, and on the Outlining toolbar, click the Demote To Body Text button.	
Display all headings and body text	On the Outlining toolbar, click the Show All Headings button.	All

Lesson 14 Quick Reference

To	Do this	Button
Display the first line of body text	On the Outlining toolbar, click the Show First Line Only button. To display all the body text, click Show First Line Only again.	
Move a block of text up in Outline view	Click a collapsed heading, and on the Outlining toolbar, click the Move Up button.	
Move a block of text down in Outline view	Click a collapsed heading, and on the Outlining toolbar, click the Move Down button.	
Create a subdocument within an existing document	Select the text you want to create as the subdocument. Then, on the Outlining toolbar, click the Create Subdocument. To save and name the subdocument, save the master document.	
Open the subdocument in a separate window	In the master document, either click the hyperlink, or double-click the subdocument icon.	
Add a bookmark to a document	Place the insertion point where you want the bookmark, and on the Insert menu, click Bookmark. In the Bookmark dialog box, type a name to identify the bookmark, and then click Add.	
Go to a bookmark in a document	On the left side of the status bar, double-click the page number. In the Find And Replace dialog box, on the Go To tab, select Bookmark, and then select the desired bookmark. Click Go To.	

15

Sending Documents Through E-mail

In this lesson you will learn how to:

- ✔ *Send a Microsoft Word document as an e-mail attachment.*
- ✔ *Send a Word document through e-mail in HTML format.*
- ✔ *Route a Word document for review by a specific order of recipients.*
- ✔ *Set up Word as your e-mail editor.*
- ✔ *Personalize outgoing e-mail messages using stationery and a signature.*

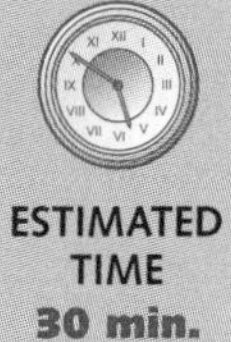

ESTIMATED TIME **30 min.**

As you work on projects with coworkers, you often want to pass files back and forth for review or further work. Using e-mail programs, such as Microsoft Outlook or Microsoft Outlook Express, you can easily send Word documents through e-mail. You can also send Word documents in HTML format for file recipients who do not have Word installed on their computers.

The routing-slip feature in Word also allows you to send a document through e-mail to a succession of recipients. Each person can review the document, making comments or changes, and then route it to the next designated recipient. In this way, all feedback occurs in one document.

You can also use Word as your e-mail editor to create customized e-mail messages with Word formatting such as bold and italic type, bulleted and numbered lists, font types and colors. In addition, you can personalize your messages with themes and special signatures.

As you complete the following exercises, if some of your results differ from those in the lesson, consult Appendix B, "Matching the Exercises" on the Microsoft Word 2000 Step by Step CD-ROM.

At Impact Public Relations, you want to send your business partner a subdocument of the outline of a client's Web site. Using Word 2000, you attach the subdocument to send in Outlook 2000 for your partner to edit in Word. To utilize the HTML formatting available in Word 2000, you send this document to your partner again in HTML format. She opens and edits it in Word. Then you route the outline document to several reviewers for their feedback. Finally, you set up Word to edit your e-mail with Word formatting.

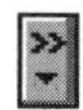

More Buttons

important

The default toolbar setting in Microsoft Word 2000 displays both the Standard and Formatting toolbars in one row at the top of your document window. This gives you maximum workspace. While working through the exercises in this book, you use toolbar buttons that may not initially be visible. If a toolbar button you need is not visible, click one of the two More Buttons drop-down arrows on the toolbar to locate the button you need. When you select a new toolbar button, it is automatically added to the visible portion of your toolbar, replacing one that is not used often.

Start Word and open a practice file

In this exercise, you start Word, open a practice file, and then save it under a new name.

1. On the Windows taskbar, click the Start button.

   The Start menu appears.

2. On the Start menu, point to Programs, and then click Microsoft Word.

   Microsoft Word 2000 opens.

Open

3. On the Standard toolbar, click the Open button.

   The Open dialog box appears.

4. Click the Look In drop-down arrow, and then select your hard disk.
5. In the list of folders, double-click the Word 2000 SBS Practice folder, and then double-click the Lesson15 folder.
6. In the file list, double-click the 15A file to open it.

   This document, which outlines Web site content for your company's client, opens in Outline view.

7. On the File menu, click Save As.

   The Save As dialog box appears.

8. Be sure that the Lesson15 folder appears in the Save In box.
9. In the File Name box, select the text, and then type **Web Outline 15**
10. Click Save.

Display formatting marks

To make it easier to edit your document, you can display formatting marks, such as paragraph marks and space marks, on your screen.

Show/Hide ¶

- If formatting marks are not currently displayed, on the Standard toolbar, click the Show/Hide ¶ button.

> **important**
>
> In this lesson, you use Word 2000 and Outlook 2000 to send documents to your own e-mail address. This will allow you to see the results of the exercises. In order to complete this lesson, you must be able to send electronic mail over a network, and you must have a Typical or Full installation of Microsoft Office 2000.

Sending Word Documents Through E-mail

Sending Word documents through e-mail is a quick way to deliver files to other team members or outside contacts. You can send a document as a file attachment to an e-mail message, or you can send it displayed directly within the message, in HTML format.

When you send a document as an attachment to an e-mail message, the file is sent unopened and appears in the message represented by a Word icon and the filename. The recipient can open and edit the file in Word (if Word is installed), and can save it to his or her own computer. If the attachment is a Web page that was created in Word, the recipient can open it in a Web browser, and then edit it in Word.

When you send a Word document displayed directly in an e-mail message, the document arrives in the recipient's inbox in HTML format. A recipient who does not have Word installed can at least read the document—with its original formatting—as displayed in the e-mail message. You might choose to send a document in HTML format in case all recipients do not have Word, or if you want to allow quick access to the document, so recipients don't have to open a separate file.

important

With Microsoft Word 2000, you can use the following e-mail programs to send a Word attachment: Outlook, Outlook Express, Microsoft Exchange Client, or another 32-bit e-mail program that is compatible with the Messaging Application Programming Interface (MAPI). To send a document in HTML format, you need to use Outlook 2000 or Outlook Express 5.0 or later versions. In addition, sending and routing documents through e-mail may not work across electronic mail gateways. A gateway refers to software or a computer running software that enables two different networks to communicate. For more about requirements for using Word with e-mail programs, see Microsoft Word Help.

Establish a connection and select the mail format

In this exercise, you establish a connection to your e-mail server and then set your Outlook mail format to Outlook Rich Text.

1. Establish a connection to your e-mail server.
2. On the Windows taskbar, click the Start button.

   The Start menu appears.
3. On the Start menu, point to Programs, and then click Microsoft Outlook.

   Microsoft Outlook 2000 opens.
4. On the Tools menu, click Options.

   The Options dialog box appears.
5. On the Mail Format tab, in the Send In This Message Format list, select Microsoft Outlook Rich Text, and click OK.
6. Close Outlook.

For more information on subdocuments, see Lesson 14, "Using Outline View and Master Documents."

Open a subdocument and attach it to an e-mail message

In this exercise, you open a subdocument within the Web Outline 15 document and attach it to an e-mail message to send to your business partner.

1. Switch back to the Word window.
2. In the Web Outline 15 document, scroll down to the hyperlink for the subdocument, *C:\Word 2000 SBS Practice\Lesson15\15B.*
3. Click the hyperlink.

   The subdocument file 15B, with the heading *Navigation Bar,* opens as a separate document, and the Web toolbar appears.

tip

If you don't see the hyperlink, be sure that the document is in Outline view. If the document is not in Outline view, on the left end of the horizontal scroll bar, click the Outline View button. Then, on the Outlining toolbar, click the Collapse Subdocuments button.

4. In the subdocument window, on the File menu, point to Send To, and then click Mail Recipient (As Attachment).

tip

If the menu item Mail Recipient (As Attachment) is not available, on the Tools menu, click Options. In the Options dialog box, on the General tab, select the Mail As Attachment check box, and click OK.

An Outlook message window opens. The subdocument is attached in the message, represented by an icon with the file name 15B. Its top-level heading is displayed in the message Subject line.

Your screen should look similar to the following illustration.

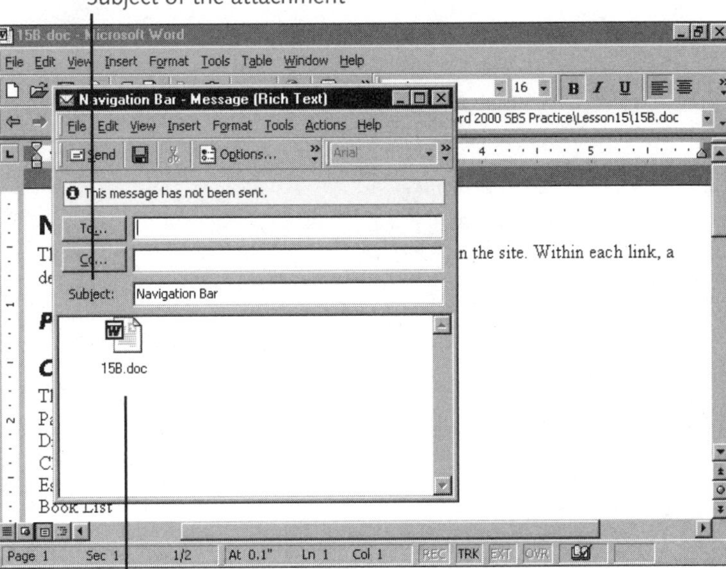

5. In the To box, type your own e-mail address.

Add text and send the message

In this exercise, you include a short text message and then send the e-mail.

1. In the message window, click to the right of the document icon, and then press Enter.
2. Type **Here's your section of the Web site outline. When you've completed it, please send it back to me. Thanks.**
3. On the Outlook Standard toolbar, click the Send button.

   The message is sent, and the subdocument 15B remains displayed in a Word window.
4. Close subdocument 15B, and leave Web Outline 15 displayed in the Word window.

Receive and open the attachment

In this exercise, you open the e-mail message that includes the attachment 15B.

1. On the Windows taskbar, click the Start button.

   The Start menu appears.
2. On the Start menu, point to Programs, and then click Microsoft Outlook.

   Microsoft Outlook 2000 opens.
3. Display the contents of your Inbox. If necessary, on the Standard toolbar in Outlook, click the Send/Receive button to get your latest mail.

   The e-mail message you sent to yourself appears in the Inbox, with the subject name *Navigation Bar*. A paper clip icon signifies that it contains an attachment.
4. Double-click the message.

   The message opens, and subdocument 15B is attached, represented by an icon, above the text that you typed.

Your screen should look similar to the following illustration.

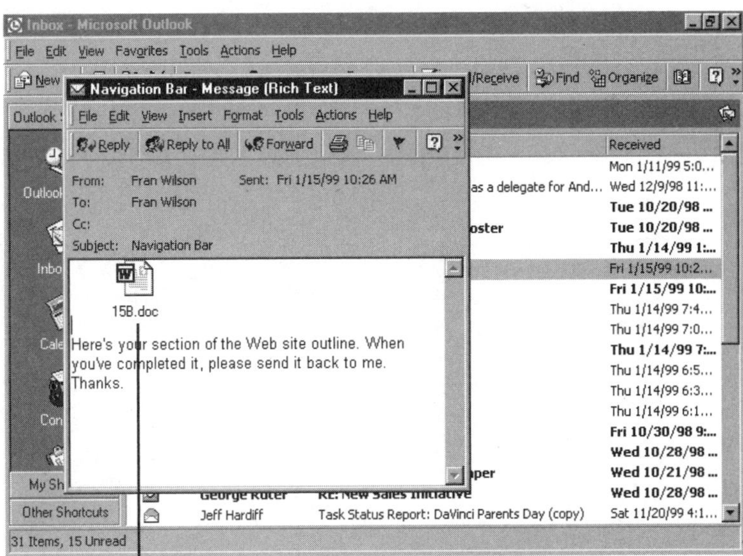

Attached document in a received mail message

5. Close the Outlook message window, and minimize Outlook.

tip

When you double-click an attached document in e-mail, you might be prompted to open the file, or save it to your hard disk. It is generally advisable to select the Save It To Disk option. This saves a copy of the file on your computer and, if you have the applicable software, enables your computer virus scanner to check the document before opening it on your computer. Scanning for viruses can prevent corrupt files from infecting your hard disk. For more about saving an attachment, see the following section, "Saving an Attached Document."

Saving an Attached Document

When you receive a message with an attached document, you can save the document on your computer. This creates a copy of the document so that you don't have to edit it as an attachment in e-mail.

You can save the document with the same filename, or rename it. Renaming the file can help you keep track of which version you edit.

Save an attached document

1. In Outlook, open the message that includes the attachment you want to save.
2. On the File menu, click Save Attachments.

   The Save Attachment dialog box appears.
3. Navigate to the folder in which you want to save the attachment.
4. In the File Name box, type a new filename, and then click Save.

   A copy of the attached document is renamed and saved to your hard disk, and the original attachment remains in the e-mail message.

Now you can work on your saved copy to make changes to the document. To send the edited file to the original sender or someone else, follow the procedure earlier in this lesson for attaching the file in an e-mail message.

You can also attach the file from within Outlook. In Outlook, open a new message window, and on the Outlook Standard toolbar, click the Insert File button.

Insert File

In the Insert File dialog box, browse the folders on your computer to locate the file you want to send, and then click Insert. An icon appears in the message that represents the file type you have inserted.

Sending Documents in HTML Format

If you are not working through this lesson sequentially, before proceeding to the next step, open the 15C file in the Lesson 15 folder, and save it as Web Outline 15.

To send a document from Word in HTML format, use the E-mail button on the Standard toolbar. When you send a document in this way, the document is displayed in the mail message window. After you send the mail, the recipient sees the document displayed in the Outlook message window, but it is now formatted in HTML rather than Word. If the mail recipient does not have HTML mail capability, and receives mail in plain text format, for example, he or she will see the mailed document as an attachment in the message.

You might want to send a message in HTML just for the immediacy of having the document appear in the mail message window. A reviewer can make changes to the document right in the message.

By sending a document in HTML format, you can preserve all the formatting that HTML makes possible, so that a Web page, for example, would be displayed intact in the mail. If the recipient does have Word, he or she can edit the document using Word as the editor.

In the following exercises, you re-send the Navigation Bar document to your business partner for editing—this time, the document is in HTML format.

Send a document in HTML format

In this exercise, you send the document Web Outline 15 in HTML format.

1. Be sure that your computer is connected to your mail server.
2. With Web Outline 15 displayed in the Word window, right-click the toolbar area to display the shortcut menu, and click Outlining toolbar and Web toolbar to turn them off.

E-mail

3. Press Ctrl+Home to move the insertion point to the top of the document, and on the Standard toolbar, click the E-mail button.

   The Outlook toolbar and address boxes are added to the Word document window.

   Your screen should look similar to the following illustration.

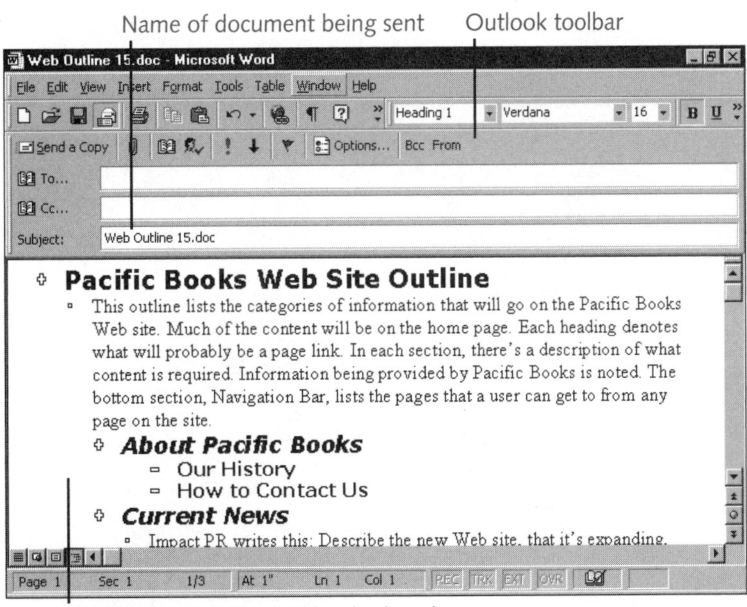

4. In the To line, type your e-mail address. (For the purposes of this lesson you're using your own e-mail address so you can review the results of the exercises.)
5. Click in the document window. On the Word Tools menu, point to Track Changes, and then click Highlight Changes.

   The Highlight Changes dialog box appears.
6. Select the Track Changes While Editing check box, select the Highlight Changes On Screen check box, and click OK.
7. In the document, click in front of the heading *Pacific Books Web Site Outline*, and press Enter.

   A new, blank paragraph mark is inserted above the heading.
8. Position the insertion point before the new paragraph mark. On the Formatting toolbar, click the Style drop-down arrow, and then select Normal.

   The paragraph mark changes to Normal style and decreases in size.
9. On the new, blank line, type **Here's the outline I'd like you to review. Please make changes using revision marks, and then send the document back to me.**

   This text is displayed with revision marks showing.

   Your screen should look similar to the following illustration.

Message text with revision marks showing

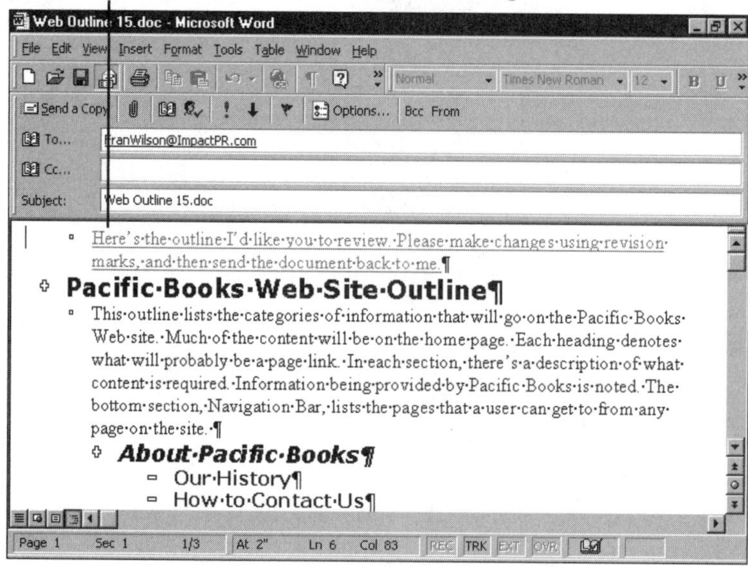

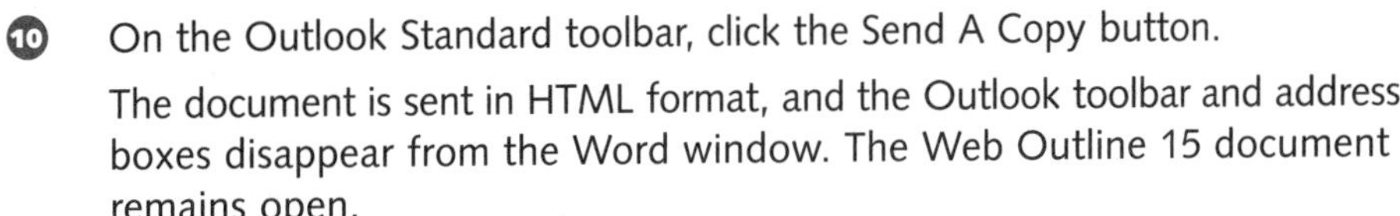

10. On the Outlook Standard toolbar, click the Send A Copy button.

    The document is sent in HTML format, and the Outlook toolbar and address boxes disappear from the Word window. The Web Outline 15 document remains open.

Save

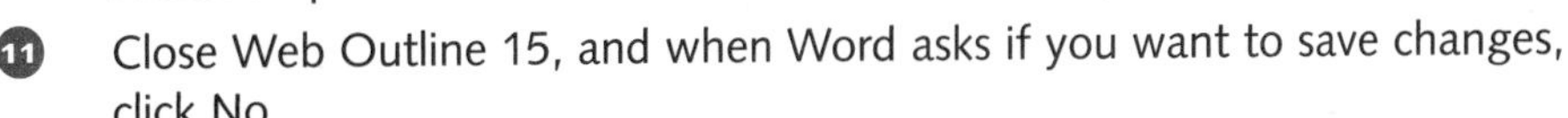

11. Close Web Outline 15, and when Word asks if you want to save changes, click No.

Open and edit the HTML message

In this exercise, you open the e-mail message from your Outlook Inbox and edit the Web Outline 15 document in Word.

1. Maximize the Outlook window. (If Outlook is not open, on the Windows taskbar, click the Start button, point to Programs, click Microsoft Outlook, and then open your Inbox.)
2. In the Outlook Inbox, double-click the message Web Outline 15.

   The message opens, and the document text is formatted in HTML.

   Your screen should look similar to the following illustration.

Received e-mail message with document formatted in HTML

Another way to edit the message in Word is to right-click the message and then on the shortcut menu, click Edit Message.

3. In the message window, on the Edit menu, click Edit Message.

   The message is displayed in a Word window, and a new, default document name is displayed in the title bar.

4. Click at the end of the first paragraph under the heading *Pacific Books Web Site Outline*, and type **[Let's include a cover sheet with a diagram of all the site links.]**

   (Remember that you are playing the role of a recipient responding to the message. If the message had actually been sent to another person, the revision marks would be in a different color from the sender's revision marks.)

E-mail

5. On the Standard toolbar, click the E-mail button.

   The Outlook menu bar and address boxes are added to the Word document window.

6. In the To box, type your own e-mail address.
7. In the Subject line, type **Edited Web Outline 15**
8. On the Outook toolbar, click the Send A Copy button.

   The document with your edits is sent. The Outlook toolbar and address boxes disappear from the Word window, and the edited document remains open.

9. Close the document, and when prompted to save the changes, click No.
10. Switch to the Outlook window and check to see that your message was received.
11. Minimize the Outlook window.

tip

If the text you typed is displayed with revision marks but isn't underlined, on the Word Tools menu, point to Track Changes, and then click Highlight Changes. In the Highlight Changes dialog box, click Options. In the Track Changes dialog box, in the Inserted Text area, click the Mark drop-down arrow, and then select Underline from the list. Click OK in the Track Changes dialog box.

Routing Documents

For more information on protecting documents for changes and comments, see Lesson 13, "Tracking Changes in Group Projects."

Using a routed document, which is sent in Word (.doc) format, simplifies the process of gathering feedback from several reviewers. Routing allows you to send one document to a succession of individual reviewers. Each reviewer makes changes or comments to the document and then sends it to the next designated reviewer.

To route a document, you attach a routing slip to it and protect the document for certain types of changes. For example, if you protect the document for Tracked Changes, all reviewers' changes are tracked with revision marks. If you protect the document for comments, recipients can insert comments, but they cannot change the document in any other way.

When you send the routed document, recipients receive it as an attachment in e-mail. Word automatically includes a message in the e-mail, explaining that the document is being routed and instructing recipients about what to do when they've completed their reviews. While the document is being routed, the originator receives a notification e-mail each time the document is sent to a new recipient. When the document has been routed to all designated recipients, and the last reviewer has completed his or her review, the document is automatically sent back to the originator, who decides which edits to accept.

You want input on the outline for a client's Web site, but you want to keep all comments and recommended changes in one document in order to save yourself time. To do this, you decide to route the Web Outline 15 document to your team members at Impact Public Relations.

important

For the purposes of this exercise, you will route the Web Outline 15 document to people in your own list of contacts in Outlook. Choose a few people that won't mind helping you with this exercise; all users should have Microsoft Office 2000 installed. If you need to create contacts, refer to the Help file in Outlook. Note that your contacts will not match the names in the illustration on the following page.

Fill out a routing slip and send the routed document

If you are not working through this lesson sequentially, before proceeding to the next step, open the 15D file in the Lesson15 folder, and save it as Web Outline 15.

In this exercise, you add a routing slip to Web Outline 15, set up a list of recipients, and send the routed document.

1. Be sure that you are connected to your mail server.
2. On the Standard toolbar, click Open, and in the Lesson15 folder, double-click Web Outline 15 to open it.

3. On the File menu, point to Send To, and then click Routing Recipient. The Routing Slip dialog box appears.

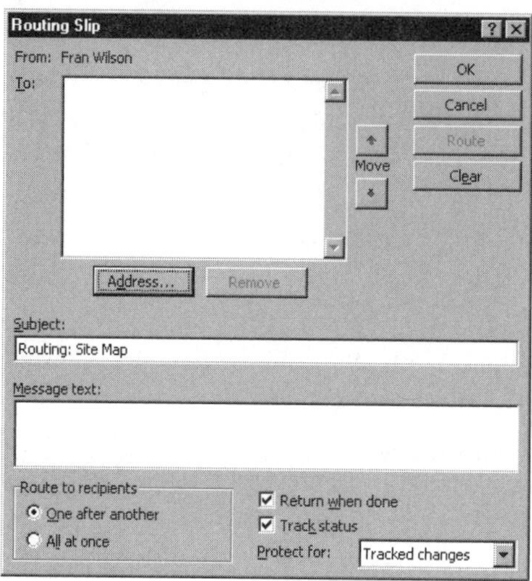

4. In the Routing Slip dialog box, click Address. The Address Book dialog box appears.

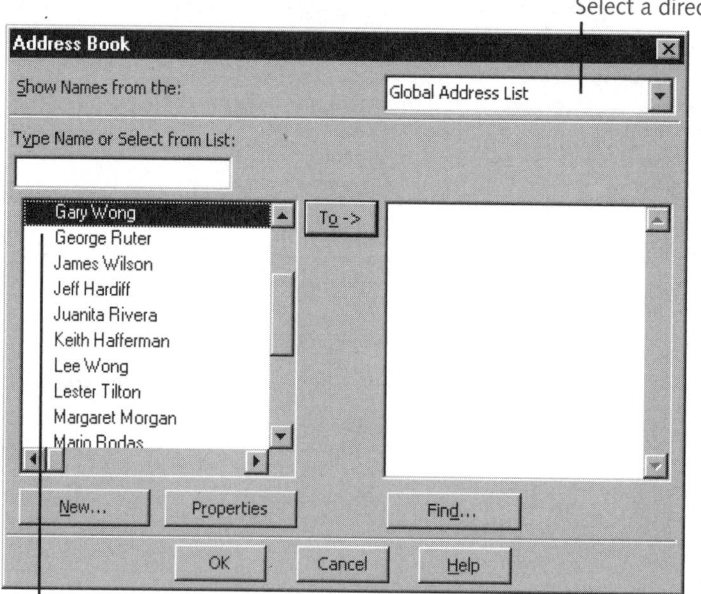

tip

Depending on the type of mailing list you have set up in your Address Book in Outlook, the options in the Show Names From The: list will vary. You could select names from the Outlook Contacts list, if you have added any, or you might have another customized list of addressees, such as a global address book. For more information about directories you can include in Outlook, see your Outlook documentation.

To change the order of names, select a name, and in the Move area, click the up or down arrow.

5. Double-click the recipients' names in the order that you want them to review the document.

   In the To list, the names are displayed in the order that the recipients will receive the routed document.
6. Click OK.

   The Address Book dialog box closes. In the Routing Slip dialog box, recipients' names appear in the To list in the order you requested.
7. In the Message Text box, type **Thanks for helping me practice routing a document. The instructions below my message will tell you how to route to the next recipient.**

   (An additional message, which tells the recipient how to route to the next recipient, is created automatically when you send the document.)
8. In the Route To Recipients area, be sure that the option One After Another is selected.
9. Be sure that the Return When Done and Track Status options are selected.
10. In the Protect For box, be sure that the item *Tracked Changes* is displayed.

    Users are allowed to edit the document or insert comments, and revision marks will be included.
11. Click Route.

    The Routing Slip dialog box closes, and Web Outline 15 remains open. A copy of the Web Outline 15 document is sent in e-mail as an attachment to the first recipient on the routing slip.

Save

12. On the Standard toolbar, click the Save button.

    The attached routing slip is saved.
13. Close the Web Outline 15 document.

tip

If you are filling out a routing slip and find that you want to make additional changes to the document before you route it, in the Routing Slip dialog box, click Add Slip. The Routing Slip dialog box closes, the routing slip is attached to the document, and the document is not routed. To route the document with the attached routing slip, on the File menu, point to Send To and then click Next Routing Recipient. The Send dialog box appears. Be sure the Route Document To (*next recipient*) option is selected, and click OK to start routing the document. To edit an attached routing slip, open the document with the routing slip you want to edit, and on the File menu, point to Send To, and then click Other Routing Recipient. Make the changes you want in the Routing Slip dialog box, and click Route to send the document.

Receiving a Routed Document

For more information on tracking changes with revision marks, see Lesson 13, "Tracking Changes in Group Projects."

When you receive a routed document, it appears as an attachment in an e-mail message. If the document has been protected for tracked changes, you can edit it and your revisions will show in a different color than other recipients' changes.

1. To save the attached document on your computer, follow the steps in the sidebar earlier in this lesson, "Saving an Attached Document."
2. In Word, on the Standard toolbar, click the Open button, and open the routed document that you saved to your hard disk.
3. Edit the document, and then save your changes.
4. On the File menu, point to Send To, and then click Next Routing Recipient.

   The Send dialog box appears.
5. Be sure that the Route Document To (next recipient) option is selected, and click OK.

   The edited document is routed to the next designated recipient. Although you can't see it, Word sends a status message informing the person who originated the routed document that the document has been sent to the next person on the routing list.

Using Word as Your E-mail Editor

Although Outlook has its own text editor, you might want to create e-mail messages using the greater range of formatting options and tools that are available in Word. By using Word as your e-mail editor, you can select font types and colors for your messages, run a Spelling and Grammar Check, use AutoFormat, create bulleted lists, select a design theme, and use other Word features.

You can designate Word as your e-mail editor from within either Word or Outlook. When you send an e-mail message from Word, your message is sent in HTML format. When you send a message from Outlook, you have the option of selecting Outlook Rich Text, Plain Text, or HTML message formats. For Word formatting to be conveyed in a message, you must choose Outlook Rich Text or HTML format. If you select rich text formatting, you type the new mail message within an Outlook message window, and you have access to the Word menus and toolbars. If you select HTML formatting, you type a new message directly in a Word window.

Note that some mail recipients might have mail servers that do not support rich text or HTML, so a message sent in these formats might not be readable for them, and you would have to send the message in plain text format.

In the following exercises, you learn how to select Word as your e-mail editor from within Word. Then, you learn how to select Word as your e-mail editor from Outlook. For the purposes of this exercise, you must have Word 2000 and either Outlook 2000 or Outlook Express 5.0 or later versions installed on your computer.

Prepare a Word window for sending an e-mail message

In this exercise, you prepare to send an e-mail message from Word.

1. If Word is not open, on the Windows taskbar, click the Start menu, point to Programs, and then click Microsoft Word.

   Microsoft Word 2000 opens.

2. On the File menu, click New.

   The New dialog box appears.

3. On the General Tab, click the E-mail Message icon.

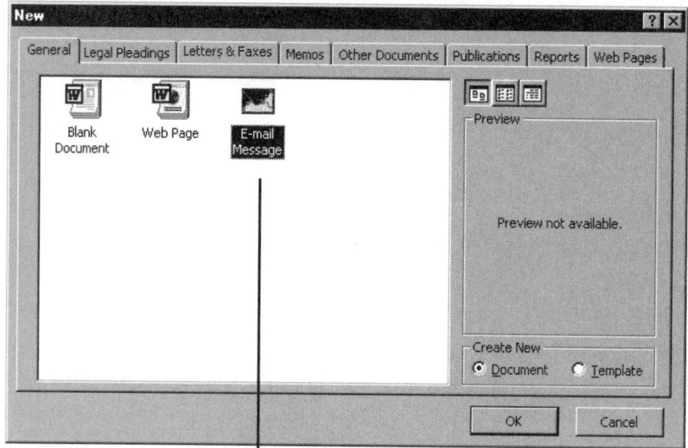

Click to send an e-mail message from Word.

New Blank Document

New E-Mail Message

4. Click OK.

   The Word document window changes to an untitled message window, and the Outlook message toolbar and address boxes appear beneath the Word menus and toolbars. On the Word Standard toolbar, the New Blank Document button changes to the New E-Mail Message button.

5. Close the untitled message window.

Set up Word as your e-mail editor from within Outlook

In this exercise, you choose Word as your e-mail editor from within Outlook.

1. Maximize Outlook. (If Outlook is not open, on the Windows taskbar, click the Start button, point to Programs, and then click Microsoft Outlook.)
2. On the Outlook Tools menu, click Options.

   The Options dialog box appears.

3. On the Mail Format tab, select the Use Microsoft Word To Edit E-mail Messages option.
4. Click the Send In This Message Format drop-down arrow, and select HTML.
5. Click OK.

New

6. On the Outlook Standard toolbar, click the New button.

   An untitled message window opens in Word, with the Outlook toolbar and address boxes beneath the Word menus and toolbars.

7. Close the untitled message window, leave Word open, and then quit Outlook.

One Step Further Customizing Outgoing E-mail Messages

By using Word as your e-mail editor, you can personalize your e-mail messages with your own stationery and special signature.

Select a theme and create a signature

If you are not working through this lesson sequentially, before proceeding to the next step, open a Word window. On the File menu, click New, and then click E-Mail Message.

In this exercise, you select a theme and create a personalized signature for your outgoing messages.

1. In Word, on the Standard toolbar, click the New E-Mail Message button.

   An untitled message window opens in Word.

2. On the Tools menu, click Options.

   The Options dialog box appears.

3. On the General tab, click E-mail Options.

   The E-mail Options dialog box appears.

4. On the Personal Stationery tab, click Theme.

   The Theme Or Stationery dialog box appears.

5. In the Choose A Theme list, select Cypress, and click OK. If you get a message asking whether to install the theme, click Install. After the theme is installed, click OK to close the Theme Or Stationery dialog box.

tip

Although a theme has a particular font style, you can choose to use another font style. To select a different font, in the E-mail Options dialog box, below the Theme button, clear the Use Theme's Font check box. In the New Mail Messages area, click Font. In the Font dialog box, select options for the font you want to use in your new e-mail messages, and click OK. In the E-mail Options dialog box, in the Replying Or Forwarding Messages area, click Font, and in the Font dialog box, select options for the font you want to use in messages you reply to, or forward. Click OK.

6. On the E-Mail Signature tab, in the Type The Title Of Your E-mail Signature Or Choose From The List box, type **Casual**

Font Size

Bold

Italic

Font Color

7. In the Create Your E-mail Signature area, click the Font drop-down arrow, and select Verdana.
8. Click the Font Size drop-down arrow, and select 10.
9. Click the Bold button, and click the Italic button.
10. Click the Font Color drop-down arrow, and select Olive Green, the third box from the left in the top row.
11. In the text area, type your name and any other text that you want to appear in messages you send.

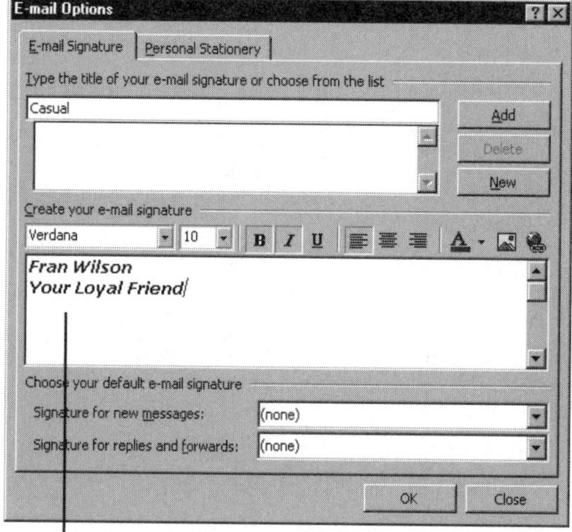

Your signature as it will appear in mail messages

12. Click Add.

    The Casual signature becomes an option in the list, and it becomes the default selection in the Signature For New Messages box and Signature for Replies And Forwards box. If you've already created other personal signatures, you'll be prompted to designate the most recently added signature as the one for all messages.
13. Click OK to close the E-mail Options dialog box, and then click OK again to close the Options dialog box.

View a sample of your stationery and signature

In this exercise, you open a new e-mail message to see your stationery and theme in the message.

1. On the Word Standard toolbar, click the New E-Mail Message button.

   A new untitled message window opens, and the message is formatted with your signature and stationery. You can now write the message and send it.

   Your screen should look similar to the following illustration.

Your stationery with theme and signature applied

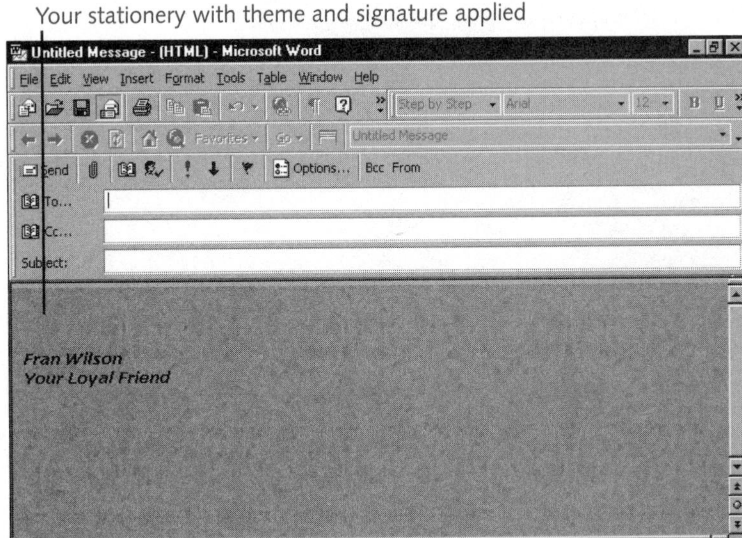

Finish the lesson

1. Close any open document or message window.
2. On the File menu, click Exit.

Lesson 15 Quick Reference

To	Do this	Button
Send a Word document as an e-mail attachment	Open the document you want to send. On the File menu, point to Send To, and then click Mail Recipient (As Attachment).	
Send a Word document in HTML format	Open the document you want to send. On the Standard toolbar, click the E-mail button.	
Use Word to edit a document sent in HTML format	In the Outlook message window, on the Edit menu, click Edit Message.	
Select Word as your e-mail editor from Word	On the File menu in Word, click New. In the New dialog box, on the General tab, click E-mail Message, and click OK.	
Route a document	Open the document you want to route. On the File menu, point to Send To, and then click Routing Recipient. Fill out the Routing Slip, and then click Route.	
Select Word as your e-mail editor from Outlook	On the Tools menu in Outlook, click Options. On the Mail Format tab, select the Use Microsoft Word To Edit E-mail Messages option. Click the Send In This Message Format drop-down arrow, and select either Outlook Rich Text or HTML. Click OK.	
Use Word to select a theme and create a signature for outgoing e-mail messages	On the Tools menu, click Options, and on the General tab, click E-mail Options. On the Personal Stationery tab, choose a theme. On the E-mail Signature tab, type a name for the new signature, and in the Create Your E-mail Signature area, set options for the new signature. Click Add.	

16

Connecting with Other Office 2000 Programs

In this lesson you will learn how to:

- ✔ *Convert a Word document to a PowerPoint slide presentation.*
- ✔ *Embed a slide presentation into a Word document.*
- ✔ *Link a section of an Excel workbook to a Word document.*
- ✔ *Update linked information.*
- ✔ *Insert a chart into a Word document.*
- ✔ *Add a hyperlink to a Word document.*

ESTIMATED TIME **30 min.**

You've already seen how easy it is to work between Microsoft Word documents. Now it's time to see how easy it is to work between Word and other Microsoft Office programs such as Microsoft PowerPoint and Microsoft Excel.

In this lesson, you create a slide presentation for your client Pacific Books, recapping the highly successful book fair event. You convert a Word document to a PowerPoint slide presentation and then incorporate PowerPoint slides into a Word document. You insert an Excel workbook containing sales figures for Pacific Books into a Word document and link them so that corrections made to the workbook are reflected in the Word document. Finally, you insert hyperlinks to create shortcuts to other programs.

Start Word and open a practice file

In this exercise, you start Word, open a practice file, and then save it with a new name.

1. On the Windows taskbar, click the Start button.
   The Start menu appears.
2. On the Start menu, point to Programs, and then click Microsoft Word.
   Microsoft Word 2000 opens.
3. On the Standard toolbar, click the Open button.
   The Open dialog box appears.

   Open

4. In the list of folders, double-click the Word 2000 SBS Practice folder, and then double-click the Lesson16 folder.
5. In the file list, double-click the 16A file to open it.
   The document opens in the document window.
6. On the File menu, click Save As.
   The Save As dialog box appears.
7. Be sure that the Lesson16 folder appears in the Save In box.
8. In the File Name box, select the text, and then type **Pacific Books 16 Slides**
9. Click Save.

Display formatting marks

To make it easier to edit your document, you can display formatting marks such as paragraph marks and space marks on your screen.

Show/Hide ¶

- If formatting marks are not currently displayed, on the Standard toolbar, click the Show/Hide ¶ button.

> **important**
> In order to complete exercises in this lesson, you must have Microsoft PowerPoint and Microsoft Excel installed on your computer.

Sending Word Documents to PowerPoint

If you are not working through this lesson sequentially, before proceeding to the next step, open the 16A file in the Lesson16 folder, and save it as Pacific Books 16 Slides.

By combining the capabilities of Microsoft Word and other Microsoft Office products, you can get extra mileage out of the documents you create. For example, you might draft an outline of a presentation using Word and then send it to Microsoft PowerPoint to be converted to a slide presentation. The outline would open in PowerPoint as a structured presentation, ready for the addition of graphics and other embellishments.

Send a Word document to PowerPoint

In this exercise, you send a Word document to PowerPoint.

- On the File menu, point to Send To, and then click Microsoft PowerPoint.

  Microsoft PowerPoint 2000 opens, and the text from the Word file is converted into PowerPoint slides. The original Word document is left intact.

  Your screen should look similar to the following illustration.

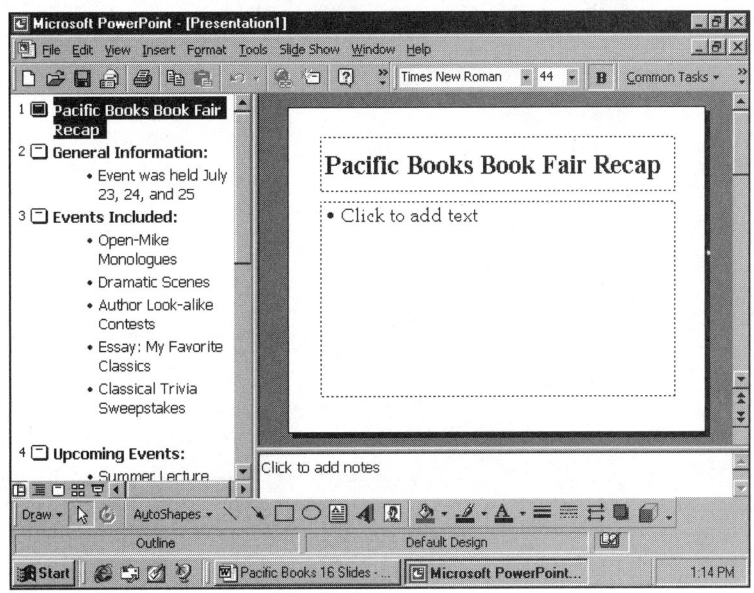

Format the slides

In this exercise, you format the PowerPoint slides you produced in the previous exercise.

1. Press Ctrl+A to select all of the slides.
2. On the PowerPoint Formatting toolbar, click the Common Tasks button, and then click Apply Design Template.

   The Apply Design Template dialog box appears.
3. In the file list, click Nature, and then click Apply.

   The slides are formatted in the Nature design.
4. In the left window, scroll up and select Slide 1.

   Your screen should look similar to the following illustration.

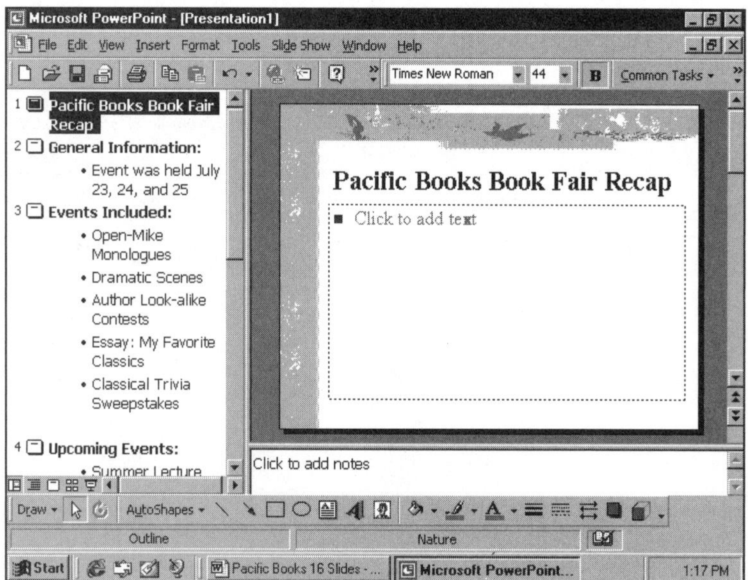

5. On the PowerPoint Formatting toolbar, click the Common Tasks button, and then click Slide Layout.

   The Slide Layout dialog box appears.
6. In the Reapply The Current Master Styles area, click the first slide on the left in the top row.

   This is called the Title Slide.

7. Click Apply.

   The slide is reformatted as a title slide.

   Your screen should look similar to the following illustration.

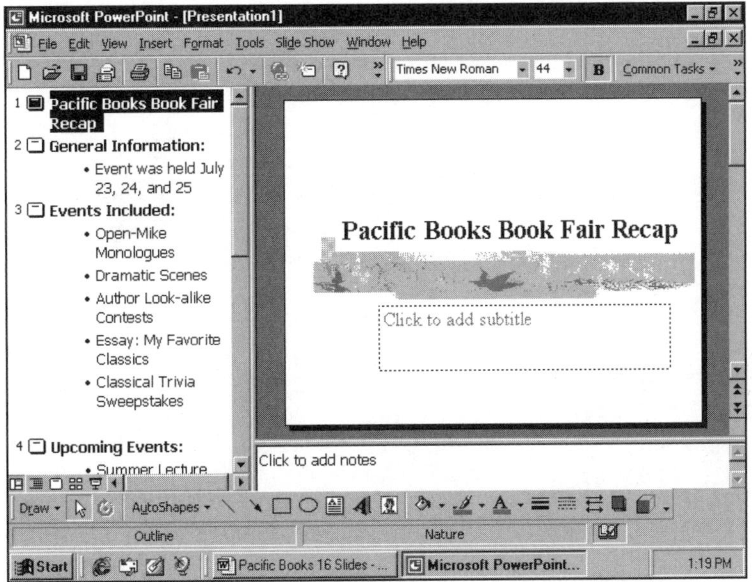

Save the presentation

In this exercise, you save the PowerPoint slide presentation created in the previous two exercises.

Save

1. On the Standard toolbar, click the Save button.

   The Save As dialog box appears.

2. Be sure that the Lesson16 folder (within the Word 2000 SBS Practice folder) appears in the Save In box.
3. In the File Name box, type **Pacific Books Slide Show** and click Save.
4. On the File menu, click Exit.

   You return to Word.

5. On the Word File menu, click Close.

   The Pacific Books 16 Slides document closes.

Sending PowerPoint Slides to Word

You can send PowerPoint presentations to Word, just as you can send Word documents to PowerPoint.

Send a PowerPoint presentation to Word

1. Start PowerPoint and open the presentation.
2. On the File menu, point to Send To, and then click Microsoft Word.
3. In the Write-Up dialog box, select a page layout option, and click OK.

   The slides and notes, or outline, appear in the Word document in the layout you selected.

Inserting PowerPoint Presentations into Word Documents

Besides converting a Word document to a PowerPoint presentation, you can also insert a PowerPoint slide presentation into a Word document. When you double-click the inserted object, the PowerPoint slide presentation is opened. Objects can be inserted as either *embedded* or *linked* objects. *Embedded presentations* are stored within the Word document. The PowerPoint program does not need to be available to display the presentation. *Linked presentations* remain stored in PowerPoint files, so the PowerPoint program must be available when you want to view these presentations.

Open a practice document

In this exercise, you open a Word document.

Open

1. On the Standard toolbar, click the Open button.

   The Open dialog box appears.
2. Be sure the Lesson16 folder (within the Word 2000 SBS Practice folder) appears in the Look In box.
3. In the file list, double-click the 16B file to open it.

   The document opens in the document window.
4. On the File menu, click Save As.

   The Save As dialog box appears.

5. In the File Name box, type **Pacific Books Activity Report**
6. Click Save. Do not close the document.

Insert a PowerPoint slide presentation

In this exercise, you insert a PowerPoint slide presentation as a linked object into the Pacific Books Activity Report.

For a demonstration of how to insert a PowerPoint slide presentation, in the Multimedia folder on the Microsoft Word 2000 Step by Step CD-ROM, double-click InsertPowerPointSlide.

1. In the Pacific Books Activity Report document, under the heading *Book Fair Recap*, click below the text *To view slide presentation, double-click icon:*
2. On the Insert menu, click Object.

   The Object dialog box appears.
3. Click the Create From File tab, and click Browse.

   The Browse dialog box appears.
4. Be sure the Lesson16 folder (within the Word 2000 SBS Practice folder) appears in the Look In box.
5. Double-click the PowerPoint presentation file 16C.

   The Object dialog box appears.
6. In the Object dialog box, on the Create From File tab, select the Link To File and Display As Icon check boxes.

   Your screen should look similar to the following illustration.

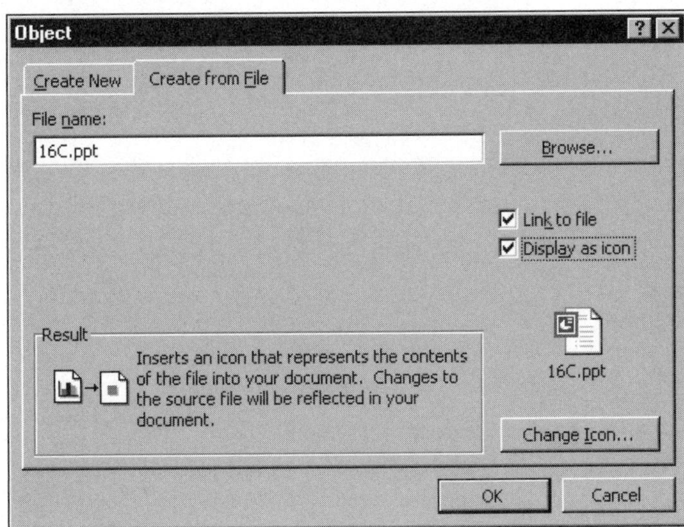

7. Click OK.

   A PowerPoint icon, labeled 16C.ppt, appears below the text.

View a slide presentation

In this exercise, you view the PowerPoint slide presentation you inserted in the Word document in the previous exercise.

1. In the Pacific Books Activity Report, double-click the PowerPoint icon.

   The first slide of the PowerPoint slide presentation is displayed.
2. Click the Pointer icon at the lower-left corner of the screen. Click Next to view each slide. Click End Show to close the presentation and return to the Word document.
3. Leave the Pacific Books Activity Report open for the next exercise.

Insert a single PowerPoint slide

In this exercise, you link a single slide from a PowerPoint presentation to a Word document.

1. On the Windows taskbar, click the Start button, and then click Open Office Document.

   The Open Office Document dialog box appears.
2. Be sure the Lesson16 folder (within the Word 2000 SBS Practice folder) appears in the Look In box.
3. Double-click the PowerPoint file 16D.

   PowerPoint opens.

Copy

4. On the PowerPoint View menu, click Slide Sorter, and then select Slide 1.
5. On the Standard toolbar, click the Copy button.
6. On the Windows taskbar, click the Pacific Books Activity Report button to display the document.

7. In the Pacific Books Activity Report document, under the heading *Pacific Books Logo*, click below the text *To view slide, double-click icon*:
8. On the Edit menu, click Paste Special.

   The Paste Special dialog box appears.
9. In the As box, be sure Microsoft PowerPoint Slide Object is selected.
10. Select the Paste Link option and Display As Icon check box.

    Your screen should look similar to the following illustration.

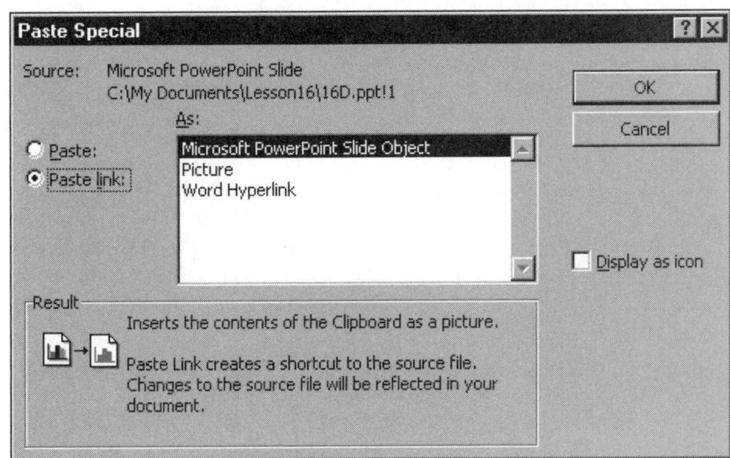

11. Click OK.

    The PowerPoint slide icon, labeled Microsoft PowerPoint Slide, is inserted and linked to the Word document.
12. Double-click the icon.

    The slide is displayed in PowerPoint.
13. On the PowerPoint File menu, click Exit.

    The Word document is displayed.
14. Save and close the Word document.

Creating a New Slide in Word

You can create a single PowerPoint slide directly from within Word.

Create a single slide in a Word document

1. Open a Word document.
2. On the Insert menu, click Object.

   The Object dialog box appears.
3. Click the Create New tab.
4. In the Object Type list, select Microsoft PowerPoint Slide.
5. If you want the object inserted as an icon, select the Display As Icon check box.
6. Click OK.

   PowerPoint opens.
7. In the PowerPoint window, format the slide.
8. Close PowerPoint.

   The Word document appears.

   You do not have to save the PowerPoint file because this slide is stored as part of the Word document.
9. Close Word.

Inserting and Linking Microsoft Excel Data

You can insert workbooks created in Microsoft Excel into Word documents. Inserting workbooks allows you to display complex data in Word using Excel features, such as formulas and numerical formatting, that are otherwise not available in Word. Inserted workbooks are static: the data does not change if the source file is updated or changed.

You can also link a workbook to a Word document. When you link a workbook, any changes made in the source workbook can be easily updated in the Word document. This eliminates the need to reinsert a workbook in your Word document each time you make a change to the original workbook.

Insert an Excel workbook into a Word document

In this exercise, you insert an Excel workbook into a Word document.

Open

1. On the Word Standard toolbar, click the Open button.

   The Open dialog box appears.
2. Be sure the Lesson16 folder (within the Word 2000 SBS Practice folder) appears in the Look In box.
3. In the file list, double-click the 16E file to open it.
4. On the File menu, click Save As.

   The Save As dialog box appears.
5. In the File Name box, type **Pacific Books Recap**
6. Click Save.
7. In the document, click before the first paragraph mark after the text *Current Sales Information*.
8. On the Insert menu, click File.

   The Insert File dialog box appears.
9. Be sure the Lesson16 folder (within the Word 2000 SBS Practice folder) appears in the Look In box.
10. Click the Files Of Type drop-down arrow and select All Files.

    Your screen should look similar to the following illustration.

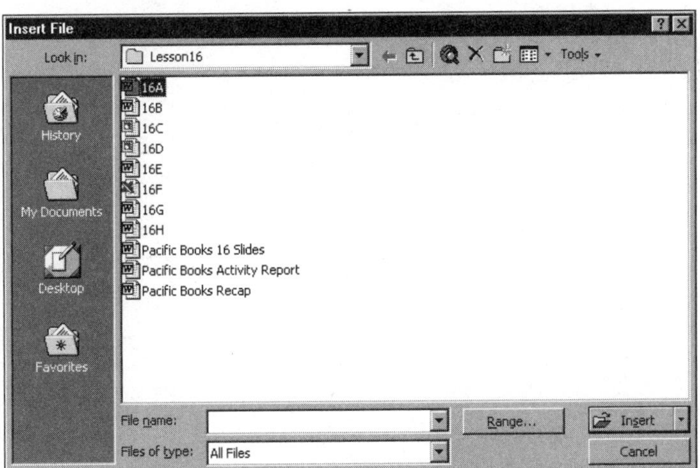

11. Select the Excel file 16F, and click Insert.

    The Open Worksheet dialog box appears.

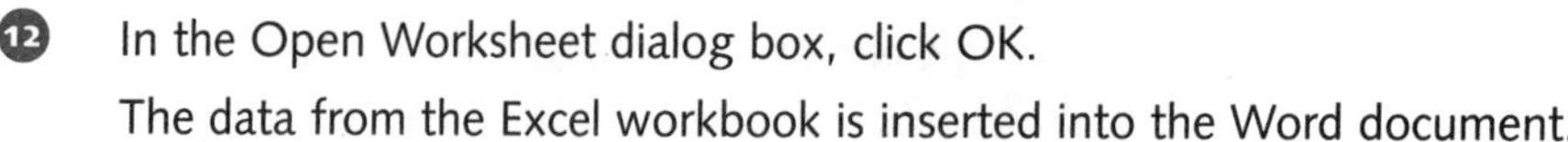

12. In the Open Worksheet dialog box, click OK.

    The data from the Excel workbook is inserted into the Word document.

Undo

13. On the Standard toolbar, click the Undo button.

    The workbook is removed from the document.

Link a workbook to a Word document

If you are not working through this lesson sequentially, before proceeding to the next step, open the 16E file in the Lesson16 folder, and save it as Pacific Books Recap.

In this exercise, you insert data from an Excel workbook into a Word document and link the two files so that changes made to the workbook source file will be reflected in the Word document.

1. Click before the first paragraph mark after the text *Current Sales Information*.
2. On the Insert menu, click File.

   The Insert File dialog box appears.
3. Be sure the Lesson16 folder (within the Word 2000 SBS Practice folder) appears in the Look In box.
4. If necessary, click the Files Of Type drop-down arrow, and select All Files.
5. Select the Excel 16F file.
6. Click the Insert drop-down arrow, and click Insert As Link.

   The Open Worksheet dialog box appears.
7. In the Open Worksheet dialog box, click OK.

   The data from the Excel workbook is inserted into the Word document as a linked file.

Save

8. Save the Word document.

Update the linked information

In this exercise, you change the Excel workbook data and update the Word link.

1. On the Windows taskbar, click the Start button, and then click Open Office Document.
2. Be sure the Lesson16 folder (within the Word 2000 SBS Practice folder) appears in the Look In box, and then double-click the 16F file to open it.
3. Click in cell F5, type **5529** and press Enter.

   The next cell is selected.

4. In cell F6, type **5364** and press Enter.
5. On the Standard toolbar, click the Save button, and on the File menu, click Exit.

   The Excel workbook is closed, and the Word document is displayed.
6. On the Edit menu, click Links.

   The Links dialog box appears.

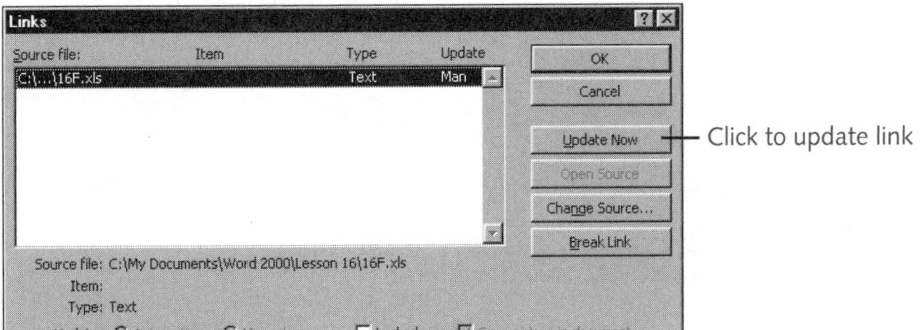

7. In the Links dialog box, click Update Now.

   The Open Worksheet dialog box appears.

   Your screen should look similar to the following illustration.
8. Click OK.

   The Excel workbook is updated in the Word document.
9. In the Links dialog box, click OK.

Break the link

Dynamic links can be intentionally broken. For example, you might want to freeze data in a Word document to show financial results at a certain point in time. In this exercise, you break the link between the Excel workbook and the Word document created in the previous exercise.

1. With the Pacific Books Recap document displayed, on the Edit menu, click Links.

   The Links dialog box appears.
2. Click Break Link, and then click Yes when prompted.

   The link is broken. Changes made to the Excel workbook will no longer be updated in the Word document.

Sort table information

In this exercise, you sort the information in the sales information table that was inserted in the Word document.

1. Click anywhere in the table below the heading *Current Sales Information*.
2. On the Table menu, click Select, and then click Table.
3. On the Table menu, click Sort.

   The Sort dialog box appears.
4. Click the Sort By drop-down arrow, select Branch, and then select the Descending option.

   Your screen should look similar to the following illustration.

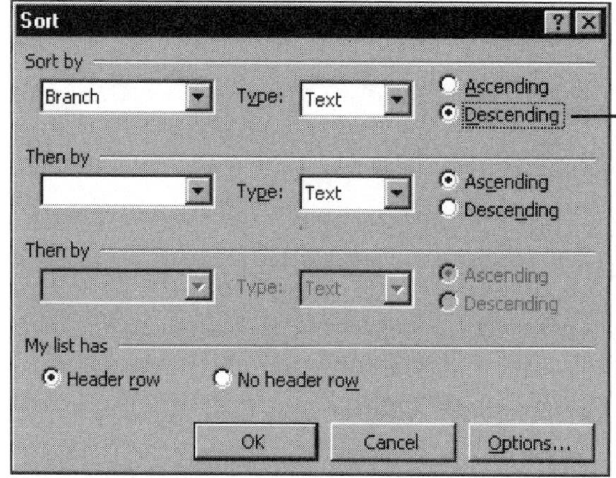

Items in the table will be sorted in descending (highest to lowest dollar amount) order.

5. Click OK.

   The table is sorted by highest to lowest sales.
6. Save the file.

Save

Creating Charts in Word Documents

If you are not working through this lesson sequentially, before proceeding to the next step, open the 16G file in the Lesson16 folder, and save it as Pacific Books Recap.

Not only can you insert presentations and worksheets into your Word documents, but you can also create and display charts in Word using the Microsoft Graph 2000 Chart tool. You can choose from any of Graph's chart styles such as line, bar, and pie. You can also format the x- and y-axes and add legends and chart titles.

Insert a chart

In this exercise, you add a chart to the Pacific Books Recap document.

1. Click below the table.
2. On the Insert menu, click Object.

   The Object dialog box appears.
3. Click the Create New tab. In the Object Type box, select Microsoft Graph 2000 Chart.
4. Click OK.

   A chart and datasheet are displayed. Your worksheet should look similar to the following illustration.

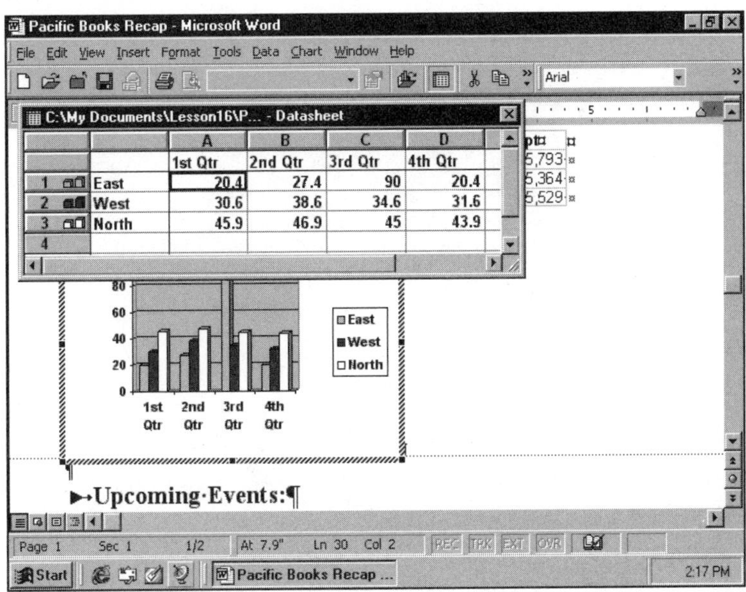

Importing Excel Data into a Web Page

Excel data can be imported to and displayed on Word Web pages.

Import Excel data into a Web page

1. Open a Web page and click where you want to insert the Excel data.
2. On the Insert menu, click File, and select the Excel workbook you want to insert.
3. Click Insert. You can also click the drop-down arrow and choose Insert As Link if you want to link the data to the Web page.
4. In the Open Worksheet dialog box, click OK.

   The Excel data is inserted into the Web page.

Modify the chart information

In this exercise, you change the display of information on each axis.

1. In the chart, click any dollar figure on the y-axis (Value Axis).

   Your screen should look similar to the following illustration.

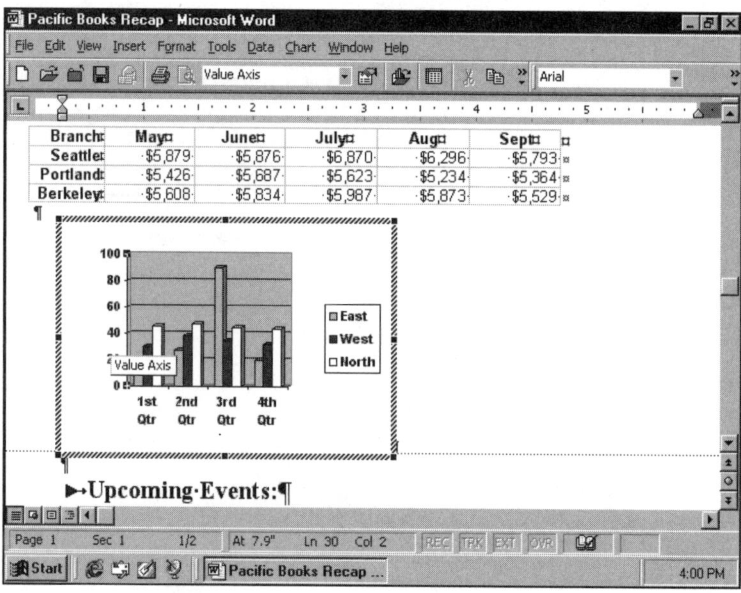

2. Right-click, and on the shortcut menu, click Format Axis.

   The Format Axis dialog box appears.

3. Click the Scale tab, and in the Maximum list, type **200**
4. Click OK.

   A zero is displayed at the bottom of the axis, and 200 is displayed at the top.

Add a chart title

In this exercise, you add a chart title.

1. Position the insertion point anywhere in the blank area of the chart, and right-click.

   A shortcut menu appears.

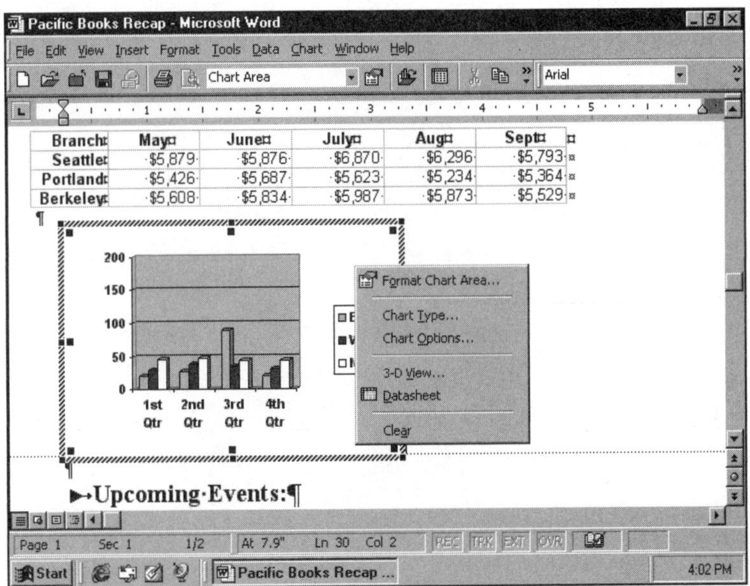

2. On the shortcut menu, select Chart Options.

   The Chart Options dialog box appears.
3. Click the Titles tab.
4. In the Chart Title box, type **Pacific Books Revenue** and click OK.
5. Click anywhere outside of the graph to cancel the selection.

   The chart is now part of the document.
6. Save your work.

One Step Further Adding Hyperlinks to Word Documents

If you are not working through this lesson sequentially, before proceeding to the next step, open the file 16H, in the Lesson16 folder, and save it as Pacific Books Recap.

You can use *hyperlinks* to connect Word users to other Microsoft Office 2000 program files. Hyperlinks, displayed in a document as text or graphics, are active areas in a document that, when clicked, take users to another program, document, or location on the Internet. For example, you can create a hyperlink that jumps from a Word document to a Microsoft Excel workbook. Hyperlinks are displayed in Word documents in text that is usually blue and underlined.

Insert a hyperlink in a workbook

In this exercise, you add a hyperlink between your Word document and an Excel workbook.

1. In the Pacific Books Recap document, click under the heading Current Sales Information, in the line below the chart.
2. Type **To open the Excel workbook, click this hyperlink:** and press the Spacebar.
3. On the Standard toolbar, click the Insert Hyperlink button.

   The Insert Hyperlink dialog box appears.
4. In the Browse For area, click File.
5. Be sure that the Lesson16 folder (within the Word 2000 SBS Practice folder) appears in the Look In box.
6. Double-click the Microsoft Excel workbook file 16F.

   Your screen should look similar to the following illustration.

Insert Hyperlink

If the Hyperlink button is not visible, on the Standard toolbar, click the More Buttons drop-down arrow to locate the button.

Name of the file that will be linked to the Word document

Text that will be displayed as the hyperlink

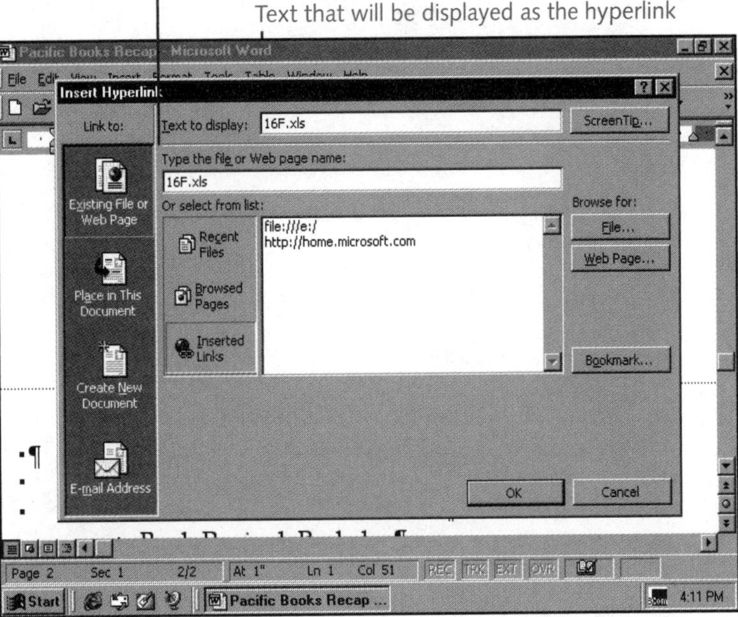

7. Click OK.

   The filename, 16F.xls, appears in blue, underlined text in your document. To jump to the Excel file, click the hyperlink.

Insert an e-mail link

In this exercise, you insert an e-mail address into a Word document.

1. Press Ctrl+End to move the insertion point to the end of the document.
2. On the Standard toolbar, click the Insert Hyperlink button.

   The Insert Hyperlink dialog box appears.
3. On the Link To bar, click E-mail Address.
4. In the E-mail Address box, type **RSmith@xxx.com** and click OK.

   The e-mail address is inserted into the Word document. To start an e-mail message to RSmith, click the hyperlink.

Save

Finish the lesson

1. On the Standard toolbar, click the Save button.

   The Pacific Books Recap document is saved.
2. On the File menu, click Close.
3. On the File menu, click Exit.

Lesson 16 Quick Reference

To	Do this	Button
Send a Word document to PowerPoint	On the File menu, point to Send To, and then click Microsoft PowerPoint.	
Format slides	In PowerPoint, press Ctrl+A to select all of the slides. On the Formatting toolbar, click the Common Tasks button, and then click Apply Design Template. In the File list, select a format, and then click Apply. On the Formatting toolbar, click the Common Tasks button, and then click Slide Layout. In the Reapply The Current Master Styles area, click a slide format, and then click Apply.	
Insert a PowerPoint slide presentation	On the Word Insert menu, click Object. Click the Create From File tab, and then click Browse. Double-click the PowerPoint presentation file. In the Object dialog box, click the Create From File tab. Select the Link To File and Display As Icon check boxes. Click OK.	
View a slide presentation	In Word, double-click the PowerPoint icon. Click the Pointer icon to view each slide or to close the presentation.	
Insert a single PowerPoint slide	Switch to PowerPoint. On the Viewmenu, click Slide Sorter, and select the slide to insert. On the Standard toolbar, click the Copy button. Switch back to Word. Position the insertion point in the document. On the Edit menu, click Paste Special. When the Paste Special dialog box appears, in the As box, select Microsoft PowerPoint Slide Object. Select the Paste Link option, and select the Display As Icon check box. Click OK.	

Lesson 16 Quick Reference

To	Do this
Insert an Excel workbook into a Word document	On the Word Insert menu, click File. Click the Files Of Type drop-down arrow, and click All Files. Select the Excel file, and click Insert. In the Open Worksheet dialog box, click OK.
Link a workbook to a Word document	On the Insert menu, click File. Click the Files Of Type drop-down arrow, and click All Files. Select the Excel file. Click the Insert drop-down arrow, and click Insert As Link. In the Open Worksheet dialog box, click OK.
Update the linked information	On the Word Edit menu, click Links. In the Links dialog box, select the source file, click Update Now, and click OK.
Break a link	On the Edit menu, click Links. In the Links dialog box, select the link to break, click Break Link, and click Yes when you are prompted.
Sort table information	Click anywhere in the table containing the data you want to sort. On the Table menu, click Select, and then click Table. On the Table menu, click Sort. Click the Sort By drop-down arrow, and in the Sort By box, click the drop-down arrow, and select the column to sort on. Click OK.
Copy chart data	Position the insertion point anywhere in the table containing the data you want to select. On the Table menu, click Select, and then click Table. On the Standard toolbar, click the Copy button.
Insert a chart	Position the insertion point where you want to insert the chart. On the Insert menu, click Object. In the Object Type box, select Microsoft Graph 2000 Chart. Click OK.

Lesson 16 Quick Reference

To	Do this	Button
Modify chart information	Position the pointer on the x- or y-axis and right-click. On the shortcut menu, click Format Axis. Choose tabs to change settings. Click OK.	
Add a chart title	Position the insertion point anywhere in the blank area of a chart, and right-click. On the shortcut menu, click Chart Options. Click the Titles tab. In the Chart Title box, type a chart title, and click OK.	
Insert a hyperlink to a workbook	On the Word Standard toolbar, click the Insert Hyperlink button. In the Insert Hyperlink dialog box, under Browse For, click File. Double-click the Excel file to create a hyperlink to it. Click OK.	
Insert an e-mail link	On the Word Standard toolbar, click the Insert Hyperlink button. On the Link To bar, click the E-mail Address button. In the E-mail Address box, type the e-mail address, and click OK.	

PART

4

Review & Practice

You will review and practice how to:

- ✔ *Track changes and add comments in a document.*
- ✔ *Reorganize a document in Outline view.*
- ✔ *Create a subdocument.*
- ✔ *Send a document through e-mail.*
- ✔ *Convert a Word document to PowerPoint slides.*

ESTIMATED TIME
15 min.

Now that you have finished Part 4, you can practice the skills you learned by working through the steps in this Review & Practice section. You practice tracking changes and adding comments in a document, reorganizing a document in Outline view, creating a subdocument, sending a document as an e-mail attachment, and converting a Word document into Microsoft PowerPoint slides.

Scenario

Impact Public Relations is developing a new Web site for its client Pacific Books. The editorial department has written the text for one of the Web pages and the lead editor wants you to review it. You review and revise the document, create a new subdocument, and then return the master document to the lead editor through e-mail. Then you convert the document into PowerPoint slides for a presentation to the client.

Step 1: Track Changes and Add Comments in a Document

In this step, you open the document, turn on Track Changes While Editing, and add suggestions using the Comments feature. To prevent any untracked revisions as the document continues through the editing process, you protect the document against untracked changes.

1. In the Review & Practice folder, within the Word 2000 SBS Practice folder, open the practice file RP04A, and then save it as **PB Web Site**
2. Turn on revision marks so that inserted text is displayed on the screen with a single underline, formatting changes are displayed with a double underline, and deleted text is displayed in strikethrough format.
3. Delete the placeholder heading *Add something about holiday specials*, and type **Celebrate the Holidays with Great Deals!**
4. At the end of the sentence you just inserted, use the Reviewing toolbar to insert the comment **How about this?**
5. Use Turquoise to highlight the heading *Books For Sale*, insert the comment **Can you spice up the wording of this heading?**
6. Protect the document against untracked changes.

For more information about	See
Tracking edits by using revision marks	Lesson 13
Adding comments	Lesson 13
Highlighting text for special attention	Lesson 13
Protecting documents	Lesson 13

Step 2: Reorganize Headings and Create a Subdocument

You decide that the pricing information should be on a separate page, linked to the page you are reviewing. In this step, you reorganize the existing headings and create a subdocument to be used as a guideline for the new page.

1. Switch to Outline view.
2. Demote the heading *Order Now* to Heading 2 level, and promote the headings *Classic Children's Books, Cookbooks: From Decadent to Diet,* and *New Books For The New Year* to Heading 2 levels.
3. Collapse the heading *New Pricing* so that the text below it is hidden.
4. Move the heading *New Pricing* and its collapsed subordinate text to the line below the *Order Now* heading.

5. Create a subdocument of the *New Pricing* section, and then save the changes.
6. In the master document, collapse the subdocument to display a hyperlink. Click the hyperlink, and on the subdocument heading, insert the comment **I think this would work better as a separate page.**
7. Close the subdocument and save changes to it.
8. In the master doucment, expand the subdocument.

For more information about	See
Promoting and demoting headings in Outline view	Lesson 14
Expanding a heading	Lesson 14
Moving a heading and its subordinate text	Lesson 14
Creating a subdocument	Lesson 14
Creating a subdocument hyperlink	Lesson 14

Step 3: Send a Document Through E-mail

Now that you've added your edits and comments, you want to send the document back to the lead editor. In this step, you send the document as an attachment in e-mail with a custom signature.

1. Attach the master document to an e-mail message. For the purposes of this exercise, address the outgoing e-mail to your own e-mail address.
2. Open Outlook to view the new message, then close the message, and close Outlook.

For more information about	See
Sending a document through e-mail	Lesson 15

Step 4: Convert a Word Document to PowerPoint Slides

You have a meeting with your Pacific Books clients to present your ideas for their updated Web site. To make your presentation, you will use PowerPoint slides. In this step, you convert the PB Web Site document into PowerPoint slides.

1. Unprotect the PB Web Site document, and then accept all changes in it.
2. Convert the subdocument back into part of the master document, and then switch to Normal view.

3. With the master document open and displayed in Normal view, open PowerPoint and convert the Word document into slides. Use Send To on the Word File menu.
4. Select all of the slides, and then apply the Bold Stripes design template.
5. Format the *Welcome to Pacific Books* (logo) slide as the title slide.
6. Save the PowerPoint file as **Pacific Books Proposal** and then exit PowerPoint.

For more information about	See
Accepting changes in a document	Lesson 13
Converting a subdocument into part of	Lesson 14
Connecting Microsoft Word 2000 with other Microsoft Office 2000 programs	Lesson 16
Converting a Word document into PowerPoint slides	Lesson 16
Applying a design template to a slide	Lesson 16
Formatting slides	Lesson 16

Finish the Review & Practice

- If you are finished using Microsoft Word for now, on the File menu, click Exit.

Index

A

B

D

E

F

I

J

K

L

M

Catapult, Inc. & Microsoft Press

Microsoft Word 2000 Step by Step has been created by the professional trainers and writers at Catapult, Inc., to the exacting standards you've come to expect from Microsoft Press. Together, we are pleased to present this self-paced training guide, which you can use individually or as part of a class.

Catapult, Inc., is a software training company with years of experience. Catapult's exclusive Performance-Based Training system is available in Catapult training centers across North America and at customer sites. Based on the principles of adult learning, Performance-Based Training ensures that students leave the classroom with confidence and the ability to apply skills to real-world scenarios. *Microsoft Word 2000 Step by Step* incorporates Catapult's training expertise to ensure that you'll receive the maximum return on your training time. You'll focus on the skills that can increase your productivity the most while working at your own pace and convenience.

Microsoft Press is the book publishing division of Microsoft Corporation. The leading publisher of information about Microsoft products and services, Microsoft Press is dedicated to providing the highest quality computer books and multimedia training and reference tools that make using Microsoft software easier, more enjoyable, and more productive.

MICROSOFT LICENSE AGREEMENT

Book Companion CD

IMPORTANT—READ CAREFULLY: This Microsoft End-User License Agreement ("EULA") is a legal agreement between you (either an individual or an entity) and Microsoft Corporation for the Microsoft product identified above, which includes computer software and may include associated media, printed materials, and "online" or electronic documentation ("SOFTWARE PRODUCT"). Any component included within the SOFTWARE PRODUCT that is accompanied by a separate End-User License Agreement shall be governed by such agreement and not the terms set forth below. By installing, copying, or otherwise using the SOFTWARE PRODUCT, you agree to be bound by the terms of this EULA. If you do not agree to the terms of this EULA, you are not authorized to install, copy, or otherwise use the SOFTWARE PRODUCT; you may, however, return the SOFTWARE PRODUCT, along with all printed materials and other items that form a part of the Microsoft product that includes the SOFTWARE PRODUCT, to the place you obtained them for a full refund.

SOFTWARE PRODUCT LICENSE

The SOFTWARE PRODUCT is protected by United States copyright laws and international copyright treaties, as well as other intellectual property laws and treaties. The SOFTWARE PRODUCT is licensed, not sold.

1. **GRANT OF LICENSE.** This EULA grants you the following rights:

   a. **Software Product.** You may install and use one copy of the SOFTWARE PRODUCT on a single computer. The primary user of the computer on which the SOFTWARE PRODUCT is installed may make a second copy for his or her exclusive use on a portable computer.

   b. **Storage/Network Use.** You may also store or install a copy of the SOFTWARE PRODUCT on a storage device, such as a network server, used only to install or run the SOFTWARE PRODUCT on your other computers over an internal network; however, you must acquire and dedicate a license for each separate computer on which the SOFTWARE PRODUCT is installed or run from the storage device. A license for the SOFTWARE PRODUCT may not be shared or used concurrently on different computers.

   c. **License Pak.** If you have acquired this EULA in a Microsoft License Pak, you may make the number of additional copies of the computer software portion of the SOFTWARE PRODUCT authorized on the printed copy of this EULA, and you may use each copy in the manner specified above. You are also entitled to make a corresponding number of secondary copies for portable computer use as specified above.

   d. **Sample Code.** Solely with respect to portions, if any, of the SOFTWARE PRODUCT that are identified within the SOFTWARE PRODUCT as sample code (the "SAMPLE CODE"):

      i. **Use and Modification.** Microsoft grants you the right to use and modify the source code version of the SAMPLE CODE, *provided* you comply with subsection (d)(iii) below. You may not distribute the SAMPLE CODE, or any modified version of the SAMPLE CODE, in source code form.

      ii. **Redistributable Files.** Provided you comply with subsection (d)(iii) below, Microsoft grants you a nonexclusive, royalty-free right to reproduce and distribute the object code version of the SAMPLE CODE and of any modified SAMPLE CODE, other than SAMPLE CODE, or any modified version thereof, designated as not redistributable in the Readme file that forms a part of the SOFTWARE PRODUCT (the "Non-Redistributable Sample Code"). All SAMPLE CODE other than the Non-Redistributable Sample Code is collectively referred to as the "REDISTRIBUTABLES."

      iii. **Redistribution Requirements.** If you redistribute the REDISTRIBUTABLES, you agree to: (i) distribute the REDISTRIBUTABLES in object code form only in conjunction with and as a part of your software application product; (ii) not use Microsoft's name, logo, or trademarks to market your software application product; (iii) include a valid copyright notice on your software application product; (iv) indemnify, hold harmless, and defend Microsoft from and against any claims or lawsuits, including attorney's fees, that arise or result from the use or distribution of your software application product; and (v) not permit further distribution of the REDISTRIBUTABLES by your end user. Contact Microsoft for the applicable royalties due and other licensing terms for all other uses and/or distribution of the REDISTRIBUTABLES.

2. **DESCRIPTION OF OTHER RIGHTS AND LIMITATIONS.**

   - **Limitations on Reverse Engineering, Decompilation, and Disassembly.** You may not reverse engineer, decompile, or disassemble the SOFTWARE PRODUCT, except and only to the extent that such activity is expressly permitted by applicable law notwithstanding this limitation.
   - **Separation of Components.** The SOFTWARE PRODUCT is licensed as a single product. Its component parts may not be separated for use on more than one computer.
   - **Rental.** You may not rent, lease, or lend the SOFTWARE PRODUCT.
   - **Support Services.** Microsoft may, but is not obligated to, provide you with support services related to the SOFTWARE PRODUCT ("Support Services"). Use of Support Services is governed by the Microsoft policies and programs described in the

user manual, in "online" documentation, and/or other Microsoft-provided materials. Any supplemental software code provided to you as part of the Support Services shall be considered part of the SOFTWARE PRODUCT and subject to the terms and conditions of this EULA. With respect to technical information you provide to Microsoft as part of the Support Services, Microsoft may use such information for its business purposes, including for product support and development. Microsoft will not utilize such technical information in a form that personally identifies you.

- **Software Transfer.** You may permanently transfer all of your rights under this EULA, provided you retain no copies, you transfer all of the SOFTWARE PRODUCT (including all component parts, the media and printed materials, any upgrades, this EULA, and, if applicable, the Certificate of Authenticity), **and** the recipient agrees to the terms of this EULA.
- **Termination.** Without prejudice to any other rights, Microsoft may terminate this EULA if you fail to comply with the terms and conditions of this EULA. In such event, you must destroy all copies of the SOFTWARE PRODUCT and all of its component parts.

3. **COPYRIGHT.** All title and copyrights in and to the SOFTWARE PRODUCT (including but not limited to any images, photographs, animations, video, audio, music, text, SAMPLE CODE, REDISTRIBUTABLES, and "applets" incorporated into the SOFTWARE PRODUCT) and any copies of the SOFTWARE PRODUCT are owned by Microsoft or its suppliers. The SOFTWARE PRODUCT is protected by copyright laws and international treaty provisions. Therefore, you must treat the SOFTWARE PRODUCT like any other copyrighted material **except** that you may install the SOFTWARE PRODUCT on a single computer provided you keep the original solely for backup or archival purposes. You may not copy the printed materials accompanying the SOFTWARE PRODUCT.

4. **U.S. GOVERNMENT RESTRICTED RIGHTS.** The SOFTWARE PRODUCT and documentation are provided with RESTRICTED RIGHTS. Use, duplication, or disclosure by the Government is subject to restrictions as set forth in subparagraph (c)(1)(ii) of the Rights in Technical Data and Computer Software clause at DFARS 252.227-7013 or subparagraphs (c)(1) and (2) of the Commercial Computer Software—Restricted Rights at 48 CFR 52.227-19, as applicable. Manufacturer is Microsoft Corporation/One Microsoft Way/Redmond, WA 98052-6399.

5. **EXPORT RESTRICTIONS.** You agree that you will not export or re-export the SOFTWARE PRODUCT, any part thereof, or any process or service that is the direct product of the SOFTWARE PRODUCT (the foregoing collectively referred to as the "Restricted Components"), to any country, person, entity, or end user subject to U.S. export restrictions. You specifically agree not to export or re-export any of the Restricted Components (i) to any country to which the U.S. has embargoed or restricted the export of goods or services, which currently include, but are not necessarily limited to, Cuba, Iran, Iraq, Libya, North Korea, Sudan, and Syria, or to any national of any such country, wherever located, who intends to transmit or transport the Restricted Components back to such country; (ii) to any end user who you know or have reason to know will utilize the Restricted Components in the design, development, or production of nuclear, chemical, or biological weapons; or (iii) to any end user who has been prohibited from participating in U.S. export transactions by any federal agency of the U.S. government. You warrant and represent that neither the BXA nor any other U.S. federal agency has suspended, revoked, or denied your export privileges.

DISCLAIMER OF WARRANTY

NO WARRANTIES OR CONDITIONS. MICROSOFT EXPRESSLY DISCLAIMS ANY WARRANTY OR CONDITION FOR THE SOFTWARE PRODUCT. THE SOFTWARE PRODUCT AND ANY RELATED DOCUMENTATION IS PROVIDED "AS IS" WITHOUT WARRANTY OR CONDITION OF ANY KIND, EITHER EXPRESS OR IMPLIED, INCLUDING, WITHOUT LIMITATION, THE IMPLIED WARRANTIES OF MERCHANTABILITY, FITNESS FOR A PARTICULAR PURPOSE, OR NONINFRINGEMENT. THE ENTIRE RISK ARISING OUT OF USE OR PERFORMANCE OF THE SOFTWARE PRODUCT REMAINS WITH YOU.

LIMITATION OF LIABILITY. TO THE MAXIMUM EXTENT PERMITTED BY APPLICABLE LAW, IN NO EVENT SHALL MICROSOFT OR ITS SUPPLIERS BE LIABLE FOR ANY SPECIAL, INCIDENTAL, INDIRECT, OR CONSEQUENTIAL DAMAGES WHATSOEVER (INCLUDING, WITHOUT LIMITATION, DAMAGES FOR LOSS OF BUSINESS PROFITS, BUSINESS INTERRUPTION, LOSS OF BUSINESS INFORMATION, OR ANY OTHER PECUNIARY LOSS) ARISING OUT OF THE USE OF OR INABILITY TO USE THE SOFTWARE PRODUCT OR THE PROVISION OF OR FAILURE TO PROVIDE SUPPORT SERVICES, EVEN IF MICROSOFT HAS BEEN ADVISED OF THE POSSIBILITY OF SUCH DAMAGES. IN ANY CASE, MICROSOFT'S ENTIRE LIABILITY UNDER ANY PROVISION OF THIS EULA SHALL BE LIMITED TO THE GREATER OF THE AMOUNT ACTUALLY PAID BY YOU FOR THE SOFTWARE PRODUCT OR US$5.00; PROVIDED, HOWEVER, IF YOU HAVE ENTERED INTO A MICROSOFT SUPPORT SERVICES AGREEMENT, MICROSOFT'S ENTIRE LIABILITY REGARDING SUPPORT SERVICES SHALL BE GOVERNED BY THE TERMS OF THAT AGREEMENT. BECAUSE SOME STATES AND JURISDICTIONS DO NOT ALLOW THE EXCLUSION OR LIMITATION OF LIABILITY, THE ABOVE LIMITATION MAY NOT APPLY TO YOU.

MISCELLANEOUS

This EULA is governed by the laws of the State of Washington USA, except and only to the extent that applicable law mandates governing law of a different jurisdiction.

Should you have any questions concerning this EULA, or if you desire to contact Microsoft for any reason, please contact the Microsoft subsidiary serving your country, or write: Microsoft Sales Information Center/One Microsoft Way/Redmond, WA 98052-6399.

PN 097-0002296

Register Today!

Return this
Microsoft® Word 2000 Step by Step
registration card today

Microsoft® Press
mspress.microsoft.com

OWNER REGISTRATION CARD

1-57231-970-4

Microsoft® Word 2000 Step by Step

FIRST NAME **MIDDLE INITIAL** **LAST NAME**

INSTITUTION OR COMPANY NAME

ADDRESS

CITY **STATE** **ZIP**

( )

E-MAIL ADDRESS **PHONE NUMBER**

U.S. and Canada addresses only. Fill in information above and mail postage-free.
Please mail only the bottom half of this page.

start
faster
go
farther